I0319236

Ghattas Eid

The Phonology of Maaloula Aramaic

Ghattas Eid

The Phonology of Maaloula Aramaic

d|u|p
düsseldorf university press

D 61 Düsseldorf

ISBN 978-3-11-144704-9
e-ISBN (PDF) 978-3-11-144712-4
e-ISBN (EPUB) 978-3-11-144722-3
DOI https://doi.org/10.1515/9783111447124

Library of Congress Control Number: 2024937101

Bibliographic information published by the Deutsche Nationalbibliothek
The Deutsche Nationalbibliothek lists this publication in the Deutsche Nationalbibliografie; detailed bibliographic data are available on the Internet at http://dnb.dnb.de.

d|u|p düsseldorf university press is an imprint of Walter de Gruyter GmbH.

Cover image: Maaloula, the Eastern Gorge. Photo: Ghattas Eid

dup.degruyter.com

Contents

Acknowledgements — IX
Abbreviations and symbols — XI
List of figures — XIII
List of tables — XIV
List of maps — XIV

1 Introduction — 1

2 Analytical framework — 6
2.1 Introduction — **6**
2.2 Language data — **6**
2.2.1 Sources of language data — **6**
2.2.2 Citation and transcription — **7**
2.3 Quantitative analysis — **8**
2.4 Morphological analysis — **10**
2.5 Phonological analysis — **13**

3 The Maaloula Aramaic Speech Corpus (MASC) — 18
3.1 Introduction — **18**
3.2 The data included in the corpus — **19**
3.3 Data computerization and annotation — **20**
3.3.1 Scanning and digitizing the transcriptions — **20**
3.3.2 Correcting errors and adding informative tags — **21**
3.3.3 Lemmatizing the transcriptions — **22**
3.3.4 Denoising the audio recordings — **24**
3.3.5 Automatically aligning the transcriptions with the recordings — **24**
3.4 Corpus structure and use — **24**
3.4.1 The transcriptions — **26**
3.4.2 The lemmatized transcriptions — **29**
3.4.3 The audio files and time-aligned phonetic transcriptions — **31**
3.4.4 The SQLite database — **32**
3.5 Discussion: Applications — **32**

4 Phoneme inventory — 35
4.1 Introduction — **35**
4.2 Consonants — **35**
4.2.1 Stops — **39**

4.2.2 Affricates — **44**
4.2.3 Fricatives — **44**
4.2.4 Nasals — **52**
4.2.5 Liquids — **53**
4.2.6 Glides — **54**
4.3 Vowels — **55**
4.3.1 Short vowels — **57**
4.3.2 Long vowels — **58**
4.3.3 Diphthongs — **59**
4.3.4 The epenthetic vowel — **62**
4.4 Conclusion — **62**

5 The distribution of bilabial stops — 64
5.1 Introduction — **64**
5.2 Singleton bilabial stops — **65**
5.2.1 Bilabial stops in postvocalic position — **65**
5.2.2 Bilabial stops in preconsonantal position — **69**
5.2.3 Bilabial stops in word-initial position — **73**
5.3 Geminate bilabial stops — **75**
5.4 Conclusion — **79**

6 Morpho-phonological alternations in feminine nouns — 80
6.1 Introduction — **80**
6.2 Feminine marker alternation — **80**
6.2.1 Spitaler's account — **81**
6.2.2 Open questions — **82**
6.2.3 Data and method — **84**
6.2.4 Results — **86**
6.2.5 Summary of results — **92**
6.2.6 Formalization — **93**
6.3 Plural marker alternation — **95**
6.3.1 Previous accounts — **96**
6.3.2 Data and method — **98**
6.3.3 Results — **99**
6.3.4 Formalization — **102**
6.4 Conclusion — **104**

7 Local and long-distance assimilation — 106
7.1 Introduction — **106**

7.2 Assimilation — **106**
7.2.1 Assimilation of the preposition *b-* — **106**
7.2.2 Assimilation of base-final /t/ — **109**
7.2.3 Assimilation of the prefixes *č-* — **111**
7.2.4 Assimilation of suffix-final /ṯ/ — **114**
7.2.5 Assimilation of /ḏ/ in *hōḏ* — **116**
7.2.6 Assimilation of preposition-final /ʕ/ — **118**
7.2.7 Assimilation of /n/ — **121**
7.2.8 Assimilation of /l/ — **123**
7.2.9 Lexically restricted assimilation — **128**
7.3 Umlaut — **129**
7.3.1 Regressive umlaut — **129**
7.3.2 Progressive umlaut — **141**
7.4 Conclusion — **143**

8 Syllable structure and syllabification — 144
8.1 Introduction — **144**
8.2 Previous accounts — **144**
8.2.1 Syllable structure and syllabification — **144**
8.2.2 Vowel epenthesis — **146**
8.2.3 Glottal epenthesis — **153**
8.3 Syllable-based analysis — **154**
8.3.1 Data and method — **156**
8.3.2 Syllable weight — **156**
8.3.3 Syllabification — **158**
8.3.4 Stray consonants — **159**
8.3.5 Vowel epenthesis and resyllabification — **161**
8.3.6 Glottal epenthesis and resyllabification — **166**
8.3.7 A cross-linguistic perspective — **168**
8.4 Two adjacent stray consonants — **169**
8.4.1 Epenthesis in the case of C′C′ — **171**
8.4.2 C′C′ yet no epenthesis — **173**
8.5 Summary and discussion — **179**
8.6 Implications — **182**

9 Gemination — 185
9.1 Introduction — **185**
9.2 Underlying and surface geminates — **187**
9.2.1 Underlying geminates — **188**

9.2.2 Surface geminates — **192**
9.3 The phonological and phonetic properties of Maaloula Aramaic geminates — **194**
9.3.1 Methodology — **195**
9.3.2 Word-medial geminates — **199**
9.3.3 Word-final geminates — **203**
9.3.4 Word-initial geminates — **208**
9.4 Conclusion — **212**

10 Stress — 214
10.1 Introduction — **214**
10.2 Stress algorithm — **214**
10.3 Stress-dependent processes — **217**
10.3.1 Pretonic raising of short mid vowels — **217**
10.3.2 Pretonic shortening of long vowels — **219**
10.4 The distribution of vowels — **224**
10.4.1 Positional restrictions on the distribution of long vowels — **224**
10.4.2 Positional restrictions on the distribution of short vowels — **230**
10.5 Summary and conclusion — **235**

11 Conclusion and outlook — 239

References — 241
Index — 247

Acknowledgements

This book is a slightly revised version of my doctoral dissertation, which I submitted and defended at the Faculty of Arts and Humanities of the Heinrich Heine University Düsseldorf. I owe a debt of gratitude to a number of people without whom I would not have been able to complete this dissertation.

I would like to express my sincere thanks and gratitude to my first supervisor and teacher Ingo Plag who helped me and supported me in many ways. He offered me a position in the English Language and Linguistics department where I taught and conducted my research for five and a half years, he provided me with all of the resources and funds that I needed for my research, he sent me abroad to participate in international conferences and attend summer schools, he supervised my dissertation, and most importantly he believed in me and my project.

My sincere thanks are due to my second supervisor Ruben van de Vijver who inducted me into the world (and also the department) of General Linguistics and who was always generous with his time, knowledge, and feedback. I also wish to express all my thanks to the members of my examining board: Kilu von Prince, Kevin Tang, and Roger Lüdeke.

I am deeply grateful to Christian Uffmann who, as a teacher and as a colleague, introduced me to many interesting topics in phonological theory and who always listened to my analyses and problems and gave me suggestions which significantly improved the quality of my analyses.

I would like to thank my native language consultant Emad Rihan who proofread and corrected the errors in the digitized transcriptions, provided new language data that I used in my studies and analyses, and promptly and passionately replied to all my detailed questions about Maaloula Aramaic. Emad made a substantial contribution to this work, and this contribution is described in detail in Section 2.2.1.

I am grateful to Simon David Stein for his help with the acoustic measurements in Chapter 9. Simon wrote the Python scripts that read segment durations in TextGrid files and transferred them into a data set.

I would like to thank the institutions and people without whom the Maaloula Aramaic Speech Corpus (MASC) would not have been created: Werner Arnold for allowing me to use the primary data from his field research in Maaloula, Harrassowitz Verlag for the permission to include the published transcriptions in the corpus, and Esther Seyffarth for creating a lemmatized version of the digitized transcriptions, denoising the audio recordings, aligning the transcriptions with the

https://doi.org/10.1515/9783111447124-202

corresponding recordings, and creating the SQLite database. This corpus is described in Chapter 3.

I am delighted to acknowledge and thank my current and former colleagues at Heinrich Heine University Düsseldorf for patiently listening to my talks about different aspects of the phonology of Maaloula Aramaic and for providing me with invaluable feedback and new insights. Special thanks go to Heidrun Dorgeloh, Dieter Stein, Tania Kouteva, Lea Kawaletz, Dominic Schmitz, Viktoria Schneider, Julia Muschalik, Julika Weber, Akhilesh Kakolu Ramarao, Christopher Geissler, Sven Kotowski, Arne Lohmann, and Marie Engemann. Special thanks also go to Ulrike Kayser for her great help with the organizational matters. I am also grateful to Lara Rüter, Ann-Sophie Haan, Nina Stratmann, Anna Stein, and Defne Cicek for proofreading the final version of my dissertation.

To the people who planted the seeds of love for this language in my heart, my late father Ḥunen and my mother Amira, I send my love and my gratitude. I thank my brother Ayman for being a great companion in the journey of language documentation and for sending me fascinating pictures of Maaloula.

Finally, I would like to thank my loving family: my wife Faten, my daughter Carla, and my son Ḥanna. Without your love, humor, and moral support I would not have completed this work.

Abbreviations and symbols

Grammatical abbreviations

Ø	zero-morph
1	first person
2	second person
3	third person
CST	construct state
DEF	definite
DTR	detransitivizing prefix
EPL	enumerative plural
F	feminine
IMP	imperative
INDF	indefinite
LM	linking morpheme
M	masculine
NE	nominal ending
OM	object marking
PL	plural
PRET	preterit
PRF	perfect
PRS	present
SBJV	subjunctive
SG	singular

General abbreviations

III	Arnold (1991a)
IV	Arnold (1991b)
V	Arnold (1990a)
VI	Arnold (2019)
FW	fieldwork
NA	not available
sthg.	something

https://doi.org/10.1515/9783111447124-203

List of figures

Fig. 3.1: Distribution of tokens by speaker —— **25**
Fig. 3.2: Distribution of tokens by age and gender —— **26**
Fig. 3.3: Screenshot from AntConc: A lemma frequency list —— **28**
Fig. 3.4: Screenshot from AntConc: A lemma containing the search string **ṭ*ʕ*n** and its word forms —— **29**
Fig. 3.5: Screenshot from the File View window in AntConc (hidden lemma tags) —— **30**
Fig. 3.6: Screenshot from Praat displaying the four tiers as well as the corresponding spectrogram and waveform —— **31**
Fig. 3.7: The structure of the database —— **32**
Fig. 3.8: Example query on the MASC database —— **33**
Fig. 3.9: The research process adopted to investigate vowel epenthesis —— **34**
Fig. 4.1: The type frequency of stops —— **43**
Fig. 4.2: The type frequency of coronal fricatives —— **48**
Fig. 6.1: Distribution of *-ṯ* and *-č* in groups 1, 2, 3, and 4 by the manner of articulation of the preceding consonant —— **92**
Fig. 9.1: Distributions of consonant duration in word-medial position —— **201**
Fig. 9.2: Distributions of the duration of short and long vowels (in ms) before word-medial singletons (sgl) and word-medial geminates (gem) —— **202**
Fig. 9.3: Distributions of consonant duration in word-final position —— **203**
Fig. 9.4: Distributions of the duration of short and long vowels (in ms) before word-final singletons (sgl) and word-final geminates (gem) —— **207**
Fig. 9.5: Distributions of consonant duration in word-initial position —— **210**
Fig. 9.6: Automatic segmentation of a TextGrid file (on the left) compared to manual segmentation (on the right) —— **211**

https://doi.org/10.1515/9783111447124-204

List of tables

Table 3.1: Extract from the lemma list —— **23**
Table 3.2: KWIC concordance of *xōla* 'food' —— **27**
Table 3.3: KWIC concordance of words containing the search string **ṭ*ʕ*n** —— **27**
Table 3.4: Extract from the MASC dataframe —— **29**
Table 3.5: KWIC concordance of the lemma *iṯḳen yiṯḳan* 'to become' —— **30**
Table 4.1: Consonant phonemes —— **35**
Table 5.1: Distribution of the geminate bilabial stops across different environments —— **78**
Table 6.1: Distribution of the feminine alternants —— **86**
Table 6.2: Distribution of the feminine alternants across the different environments in which they occur —— **86**
Table 6.3: Distribution of the feminine alternants across the different phonological environments with the templatic pattern as a grouping factor —— **87**
Table 6.4: Distribution of *-ṯ* and *-č* in groups 1, 2, 3, and 4 by the manner of articulation of the preceding consonant —— **91**
Table 6.5: Accuracy of predicting the distribution of *-ṯ* and *-č* when all three variables are used —— **93**
Table 6.6: The environments in which the feminine alternants occur —— **94**
Table 6.7: Distribution of the plural alternants —— **99**
Table 6.8: Distribution of the plural alternants with the properties of the underlying bases as the grouping factor —— **99**
Table 9.1: Distribution of singletons and geminates —— **197**
Table 9.2: Distribution of short and long vowels before medial and final consonants —— **198**
Table 9.3: Duration of word-medial consonants in milliseconds —— **201**
Table 9.4: Duration of vowels (in ms) before word-medial consonants —— **203**
Table 9.5: Duration of word-final consonants in milliseconds —— **204**
Table 9.6: Duration of vowels (in ms) before word-final consonants —— **207**
Table 9.7: Duration of word-initial consonants in milliseconds —— **210**

List of maps

Map 1.1: Location of Maaloula (60 km northeast of Damascus) —— **2**
Map 1.2: Location of Maaloula with respect to Jubbaadin and Bakhaa (Al-Sarkha) —— **3**

https://doi.org/10.1515/9783111447124-205

1 Introduction

Aramaic is a Semitic language that has been spoken in the Middle East for more than three millennia. It has survived, however, not as a single language but as a number of varieties collectively given the hypernym 'Neo-Aramaic'. These Neo-Aramaic varieties fall into four groups: Western Neo-Aramaic, Central Neo-Aramaic, North-Eastern Neo-Aramaic (NENA), and Neo-Mandaic (Heinrichs 1990: x–xv; Khan & Noorlander 2021: xvii).

Western Neo-Aramaic, which is the variety described in this work, is spoken in the two villages Maaloula and Jubbaadin (at the time of writing this book). Before the Syrian Civil War, it was also spoken in a third village, named Bakhaa (also known as Al-Sarkha). During the war, however, Bakhaa was destroyed and subsequently deserted by its inhabitants (Duntsov, Häberl & Loesov 2022: 359). These three villages have their own dialects of Western Neo-Aramaic (Heinrichs 1990: xi; Arnold 2011: 685). In this work, I focus only on the dialect spoken in Maaloula and use the term 'Maaloula Aramaic' to refer to it. I keep using the term 'Western Neo-Aramaic' to refer to the three dialects collectively.

These Aramaic-speaking villages are located in the Qalamoun Mountains in Syria. The geographical location of Maaloula with respect to the capital city, Damascus, is displayed in Map 1.1, and its location with respect to the two other villages is shown in Map 1.2. The remaining inhabitants of these villages also speak Arabic (Heinrichs 1990: xi; Arnold 1990a: xix). In addition to the inhabitants of these villages, the native speakers who moved to bigger cities, such as Damascus and Beirut, still speak Western Neo-Aramaic (Arnold 2011: 685).

Western Neo-Aramaic is considered "definitely endangered" by the UNESCO Atlas of the World's Languages in Danger (Moseley 2010). A language is considered definitely endangered when it "is no longer being learned as the mother tongue by children in the home. The youngest speakers are thus of the parental generation"(Moseley 2010: 12). Similarly, Ethnologue (Eberhard, Simons & Fennig 2023) considers Western Neo-Aramaic "endangered". According to Ethnologue, a language is endangered when "it is no longer the norm that children learn and use this language". Ethnologue reports that the Expanded Graded Intergenerational Disruption Scale (EGIDS) level for Western Neo-Aramaic is 7 (Shifting). Level 7 is exactly between 6b (Threatened) and 8a (Moribund).

https://doi.org/10.1515/9783111447124-001

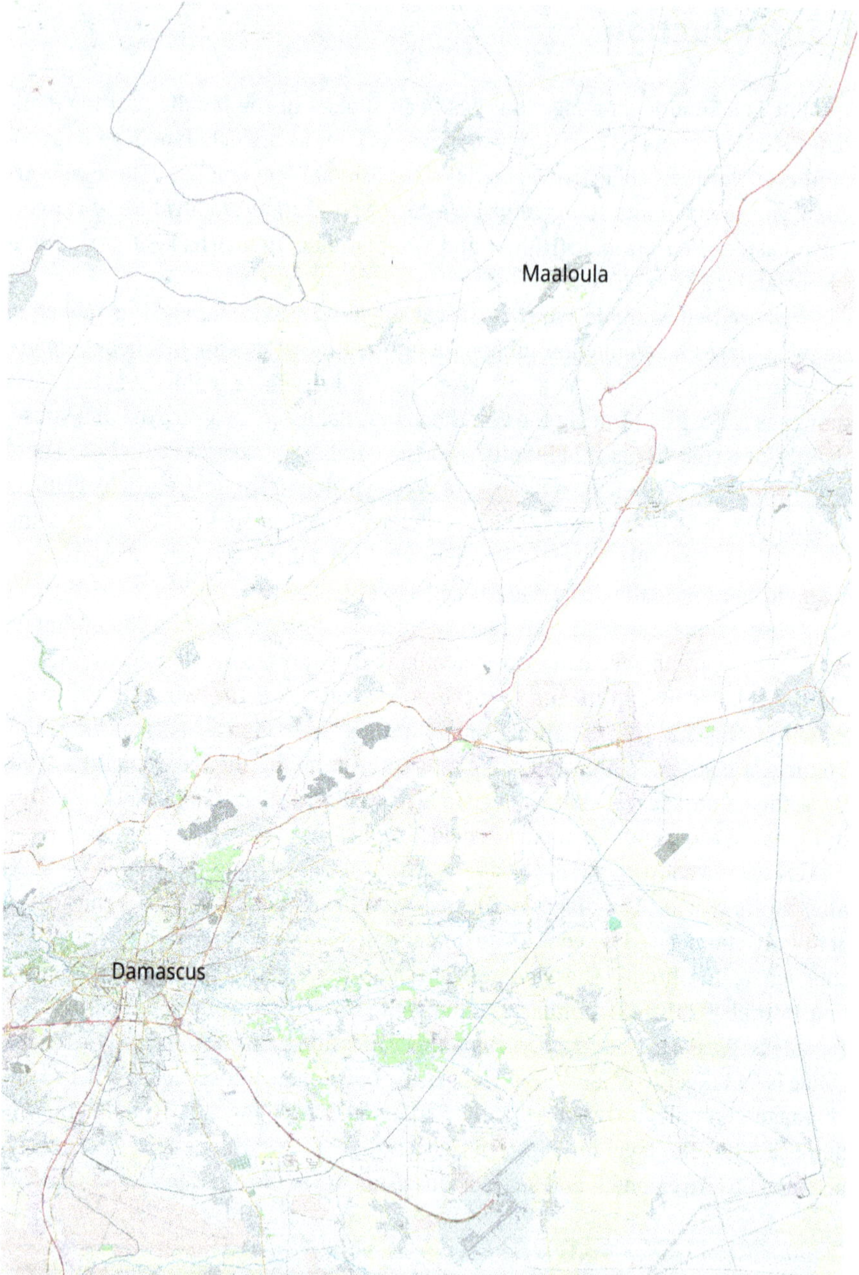

Map 1.1: Location of Maaloula (60 km northeast of Damascus) (© OpenStreetMap contributors, retrieved from https://www.openstreetmap.org)

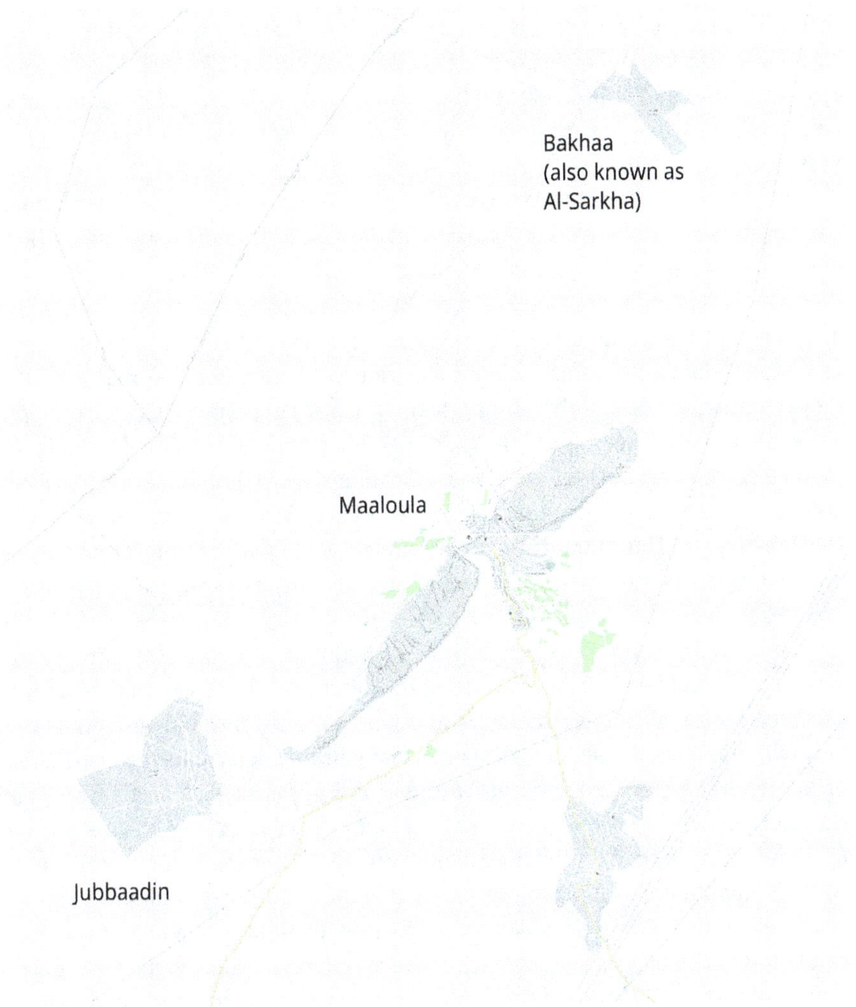

Map 1.2: Location of Maaloula with respect to Jubbaadin and Bakhaa (Al-Sarkha) (© OpenStreetMap contributors, retrieved from https://www.openstreetmap.org)

The phonology of Maaloula Aramaic has been described in the grammars of Spitaler (1938) and Arnold (1990a). These works, as well as subsequent publications (e.g., Arnold 1990b, 2006, 2008, 2011), provide descriptive generalizations which serve as an essential starting point for anyone who intends to conduct linguistic research into the phonology or morpho-phonology of Maaloula Aramaic. Linguistic research can also benefit from the primary language data collected during fieldwork. These data have been made accessible to the scientific community in paper format (see, e.g., the transcripts published in Bergsträsser 1915, 1918, 1933; Reich 1937; Spitaler 1957; Arnold 1991a, 1991b, 2002) and (in the more recent fieldwork) in audio format (see the *Semitisches Tonarchiv* 'Semitic Sound Archive' website of Heidelberg University, Arnold 2003).

In addition to these academic publications, there are a few textbooks which have been written and published locally by Maaloula Aramaic language teachers who are members of the speech community (e.g., Rizkallah 2010; Rihan 2017). Although these textbooks are designed for language learners, rather than for linguists, and although their aim is to provide grammar rules, rather than a phonological analysis of Maaloula Aramaic, they are a valuable source for two reasons. First, they contain a few descriptive observations which are not captured by the previous academic research (see, e.g., Rihan's 2017: 87 description of the distribution of the plural marker alternants *-ō* ~ *-yō* in feminine nouns, which I review in Section 6.3.1). Second, they give an insight into how native speakers describe the grammar of their own language and how they distinguish (or do not distinguish) the different outputs of phonological processes (i.e., allophones and allomorphs) in the transcriptions of their examples.

However, these previous (scholarly and community-produced) resources leave a number of problems unsolved. First, at the descriptive level, the generalizations provided by the available grammars and textbooks are incomplete. To mention only two examples, the phonological environments that determine the distribution of the feminine marker alternants *-ṯ* and *-č* are not clear (see Section 6.2), and certain cases where vowel epenthesis cannot apply are not reported (see Sections 8.2.2 and 8.4.2). Second, at the methodological level, the proposed generalizations call for quantitative empirical research that may be able to account for the gradience in the variation. However, conducting quantitative empirical research, given the available format of the above-mentioned primary data, is nearly impossible. The transcripts are published in paper format, and the audio files are not supplemented by time-aligned transcriptions. Third, at the theoretical level, the generalizations presented are entirely language-specific and lack a perspective that speaks to broader issues in phonological theory.

The overarching goal of this book is to provide a phonology of Maaloula Aramaic which addresses these unsolved problems at the descriptive, methodological, and theoretical levels. At the descriptive level, I aim to revisit the phonological rules provided in the previous accounts, describe all the environments where they apply, and account for the cases where certain rules are blocked.

At the methodological level, I (with the help of co-authors) aim to create and publish a machine-readable speech corpus that can facilitate empirical research in this and future work (see Chapter 3). Using this corpus, I aim to conduct empirical studies to investigate the distribution of allophones and allomorphs and to examine the phonological environments where phonological rules apply (for an introduction to the corpus-based analysis adopted in this work, see Section 2.3).

At the theoretical level, I will discuss the results of the empirical studies from the perspective of phonological theory in order to make the phonology of Maaloula Aramaic relevant and accessible to phonologists in general, who may not necessarily be familiar with Aramaic or Semitic languages. With this aim in mind, I will formalize synchronic phonological rules, show how different phonological rules interact with each other, and (whenever possible) make cross-linguistic comparisons. I will also provide the relevant morphological background whenever a morpho-phonological process is being discussed (see Section 2.4).

This book is structured as follows. In Chapter 2, I will introduce the analytical framework that I have adopted in this book. Chapter 3 will present the electronic speech corpus that we created and published to facilitate empirical linguistic research. Most of the language data used in this work come from this corpus. In Chapter 4, I will describe the phoneme inventory of Maaloula Aramaic. In Chapter 5, I will investigate the distribution of bilabial stops and formulate the phonological rules that are responsible for their distribution. In Chapter 6, I will investigate two morpheme-specific alternations that occur in feminine nouns. In Chapter 7, two types of assimilation will be presented and discussed: local assimilation and long-distance assimilation (or umlaut). In Chapter 8, I will discuss syllable structure, syllabification, and epenthesis. In Chapter 9, I will investigate geminates by grouping them according to their provenance and position and by studying their phonological and phonetic properties. In Chapter 10, I will describe word stress, formulate stress-dependent rules, and review the restrictions on the distribution of vowels in stressed, pretonic, and post-tonic positions. Chapter 11 will conclude this book.

The topics discussed in Chapters 4–10 move from the segmental phonology to the prosodic phonology of Maaloula Aramaic. The choice as to what topics to include in these chapters was made based on whether there are phonological or morpho-phonological alternations that can be accounted for by proposing a synchronic analysis. For example, the alternation between [b] and [p] in two inflected forms of the same lemma (e.g., *irxe**b*** 'he rode' vs. *rix**p**iṯ* 'I rode') made it necessary to dedicate a chapter to investigate the distribution of these bilabial stops (see Chapter 5). However, the sounds that do not show any alternations, including the sounds that used to have an allophonic relationship at an earlier stage of Aramaic (e.g., *k* and *x*) but do not show any alternations in modern Maaloula Aramaic, were not included in the topics to be examined.

2 Analytical framework

2.1 Introduction

In this chapter, I introduce the analytical framework that I have adopted in this book. I start by providing an overview of the language data used in this work. I then present the three types of analyses that I conducted on the language data: the quantitative analysis, the morphological analysis, and the phonological analysis.

2.2 Language data

This section introduces the sources of language data and the method used in order to cite and transcribe the examples taken from these sources.

2.2.1 Sources of language data

The language data that I use in this work come from three sources. The first source, which provides most of the language data, is the Maaloula Aramaic Speech Corpus (MASC, Eid et al. 2022) (for the primary data, see Arnold 1991a, 1991b, 2003). This corpus is introduced and described in detail in Chapter 3.

The second source of language data is my native speaker consultant, Emad Rihan. Emad is a 37-year-old male who is bilingual in Maaloula Aramaic and Arabic, and he also speaks English. He lived in Syria until 2018 and in Lebanon between 2018 and 2020 and has lived in Canada since 2020. He has a bachelor's degree in biology from Damascus University, and he worked as a biology teacher in Maaloula's High School before leaving his homeland. He taught Maaloula Aramaic at the Aramaic Language Center in Maaloula and at the Higher Language Institute at Damascus University. He designed and published a textbook (Rihan 2017) for the courses that he taught.

To collect language data from Emad, I conducted several elicitation sessions with him. These elicitation sessions were held online because we live in different countries. In addition to these sessions, Emad and I exchanged different forms of emails and messages (e.g., text, picture, and voice messages) and collaborated on shared documents. This collaboration had the aim of generating inflectional forms which are not attested in the corpus and of verifying whether certain word forms are grammatical or not. Emad also had an important role in the creation of MASC

https://doi.org/10.1515/9783111447124-002

(see Chapter 3). He matched the scanned texts with the original transcriptions and audio files, he corrected the spelling errors and inconsistencies (see Section 3.3.2), and he helped in creating a comprehensive lemma list by supplying 12,220 word forms with their lemmas and roots as they appear in Arnold's (2019) Aramaic-German dictionary (see Section 3.3.3).

The third (and least used) source of language data is the various publications on Maaloula Aramaic which were not included in MASC. These sources fall into two categories: academic publications (e.g., Bergsträsser 1915, 1918; Spitaler 1938, 1957; Arnold 1990a, 1990b, 2002, 2006, 2008, 2019) and community-produced materials (e.g., Rizkallah 2010; Rizkallah & Saadi 2016; Rihan 2017). I only took individual examples from these sources. All of these examples were also checked by my native speaker consultant.

2.2.2 Citation and transcription

In order to cite the primary sources of the examples listed in this work, I use the Roman numbers III, IV, V, and VI to refer respectively to Arnold's volumes (1991a, 1991b, 1990a, and 2019). I have chosen these numbers following Arnold's original numbering of his volumes (see the references at the end of the book). I use Arabic numbers to refer to page numbers. For example, III.28 refers to Arnold (1991a: 28). Arabic numbers are also used occasionally (in Section 3.4) to refer to text file (i.e., narrative) numbers, but in this case they are followed by *.txt*. For example, III.28.txt refers to the 28th narrative in Arnold (1991a). The examples which do not come from Arnold's four volumes (III, IV, V, and VI) are cited normally. The examples marked 'FW' are from my native language consultant.

Throughout this book, I adopt the transcription system traditionally used in the linguistic publications on Semitic languages. Specifically, I use the version adopted by Arnold (1990a, 1991a, 1991b). The correspondences between the adopted transcription symbols and the IPA symbols are given in (1). Only the symbols which differ from the IPA symbols are shown (see Chapter 4 for a detailed description of the phoneme inventory).

(1) *Correspondences between the adopted transcription and the IPA symbols*

Transcription	IPA	Transcription	IPA
ṯ	/θ/	ṣ	/sˤ/ or /sˠ/
ḏ	/ð/	ẓ	/zˤ/ or /zˠ/
š	/ʃ/	ṭ	/tˤ/ or /tˠ/
č	/tʃ/	ḍ	/ðˤ/ or /ðˠ/

Transcription	IPA	Transcription	IPA
ž	/ʒ/	*y*	/j/
x	/χ/	*ī*	/i:/
ġ	/ʁ/	*ū*	/u:/
ḥ	/ħ/	*ē*	/e:/
k	/kʲ/ or /k̟/	*ō*	/o:/
ḳ	/k̠/ or /k/	*ā*	/a:/

Although this adopted system is meant to represent surface forms, the outputs of a few phonological processes are consistently absent from it. For example, the glottal stops that are inserted at the beginning of word-initial onsetless syllables are not represented, as can be seen in (2a). The geminate consonants which undergo degemination in preconsonantal position are transcribed as geminates, rather than singletons, as in (2b) (see Sections 8.2.3 and 8.3.6 for glottal epenthesis and Section 9.3.2 for preconsonantal degemination). In this work, I have adopted the original transcription system without modifying it, but I have provided the actual surface representations in square brackets whenever a more accurate representation is needed. Throughout the book, I use bold text to draw attention to the relevant segments in the examples.

(2) *Cases where the transcribed forms differ from surface forms*

	Transcribed form			Surface form
(a)	*ana*	'I'	III.28	[**ʔ**ana]
	anaḥ	'we'	III.260	[**ʔ**anaḥ]
	orḥa	'once'	III.294	[**ʔ**orḥa]
(b)	*ḏo**kk**ṯa*	'place'	IV.306	[ḏo**k**ṯa]
	*mʕa**rr**ṯa*	'cave'	III.368	[mʕa**r**ṯa]
	*xa**ff**ṯa*	'shoulder'	IV.228	[xa**f**ṯa]

2.3 Quantitative analysis

In this work, I quantitatively investigate the descriptive generalizations found in previous research as well as the observations that my language consultant and I made while computerizing and proofreading the transcriptions that we included in MASC. As discussed in Section 2.2.1, the empirical research conducted in this work is primarily based on corpus data. I accessed the plain and lemmatized transcriptions in MASC using the corpus analysis toolkit AntConc (Anthony 2020).

All of the concordances presented in this work were generated with this corpus analysis toolkit. I accessed the audio files and the time-aligned phonetic transcriptions using the speech analysis software Praat (Boersma & Weenink 2021). All of the spectrograms and waveforms displayed in this work were generated with this software.

I conducted quantitative analyses, using the data set called "MASC_dataframe.csv", which is also downloadable with MASC (see Section 3.4.1 for more details on this data set). For most of these analyses, I added more variables to the original MASC dataframe. For example, to investigate the feminine marker alternation, I used a subset of the MASC dataframe, which only contained the nouns ending with the feminine marker, and I added a number of variables which I expected the distribution of the feminine marker alternants to be influenced by (see Section 6.2.3). For example, I created the variable ENVIRONMENT to identify the phonological environments in which the feminine marker occurs, the variable TEMPLATICPATTERN to identify the templatic patterns of the feminine nouns, and the variables PRECEDINGSEGMENT and MANNER to identify the immediately preceding segment and its manner of articulation. An abbreviated extract from the subset used in this study is shown in (3) (see Section 6.2.3 for the original extract and Section 6.2 for the entire study).

(3) *Extract from the data set used to investigate the feminine marker alternation*

SG FORM	FEM MARKER	ENVIRONMENT	TEMPLATIC PATTERN	PRECEDING SEGMENT	MANNER
baḥərṯa	ṯ	CC___	CVCCCa	r	Rhotic
balbalča	č	VC___	CVCCVCCa	l	Lateral
ballōrča	č	VVC___	CVGGVVCCa	r	Rhotic
barəmṯa	ṯ	CC___	CVCCCa	m	Nasal

To conduct quantitative analyses of the data provided by data sets, such as the one presented in (3), I used spreadsheet software and the programming language for statistical computing R (R Core Team 2021).[1] The bar charts and mosaic plots displayed in this work were generated with this programming language. The boxplots were created with the `lattice` package (Sarkar 2008).

1 These data sets and R scripts can be found online at: https://osf.io/36pgv/.

2.4 Morphological analysis

Although this work focuses on the phonology (rather than the morphology) of Maaloula Aramaic, many of the alternations discussed in this book are morpheme-specific. Cases of phonologically conditioned allomorphy cannot be explained and discussed unless the relevant morphological background is presented. In all cases where allomorphy plays a role, the pertinent morphological phenomena are presented as we go along.

In order to understand the numerous phenomena discussed in this work, the reader necessitates an understanding of some general properties of Maaloula Aramaic word structure (for more details on the morphology of Maaloula Aramaic, see Spitaler 1938; Arnold 1990a).

In Maaloula Aramaic, as well as in other Semitic languages, words are derived from consonantal roots. The majority of these roots are triliteral, but there are also quadriliteral and biliteral roots. Each root has a broad meaning (e.g., *ṭʕn* 'carrying', *bšl* 'cooking', *šmṭ* 'fleeing; escaping'). Derivatives are generated from these roots according to templatic patterns, as in (4). This type of non-concatenative morphology is referred to as 'root-and-pattern morphology' (for root-and-pattern morphology in Semitic languages in general, see Gensler 2011: 283–287; for Arabic see, e.g., Watson 2002: 3–4; Hellmuth 2013: 47). The symbols C_1, C_2, and C_3 in (4) refer to the three consonants (or radicals) which make up the triliteral root.

(4) *Words generated from the triliteral root ṭʕn ($C_1C_2C_3$) 'carrying'*

Word	Meaning	Pattern	Part of speech	
iṭʕan	'he carried'	$iC_1C_2aC_3$	preterit verb	V.55
yiṭʕun	'(that) he carries'	$yiC_1C_2uC_3$	subjunctive verb	V.55
ṭʕōn	'carry (2M.SG)!'	$C_1C_2\bar{o}C_3$	imperative verb	V.55
ṭōʕen	'he carries'	$C_1\bar{o}C_2eC_3$	present verb	V.55
iṭʕen	'he is carrying'	$iC_1C_2eC_3$	perfect verb	V.55
ṭʕōna	'(the act of) carrying'	$C_1C_2\bar{o}C_3a$	noun	VI.850
ṭaʕna	'load'	$C_1aC_2C_3a$	noun	VI.850

The verbal derivatives which are derived from triliteral roots are created following eleven fixed patterns (Arnold 1990a: 53–55). These patterns, in Semitic languages generally, are called 'binyanim' in some references (e.g., Gensler 2011: 284) and 'verb forms' (or 'forms' for short) in other references (e.g., Watson 2002: 134). In this work, I use the latter, but I capitalize the first letter (i.e., *Form*) in order to distinguish between *Forms* in the sense of 'verb forms' and *forms* (non-capitalized) in the sense of ‘word forms’ or ‘grammatical words’ (which are usually contrasted with lexemes).

The eleven verb Forms in Maaloula Aramaic are shown in (5). For the sake of simplicity, only one representative example is shown for every Form. Complications, variations, exceptional cases, and non-triliteral verb Forms are ignored here. The Forms in (5) are taken from Arnold (1990a: chap. 3). All the examples are preterit verbs inflected for the third person masculine singular. The symbols GG refer to a geminate consonant (for gemination, see Chapter 9).

(5) *Maaloula Aramaic verb Forms (based on Arnold 1990a: chap. 3)*

Form	Pattern	Example	Meaning	
I	iC$_1$C$_2$eC$_3$	*iḏmex*	‘he slept’	V.56
II	C$_1$aG$_2$G$_2$eC$_3$	*zappen*	‘he sold’	V.60
III	C$_1$ōC$_2$aC$_3$	*sōfar*	‘he travelled’	V.60
IV	aC$_1$C$_2$eC$_3$	*arkeš*	‘he woke up’	V.61
I$_2$	ičC$_1$C$_2$eC$_3$	*iččxel*	‘he trusted (in God)’	V.62
II$_2$	čC$_1$aG$_2$G$_2$aC$_3$	*čʕažžab*	‘he marveled’	VI.139
III$_2$	čC$_1$ōC$_2$aC$_3$	*čḥōṣar*	‘he was besieged’	V.63
IV$_2$	ččaC$_1$C$_2$aC$_3$	*ččarnaḥ*	‘he was put/laid’	V.63
I$_7$	inC$_1$C$_2$aC$_3$	*inəfṭaḥ*	‘it (M) was opened’	V.64
I$_8$	iC$_1$čC$_2$aC$_3$	*inəčġab*	‘it (M) was stolen’	V.65
I$_{10}$	sčaC$_1$C$_2$eC$_3$	*sčaṣʕeb*	‘he found (sthg.) difficult’	V.66

In addition to these non-concatenative processes, affixation (which is a concatenative process) is an essential part of the morphology of Maaloula Aramaic. The examples in (6) show affixed words in Maaloula Aramaic.

(6) *Affixed words exemplified*

xif-ō
stone-PL
‘stones’ III.192

ešm-ax
name-2M.SG
‘your name’ III.144

zabn-iṯ
buy.PRET-1SG
‘I bought’ III.52

zaʕḳ-aṯ
call.PRET-3F.SG
‘she called; she screamed’ IV.68

y-nufḳ-an	*ni-m-baššl-in*
3-go out.SBJV-F.PL	1-PRS-cook-M.PL
'(that) they (F) go out' III.52	'we (M) cook' III.38

Throughout this work, I provide morpheme-by-morpheme glosses, such as the ones shown in (6), only when understanding the morphological structure is essential for understanding the phonological or morpho-phonological process to be introduced in a certain section. Once the relevant morphological background has been provided, the remaining examples in the section are presented without glosses and are analyzed from a phonological perspective (see Section 2.5).

By the term 'morpheme', I refer to the smallest unit that has a meaning (Hayes 2009: 103; Lieber 2009: 3; Plag 2018: 10). The examples in (6) above show that each morpheme has its own form (in the upper line) and meaning (in the line below it) (for the morpheme as a unit of form and meaning, see Plag 2018: sec. 2.1). In the cases where a morpheme does not have a form to express its meaning, I have used the zero-morph (Ø), as in (7) (for more details on the notion of the zero-morph (or zero affix), see Haspelmath & Sims 2010: 64; Plag 2018: 22).

(7) *Using the zero-morph in glossed examples*

Ø-m-ayṯy-an	*ḳaṭʕ-Ø-il*	*xōl-a*
3-PRS-bring-F.PL	cut.PRET-3M.SG-OM	food-NE
'they (F) bring' IV.156	'he stopped eating' IV.88	

It should be noted that the morphemes presented in this work and those presented in the previous literature (e.g., Spitaler 1938; Arnold 1990a) are not always in a one-to-one correspondence. The historical morphemes which used to have a meaning at earlier stages of the language but do not carry any meaning now are not treated as morphemes in this work (for a similar argument for the need to separate morphology from etymology, see Plag 2018: 24–25). For example, both Spitaler (1938: 88–90) and Arnold (1990a: 353–355) consider *-ōna* a suffix which occurs at the end of a number of masculine nouns, as in (8).

(8) *Masculine nouns ending in -ōna (Arnold 1990a: 353)*

ḥōna	'brother'
psōna	'boy'
ʕaḳōna	'crow; raven'
ṣafrōna	'(small) bird'
ġabrōna	'man'

According to Arnold (1990a: 353), *-ōna* in the examples above used to be the diminutive ending at earlier stages of Aramaic. However, this historical suffix does not express the diminutive anymore and does not carry any particular meaning in the Neo-Aramaic variety spoken in Maaloula. For this reason, I do not consider *-ōna* to be a morpheme in this work. I consider the nouns in (8) to have the following morphological structure: a nominal base + the nominal ending *-a* (which occurs at the end of the citation form of most nouns). This analysis is shown in (9).

(9) *The adopted analysis of the masculine nouns ending in the historical suffix -ōna*

ḥōn-a	*psōn-a*	*ʕaḳōn-a*	*ṣafrōn-a*	*ġabrōn-a*
brother-NE	boy-NE	crow-NE	bird-NE	man-NE
'brother'	'boy'	'crow; raven'	'(small) bird'	'man'

There are also other cases where the morphemes presented in the previous literature and the morphemes presented in this work are not in a one-to-one relation. In some of these cases, I divide what is considered one morpheme in the previous literature into two or more morphemes if each of these smaller morphemes carries its own meaning. For example, I divide the feminine plural ending *-ōṯa* ~ *-yōṯa* (according to Arnold 1990a: 292) into three morphemes: the plural marker itself *-ō* ~ *-yō*, the feminine marker *-ṯ*, and the nominal ending *-a* (see Sections 6.3 and 6.2 for the rationale). The examples in (10) (from Section 6.3) illustrate this analysis.

(10)

ḏukk-ō-ṯ-a	*mašču-yō-ṯ-a*
place-PL-F-NE	wedding-PL-F-NE
'places' III.200	'weddings' III.374

2.5 Phonological analysis

I present the phonological analysis in a rule-based format without commitment to potential theoretical underpinnings of a rule-based approach. An alternative constraint-based approach should also be feasible. For example, using the Stratal Optimality Theory model applied to Arabic by Kiparsky (2003) to analyze syllabification and vowel epenthesis in Maaloula Aramaic is also possible. I will not engage in a comparison between the rule-based and the constraint-based approaches, as none of my main points hinges on the choice of framework.

I express the phonological rules in formal notation to show how surface forms are derived from underlying forms. For example, I will show in Section 10.3.1 that the mid vowels /e/ and /o/ are realized as [i] and [u] respectively in pretonic position (see also Spitaler 1938: 4–5, 9; Arnold 1990a: 26). This pretonic raising rule is expressed in (11).

(11) *Pretonic raising of short mid vowels (from Section 10.3.1)*

$$\begin{bmatrix} \text{+syllabic} \\ \text{-long} \\ \text{-high} \\ \text{-low} \end{bmatrix} \rightarrow \text{[+high]} \ / \_\_ \ C_0 \begin{bmatrix} \text{+syllabic} \\ \text{+stress} \end{bmatrix}$$ [2]

Local and long-distance assimilation rules are expressed in feature-geometrical notation (see Chapter 7). For example, the assimilation of /l/ to a following coronal, which I discuss in Section 7.2.8, is formalized in (12) (see also Spitaler 1938: 34–35; Arnold 1990a: 19).

(12) *Assimilation of /l/ to a following coronal (from Section 7.2.8)*

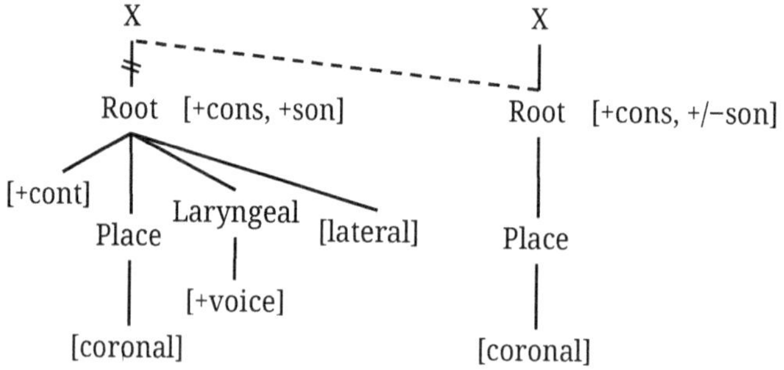

Syllable-related processes such as syllabification, vowel epenthesis, and resyllabification are expressed in moraic representations. For example, in (13) I show how syllabification applies in Maaloula Aramaic, using a moraic representation of the word *payṯaḥ* 'our home' III.60 (see Section 8.3.3 for the original analysis).

2 C_0 refers to any number of consonants.

(13) *Syllabification scheme exemplified (from Section 8.3.3)*

(a) Nucleus formation (b) Onset formation (c) Coda formation

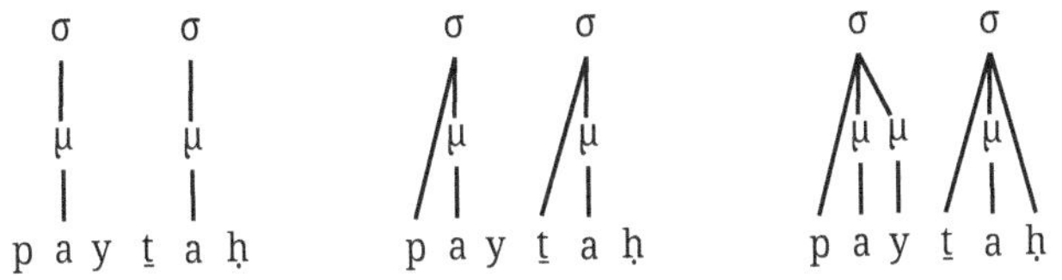

/payṯ-aḥ/ → [ˈpay.ṯaḥ] 'our home' III.60

Following Kiparsky (1982, 2003), I argue that the phonological processes apply at two distinct levels: the lexical level and the postlexical level. The lexical level is the word domain. I assume that, like in other languages such as Greek or Latin (e.g., Nespor & Vogel 2007: 110ff), the phonological word and the syntactic word coincide in Maaloula Aramaic. The syntactic word is the smallest syntactic unit (including affixes) that has a syntactic category specification, i.e., part of speech ("the terminal element of the syntactic tree", Nespor & Vogel 2007: 110). The phonological word in Maaloula Aramaic is coextensive with the syntactic word and constitutes the domain in which certain phonological processes do, or do not, apply.

According to these definitions, lexemes appearing in their citation forms, as in (14a), are considered words because each of them belongs to one part of speech and has one main stress. Inflectional word forms, such as the ones in (14b), are also considered words because they are syntactic units in the above sense. However, the clitic groups in (14c), each of which consists of a clitic and its host (e.g., a prepositional clitic and a prepositional complement), cannot be considered words. I will use vowel epenthesis, which is a postlexical process, to illustrate the different behavior of words versus clitic groups. Words starting with a CCC cluster (#CCC), such as the first word in (14b), differ from clitic groups which start with the same cluster (C#CC), such as the two examples in (14c). While we see an epenthetic schwa within the CCC cluster in the clitic group, vowel epenthesis is ruled out within the word (e.g., *nčḳalle* and not **nəčḳalle*). This will be discussed in more detail in Sections 8.4 and 8.5.

(14) (a)	*ṯarʕa*	'door'	IV.264
	xallṯa	'daughter-in-law'	IV.130
(b)	*nčḳalle*	'she met him'	IV.154
	mašəphōš	'she looks like you (F)'	IV.176
(c)	*bə-klēsya*	'in the church'	III.152
	lə-ʕrōba	'until the evening'	III.102

The postlexical level is where processes apply across word boundaries, within the phonological phrase. The examples in (15) (from Section 5.2.1) show how lexical and postlexical processes apply to derive surface forms from underlying forms. Throughout this work, I mark morpheme boundaries with hyphens in the underlying representations.

(15) *Deriving surface forms from underlying forms (from Section 5.2.1)*

Underlying forms		Surface forms		
/āsep/	→	[ˈʔō.seb]	'he takes'	FW
/āsep-l-a/	→	[ʔa.ˈseb.la]	'he takes her (as a wife)'	IV.132
/n-usp-l-ē-l-e/	→	[nu.səp.ˈlē.le]	'(that) I take (sthg. DEF) to him'	IV.58

/āsep/	/āsep-l-a/	/n-usp-l-ē-l-e/		
āse**b**	āse**bla**	–	bilabial stop voicing	lexical
ā.seb	ā.seb.la	nus.⟨p⟩.lē.le	syllabification	
ˈ**ā**.seb	ā.ˈ**seb**.la	nus.⟨p⟩.ˈ**lē**.le	stress assignment	
–	**a**.ˈseb.la	–	pretonic shortening	
ˈ**ō**.seb	–	–	/ā/ rounding	
–	–	nus.**ə**⟨p⟩.ˈlē.le	vowel epenthesis	postlexical
–	–	nu.**səp**.ˈlē.le	resyllabification	
ˈ**ʔ**ō.seb	**ʔ**a.ˈseb.la	–	glottal epenthesis	
[ˈʔō.seb]	[ʔa.ˈseb.la]	[nu.səp.ˈlē.le]		

I use derivations, such as the one shown in (15), to illustrate how phonological processes interact with each other. The derivation in (15) shows three interesting interactions that I will introduce briefly to exemplify what I mean by interacting phonological processes. The first interaction is between syllabification and vowel epenthesis, the second between pretonic shortening and /ā/ rounding, and the third between vowel epenthesis and bilabial stop voicing.

When syllabification applies to the underlying form /n-usp-l-ē-l-e/, the consonant /p/ remains unsyllabified (or stray) (see Section 8.3.3 for syllabification and Section 8.3.4 for stray consonants). Since this stray consonant is immediately preceded by a coda consonant, an epenthetic vowel can be inserted between them (for vowel epenthesis see Sections 8.2.2 and 8.3.5). Here, syllabification creates a phonological environment where vowel epenthesis can apply. In rule-ordering terminology, syllabification feeds vowel epenthesis (for a clear introduction to rule-ordering terminology, see Hayes 2009: 183–185).

Pretonic shortening turns /ā/ in /āsep-l-a/ into [a] because /ā/ occurs in a pretonic syllable (for pretonic shortening, see Section 10.3.2). If pretonic shortening had not applied, then /ā/ rounding would have applied (as it actually did to /āsep/ in the first column). Here, pretonic shortening prevents /ā/ rounding from applying. In rule-ordering terminology, pretonic shortening bleeds /ā/ rounding.

Bilabial stop voicing turns the voiceless bilabial stop /p/ into [b] in postvocalic position (for the bilabial stop voicing rule, see Section 5.2.1). For this reason, this voicing rule applies to postvocalic [p] in /āsep/ and /āsep-l-a/, but not to postconsonantal [p] in /n-usp-l-ē-l-e/. Vowel epenthesis inserts a schwa before the stray consonant ⟨p⟩ in /n-usp-l-ē-l-e/, making ⟨p⟩ postvocalic. Although ⟨p⟩ is postvocalic now, bilabial stop voicing cannot apply to it. This is because vowel epenthesis is ordered after (rather than before) bilabial stop voicing, and it therefore fails to feed it. In rule-ordering terminology, vowel epenthesis counterfeeds bilabial stop voicing.

3 The Maaloula Aramaic Speech Corpus (MASC)

3.1 Introduction

This chapter presents the Maaloula Aramaic Speech Corpus (MASC, Eid et al. 2022), the first electronic speech corpus of Maaloula Aramaic and the main source of language data that I use in this book.[1] MASC is available to the scientific community at https://doi.org/10.5281/zenodo.6496714.

Before creating MASC, neither a text corpus in electronic format nor a speech corpus with audio files and time-aligned transcriptions had been available. This does not imply, however, that there was no well-documented written or audio material on Maaloula Aramaic. Transcriptions of authentic narratives coming from fieldwork trips have been published sporadically for more than a century (e.g., Bergsträsser 1915, 1933; Reich 1937; Spitaler 1957; Arnold 1991a, 1991b). An online archive of audio files, albeit without accompanying transcriptions, has existed for around 20 years (see Section 3.2).

The importance of such transcriptions and audio archives to language documentation and preservation is undeniable, but the extent to which they can facilitate empirical linguistic research in their available format is rather limited. For example, a phonetician interested in the acoustic properties of the Maaloula Aramaic sounds would need to listen to the audio files and simultaneously go through the textbook pages to match the transcriptions with the pronounced segments. This is because these transcriptions are mainly available in paper format. By the same token, a morphologist studying a certain inflectional process would need to collect the examples manually from these textbooks.

The electronic corpus presented in this chapter meets these and other empirical research requirements by benefitting from and complementing the existing resources. The existing resources are the result of many hours of work involving finding the native speakers, recording their speech in situ, and painstakingly transcribing the recordings. Therefore, turning part of them into a speech corpus is a more efficient process than having to repeat all these steps from the beginning.

However, compiling a corpus that would cover a wide array of potential research needs should go beyond the digitization of available transcriptions. For that reason, we decided to design a multi-purpose corpus and make it available to the scientific community in four different formats: (1) transcriptions (e.g., for lexical

1 An earlier version of this chapter was published in Eid, Seyffarth & Plag (2022).

https://doi.org/10.1515/9783111447124-003

and sociolinguistic analysis), (2) lemmatized transcriptions (e.g., for morphological and lexicographical analysis), (3) audio files and time-aligned phonetic transcriptions (e.g., for phonetic and phonological analysis), and (4) an SQLite database, through which the data can be accessed at the level of tokens, types, lemmas, sentences, narratives, or speakers, thus enabling all sorts of inquiries at any of these levels.[2] Such formats are now considered state-of-the-art, as evidenced by the growing number of speech corpora which include time-aligned phonetic transcriptions, such as the TIMIT corpus (Garofolo et al. 1993), the Switchboard corpus (Godfrey, Holliman & McDaniel 1992; Godfrey & Holliman 1993), and the Buckeye Corpus (Pitt et al. 2007).

3.2 The data included in the corpus

The data chosen for inclusion in the Maaloula Aramaic Speech Corpus consist of the transcriptions of tape-recorded narratives that Werner Arnold collected during his field research in Maaloula between 1985 and 1987. These transcriptions alongside the translation into German appear in two publications (Arnold 1991a, 1991b). These two particular sources were chosen for two main reasons.

First, the audio files of these narratives are available at the *Semitisches Tonarchiv* 'Semitic Sound Archive' website of Heidelberg University (see Arnold 2003). They are fully accessible to the scientific community as the Semitisches Tonarchiv "was established by support of the Deutsche Forschungsgemeinschaft and it can therefore be used by all scientists for research purposes" (Arnold, private communication). Each audio file is further supplemented by valuable metadata (e.g., name, gender, age, and occupation of the speaker; the year and place of recording; and reference to the textbook that contains the transcription).

Second, these texts are varied with regard to their content and the sociolinguistic variables pertaining to their narrators. In terms of content, these texts consist of 173 monologues that belong to different text types, such as fairy tales, fables, and legends; local and religious traditions, customs, and beliefs; personal experiences and autobiographies; daily, occupational, and agricultural activities; jokes and anecdotes; songs and poems (see Arnold 1991a: vii–x, 1991b: vii–ix for a comprehensive classification of the individual narratives).

In terms of their sociolinguistic properties, these monologues are also varied as they were narrated by 45 native speakers (32 males, 13 females) between the ages

2 The pronoun *we* in this chapter refers to the team that was responsible for creating MASC. This team consisted of Ghattas Eid, Esther Seyffarth, Emad Rihan, Werner Arnold, and Ingo Plag.

of 13 and 89. There are no substantial differences between the age of female speakers (mean = 50.85 years) and male speakers (mean = 52.62 years) (see Arnold 1991a: 381–382, 1991b: 345–346 for the name, age, and occupation of each speaker).

Now I turn to how we computerized and annotated these transcriptions.

3.3 Data computerization and annotation

This step involved carrying out the following tasks:

- scanning and digitizing the transcriptions
- correcting the errors manually and adding informative tags
- lemmatizing the transcriptions
- denoising the audio recordings
- automatically aligning the transcriptions with the corresponding recordings

In what follows, each task will be introduced and explained individually.

3.3.1 Scanning and digitizing the transcriptions

The two volumes (Arnold 1991a, 1991b) were scanned, and the transcriptions were computerized with the help of the optical character recognition (OCR) software ABBYY FineReader 10.[3] However, since Maaloula Aramaic is not one of the languages that the OCR software can recognize, the computerized text was far from perfect, as example (1) shows:

(1) **OCR output:** *anah höxa bd-blöta nmiScabrill Sinbö mastra ra?isô P-blöta*
Desired text: *anaḥ hōxa bə-blōta nmiʕčabrill ʕinbō maṣtra raʔisō lə-blōta*
'We, here in the village, consider grapes to be a main source for the village.'
III.28

While some errors were predictable and somehow automatically correctable (e.g., *S*, *c*, and *ö* ~ *ô* could be replaced with *ʕ*, *č*, and *ō* respectively), other errors were impossible to correct automatically. For example, the contrast between similarly written characters (e.g., *š* and *ṣ*, *ḳ* and *k*, *ḥ* and *h*) was neutralized completely by the

3 We are grateful to the Harrassowitz Publishing House for allowing us to use the published transcriptions.

OCR software, which displayed all these characters without the diacritic marks (e.g., *anah* rather than *anaḥ* 'we' in (1)). As a result, manual correction was inevitable.

3.3.2 Correcting errors and adding informative tags

In order to produce an error-free text, we compared the scanned texts with both the original transcriptions and audio files. During this phase, two types of errors, spelling inconsistencies, and mismatches were identified and corrected. The first type consists of spelling errors and inconsistencies in the original transcription, such as the words in (2). The errors, here, were not made by the original narrators. They are the result of the transcription process itself. Therefore, we corrected them without adding any textual marking.

(2)

Misspelled	Corrected		
sōləfṯa	*soləfṯa*	'story'	IV.140
bēʕṯa	*beʕṯa*	'egg'	III.326
ḳuttōra	*ḳuṭṭōra*	'quarrel; fight'	IV.8
m-ʕa	*maʕ*	'from; about'	IV.8
ḳʕōle ~ *kʕōle*	*ḳʕōle*	'he sat'	III.304 ~ IV.8

The second type consists of errors made by the narrators themselves. In these cases, we tried to remain as faithful as possible to the audio files even if this meant that some of our new passages would be different from the original transcriptions. For this type, we added explicit textual marking. Whenever a narrator made an error, we would transcribe their words the way they were said, but we would mark the error by inserting *sic* in square brackets immediately after it and give our language consultant's suggested correction in parentheses without changing the narrators' actual words, as shown in (3). In this example, the narrator inadvertently made a subject-verb agreement error. He used the verb *ṯōle* which is inflected for the third person masculine singular although it is followed by the feminine subject *eḥḏa*.

(3) *ṯōle* [sic] (= *ṯalla*) *eḥḏa*

ṯō-l-e	(=*ṯ-al-l-a*)	*eḥḏ-a*
come.PRET-OM-3M.SG	come.PRET-3F.SG-OM-3F.SG	one-F

'Someone (F) came.' III.132

In the original transcriptions, only one form appears (usually the corrected one). The second type also includes false starts, self-corrections, and extraneous remarks. Whenever a narrator reformulated their words after a false start or some hesitation, both forms would be kept, but the false start would be followed by points of ellipsis, as example (4) shows. This practice was already adopted in the original transcriptions, but we extended it to cover all similar cases.

(4) *battax... battaḥ nibəx baḥar, lōb ṭaššrīčnaḥ*

batt-ax	*batt-aḥ*	*ni-bəx*	*baḥar*	*lōb*	*ṭaššr-īč-n-aḥ*
will-2M.SG	will-1PL	1-cry.SBJV	a lot	if	leave.PRET-2M.SG-LM-1PL

'You (M.SG) will... We will cry a lot if you (M.SG) leave us.' IV.116

If a word is interrupted, it is marked with two consecutive hyphens (--) (e.g., *amrō-- amrōle* 'she said to him' IV.14). We chose a different symbol for interrupted words to distinguish them from false starts, self-corrections, and extraneous remarks. This is because the interrupted words are always ungrammatical as they are cut off before reaching their end (e.g., **amrō*). They are not part of the lexicon of the language. However, the words followed by points of ellipsis are meaningful and grammatical on their own (e.g., *battax* 'you (M.SG) will' in (4)), but they are either redundant or in disagreement with the following syntactic units.

We kept the punctuation marks and numbering of the individual sentences as they appear in the original text. We also kept the original loanword annotation which marks the non-aramaicized, infrequently occurring Arabic loanwords (Arnold 1991a: 24). We only changed the symbols used in this annotation from the original superscript *A* letters, as in (5a), to the tags <ar> and </ar>, as in (5b).

(5) (a) Original text: ^{A}*fa*^{A} *bess yiṯḳan aylul*
(b) Corpus text: <ar> *fa* </ar> *bess yiṯḳan aylul*
'When September comes.' III.28

3.3.3 Lemmatizing the transcriptions

Lemmatization is a type of corpus tagging whereby the inflected word forms are linked to their lemmas. Lemmatization is a handy feature for many research tasks and is particularly useful for highly inflectional languages (McEnery, Xiao & Tono 2006: 35–36). Being a Semitic language with complex morphology, Maaloula Aramaic is such a language. This is illustrated in (6).

(6) Lemma / Word form

Lemma			Word form		
ḏōḏa	'uncle'	III.220	*ḏaḏōye*	'his uncles'	III.256
ḏōrča	'house'	IV.138	*ḏaryōṯa*	'houses'	IV.68

We decided to lemmatize the transcriptions to maximize the benefit of this corpus. Since there were no electronic resources available for Aramaic that would have allowed automatic lemmatization, we did this manually, implementing the following procedure.

As a first step, we created a word list, which consisted of all of the 12,220 unique word forms, and supplied each word form with its lemma and root as they appear in Arnold's (2019) Aramaic-German dictionary. We excluded 614 forms because they were interrupted or misspoken words, individual letters, Arabic loanwords, or proper nouns. Although we kept these word forms in the list, we provided them with tags rather than lemmas, such as [interrupted], [sic], [NA], [loanword], and [proper noun].[4] The resulting lemma list (exemplified in Table 3.1) consists of 3,781 different lemmas derived from 1,932 roots.

Table 3.1: Extract from the lemma list

Root	Lemma	Word form
zbn	zappen yzappen	mzappnin
zbn	zappen yzappen	nimzappella
zbn	zappen yzappen	nimzappen
zbn	zappen yzappen	nimzappnilla
zbn	zappen yzappen	nimzappnille
zbn	zappen yzappen	nzappīlle
zbn	zappen yzappen	nzappillēle

Based on the hand-crafted list of form-lemma mappings, the transcription files were enhanced to indicate the lemma for each word form. Lemmas were added in angled brackets immediately after the word form, making this version of the corpus easy to use with AntConc (Anthony 2020) (see Section 3.4.2 for the advantages of this format).

4 We noticed later that we could exclude more Arabic loanwords and proper nouns, but we did not proceed because classifying a word as aramaicized or not did not prove straightforward.

3.3.4 Denoising the audio recordings

Since the original audio files were tape-recorded several decades ago, some amount of noise was present in the data. We used the REAPER Digital Audio Workstation software with the ReaFIR plugin to create a noise profile for the audio files and to generate a denoised version of each file.[5]

3.3.5 Automatically aligning the transcriptions with the recordings

One of the goals of this work was the creation of Praat TextGrid files in which the audio files are aligned with their transcriptions. Since Maaloula Aramaic is a relatively small and underdocumented language, no pre-trained language-specific alignment tool is available for it. We used the WebMAUS tool (Schiel 1999, 2015) provided by BAS Web Services (Kisler, Reichel & Schiel 2017) to align the denoised audio files with the transcription files.[6] WebMAUS provides a language-agnostic model which can align speech signals with phonetic transcriptions represented in SAMPA format.

We created a mapping of the characters appearing in our corrected transcription files to their corresponding SAMPA characters and used a SAMPA-encoded version of our text files as input to WebMAUS, together with the denoised audio files. Denoising the audio files prior to processing led to significantly better results with regard to alignment quality. For instance, noisy periods in the original audio files were often analyzed as long fricatives by WebMAUS, while the denoised files allowed WebMAUS to more reliably recognize pauses. The TextGrid files were then extended by a sentence tier, in addition to the word- and phoneme-level tiers provided by the WebMAUS output.

3.4 Corpus structure and use

In this section, we describe the composition of the corpus. We present statistics on the word tokens that make up the corpus (i.e., the number of word tokens per file,

5 The REAPER Digital Audio Workstation software is available at https://reaper.fm (accessed April 18, 2024).

6 BAS Web Services is available at https://clarin.phonetik.uni-muenchen.de/BASWebServices/interface (accessed April 18, 2024).

per speaker, per gender, and per age group). We also describe the different formats in which the corpus is available, where to find the corpus, and how to use it.

Following Arnold's original organization of texts and audio files, we divided the transcriptions into 173 text files, which contain 64,845 tokens in total, and saved them in UTF-8 format.[7] The speech data vary considerably in the number of tokens per file (mean = 374.8, median = 227, minimum = 19, maximum = 4,340, standard deviation = 470) and in the number of tokens per speaker (mean = 1,441, median = 754, minimum = 42, maximum = 10,688, standard deviation = 2,232.9). As can be seen from Figure 3.1, four speakers (represented by the leftmost bars) provided many more tokens than any of the other speakers. They produced 31,988 tokens, making up 49.3% of the entire corpus, whereas all the other 41 speakers produced a total of 32,857 tokens (50.7%).

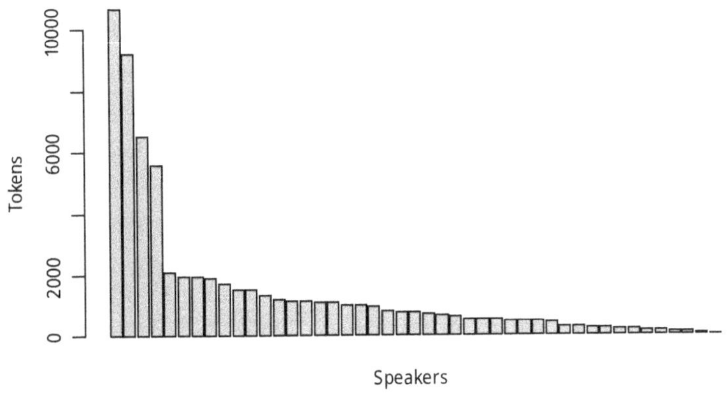

Fig. 3.1: Distribution of tokens by speaker

Around 63% of the produced speech data come from older speakers (aged 50-79) (see Figure 3.2). This trend is more prominent for female speakers where 86% of the tokens come from these age groups. Although the same trend is noticeable for male speakers, the 10,688 tokens produced by only one 26-year-old speaker (represented by the leftmost bar in Figure 3.1 above) have partly masked this trend by giving more weight to age group 20-29.

7 Corpus users will notice, however, that the corpus consists of 65,722 tokens, which additionally include the informative tags, *sic* and *ar*, and corrected words in parentheses.

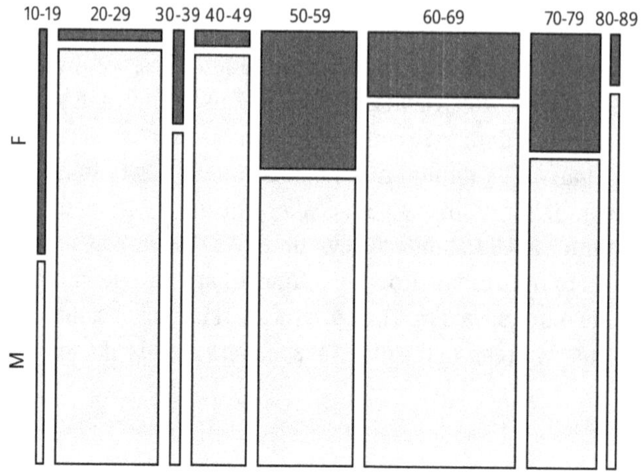

Fig. 3.2: Distribution of tokens by age and gender

Figure 3.2 also clearly shows that the corpus contains more words spoken by male speakers (53,922 tokens, 83.2%) than by female speakers (10,923 tokens, 16.8%). This distribution is expected, given that the male speakers outnumber the female speakers (see Section 3.2), and the four main speakers are all men.

As already mentioned in the introduction above, the corpus is available to the research community at https://doi.org/10.5281/zenodo.6496714 in four formats: (1) transcriptions, (2) lemmatized transcriptions, (3) audio files and time-aligned phonetic transcriptions, and (4) an SQLite database.

3.4.1 The transcriptions

These text files are the digitized transcriptions that contain no annotation at all (except for the informative tags presented in Section 3.3.2, e.g., [sic], <ar>, </ar>). These plain transcription files (as well as the lemmatized transcription files presented in Section 3.4.2) can be used with any regular programming language, such as Python. Researchers not familiar with programming can access and analyze these files via a corpus analysis toolkit. We chose to set up the files in a format compatible with the corpus tool AntConc (Anthony 2020) because it is user-friendly, free, and available to Windows, Macintosh OS X, and Linux users.

Using the corpus analysis toolkit, researchers can investigate the unannotated corpus by carrying out basic tasks, such as generating frequency lists, examining concordances, and analyzing collocations and keywords. For example, Table 3.2 shows part of the key word in context (KWIC) display for *xōla* ‘food’ within a window of two words to the left and right.

Table 3.2: KWIC concordance of *xōla* ‘food’

KWIC			File
xett mišwin	xōla	alūla aw	III.55.txt
čiḳʕēx billa	xōla	?” (15) amelle	IV.23.txt
“ē, šwēn	xōla	atar, baḥ	III.23.txt
htīṭa aw	xōla	aw ščū	III.52.txt
ʕammaxell lanna	xōla	.” (28) aḳa bib-	IV.07.txt
ʕammaxlōl lanna	xōla	. (29) aḳa ḥakīna	IV.07.txt
ḏikkil iṭlab	xōla	, aḳam hann	IV.33.txt

Using wild cards, such as the asterisk, researchers can conduct basic morphological analyses. For example, to generate a list of the words that contain the root *ṭʕn*, the search string *ṭ*ʕ*n* can be used. Table 3.3 shows only seven out of the 197 concordance hits that this search finds in the corpus.

Table 3.3: KWIC concordance of words containing the search string *ṭ*ʕ*n*

KWIC			File
čimbaṭṭel	čiṭʕun	ḥ-ḥaṣṣax?” (6)	IV.22.txt
amrillax lā	čiṭʕun	ḥ-ḥaṣṣax?” (11)	IV.22.txt
w čzellax	čiṭʕun	ḥ-ḥaṣṣax?” (19)	IV.22.txt
batta	čšaṭiʕenne	šaṭranž. (19)	IV.15.txt
lā baḳḳrič	čṭuʕnenne	w čišwenne	IV.34.txt
w hanna	ʕamṭōʕen	ḥ-ḥaṣṣe, bann	IV.22.txt
mazal čū	ʕamṭōʕna	ḳuṭʕā w	IV.55.txt

However, raw data like these may contain many irrelevant words. For example, although the fourth word, *čšaṭiʕenne* ‘play (SBJV.3F.SG) [e.g., chess] with him’, contains the search string *ṭ*ʕ*n*, it should be weeded out manually because its root is *šṭʕ* rather than *ṭʕn* (see Arnold 2019: 761).

The lemma list we provide as part of our corpus is a more elegant and timesaving solution to the problem of having to find and remove the irrelevant results manually. This solution enables the corpus users to investigate the lemmas as well as all their inflectional variants by uploading a lemma list to the corpus tool. For the lemma list (presented in Section 3.3.3) to be processed by AntConc, its layout was modified slightly. Example (7) shows the modified layout of the lemma list whereby the lemma is separated from its word form(s) by an arrow (->).

(7) *The AntConc-friendly lemma list layout*

ḥaẓẓūra -> ḥaẓẓūr, ḥaẓẓūra, ḥaẓẓurō
ḥbōka -> ḥbōka
hbulya -> hbulya
ḥḏawṯa -> əḥḏawōṯa, ḥḏawōṯa
ḥḏučča -> əḥḏuččaḥ, ḥḏučča, ḥḏučče, ḥḏuččōṯa, ḥḏuččun
ḥḏūṯa -> əḥḏūṯa, ḥḏūṯ, ḥḏūṯa, ḥḏuṯō

For the corpus users to load the lemma list to AntConc, they need to upload the Maaloula Aramaic Speech Corpus first, and then choose the Word List category in the Tool Preferences tab and click on the Lemma List Load button. When a word list is created, the lemma (rather than the word form) and its frequency are given first, followed by the individual word forms and their frequencies, as in Figure 3.3.

Rank	Freq	Lemma	Lemma Word Form(s)
1	4647	w	w 4638 wə 8 wəl 1
2	1948	b-	b 1038 bib 21 bil 15 bā 96 bāx 1 bāḥ 4 bī 3 bīš 2 bōn 29 bōnxun
3	1925	amar yīmar	amar 4 amell 38 amella 185 amelle 393 amellen 2 amellon 95 am
4	1607	ʕa/ʕal	aʕlax 21 aʕle 170 aʕli 5 aʕliš 4 aʕəl 27 əʕ 4 ʕ 308 ʕa 786 ʕal 135 ʕl

Fig. 3.3: Screenshot from AntConc: A lemma frequency list

Using the same search string (i.e., **ṭ*ʕ*n**) in the Word List pane and the numbers in the Search Only box, we can examine the lemmas that contain the root *ṭʕn*. The search yields only six results this time, three of which contain the root *ṭʕn*, and three are irrelevant. Figure 3.4 illustrates one of these six lemmas (highlighted). It can be seen that all the inflectional forms of this lemma which the corpus contains are listed together with their frequencies to the right of the lemma.

Rank	Freq	Lemma	Lemma Word Form(s)
51	202	hōxa	hōxa 109 ōxa 93
52	202	iṭʕan yiṭʕun	iṭʕan 2 iṭʕen 6 niṭʕill 1 nṭaʕell 3 nṭaʕnilla 1 nṭōʕen 1 yiṭʕun 2 yṭuʕnenne
53	201	yīb	nīb 1 nība 1 nībin 15 yīb 153 yībun 1 čīb 23 čība 5 čībin 2

Fig. 3.4: Screenshot from AntConc: A lemma containing the search string **ṭ*ʕ*n** and its word forms

For the corpus users who want to conduct further analyses and, therefore, need the output to be organized in a dataframe with each variable receiving a column, we provide a spreadsheet for this purpose. The spreadsheet is called "MASC_dataframe.csv" and is downloadable with the corpus. It contains all the 12,220 unique word forms, their frequencies, their lemmas, the frequencies of their lemmas, and their roots. Table 3.4 shows the first few rows of the spreadsheet.

Table 3.4: Extract from the MASC dataframe

Root	Lemma	LemmaFreq	Word_form	Word_formFreq
w	w	4647	w	4638
w	w	4647	wə	8
w	w	4647	wəl	1
b	b-	1948	b	1038
b	b-	1948	bā	96
b	b-	1948	bāḥ	4

3.4.2 The lemmatized transcriptions

In these files, each word is followed by the citation form of its lemma in angled brackets, as in (8). These files are the result of the lemmatization process introduced in Section 3.3.3.

(8) *Two lemmatized sentences from file III.01.txt*

(2) anaḥ<anaḥ> hōxa<hōxa> bə<b->-blōta<blōta> nmiʕčabrill<iʕčbar yiʕčbar> ʕinbō<ʕenəpṯa> maṣtra<maṣtra> raʔisō<raʔīsa> lə<l>-blōta<blōta>. (3) <ar<[annotation]>> fa<fa> </ar<[annotation]>> bess<bess/bessi> yiṯḳan<iṯḳen yiṯḳan> aylul<aylun/aylul> yiščawyan<iščwi yiščwi> ʕinbō<ʕenəpṯa> ʕa<ʕa/ʕal> maẓbuṭ<maẓbuṭ>, tōr<tōr> batte<batt-> yizlullun<zalle yzelle> ʕa<ʕa/ʕal> šṭōḥa<šṭōḥa>.

Researchers can use this lemmatized corpus in different ways, using a corpus analysis toolkit. For example, they can search for the lemma itself, as in Table 3.5. In this example, the search for the lemma *iṯḳen yiṯḳan* 'to become' (a lemma chosen from example (8) above) yields 476 hits, seven of which are shown in the table.

Table 3.5: KWIC concordance of the lemma *iṯḳen yiṯḳan* 'to become'

KWIC			File
iṯḳen<	iṯḳen yiṯḳan	>. amelle<amar yīmar>	III.32.txt
yiṯḳan<	iṯḳen yiṯḳan	>." (18) amellon<amar	IV.20.txt
ṯōḳna<	iṯḳen yiṯḳan	>." (13) amrōle<amar	IV.56.txt
ṯiḳniṯ<	iṯḳen yiṯḳan	> ana<ana> nnōḥeč<inḥeč	III.53.txt
ṯiḳniṯ<	iṯḳen yiṯḳan	> ana<ana> yaṯma<yaṯma>	III.99.txt
ṯōḳen<	iṯḳen yiṯḳan	>, ana<ana> mn<m-/mn->	IV.15.txt
ṯiḳninnaḥ<	iṯḳen yiṯḳan	> ana<ana> w<w>	IV.58.txt

If a researcher is not sure what the exact lemma is, they can look it up by searching for any of its word forms.

AntConc provides the option of hiding these tags completely or partially (from the Tags category in the Global Settings tab). If the option Hide Tags is chosen, the tags will be hidden completely, and the files will appear in their plain form (as in Section 3.4.1). However, if the option Hide Tags (Search in Conc/Plot/File View) is chosen and the lemma is typed explicitly in the search window with the surrounding brackets and a preceding asterisk (e.g., *<iṯḳen yiṯḳan>), then the lemma itself will not be revealed, but the relevant word forms will be marked.

Figure 3.5 is a screenshot from the File View window in AntConc. All tags, including the searched lemma *iṯḳen yiṯḳan* 'to become', are hidden, but the relevant word forms *yṯuḳnun* 'become (SBJV.3M.PL)' and *ṯōḳnin* 'become (PRS.3M.PL)' are marked in blue.

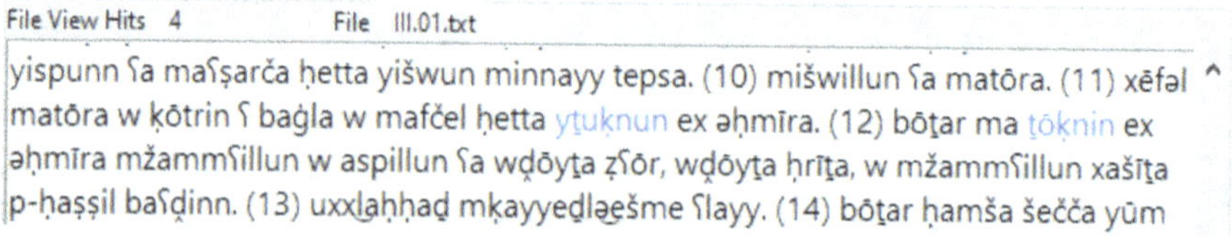
File View Hits 4
File III.01.txt
yispunn ʕa maʕṣarča ḥetta yišwun minnayy tepsa. (10) mišwillun ʕa matōra. (11) xēfəl
matōra w ḳōtrin ʕ baġla w mafčel ḥetta yṯuḳnun ex əḥmīra. (12) bōṯar ma ṯōḳnin ex
əḥmīra mžammʕillun w aspillun ʕa wḏōyṯa ẓʕōr, wḏōyṯa ḥrīṯa, w mžammʕillun xašīṯa
p-ḥaṣṣil baʕḏinn. (13) uxxlaḥḥaḏ mḳayyeḏlæšme ʕlayy. (14) bōṯar ḥamša šečča yūm

Fig. 3.5: Screenshot from the File View window in AntConc (hidden lemma tags)

3.4.3 The audio files and time-aligned phonetic transcriptions

The audio files are included in our corpus in the form of 176 mp3 files (10 hours of audio material).[8] Both the original and denoised audio files are available and can be opened in Praat (Boersma & Weenink 2021) together with their corresponding TextGrid files to conduct different types of acoustic analyses, such as measuring segment duration, vowel formants, and pitch.

The TextGrid annotations consist of four tiers, as shown in Figure 3.6. The first tier represents the sentence level. The second and third tiers represent the word level in the normal script (Tier 2) and SAMPA (Tier 3). The fourth tier represents the segment level, which is also transcribed in SAMPA.

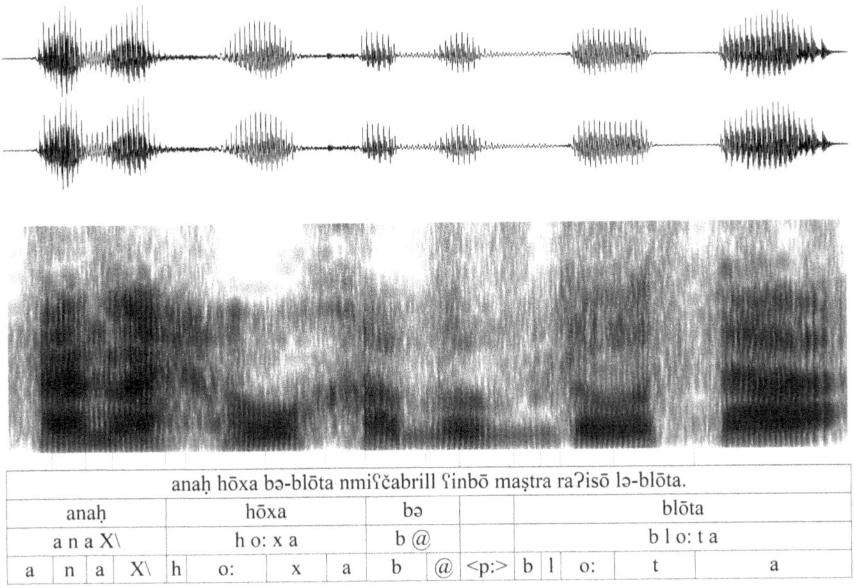

Fig. 3.6: Screenshot from Praat displaying the four tiers as well as the corresponding spectrogram and waveform

8 During the time alignment process, we had to divide a 44-minute audio file into four pieces. This explains why we have 176 (rather than 173) mp3 files.

3.4.4 The SQLite database

The SQLite database consists of eight interconnected tables in which the tokens, types, lemmas, sentences, narratives, speakers, audio files, and transcription files that appear in the corpus are associated with each other. The structure of the database is visualized in Figure 3.7.

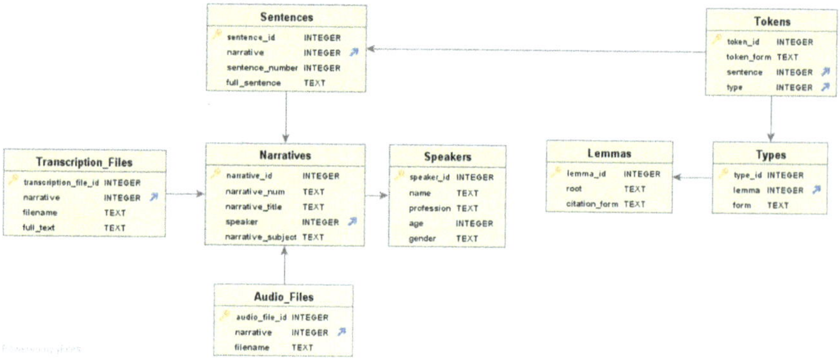

Fig. 3.7: The structure of the database

This database provides a way to conduct statistical analyses that optionally take metadata into account. For instance, the database can be queried to answer questions such as: Which words are most often used by female speakers, and which words are most often used by male speakers? Which words are specific to one subject area, and which words appear in the context of a variety of topics? Which words are exclusively used by speakers belonging to a particular profession? Do younger speakers produce longer or shorter sentences than older speakers? An example query selecting all sentences uttered by female speakers under 40 is presented in Figure 3.8.

3.5 Discussion: Applications

As previously noted, one of the main goals of creating the Maaloula Aramaic Speech Corpus is to facilitate empirical linguistic research. This goal has been put to the test in the different studies conducted in this book.

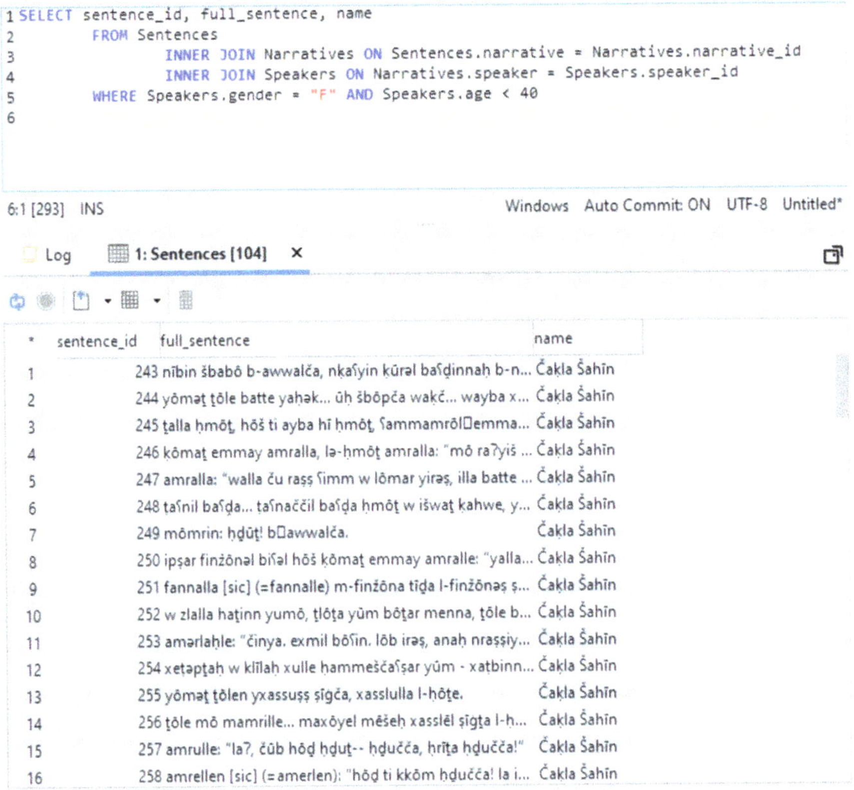

Fig. 3.8: Example query on the MASC database

To mention only two examples, MASC was an essential component of the research process that I adopted in order to investigate vowel epenthesis in Maaloula Aramaic (see Section 8.3.1). As can be seen in Figure 3.9, I used MASC to extract the words that exemplify a descriptive generalization found in previous accounts as well as the words that represent counterexamples not captured by the generalization. The numerous examples and counterexamples provided by the corpus helped me reformulate and formalize the generalization.

In a different study employing acoustic analyses, I used the TextGrid files to measure the durational differences between singletons and geminates on the one hand and between the vowels preceding them on the other hand (see Section 9.3).

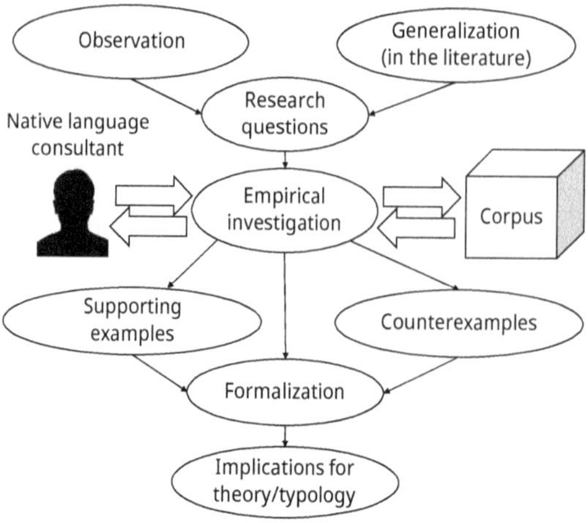

Fig. 3.9: The research process adopted to investigate vowel epenthesis

Further studies based on MASC are possible in the future. For example, since the corpus provides authentic speech production data, it may be useful for studies of speech production that want to test the effect of word frequency or morphological processes (e.g., affixation) on phonetic implementation in a language that has never been explored from this perspective.

4 Phoneme inventory

4.1 Introduction

This chapter introduces the phoneme inventory of Maaloula Aramaic. It is divided into two sections. In the first section, I introduce the consonants, which I group according to their manner of articulation (i.e., stops, affricates, fricatives, nasals, liquids, and glides). In the second section, I present the vowels, which are categorized as short vowels and long vowels, and I discuss the phonemic status of diphthongs and the epenthetic vowel.

4.2 Consonants

Maaloula Aramaic has twenty-eight consonant phonemes, shown in Table 4.1. In addition, there are three marginal phonemes, appearing in parentheses, which occur only in loanwords (Arnold 1990a: 12, 2006: 1, 2011: 686). In the table, the left-aligned consonants are voiceless, and the right-aligned consonants are voiced.

Table 4.1: Consonant phonemes; marginal phonemes in parentheses (adapted from Arnold 2006: 1) (see also Duntsov, Häberl & Loesov 2022: 363)

	Labial	**Dental**	**Alveolar**	**Palato-alveolar**	**Palatal/ Post-palatal**	**Velar/ Post-velar**	**Uvular**	**Pharyn-geal**	**Glottal**
Stop	*p* *b*		*t* *(d)*		*k*	*ḳ* *(g)*			*(ʔ)*
emphatic			*ṭ*						
Affricate				*č*					
Fricative	*f*	*ṯ* *ḏ*	*s* *z*	*š* *ž*			*x* *ġ*	*ḥ* *ʕ*	*h*
emphatic		*ḏ̣*	*ṣ* *ẓ*						
Nasal	*m*		*n*						
Rhotic			*r*						
Lateral			*l*						
Glide	*w*				*y*				

https://doi.org/10.1515/9783111447124-004

The geminate consonants, which are transcribed as two identical letters (e.g., *ḥaṣṣa* 'back' IV.200), are not included in the phoneme inventory as most of them are formed by morphological and phonological processes (see Section 9.2).

The correspondences between the adopted transcription symbols and the IPA symbols are given in (1), repeated in part from Section 2.2.2 for convenience. Only the symbols which differ from the IPA symbols are shown (see Section 2.2.2 for more details on the transcription system).

(1) *Correspondences between the adopted transcription and the IPA symbols*

Transcription	IPA	Transcription	IPA
t̠	/θ/	*ṭ*	/tˤ/ or /tˠ/
d̠	/ð/	*ḏ̣*	/ðˤ/ or /ðˠ/
š	/ʃ/	*ṣ*	/sˤ/ or /sˠ/
č	/tʃ/	*ẓ*	/zˤ/ or /zˠ/
ž	/ʒ/	*k*	/kʲ/ or /k̟/
x	/χ/	*ḳ*	/k̠/ or /k/
ġ	/ʁ/	*y*	/j/
ḥ	/ħ/		

It should be noted that the dots placed under certain letters may cause a notational problem to the reader because these dots do not consistently refer to the same articulatory properties. Whereas the dot marks the emphatics *ṭ ḏ̣ ṣ ẓ* (see (4) below), it is also placed under two non-emphatic phonemes, i.e., the (post-)velar stop *ḳ* and the voiceless pharyngeal fricatives *ḥ*.

For Maaloula Aramaic, I adopt a model of feature geometry (shown in (2)) based on proposals made by Sagey (1986) and Halle (1992, 1995) (see Uffmann 2011: 650 and Zsiga 2013: 293 for the two models that directly inspired this model). This model is considered articulator-based because "priority is given to articulatory considerations in the grouping of features in the geometry" (Uffmann 2011: 649).

Apart from the emphatic and glottal consonants, the Maaloula Aramaic consonants are characterized by one place feature: [labial], [coronal], [dorsal], or [pharyngeal], as in (3).

The emphatic consonants deserve special attention. The term 'emphatic' indicates a consonant with a specific type of secondary articulation (e.g., the emphatic consonants /ṭ ḏ̣ ṣ ẓ/ vs. the non-emphatic counterparts /t d̠ s z/). There seems to be no agreement on the term to be used to describe the exact nature of this secondary articulation in the literature on Semitic phonology. Whereas some references on Aramaic phonology refer to it as velarization (see, e.g., Arnold 1990a: 16 on Western

Neo-Aramaic; Jastrow 1993: 3 on Turoyo), other references on Arabic phonology refer to it as pharyngealization (see, e.g., Watson 2002: 38, 269).

(2) *A feature geometry model for Maaloula Aramaic*

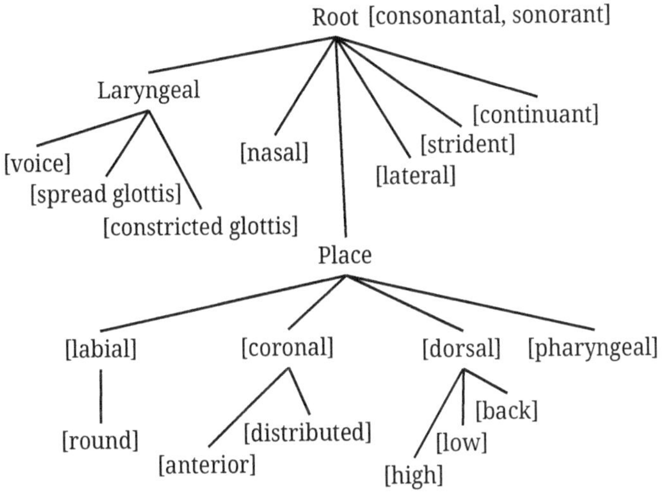

(3) *Place features*

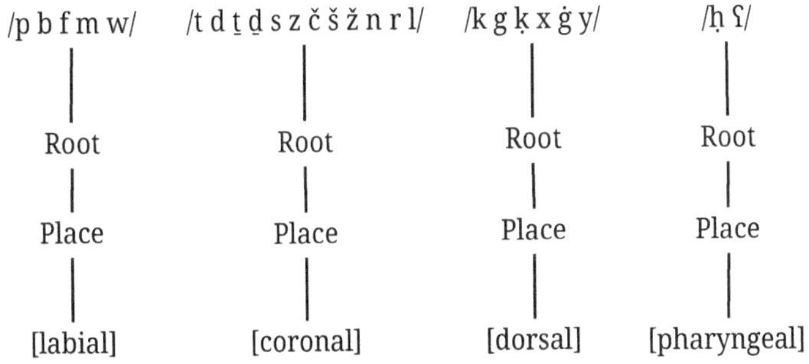

Since laboratory analyses that would investigate the articulatory correlates of emphasis in this variety do not exist yet, I will adopt the following terminology. For the descriptive parts of this book, I will use the cover term 'emphatic'. For the parts which involve formalization, the emphatic consonants /ṭ ḍ ṣ ẓ/ will be characterized by the primary feature [coronal] and the secondary feature [+low]. By choosing [+low] to represent the secondary articulation, I am tacitly assuming that emphasis is pharyngealization, rather than velarization. Using the feature [+low] for pharyngealization is common in phonological theory (see, e.g., Hayes 2009: 88; Zsiga 2013: 267). However, the choice between velarization and pharyngealization is of little consequence to the phonology because whereas the distinction between emphasized and plain pronunciation is contrastive in Maaloula Aramaic, the distinction between velarization and pharyngealization is not contrastive.

The remaining question about the emphatic consonants is: How can the primary feature [coronal] be distinguished from the secondary feature [+low] in the feature tree? One of the solutions proposed to mark the difference between a primary and secondary articulation in the articulator-based model is to extend a pointer from the Root node to the primary feature (Sagey 1986: 207; Halle, Vaux & Wolfe 2000: 390; Uffmann 2011: 653). This solution is illustrated in (4).

(4) *Emphatic consonants: Distinguishing the primary from secondary articulation*

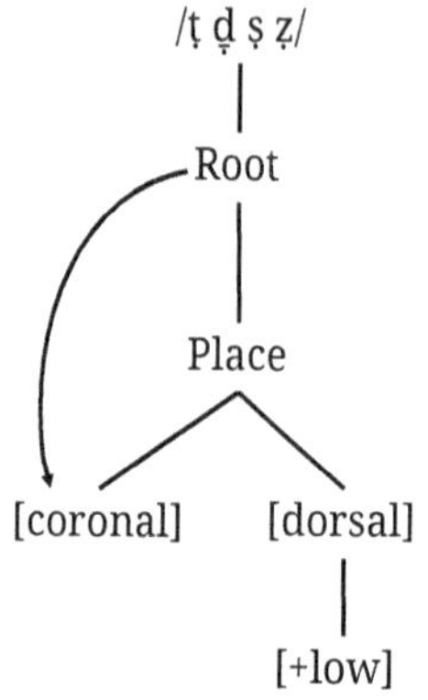

The glottal consonants /h ʔ/ are connected to the Laryngeal node rather than the Place node and are characterized by the features [spread glottis] and [constricted glottis] respectively, as in (5).

(5) *The glottal consonants* /h ʔ/

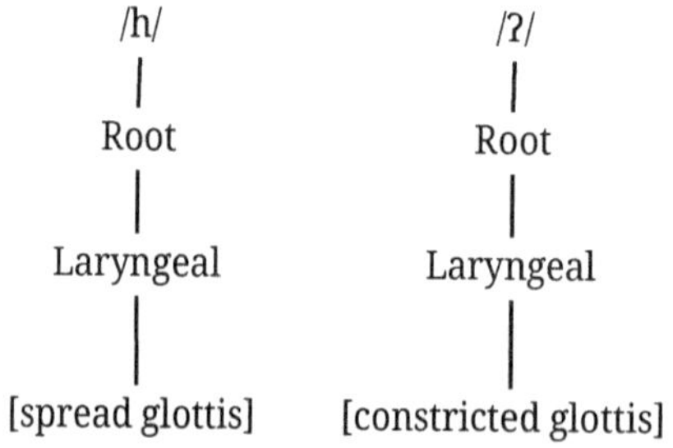

In what follows, the Maaloula Aramaic consonants will be grouped according to their manner of articulation. Within each section, the distinctive features of each group of consonants will be displayed, then the consonants will be further divided according to their place and manner of articulation (e.g., coronal stops, dorsal fricatives). For each consonant, three examples are presented to show that the consonant can occur in word-initial, word-medial, and word-final positions.

When two (or more) consonants share common articulatory properties, minimal pairs are provided to demonstrate that they are contrastive. Arnold (1990a: 13–14) presents a different set of minimal pairs for the consonant phonemes that historically used to have an allophonic relationship (e.g., *p* and *b*, *č* and *ṯ*, *t* and *ḏ*, *k* and *x*, *k* and *ġ*). The minimal pairs presented in this work are not based on the historical change that these sounds have undergone but rather on their current articulatory positions. The readers interested in the historical development of Maaloula Aramaic consonants are referred to previous publications (e.g., Bergsträsser 1928; Spitaler 1938; Arnold 1990a, 2008).

4.2.1 Stops

Maaloula Aramaic has the following stops, which are presented with their distinctive features:

(6) *Stops in Maaloula Aramaic*

	Consonantal	Sonorant	Continuant	Voice	Constricted glottis	Labial	Coronal	Dorsal	Back	Low
p	+	–	–	–		+				
b	+	–	–	+		+				
t	+	–	–	–			+			
ṭ	+	–	–	–			+			+
d	+	–	–	+			+			
k	+	–	–	–				+	–	
ḳ	+	–	–	–				+	+	
g	+	–	–	+				+		
ʔ	+	–	–		+					

According to their place of articulation, stops can be divided into bilabial, coronal, dorsal, and glottal.

Bilabial stops

Maaloula Aramaic has the bilabial stops /p/ and /b/ which mainly differ in voicing. The minimal pairs given in (7) show that /p/ and /b/ are two different phonemes. The first pair is from Arnold's (1990a: 13) grammar:

(7) *Minimal pairs for* /p/ *and* /b/

*ḥal**pa***	'he milked it (F)/her'	V.13
*ḥal**ba***	'milk'	V.13
*aš**pah***	'he resembled'	FW
*aš**bah***	'braver'	IV.210

Although both bilabial stops are attested in word-initial, word-medial, and word-final positions, as (8) shows, there are certain positional restrictions on the distribution of these two bilabial stops. These restrictions are presented and discussed in Chapter 5.

(8) /b/ *and* /p/ *in word-initial, word-medial, and word-final positions*

/b/:	***b**esra*	'meat'	IV.282
	*ʕi**b**raṯ*	'she entered'	III.272
	*ačʕe**b***	'he felt tired'	IV.86
/p/:	***p**ayṯa*	'house'	IV.228
	*xal**p**a*	'dog'	IV.278
	*ḏinə**p***	'tails (EPL)'	III.286

Coronal stops

Maaloula Aramaic has the three coronal stops /t/, /ṭ/, and /d/, but since /d/ is a borrowed sound "with only marginal phoneme status" (Arnold 2011: 686), it will be presented later with the two other marginal phonemes /g/ and /ʔ/. The phonemes /t/ and /ṭ/ have the same primary place of articulation, manner of articulation, and voicing (both being voiceless), but they differ in that /ṭ/ is emphatic whereas /t/ is plain. This secondary articulation is contrastive in Maaloula Aramaic, as the minimal pairs in (9) demonstrate.

(9) *Minimal pairs for* /t/ *and* /ṭ/

tefla	'dregs'	VI.809
ṭefla	'child'	III.62
atar	'but; so; then'	III.276
aṭar	'he/they flew'	IV.104
intar	'he/they went around'	III.158
inṭar	'he/they waited'	III.328

Both /t/ and /ṭ/ occur in word-initial, word-medial, and word-final positions, as (10) shows.

(10) /t/ *and* /ṭ/ *in word-initial, word-medial, and word-final positions*

/t/:	*tarba*	'road'	III.332
	blōta	'village'	IV.12
	emmat	'when'	III.310
/ṭ/:	*ṭūra*	'mountain'	IV.334
	ḥūṭa	'thread'	III.62
	arheṭ	'he ran'	IV.16

Dorsal stops (except for marginal /g/)

Maaloula Aramaic has the dorsal stops /k/ and /ḳ/. According to the available literature, /k/ is described as a "strongly palatalized" stop (Bergsträsser 1915: xviii; Arnold 1990a: 15, 2011: 686), and /ḳ/ is described as a velar (Bergsträsser 1915: xviii) or "slightly post-velar" stop (Arnold 2011: 686). In terms of features, /k/ which is more advanced or fronted can be differentiated by the feature [−back], whereas /ḳ/ which is more retracted can be characterized as [+back] (see (6) above). These two sounds are contrastive, as the minimal pairs in (11) show.

(11) *Minimal pairs for* /k/ *and* /ḳ/

koppṯa	'one ball of kibbeh (a dish)'	VI.434
ḳoppṯa	'dome'	IV.70
kallel	'he/they married'	IV.258
ḳallel	'little; not enough'	IV.186

The phonemes /k/ and /ḳ/ occur in all positions:

(12) */k/ and /ḳ/ in word-initial, word-medial, and word-final positions*

/k/:	***k**orsa*	'chair'	III.208
	*ḏī**k**a*	'rooster'	IV.22
	*ani**k***	'where'	III.86
/ḳ/:	***ḳ**aʕpra*	'mouse'	IV.20
	*ḏlū**ḳ**a*	'firewood'	IV.16
	*summu**ḳ***	'red (INDF.M.SG)'	III.358

Marginal phonemes

The previous accounts on Maaloula Aramaic consider /d/, /g/, and /ʔ/ to be marginal phonemes. Spitaler (1938: 12) and Arnold (1990a: 12, 2006: 1) point out that /d/ and /g/ occur only in loanwords. This argument is supported by the corpus data. The examples in (13) show six loanwords in which the sounds /d/ and /g/ occur in word-initial, word-medial, and word-final positions. For each example, I also provide the original word in the source language according to Arnold's (2019) dictionary.

(13) */d/ and /g/ in word-initial, word-medial, and word-final positions*

/d/:	***d**urbakke*	'darbuka (a goblet drum)'	III.160
		< *dərbakke* (Arabic)	VI.228
	*bana**d**ōra*	'tomato'	III.324
		< *banadōra* (Syrian Arabic) < *pomodoro* (Italian)	VI.170
	*barrā**d***	'refrigerator'	III.328
		< *barrād* (Arabic)	VI.175
/g/:	***g**rāfe*	'necktie'	III.240
		< *grāfe* (Syrian Arabic) < *cravate* (French)	VI.300
	*ʕu**g**ōle*	'his agal (traditional headband)'	III.130
		< *ʕgāl* (Bedouin Arabic)	VI.76
	*fran**g***	'franc; five piasters (obsolete currency)'	IV.48
		< *franc* (French)	VI.281

The sound /ʔ/ represents a more complicated case. Arnold (1990a: 12) considers word-medial /ʔ/ as restricted to loanwords, as in (14a), but he does not comment on word-final /ʔ/. The corpus data show that word-final /ʔ/ is even less frequent, occurring only in six word forms exemplified in (14b).

(14) *Distribution of non-initial /ʔ/*

(a)	*su**ʔ**ōla*	'question'	III.210
		< derived from the Arabic root *sʔl*	VI.678
(b)	*žizə**ʔ***	'parts (EPL)'	III.258
		< *ǧizʔ* (Arabic)	VI.997

On the other hand, word-initial glottal stops are common and by no means restricted to loanwords. These glottal stops occur (phonetically but not necessarily always orthographically) at the beginning of words which have undergone glottal epenthesis (e.g., ***ʔ**ommṯa* 'people' IV.112). However, in the case of glottal epenthesis, this word-initial [ʔ] has no phonemic status and no underlying representation. It is an epenthetic consonant that is inserted by a phonological process. For this reason, it will be discussed in Sections 8.2.3 and 8.3.6 (see also Spitaler 1938: 25 and Arnold 1990a: 12).

The marginal status of /d/, /g/, and (non-initial) /ʔ/ can be investigated by calculating the frequency of occurrence of these phonemes. I calculated the type frequency of all stops and found that /d/, /g/, and non-initial /ʔ/ are indeed the least frequent stops in the corpus, as shown in Figure 4.1. By 'type frequency' of a segment, I mean the number of different word forms (i.e., word types) that contain the segment in the corpus (see Plag 2018: 52).

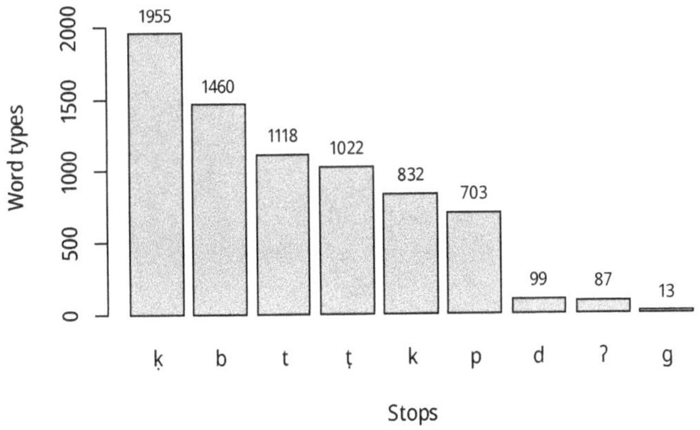

Fig. 4.1: The type frequency of stops

4.2.2 Affricates

Maaloula Aramaic has only one affricate, the voiceless palato-alveolar affricate /č/, which is characterized by the distinctive features presented in (15):

(15) *The affricate* /č/

	Consonantal	Sonorant	Continuant	Voice	Strident	Coronal	Anterior
č	+	−	−	−	+	+	−

The phoneme /č/ can occur in word-initial, word-medial, and word-final positions, as (16) shows:

(16) /č/ *in word-initial, word-medial, and word-final positions*

***č**išrin ṯēn*	'November'	III.346
*xō**č**ma*	'ring'	IV.66
*ṯar**č***	'two (F)'	III.274

4.2.3 Fricatives

Maaloula Aramaic has 15 fricatives, which are presented with their distinctive features in (17).

(17) *Fricatives in Maaloula Aramaic*

	Consonantal	Sonorant	Continuant	Voice	Spread glottis	Strident	Labial	Coronal	Anterior	Dorsal	Pharyngeal	Low
f	+	−	+	−			+					
ṯ	+	−	+	−		−		+	+			
ḏ	+	−	+	+		−		+	+			
ḏ̣	+	−	+	+		−		+	+			+

	Consonantal	Sonorant	Continuant	Voice	Spread glottis	Strident	Labial	Coronal	Anterior	Dorsal	Pharyngeal	Low
s	+	−	+	−		+		+	+			
ṣ	+	−	+	−		+		+	+			+
z	+	−	+	+		+		+	+			
ẓ	+	−	+	+		+		+	+			+
š	+	−	+	−		+		+	−			
ž	+	−	+	+		+		+	−			
x	+	−	+	−						+		
ġ	+	−	+	+						+		
ḥ	+	−	+	−							+	
ʕ	+	−	+	+							+	
h	−	−	+	−	+							

According to their place of articulation, fricatives can be divided into labial, coronal, dorsal, pharyngeal, and glottal.

Labial fricatives

Maaloula Aramaic has only one labial fricative, the voiceless labiodental fricative /f/, which can occur in word-initial, word-medial, and word-final positions, as (18) shows:

(18) /f/ *in word-initial, word-medial, and word-final positions*

***f**elka*	'half'	IV.12
*ḳu**f**ōla*[1]	'lid; cover'	III.346
*aḥre**f***	'he/they replied'	IV.84

Coronal fricatives

Maaloula Aramaic has the coronal fricatives /ṯ ḏ ḏ̣ s z ṣ ẓ š ž/ whose phonemic status is illustrated by the minimal pairs, triplets, and quadruplets given in (19).

1 It is transcribed as *ḳuffōla* in the original text.

(19) *Minimal pairs, triplets, and quadruplets for the coronal fricatives*

(a) Minimal quadruplets for /ṯ/, /s/, /z/, and /š/

imṯaḥ	'he stretched'	VI.576
imsaḥ	'he wiped'	VI.568
imzaḥ	'he joked'	VI.583
imšaḥ	'he anointed'	VI.570

(b) Minimal quadruplets for /ḏ/, /ḏ̣/, /s/, and /ṣ/

aḏab	'it (M) melted'	III.32
aḏ̣ab	'he packed'	VI.248
asab	'he took'	III.276
aṣab	'he poured'	VI.779

(c) Minimal quadruplets for /s/, /ṣ/, /š/, and /ž/

sīrča	'conduct; behavior'	IV.120
ṣīrča	'(sheep) pen'	VI.802
šīrča	'the rest'	IV.256
žīrča	'neighborhood'	III.42

(d) Minimal triplets for /ṯ/, /z/, and /ž/

ṯamra	'fruit'	IV.278
zamra	'reed pipe music'	III.184
žamra	'embers'	III.72

(e) Minimal triplets for /ṯ/, /ḏ̣/, and /š/

ifṯaḥ	'he opened'	VI.291
ifḏ̣aḥ	'he disgraced'	VI.261
ifšaḥ	'he strode'	VI.288

(f) Minimal triplets for /ḏ/, /z/, and /š/

eḏna	'ear'	III.266
ezna	'permission'	IV.84
ešna	'year'	IV.116

(g) Minimal triplets for /ḏ̣/, /ṣ/, and /ž/

aḏ̣ar	'he harmed/hurt'	VI.252
aṣar	'he wrapped/tied up'	VI.795
ažar	'he dragged'	VI.991

(h) Minimal triplets for /s/, /š/, and /ẓ/

safərṯa	'trip; journey'	IV.132
šafərṯa	'razor blade'	III.296
ẓafərṯa	'the floating fat that is skimmed off when meat is cooked'	III.152

(i) Minimal pairs for /ṯ/ and /ḏ/

ṯiḳniš	'you (F.SG) became'	IV.292
ḏiḳniš	'your (F.SG) chin/beard'	III.276

(j) Minimal pairs for /ṯ/ and /ṣ/

ṯlōṯa	'three (F)'	IV.168
ṣlōṯa	'prayer; Mass'	III.162

(k) Minimal pairs for /ḏ̣/ and /z/

aḏ̣aʕ	'he got lost'	IV.100
azaʕ	'he felt afraid'	IV.260

(l) Minimal pairs for /ḏ̣/ and /ẓ/ (also found in Arnold 1990a: 16)

ḏ̣arfa	'waterskin'	IV.250
ẓarfa	'envelope'	IV.92

(m) Minimal pairs for /ṣ/ and /z/

ṣahra	'moon'	IV.94
zahra	'flowers; blossoms'	III.154

There are fewer minimal pairs for /ẓ/ than for any of the other coronal fricatives. There might be two reasons for this limited number of minimal pairs for this specific phoneme. First, /ẓ/ is the least frequent coronal fricative in Maaloula Aramaic. This can be seen in Figure 4.2 which illustrates the type frequency of all coronal fricatives.

Second, the literature on Maaloula Aramaic (e.g., Spitaler 1938: 33; Arnold 1991b: 228, 2019: 960, 967, 972, 1000) reports that some words are pronounced with [ẓ] by some speakers and [z] by other speakers, as in (20). All examples are from the literature.

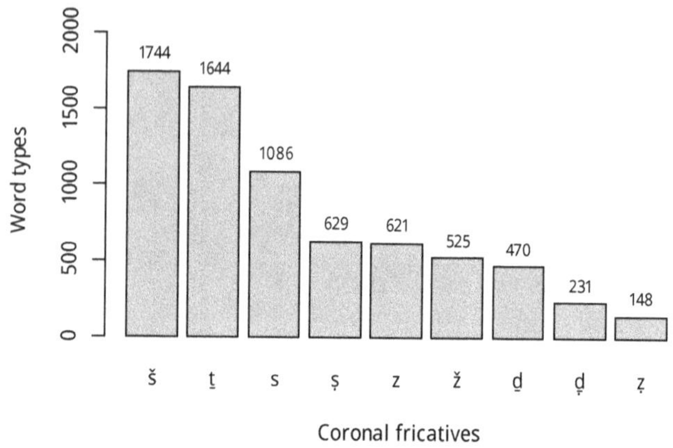

Fig. 4.2: The type frequency of coronal fricatives

(20) *iẓʕur*	~ *izʕur*	'small (M.SG)'	Spitaler 1938: 33
ẓxy	~ *zxy*	[as a root] 'to defeat'	Arnold 2019: 972
muẓrōba	~ *muzrōba*	'gutter; downspout'	Arnold 2019: 967
ẓunnōra	~ *zunnōra*	'belt'	Arnold 2019: 1000
ẓahrō	~ *zahrō*	'dried flowers and herbs for herbal tea'	Arnold 2019: 960

Spitaler argues that the [ẓ] in *iẓʕur* (see the first example above) is the result of a regressive assimilation process whereby emphasis spreads from /ʕ/ to the preceding /z/ (Spitaler 1938: 33). However, this analysis cannot account for the occurrence of [ẓ] in the other examples which currently have no emphatic segments. Arnold (2019) points out in some of his dictionary entries (e.g., the last two words in (20) above) that the variation between [ẓ] and [z] is age-based (i.e., [z] by older speakers and [ẓ] by younger speakers).

Arnold's explanation seems to be plausible because my language consultant, who belongs to an even younger generation, consistently pronounces these words with [ẓ]. He also pronounces some other words with [ẓ], which are transcribed with [z] in Arnold's (1991a, 1991b) transcripts, see (21).

(21) Arnold (1991a, 1991b)	My language consultant		
zarʕa	*ẓarʕa*	'crops'	IV.220
zrōʕa	*ẓrōʕa*	'sowing; planting'	III.84
zōyrin	*ẓōyrin*	'they (M) visit'	III.264
zxīčən	*ẓxīčən*	'you (M.SG) defeated me'	IV.138

The current situation can be summarized, as in (22). Set 1 represents the words which all speakers pronounce with [z]. This set is exemplified by the word *azaʕ* 'he felt afraid' IV.260. Set 2 represents the words which older speakers pronounce with [z] but younger speakers pronounce with [ẓ] (exemplified by *izʕur* ~ *iẓʕur* 'small (M.SG)' III.80). Set 3 represents the words which all speakers pronounce with [ẓ] (exemplified by *ẓarfa* 'envelope' IV.92).

(22)	Set 1: [z]	Set 2: [z] ~ [ẓ]	Set 3: [ẓ]
Older speakers	*azaʕ*	*izʕur*	*ẓarfa*
Younger speakers	*azaʕ*	*iẓʕur*	*ẓarfa*

Whether the variation between [z] and [ẓ] in Set 2 is only aged-based or is also due to other sociolinguistic factors is a question which future studies can investigate. What is clear from the previous accounts, the corpus data, and my consultant's judgements, however, is that [z] and [ẓ] have no allophonic relationship. The variation is speaker-based and has nothing to do with the environments in which these sounds occur. Moreover, this variation is limited to Set 2. I will still assume that the two sounds [z] and [ẓ] represent two different phonemes (i.e., /z/ and /ẓ/) although I could not find minimal pairs to show that they are contrastive. I will also assume that the underlying phoneme in Set 2 is /z/ for the older speakers and /ẓ/ for the younger speakers.

With regard to distribution, the Maaloula Aramaic coronal fricatives can occur in word-initial, word-medial, and word-final positions, as (23) shows:

(23) *The coronal fricatives in word-initial, word-medial, and word-final positions*

/ṯ/:	*ṯelka*	'snow'	III.84
	bisnīṯa	'girl'	IV.88
	payṯ	'my home'	IV.266
/ḏ/:	*ḏwōṯa*	'hands'	IV.30
	ḏōḏa	'paternal uncle'	III.220
	imōḏ	'today'	III.196
/ḏ̣/:	*ḏ̣abʕa*	'hyena'	IV.14
	ḳōḏ̣ya	'judge'	IV.146
	aḥfeḏ̣	'he protected; saved'	IV.168
/s/:	*semla*	'ladder'	IV.146
	klēsya	'church'	III.322
	ḳalles	'a little'	IV.264

/z/:	*zawʕa*	'fear'	IV.84
	ġawza	'walnut'	IV.340
	nōz	'I am going'	III.50
/ṣ/:	*ṣafrōna*	'(small) bird'	VI.782
	nīṣa	'porcupine'	III.350
	irəṣ	'he/they accepted'	IV.226
/ẓ/:	*ẓolma*	'injustice'	IV.10
	maẓbuṭ	'right; correct (M)'	III.196
	aḥfēẓ	'memorize (2M.SG)!'	III.362
/š/:	*šenna*	'rock'	III.370
	barnōša	'person'	IV.332
	hōš	'now'	III.48
/ž/:	*žamra*	'embers'	III.72
	ʕaža	'why'	IV.186
	yōḥež	'(that) he goes on a pilgrimage'	IV.294

Dorsal fricatives

Maaloula Aramaic has the two dorsal fricatives /x/ and /ġ/ which differ in voicing. The minimal pairs in (24) show that /x/ and /ġ/ are contrastive.

(24) *Minimal pairs for* /x/ *and* /ġ/

axla	'he ate it'	IV.76
aġla	'dearer'	IV.168
xayra	'goodness'	IV.28
ġayra	'another (F)'	IV.56
inəčxab	'they chose/decided'	III.312
inəčġab	'it (M) was stolen'	IV.102

Both dorsal fricatives can occur in word-initial, word-medial, and word-final positions, as (25) shows:

(25) /x/ *and* /ġ/ *in word-initial, word-medial, and word-final positions*

/x/:	*xēfa*	'stone'	IV.188
	hōxa	'here'	III.28
	ōbux	'your (M.SG) father'	IV.268

/ġ/:	*ġamla*	'camel'	IV.228
	boġta	'rug'	III.110
	zawġ	'pairs (EPL)'	III.100

Pharyngeal fricatives

Maaloula Aramaic has the pharyngeal fricatives /ḥ/ and /ʕ/ which mainly differ in voicing. From a phonetic perspective, however, doubts have been expressed as to whether these sounds in Semitic languages are truly pharyngeal and fricative or instead should be called epiglottal and approximant (see Ladefoged & Maddieson 1996: 167–169 for a detailed discussion). Nevertheless, in this work I maintain the phonological proposition that these sounds are pharyngeal fricatives.

The minimal pairs in (26) show that /ḥ/ and /ʕ/ are two different phonemes.

(26) *Minimal pairs for /ḥ/ and /ʕ/*

ḥamra	'wine'	III.322
ʕamra	'wool'	III.110
ḥōna	'brother'	III.300
ʕōna	'sheep (PL)'	IV.174
ḥīlča	'trick; ruse'	IV.8
ʕīlča	'donkey foal (F)'	IV.280

Both pharyngeal fricatives can occur in word-initial, word-medial, and word-final positions, as (27) shows:

(27) */ḥ/ and /ʕ/ in word-initial, word-medial, and word-final positions*

/ḥ/:	*ḥašoppa*	'Sunday'	III.152
	mešḥa	'oil'	III.212
	anaḥ	'we'	IV.10
/ʕ/:	*ʕakkōra*	'roof'	IV.288
	arʕa	'earth; ground'	III.368
	arpaʕ	'four (M)'	III.348

Glottal fricatives

Maaloula Aramaic has the voiceless glottal fricative /h/ which can occur in word-initial, word-medial, and word-final positions, as (28) shows:

(28) /h/ *in word-initial, word-medial, and word-final positions*

/h/:	***h**ašš*	'you (F.SG)'	IV.66
	*no**h**ra*	'light'	III.42
	*iṣə**h***	'he felt thirsty'	III.360

4.2.4 Nasals

Maaloula Aramaic has the nasals /m/ and /n/, which are presented with their distinctive features in (29).

(29) *Nasals in Maaloula Aramaic*

	Consonantal	Sonorant	Continuant	Nasal	Voice	Labial	Coronal
m	+	+	−	+	+	+	
n	+	+	−	+	+		+

The minimal pairs in (30) show that /m/ and /n/ are contrastive.

(30) *Minimal pairs for* /m/ *and* /n/

*eš**m**a*	'name'	IV.154
*eš**n**a*	'year'	IV.116
*eḏ**m**a*	'blood'	III.94
*eḏ**n**a*	'ear'	III.266
***m**īṯa*	'dead (one)'	IV.302
***n**īṯa*	'intention'	IV.128

Both nasals can occur in word-initial, word-medial, and word-final positions, as (31) shows:

(31) /m/ *and* /n/ *in word-initial, word-medial, and word-final positions*

/m/:	***m**alka*	'king'	IV.14
	*yō**m**a*	'day'	III.62
	*iḳḏu**m***	'before'	IV.134

/n/:	***nawella***	‘(weaving) loom’	III.310
	*ḥō**n**a*	‘brother’	III.300
	*mō**n***	‘who’	IV.296

4.2.5 Liquids

Maaloula Aramaic has the liquids /r/ and /l/, which are presented with their distinctive features in (32).

(32) *Liquids in Maaloula Aramaic*

	Consonantal	Sonorant	Continuant	Coronal	Voice	Lateral
r	+	+	+	+	+	
l	+	+	+	+	+	+

The minimal pairs in (33) show that /r/ and /l/ are contrastive.

(33) *Minimal pairs for* /r/ *and* /l/

*aġ**r**a*	‘wage; pay’	III.110
*aġ**l**a*	‘dearer’	IV.168
*ḥa**r**ba*	‘war’	IV.268
*ḥa**l**ba*	‘milk’	III.34
*ḥī**r**ča*	‘confusion; puzzlement’	IV.8
*ḥī**l**ča*	‘trick; ruse’	IV.8

Both liquids can occur in word-initial, word-medial, and word-final positions, as (34) shows:

(34) /r/ *and* /l/ *in word-initial, word-medial, and word-final positions*

/r/:	***r**ayša*	‘head’	IV.44
	*nū**r**a*	‘fire’	III.174
	*baḥa**r***	‘a lot; very’	III.146

/l/: ***leḥma*** ‘bread’ III.104
lēlya ‘night’ IV.32
elʕel ‘above’ III.194

The phoneme /l/ has an emphatic counterpart /ḷ/, which occurs only in the word ***aḷō*** ‘God’ III.344 and the words derived from it (e.g., *paʕḷō* IV.82, *yībaʕḷō* IV.28, *ḏībaʕḷō* III.232 ‘God willing’) (see Bergsträsser 1915: xix).[2] This is similar to Arabic where “/ḷ/ is found exclusively in *aḷḷāh* ‘God’ and derivatives” (Watson 2002: 16). Based on this similarity, I follow Watson (2002: 20–21) in considering /ḷ/ a marginal phoneme.

4.2.6 Glides

Maaloula Aramaic has the glides /w/ and /y/, which are presented with their distinctive features in (35).

(35) *Glides in Maaloula Aramaic*

	Consonantal	Sonorant	Continuant	Dorsal	Voice	Labial
w	–	+	+	+	+	+
y	–	+	+	+	+	

The minimal pair in (36) shows that /w/ and /y/ are contrastive.

(36) *A minimal pair for* /w/ *and* /y/

ʕwōra ‘blind (M.SG)’ IV.290
ʕyōra ‘measure(ment)’ III.346

Both glides can occur in word-initial, word-medial, and word-final positions, as (37) shows:

2 These words are transcribed as *alō*, *ppaʕlō*, *yīb baʕ-alō*, and *ḏī baʕ-lō* in the original text.

(37) /w/ *and* /y/ *in word-initial, word-medial, and word-final positions*

/w/:	***wakča***	'time'	III.172
	ḥaṯawōṯa	'sisters'	IV.248
	išw	'he made'	III.318
/y/:	***yawna***	'pigeon'	III.280
	mōya	'water'	III.284
	ayṯāy	'bring (2F.SG)!'	IV.308

4.3 Vowels

Previous accounts (e.g., Spitaler 1938: 2–12; Arnold 1990a: 20–21, 2011: 686) have shown that Maaloula Aramaic has ten monophthongs and two diphthongs. The ten monophthongs are equally divided into five short vowels and five long vowels. According to the adopted transcription system, the long vowels are marked by a macron above the letter. The complete inventory of vowel phonemes is shown in (38).

(38) *Vowel phonemes (Arnold 1990a: 20)*

Long vowels			Short vowels		
ī		*ū*	*i*		*u*
ē		*ō*	*e*		*o*
	ā			*a*	

Diphthongs

aw *ay*

Although I agree that Maaloula Aramaic has ten monophthongs, I show in Section 4.3.3 that *aw* and *ay* are not the only diphthongs attested in the corpus. Furthermore, I argue, in the same section, for considering all of the attested diphthongs as combinations of two phonemes (i.e., sequences of vowels and glides), rather than single diphthongal phonemes.

In addition to the vowels presented in (38), Maaloula Aramaic has the epenthetic vowel [ə] which is inserted to break up a consonant cluster but has no phonemic status (Arnold 1990a: 20, 2011: 686) (see Section 4.3.4).

The ten monophthongs can be represented by the features shown in (39).

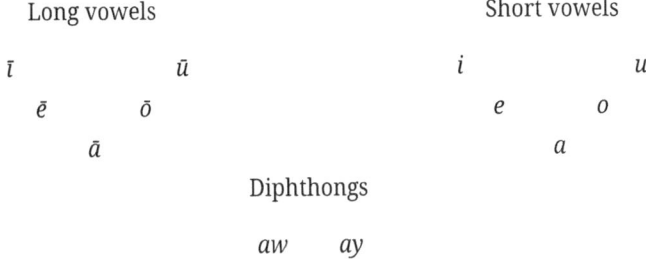

(39) *Monophthongs in Maaloula Aramaic*

	Consonantal	Sonorant	Continuant	Voice	Back	High	Low	Round
i, ī	–	+	+	+	–	+	–	–
u, ū	–	+	+	+	+	+	–	+
e, ē	–	+	+	+	–	–	–	–
o, ō	–	+	+	+	+	–	–	+
a, ā	–	+	+	+	+	–	+	–

In addition, the features [syllabic], [long], and [stress] can be used to distinguish vowels [+syllabic] from glides [−syllabic], long vowels [+long] from short vowels [−long], and stressed vowels [+stress] from unstressed vowels [−stress]. However, these features are abandoned in some models in phonological theory, such as feature geometry models and moraic theory models. For example, in Hayes's (1989) version of moraic theory, long and short vowels can be differentiated by the number of moras which they receive, rather than by the feature [long] (see Section 8.3.2). In this work, whenever I am not using feature geometry or moraic models, I will keep using the features [syllabic], [long], and [stress] as they can account for alternations in a simple way and help formalize clear phonological rules.

To illustrate how vowels can be represented from the perspective of an articulator-based feature geometry model (Sagey 1986; Halle 1992, 1995), I will show a representation of the vowel /i/ in (40).

A competing model to the articulator-based model (see, e.g., Clements & Hume 1995) proposes that consonants and vowels should be represented by a unified set of features. According to this model, the same features [labial], [coronal], [dorsal], and [pharyngeal] are used for consonants and for vowels, in the latter case replacing respectively the features [+round], [−back], [+back], and [+low] (Clements & Hume 1995: 280; Uffmann 2011: 651). For example, front vowels are characterized by the feature [coronal], and back vowels by the feature [dorsal]. This model also proposes a vocalic place (or V-place) node which occurs on a different tier from that of the C-place node (Clements & Hume 1995; Uffmann 2011).

(40) *The vowel /i/ represented according to the articulator-based model*

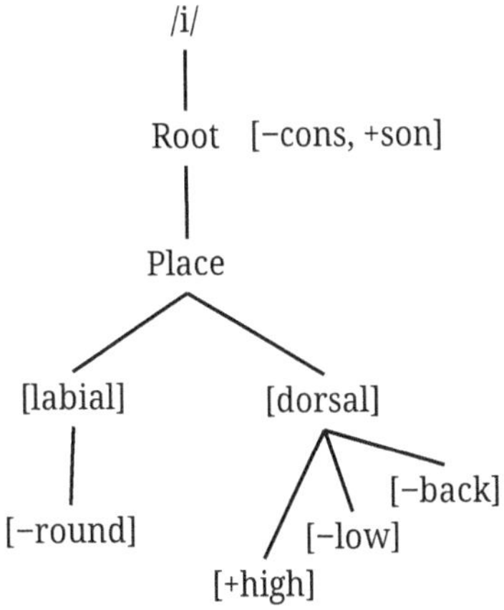

Although this competing model has its own advantages (see Uffmann 2011 for a comprehensive comparison of the two proposals), I adopt an articulator-based model because the rule-based analyses and phonological rules presented throughout the book depend on articulator-based features, including [round], [back], and [low]. Assuming a model of feature geometry which has no place for these features would not be consistent with the adopted approach.

The rest of this chapter proceeds as follows. In sections 4.3.1 and 4.3.2, I present examples of the short and long vowels respectively in word-initial, word-medial, and word-final positions. Unlike the previous sections on consonants, these sections will not contain minimal pairs for vowels. This is because the phonemic status of the Maaloula Aramaic vowels is already demonstrated by the comprehensive sets of minimal pairs provided by Arnold (1990a: 29–37). In section 4.3.3, I show examples of the attested diphthongs and discuss their status. In section 4.3.4, I present the epenthetic vowel [ə].

4.3.1 Short vowels

The short vowels /i u e o a/ can occur in word-initial, word-medial, and word-final positions:

(41) *The short vowels in word-initial, word-medial, and word-final positions*

/i/:	***i**mōma*	'day'	III.136
	*š**i**mša*	'sun'	III.292

	ti	'who(m); which'	IV.114
/u/:	*uxxul*	'every'	III.136
	rumiš	'yesterday'	III.100
	ōbu	'his father'	IV.18
/e/:	*emʕa*	'hundred'	IV.298
	ġerma	'bone'	IV.54
	ḳahwe	'coffee'	III.72
/o/:	*ommṯa*	'people'	IV.110
	xoṯla	'wall'	III.232
	inno[3]	'that'	IV.132
/a/:	*arʕa*	'earth; ground'	III.368
	yarḥa	'month'	III.162
	ḏahba	'gold'	IV.70

There are certain positional restrictions on the distribution of the short mid vowels. These restrictions are presented and discussed in Section 10.4.2.

4.3.2 Long vowels

The long vowels /ī ū ē ō ā/ are attested in word-initial, word-medial, and word-final positions, as in (42). In general, they are least frequent (some of them extremely infrequent, i.e., /ū/, /ē/, /ā/) in word-initial position and most frequent in word-medial position.

(42) *The long vowels in word-initial, word-medial, and word-final positions*

/ī/:	*īḏa*	'hand'	IV.162
	šunīṯa	'woman'	IV.262
	hī	'she'	IV.176
/ū/:	*ūle*	'he has'	III.108
	maščūṯa	'wedding'	III.362
	hū	'he'	III.294
/ē/:	*ētra*	'threshing floor'	VI.43
	ʕēḏa	'feast (day)'	IV.308

3 It is transcribed as *innu* in the original text (see Section 10.4.2 for a discussion of post-tonic [o]).

	bē	'with/in it (M)'	III.100
/ō/:	***ōlef***	'thousand'	IV.294
	*ġabr**ō**na*	'man'	IV.8
	*aḷ**ō*** [4]	'God'	III.344
/ā/:	***ās***	'myrtle'	III.264 (a loanword)
	*ṯ**ā**x*	'come (2M.SG)!'	III.52
	*ḥm**ā***	'look (2M.SG)!'	III.330

In most words, the underlying vowel /ā/ either undergoes shortening and surfaces as an [a] when it occurs in pretonic position (as will be shown in Section 10.3.2) or surfaces as an [ō] elsewhere due the /ā/ rounding rule (as will be shown in Section 7.3.1). It is unclear whether the words with a surface [ā], such as *ṯ**ā**x* and *ḥm**ā***, have an underlying /ā/ which avoids /ā/ rounding or have an underlying /a/ which undergoes lengthening. These analyses will be presented and discussed in Section 10.4.1. I will also discuss the positional restrictions on the distribution of long vowels in general in the same section.

4.3.3 Diphthongs

The previous grammars (e.g., Spitaler 1938: 11–12; Arnold 1990a: 20, 2011: 686) indicate that Maaloula Aramaic has the two diphthongs /aw/ and /ay/. These diphthongs are attested in the corpus in word-initial, word-medial, and word-final positions:

(43) /aw/ *and* /ay/ *in word-initial, word-medial, and word-final positions*

/aw/:	***aw**rab*	'bigger'	IV.8
	*m**aw**ṯa*	'death'	III.218
	aw	'or'	III.364
/ay/:	***ay**ṯā*	'bring (2M.SG)!'	III.312
	*ʕ**ay**na*	'eye'	III.278
	*emm**ay***	'my mother'	III.58

4 It is transcribed as *alō* in the original text.

In this work, I treat /aw/ and /ay/ as combinations of two phonemes (i.e., sequences of vowels and glides), rather than single diphthongal phonemes. I present four arguments to support my decision.

First, these vowel-glide combinations do not consistently meet the theoretical criteria which would enable them to be classified as diphthongs. According to Hayes (2009: 14–15), a diphthong "is a sequence of two vowels that functions as a single sound. Further, a diphthong always forms just one syllable, whereas a two-vowel sequence forms two." Although these vowel-glide combinations do occur in one syllable in some word forms (as the definition points out), they may be separated by syllable boundaries in other word forms that share the same lemma, as the pairs of examples in (44) show. In the examples presented in this section, the syllable boundaries are set according to Arnold's (1990a: 39) syllabification scheme (see Section 8.3 for an alternative syllabification scheme).

(44)	*ḥḏ**aw**.ṯa*	'joy; wedding (party)'	VI.353
	*ḥḏ**a.w**ō.ṯa*	'wedding (parties)'	VI.353
	*l**ay**.šil.le*	'they knead it (M)'	III.150
	*l**a.y**eš.le*	'he kneads it (M)'	III.42

The ability of these vowel-glide combinations to be separated across syllable boundaries challenges the basic principle that the vowel and the glide must function as a single sound.

Second, with respect to syllable weight and interaction with stress, a syllable with a vowel-glide sequence (e.g., [lay]$_\sigma$ and [čay]$_\sigma$ in (45)) behaves like a CVC syllable, and not like a CVV syllable (e.g., [lō]$_\sigma$ and [čō]$_\sigma$ in (45)) (see Section 8.3.2 for syllable weight where I adopt Hayes's 1989 version of moraic theory, and see Section 10.2 for stress assignment). Word-final CVV syllables are heavy and therefore attract stress, as the first example in each pair in (45) shows. For clarity, the stressed syllables are marked by an acute accent. In contrast, word-final CVC syllables (and similarly word-final syllables with vowel-glide sequences) are light. For this reason, they do not attract stress, as the second example in each pair in (45) shows.

(45)	*mʕal.l**ṓ***	'Maaloulian (from Maaloula) (DEF.M.SG)'	IV.218
	*mʕál.l**ay***	'Maaloulian (from Maaloula) (INDF.M.SG)'	III.182
	*ṯič.č**ṓ***	'from Ain Al-Tinah (DEF.M.SG)'	III.330
	*ṯíč.č**ay***	'from Ain Al-Tinah (INDF.M.SG)'	III.130

Third, the monophthongal vowels and the vowel-glide sequences /aw/ and /ay/ seem to form different phonological environments in Maaloula Aramaic. Here are two examples. Geminate consonants are common between two monophthongal vowels but not between a vowel-glide sequence and a monophthongal vowel (for geminates, see Chapter 9). The singleton [p] does not occur between two monophthongal vowels, but it is attested between a vowel-glide sequence and a monophthongal vowel (e.g., *awpillaḥle* 'we brought/took him' III.308) (see Section 5.2.1).

Fourth, the corpus (as well as Arnold's 2019 dictionary) shows that a number of additional vowel-glide combinations, such as the ones shown in (46), can occur in Maaloula Aramaic words. The presence of these vowel-glide sequences poses a challenge to the view that /aw/ and /ay/ are the only available diphthongs.

(46) *Additional vowel-glide combinations attested in Maaloula Aramaic*

/uw/:	*č**uw**rīḳa*	'removed/removing leaves'	IV.338
	*ḥ**uw**war*	'white (INDF.M.SG)'	IV.94
/ōw/:	*t**ōw**wut* [5]	'David (proper noun)'	III.122
	*čs**ōw** yičs**ōw***	[as a lemma] 'to come to an agreement'	VI.714
/iy/:	***iy**yar*	'May'	III.162
	*laban**iy**ye*	'labaniyye (cooked yogurt sauce)'	III.40
/uy/:	*m**uy**lōfča*	'teaching'	VI.942
	*ḥ**uy**yōṭa*	'sewing'	III.252
/ōy/:	*ṯulṯ**ōy**ṯa*	'(medium-sized) clay jar'	IV.144
	*ḳury**ōy***	'Christians'	III.268
/ūy/:	*šč**ūy***	'my drink/drinking'	IV.116
	*xuss**ūy***	'my clothes/clothing'	IV.116
/āy/:	*ayṯ**āy***	'bring (2F.SG)!'	IV.308
	*ḥm**āy***	'look (2F.SG)!'	IV.124

Based on the presented arguments, I treat all sequences of vowels and glides, including /aw/ and /ay/, as sequences of two separate phonemes regardless of whether they occur in one syllable or not. Consequently, in all of the phonological rules formalized in this book, the term *vowel* and the symbols *V* and *VV* will be used to refer exclusively to monophthongal vowels.

5 It is transcribed as ***tōwt*** in the original text. However, the vowel-glide sequence is present in both spellings.

4.3.4 The epenthetic vowel

Arnold (1990a: 20, 2011: 686) points out that Maaloula Aramaic has the epenthetic vowel [ə] which is inserted to break up a consonant cluster. This vowel occurs frequently in the corpus:

(47) *The epenthetic vowel* [ə]

ṯarəč	'two (F)'	III.274
ʕisər	'twenty'	III.304
yarəḥ	'months (EPL)'	IV.142
ḏinəp	'tails (EPL)'	III.286
ġabərnō	'men'	III.364
berəkṯa	'Saint Thecla'	III.180
šabəkṯa	'net'	IV.58
sčafəḳte	'he checked up on him'	IV.214

I follow Arnold in assuming that this vowel has no phonemic status. I assume that it has no underlying representation but is inserted when the phonological process of vowel epenthesis applies (e.g., /ṯarč/ → [ˈṯa.rəč] in (47) above). This process is discussed in detail and is analyzed from a syllable-based perspective in Chapter 8.

4.4 Conclusion

In this chapter, I have introduced the phonemes of Maaloula Aramaic, showing sets of minimal pairs to test their phonemic status and examples to illustrate the different positions in which they can occur. Following Arnold (1990a, 2006, 2011), I have shown that Maaloula Aramaic has twenty-eight consonant phonemes /p b t ṭ k ḳ č f ṯ ḏ ḏ̣ s z ṣ ẓ š ž x ġ ḥ ʕ h m n r l w y/ and three marginal phonemes /d g ʔ/. In addition, I have suggested that /ḷ/, which is the emphatic counterpart of /l/, could be considered another marginal phoneme that occurs only in the word *aḷō* 'God' and the words derived from it (for a similar situation in Arabic, see Watson 2002). I have also shown, following previous accounts (e.g., Spitaler 1938; Arnold 1990a, 2011), that Maaloula Aramaic has ten monophthongs which are equally divided into five short vowels /i u e o a/ and five long vowels /ī ū ē ō ā/.

I disagreed with the previous accounts on the number and status of diphthongs. Whereas the previous accounts indicate that only the two diphthongs /aw/ and /ay/ exist, the corpus data clearly show that a number of other vowel-glide combinations can occur in Maaloula Aramaic words (e.g., /uw/, /ōw/, /iy/, /ōy/, /āy/). I presented an argument for considering these so-called diphthongs as combinations of two phonemes, rather than single diphthongal phonemes.

I have also introduced the features which can be used to represent all of the Maaloula Aramaic phonemes. I adopted a model of feature geometry based on proposals made by Sagey (1986) and Halle (1992, 1995). These features will be used in the following chapters to formalize the phonological processes in Maaloula Aramaic.

5 The distribution of bilabial stops

5.1 Introduction

Although /p/ and /b/ are contrastive, as the minimal pairs in Section 4.2.1 have demonstrated, the corpus data show that there are strict restrictions on the distribution of these two sounds. For example, the singleton [p] is not attested in the environments V__V and V__#.[1] For instance, strings of segments such as *opa*, *upi*, *īp#*, and *ep#* are not attested in any words in the corpus. On the other hand, the singleton [b] occurs commonly in these two environments, as in (1c, d).

(1) [p] *and* [b] *in the environments V__V and V__#*

(a) [p] / V__V (not attested)

(b) [p] / V__# (not attested)

(c) [b] / V__V (common)

*ḏē**b**a*	'wolf'	IV.198
*šbō**b**a*	'neighbor'	IV.144
*ʕrō**b**a*	'evening'	IV.256

(d) [b] / V__# (common)

*irxe**b***	'he rode'	IV.168
*asa**b***	'he took'	III.276
*ġarre**b***	'try (2M.SG)!'	IV.38

In the case of geminate bilabial stops (i.e., [pp] and [bb]), the distribution is reversed. In the same two environments (i.e., V__V and V__#), the geminate [pp] is what occurs commonly whereas the geminate [bb] is barely attested (see Spitaler 1938: 15).

1 'V', here, refers exclusively to a phonemic monophthong regardless of its length. It does not refer to diphthongs or epenthetic vowels (see Sections 4.3.3 and 4.3.4 for the discussions).

https://doi.org/10.1515/9783111447124-005

(2) [pp] *and* [bb] *in the environments V__V and V__#*

(a) [pp] / V__V (common)

*ḥaš**oppa***	'Sunday'	III.152
*t**oppa***	'bear'	IV.256

(b) [pp] / V__# (less common)

*l**ipp***	'my heart'	IV.170
*š**app***	'young men (EPL)'	III.238

(c) [bb] / V__V (rare)

*r**abbi***	'big (INDF.M.SG)'	IV.54
*ṭ**abbi***	'alive (INDF.M.SG)'	IV.300

(d) [bb] / V__# (rare)

*r**abb***	'big (INDF.M.SG)'	IV.58
*ṭ**abb***	'alive (INDF.M.SG)'	III.306

In this chapter, I will investigate the distribution of the bilabial stops and provide the phonological rules which are responsible for their distribution. In Section 5.2, I will examine singleton bilabial stops, and in Section 5.3, I will investigate geminate bilabial stops.

5.2 Singleton bilabial stops

There are restrictions on the distribution of [p] and [b] in three positions: in postvocalic position (which includes the environments V__V and V__# that I have briefly touched upon in the introduction), in preconsonantal position, and in word-initial position.

5.2.1 Bilabial stops in postvocalic position

The previous literature on Maaloula Aramaic (e.g., Bergsträsser 1928: 80; Spitaler 1938: 12–15; Arnold 1990a: 12–13, 2008: 171–172) describes the phonemes /p/ and /b/ as the result of complex historical processes and takes a diachronic approach to account for their current status. According to this literature, earlier stages of Aramaic used to have [b] and [ḇ] ([β] in IPA) as allophones of the phoneme /b/. This allophonic relation was due to a general spirantization process whereby the

Aramaic stops /b g d k p t/ were realized as fricatives “after vowels and after zero or murmured vowels resulting from the disappearance of an original vowel” (Rosenthal 1961: 13, on Biblical Aramaic). Gradually, the allophones of the Aramaic stops (including [b] and [ḇ]) have developed into distinct phonemes in Maaloula Aramaic. The change of the allophones [b] and [ḇ] into the current phonemes /p/ and /b/ respectively is illustrated in (3).

(3) *The sound change resulting in /p/ and /b/ (Spitaler 1938: 14–15; Arnold 2008: 171)*

b	>	*p*	(e.g., *kal**bā***	>	*xal**pa***	‘dog’)
ḇ	>	*b*	(e.g., *dē**ḇā***	>	*ḏē**ba***	‘wolf’)

Guided by the corpus data and benefitting from the insights of the historical background presented in the previous literature, I make a general assumption that combines the two environments V__V and V__#. I assume that the distribution of [p] and [b] reflects a case of positional neutralization whereby the contrast between the underlying /p/ and /b/ is neutralized to [b] in postvocalic position, as (4) shows.

(4) *Neutralization of the bilabial stops in postvocalic position*

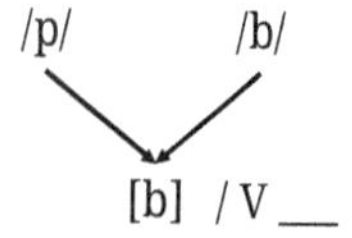

I argue that the phonological rule that is responsible for this positional neutralization is a postvocalic voicing rule, which I formalize in (5).

(5) *Postvocalic voicing of bilabial stops*

$$\begin{bmatrix}\text{+labial}\\ \text{-son}\\ \text{-cont}\end{bmatrix} \rightarrow [\text{+voice}]/\begin{bmatrix}\text{+syllabic}\\ \text{-cons}\end{bmatrix}\_\_$$

This rule is illustrated in (6). The examples are given in pairs, and each pair represents two inflected forms of the same verb. The bilabial stops occur in postvocalic position (where the voicing rule applies) in the first example of each pair and in postconsonantal position (which is one of the “elsewhere” environments) in the second example. The second column represents the underlying representations of these examples. I follow the usual practice in phonological theory in assuming that the underlying phoneme is determined based on the “elsewhere” case of a given phonological rule (see, e.g., Hayes 2009: 29; Zsiga 2013: 209). For this reason, I assume that the verbs in (6a) have /p/ in their underlying forms, and the verbs in (6b) have /b/ in their underlying forms.

(6) (a) /p/ → [b] / V__

*ʕrī**b**a*	/ʕrī**p**-a/	‘gone down (3F.SG)’	III.360
*ʕir**p**at̲*	/ʕir**p**-at̲/	‘it (F) went down’	III.106
*irxe**b***	/irxe**p**/	‘he rode’	IV.168
*rix**p**it̲*	/rix**p**-it̲/	‘I rode’	III.356
*naġe**b**le*	/nāġe**p**-l-e/	‘he kidnaps him’	IV.252
*naġ**p**it̲*	/naġ**p**-it̲/	‘I stole’	IV.66
*xt̲ī**b**a*	/xt̲ī**p**-a/	‘written (3F.SG)’	IV.334
*xōt̲**p**a*	/xāt̲**p**-a/	‘she writes’	IV.160
*ase**b**la*	/āse**p**-l-a/	‘he takes her (as a wife)’	IV.132
*as**p**ačča*	/as**p**-ačč-a/	‘she took her’	IV.170

(b) /b/ → [b] / V__

*xṭī**b**a*	/xṭī**b**-a/	‘engaged (3F.SG)’	III.220
*xaṭ**b**it̲*	/xaṭ**b**-it̲/	‘I got engaged’	III.372
*iḳle**b***	/iḳle**b**/	‘overturned (3M.SG)’	III.356
*ḳal**b**e*	/ḳal**b**-e/	‘he turned it (M) over’	III.120
*ačʕe**b***	/ačʕe**b**/	‘he felt tired’	IV.86
*ačəʕ**b**at̲*	/ačʕ**b**-at̲/	‘she felt tired’ [2]	IV.24
*ġarre**b***	/ġarre**b**/	‘try (2M.SG)!’	IV.38
*ġarr**b**iččun*	/ġarr**b**-ičč-un/	‘I tried them (M)’	III.80
*ʕi**b**rat̲*	/ʕi**b**r-at̲/	‘she entered’	III.272
*niʕ**b**ar*	/n-iʕ**b**ar/	‘(that) I enter’	IV.26

The derivation in (7) illustrates the bilabial stop voicing rule. The first and second words are from (6a), and the third and fourth words are from (6b). The bilabial stop voicing rule turns the underlying /p/ in /ʕrī**p**-a/ to [b] but does not apply to /ʕir**p**-at̲/ because the /p/ is not postvocalic. It applies vacuously to /xṭī**b**-a/ whose bilabial stop

2 This is the literal meaning. In the narrative, the intended (figurative) meaning was that the situation ‘has become bad’.

is already voiced, making no changes to its underlying form. It does not make changes to /xaṭ**b**-iṯ/ either because the conditions of this rule are not satisfied.

(7) *A derivation to illustrate the bilabial stop voicing rule*

'gone down (3F.SG)'	'it (F) went down'	'engaged (3F.SG)'	'I got en-gaged'	
/ʕrī**p**-a/	/ʕir**p**-aṯ/	/xṭī**b**-a/	/xaṭ**b**-iṯ/	
ʕrī**b**a	–	–	–	bilabial stop voicing
[ʕrī**b**a]	[ʕir**p**aṯ]	[xṭī**b**a]	[xaṭ**b**iṯ]	

Bilabial stop voicing is a lexical rule which is confined to the word domain. For example, the underlying /p/ in *hanna* ***p****ayṯa* 'this house' IV.302 is not realized as [b] although it is preceded by a vowel. This is because there is a word boundary between the vowel and the following bilabial stop.

There are examples in the corpus where [p] occurs after the epenthetic vowel, as in (8). These examples show that, unlike the phonemic vowels, the epenthetic vowel does not trigger the bilabial stop voicing rule (for vowel epenthesis, see Sections 8.2.2 and 8.3.5).

(8)	*nusə****p****lēle*	/n-us**p**-l-ē-l-e/	'(that) I take (sthg. DEF) to him'	IV.58
	*naġə****p****lēle*	/naġ**p**-l-ē-l-e/	'he stole (sthg. DEF) from him'	IV.86
	*mašə****p****hōš*	/m-aš**p**h-ā-š/	'she looks like you (F)'	IV.176
	*xuṯə****p***	/xuṯ**p**-i/	'write (2M.SG) me!'	III.374
	*ḏinə****p***	/ḏin**p**/	'tails (EPL)'	III.286

The question, then, is: Why does the underlying /p/ not undergo bilabial stop voicing although at the surface level it is preceded by the vowel [ə]? There seems to be an opaque interaction between vowel epenthesis and bilabial stop voicing. To account for this opacity, I assume that vowel epenthesis (which is a postlexical rule) is ordered after bilabial stop voicing (which is a lexical rule). The following derivation for different inflected forms of the verb 'to take' (from (6a) and (8) above) illustrates this interaction between vowel epenthesis and bilabial stop voicing. It shows why the underlying vowel /e/ in /āsep/ and /āsep-l-a/ triggers bilabial stop voicing while the epenthetic vowel [ə] does not. The other phonological rules involved in this derivation will be presented and discussed in subsequent sections: stress assignment in Section 10.2, pretonic shortening in Section 10.3.2, /ā/ rounding in Section 7.3.1, and glottal epenthesis in Sections 8.2.3 and 8.3.6.

(9) *The interaction between vowel epenthesis and bilabial stop voicing*

'he takes'	'he takes her'	'she took her'	'(that) I take (sthg. DEF) to him'	
/āse**p**/	/āse**p**-l-a/	/as**p**-ačč-a/	/n-us**p**-l-ē-l-e/	
āse**b**	āse**b**la	–	–	**bilabial stop voicing**
'**ā**seb	ā'**seb**la	as'**pačča**	nusp'**lē**le	stress assignment
–	**a**'sebla	–	–	pretonic shortening
'**ō**seb	–	–	–	/ā/ rounding
–	–	–	nusəp'lēle	**vowel epenthesis**
'**ʔ**ōseb	**ʔ**a'sebla	**ʔ**as'pačča	–	glottal epenthesis
['ʔōse**b**]	[ʔa'se**b**la]	[ʔas'**p**ačča]	[nusə**p**'lēle]	

If vowel epenthesis were ordered before bilabial stop voicing, then the wrong output *[nusə**b**lēle] would be produced, as in (10).

(10) *A derivation that gives the wrong output*

'he takes'	'he takes her'	'she took her'	'(that) I take (sthg. DEF) to him'	
/āse**p**/	/āse**p**-l-a/	/as**p**-ačč-a/	/n-us**p**-l-ē-l-e/	
'**ā**sep	ā'**sep**la	as'**pačča**	nusp'**lē**le	stress assignment
–	**a**'sepla	–	–	pretonic shortening
'**ō**sep	–	–	–	/ā/ rounding
–	–	–	nusəp'lēle	**vowel epenthesis**
'ōse**b**	a'se**b**la	–	nusə**b**'lēle	**bilabial stop voicing**
'**ʔ**ōseb	**ʔ**a'sebla	**ʔ**as'pačča	–	glottal epenthesis
['ʔōse**b**]	[ʔa'se**b**la]	[ʔas'**p**ačča]	*[nusə**b**'lēle]	

5.2.2 Bilabial stops in preconsonantal position

In contrast to the expected neutralizing effect of bilabial stop voicing in postvocalic position, both [p] and [b] surface in the V__C environment, as the examples in (11) show. If bilabial stop voicing were the only rule at work, then the words in (11a) would surface with [b] rather than [p] in this postvocalic environment.

(11) [p] *and* [b] *in the environment V__C*

(a) [p] / V__C (common)

ipḥaš 'he dug' IV.22

*i**p**xel*	'stingy (INDF.M.SG)'	IV.282
*ʕžī**p**ča*	'miracle'	III.226

(b) [b] / V__C (common)

*naġe**b**le*	'he kidnaps him'	IV.252
*ʕi**b**raṯ*	'she went inside'	III.272
*si**b**ʕaṯ*	'she ate her fill'	IV.128

The words in (11a) are simply the result of another phonological rule whereby /b/ assimilates in voicing to a following voiceless consonant (Spitaler 1938: 34; Arnold 1990a: 18, 153). This means that the postvocalic [p] in (11a) is nothing but a devoiced /b/ which immediately precedes the voiceless consonants [ḥ x č]. This phonological rule can be formalized in (12).

(12) *Devoicing of bilabial stops*

$$\begin{bmatrix} \text{+labial} \\ \text{-son} \\ \text{-cont} \end{bmatrix} \rightarrow \text{[-voice]/\_\_[-voice]}$$

This rule is further exemplified in (13). The examples are given in pairs, and each pair represents two word forms of the same lemma. The phoneme /b/ is realized as [p] in the first word form (of each pair) and as [b] in the second word form, depending on the voicing of the following segment.

(13) *Pairs of word forms illustrating the effect of the devoicing rule*

*i**p**ḥaš*	/i**b**ḥaš/	'he dug'	IV.22
***b**ōḥeš*	/**b**āḥeš/	'he digs'	IV.22
*i**p**xel*	/i**b**xel/	'stingy (INDF.M.SG)'	IV.282
***b**ixlin*	/**b**ixl-in/	'stingy (INDF.M.PL)'	III.128
*ʕžī**p**ča*	/ʕžī**b**-T-a/ [3]	'miracle'	III.226
*ʕži**b**ōṯa*	/ʕžī**b**-ā-T-a/	'miracles'	III.226

3 /T/ indicates the {FEMININE} marker that I intend to leave unspecified in underlying representations. At the surface level, this morpheme has the two allomorphs [č] and [ṯ]. However, there is a specific set of lexical exceptions in which the feminine marker is specified underlyingly as /ṯ/, rather than /T/ (e.g., *xawkapṯa* /xawkab-ṯ-a/ 'star') (see Section 6.2.6).

*xawka**p**ṯa*	/xawka**b**-ṯ-a/	'star'	III.114
*xawk**bō**ṯa*	/xawk**b**-ā-T-a/	'stars'	VI.930
***p**sōna*	/**b**sōn-a/	'boy'	III.62
***b**isinō*	/**b**isin-ā/	'boys'	III.282

The derivation in (14) illustrates the bilabial stop devoicing rule. The four examples presented in it are two of the pairs given in (13). The derivation shows that bilabial stop devoicing is ordered after bilabial stop voicing. This ordering explains why the forms [ʔi**p**ḥaš] and [ʔi**p**xel] do not undergo the bilabial stop voicing rule although the [p] sounds occur postvocalically.

(14) *A derivation to illustrate the bilabial stop devoicing rule*

'he dug'	'he digs'	'stingy (INDF.M.SG)'	'stingy (INDF.M.PL)'	
/i**b**ḥaš/	/**b**āḥeš/	/i**b**xel/	/**b**ixl-in/	
–	–	–	–	**bilabial stop voicing**
–	bōḥeš	–	–	/ā/ rounding
ʔibḥaš	–	**ʔ**ibxel	–	glottal epenthesis
ʔi**p**ḥaš	–	ʔi**p**xel	–	**bilabial stop devoicing**
[ʔi**p**ḥaš]	[**b**ōḥeš]	[ʔi**p**xel]	[**b**ixlin]	

Both Spitaler (1938: 34) and Arnold (1990a: 18) note that this process is not without exceptions although such exceptions are rare. The examples in (15) are attested in the corpus, the first two of which were first pointed out by Spitaler. In these examples, [b] is not devoiced although it immediately precedes the voiceless consonants [š ḥ]. However, whether the stops in these examples are really voiced or not is a phonetic question as the difference between [b] and [p] in these words is not contrastive.

(15)	*ḏe**b**ša*	/ḏe**b**š-a/	'honey'	III.316
	*ṭlu**b**ḥō*	/ṭlu**b**ḥ-ā/	'lentils'	IV.228
	*ka**b**ša*	/ka**b**š-a/	'ram'	IV.172
	*sō**b**ḥa*	/sā**b**ḥ-a/	'she crawls'	III.228

In addition to these few exceptions, there are non-random cases in which the bilabial stop devoicing process is completely blocked. Spitaler (1938: 34) points out that /b/ does not assimilate in voicing to a following voiceless consonant unless it is immediately adjacent to it. For example, as the corpus data in (16) show, when an epenthetic schwa separates the voiced bilabial stop from the following voiceless consonant, the bilabial stop devoicing rule does not apply.

(16) *ša**b**əkṯa*	/ša**b**k-T-a/	'net'	IV.58
*ta**b**əkṯa*	/ta**b**k-T-a/	'dabke (a folk dance)'	III.184
*mi**b**əčlaš*	/m-i**b**člaš/	'he starts'	IV.178
*ma**b**ətya*	/m-a**b**ty-a/	'she begins'	III.184

To account for this blocking, I assume that vowel epenthesis is ordered before the bilabial stop devoicing process. The following derivation for two different inflected forms of the noun meaning 'net' illustrates this interaction between vowel epenthesis and bilabial stop devoicing. The singular form /ša**b**k-T-a/ undergoes vowel epenthesis, and therefore does not undergo the bilabial stop devoicing rule. The plural form /ša**b**k-ā-T-a/ does not undergo vowel epenthesis because the conditions are not met (see Sections 8.2.2 and 8.3.5). Since /b/ is immediately followed by the voiceless consonant /k/, the devoicing rule applies (for /T/ spirantization, see Section 6.2.6).

(17) *The interaction between vowel epenthesis and bilabial stop devoicing*

'net'	'nets'	
/ša**b**k-T-a/	/ša**b**k-ā-T-a/	
šabk**ṯ**a	šabkā**ṯ**a	/T/ spirantization
–	šabk**ō**ṯa	/ā/ rounding
šab**ə**kṯa	–	**vowel epenthesis**
–	ša**p**kōṯa	**bilabial stop devoicing**
[ša**b**əkṯa]	[ša**p**kōṯa]	

If the bilabial stop devoicing process were wrongly ordered before vowel epenthesis, the derivation would give the ungrammatical form *[ša**p**əkṯa], as in (18).

(18) *A derivation that gives the wrong output*

'net'	'nets'	
/ša**b**k-T-a/	/ša**b**k-ā-T-a/	
šabk**ṯ**a	šabkā**ṯ**a	/T/ spirantization
–	šabk**ō**ṯa	/ā/ rounding
ša**p**kṯa	ša**p**kōṯa	**bilabial stop devoicing**
šap**ə**kṯa	–	**vowel epenthesis**
*[ša**p**əkṯa]	[ša**p**kōṯa]	

In summary, vowel epenthesis is ordered before bilabial stop devoicing (as I argue in this section) but after bilabial stop voicing (as I argued in Section 5.2.1). This ordering of these three phonological rules plays a crucial role in determining the surface realization of the bilabial stops (as I have shown in the derivations above). The proposed rule ordering is presented in the diagram in (19).

(19) *Ordering of the rules which determine the realization of bilabial stops*

bilabial stop voicing
↓
vowel epenthesis
↓
bilabial stop devoicing

Bilabial stop devoicing is a postlexical process that can apply within and across word boundaries (see Arnold 1990a: 18). To illustrate the ability of this rule to apply across word boundaries, I will present a derivation that shows how the preposition *b-* 'in; at' undergoes bilabial stop devoicing if it precedes a word-initial voiceless consonant, unless an epenthetic vowel is inserted between them (see Spitaler 1938: 34, Arnold 1990a: 383, and Section 7.2.1 in this work for the different realizations of this preposition).

(20) *A derivation to illustrate the ability of bilabial stop devoicing to apply across word boundaries*

'in Damascus'	'in the vineyard'	'in/with wood'	
IV.238	III.98	III.334	
/**b**-ḏemseḳ/	/**b**-xarm-a/	/**b**-xšūr-a/	
–	–	**b**ə-xšūra	vowel epenthesis
–	**p**-xarma	–	bilabial stop devoicing
[**b**-ḏemseḳ]	[**p**-xarma]	[**b**ə-xšūra]	

5.2.3 Bilabial stops in word-initial position

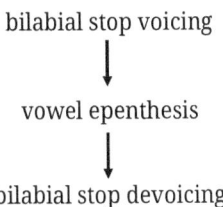

The previous literature (e.g., Spitaler 1938: 14; Arnold 1990a: 153, 2008: 172–173) indicates that it is the singleton [b] that occurs in word-initial position, and that the exceptions where [p] occurs word-initially are rare (e.g., ***p**ayṯa* 'house' Spitaler 1938: 14). The corpus data provide support for this generalization. Word-initial [b] occurs in 335 word types whereas word-initial [p] occurs in 25 word types.[4] To gain a deeper understanding of this distribution, I will break the word-initial environment down into the two environments #__V and #__C.

The literature on Maaloula Aramaic (e.g., Spitaler 1938: 13–15; Arnold 1990a: 13, 2008: 172–173) accounts for the distribution of [p] and [b] in the environment #__V from a diachronic perspective. According to this account, Maaloula Aramaic underwent a sound change whereby the fricatives, which had originally developed from stops through the spirantization process (explained in Section 5.2.1), spread to word-initial positions. As a result, fricatives like [ḇ] rather than stops like [b] occupied all word-initial positions. Subsequently, the fricative [ḇ] has developed into the current phoneme /b/ but has maintained its word-initial position, and the plosive [b] has become the current phoneme /p/ which still does not occur in word-initial position. This account explains why in the corpus there are considerably more word types with [b] than with [p] in the environment #__V.

(21) [p] *and* [b] *in the environment #__V*

(a) [p] / #__V (in 18 word types)

payṯa	'house'	IV.228
pulpel	'a place name'	IV.340
paʕḷō [5]	'God willing'	IV.82

(b) [b] / #__V (in 291 word types)

boġta	'rug'	III.110
besra	'meat'	IV.282
baḥar	'a lot; very'	III.146

From a synchronic perspective, I do not believe that there is any need to formulate a rule to account for the distribution of [p] and [b] in the environment #__V. This is because the environment #__V is already one of the "elsewhere" environments in both the bilabial stop voicing rule and the bilabial stop devoicing rule, which have been formalized respectively in (5) and (12) above. In other words, I assume that the surface forms and the underlying forms of the bilabial stops in the #__V environment are in one-to-one correspondence.

4 The non-aramaicized loanwords and the interrupted and mispronounced words are not included.

5 It is transcribed as *ppaʕlō* in the original text.

With regard to the distribution of [p] and [b] in the environment #__C (exemplified in (22)), I follow Spitaler (1938: 14, 34) in assuming that words like ***psōna***, ***pšōṯa***, and ***pčalšiṯ*** are the result of the bilabial stop devoicing rule (see the previous section). In other words, the underlying stop in all the words in (22) is /b/ which is realized as [p] in (22a) and as [b] in (22b), depending on the voicing of the following segment, a case similar to (11) above.

(22) [p] *and* [b] *in the environment #__C*

(a) [p] / #__C (in seven word types)

psōna	'boy'	III.62
pšōṯa	'raisins'	III.28
pčalšiṯ	'I started (to)'	III.106

(b) [b] / #__C (in 44 word types)

blōta	'village'	IV.12
bnōṯax	'your (M.SG) daughters'	III.340
bḏ̣ōʕča	'goods'	IV.102

5.3 Geminate bilabial stops

Spitaler (1938: 15) points out that a geminate bilabial stop is realized as voiceless (e.g., *xo**pp**a* 'thorn', *ra**pp**a* 'big (DEF.M.SG)', *le**pp**a* 'heart'), but he lists a few counterexamples (e.g., *ra**bb**i* 'big (INDF.M.SG)', *ṭa**bb**i* 'alive (INDF.M.SG)'). The corpus data provide support for Spitaler's generalization. The geminate [pp] occurs in 248 word types whereas the geminate [bb] occurs only in six word types.[6] Spitaler's observation can be interpreted from a synchronic perspective as a case of neutralization whereby the contrast between the underlying /pp/ and the underlying /bb/ is neutralized to [pp], as (23) shows.

6 The non-aramaicized loanwords and the interrupted and mispronounced words were not included. I also excluded the words in which the geminate bilabial stop is followed by a consonant because these geminates undergo preconsonantal degemination and surface as singletons (e.g., *šo**pp**ṯa* [šopṯa] 'week' III.46, *ḳo**pp**ṯa* [ḳopṯa] 'dome' IV.70) (see Section 9.3.2 and Arnold 1990a: 17).

(23) *Neutralization of geminate bilabial stops*

/pp/ /bb/

[pp]

I assume that the phonological rule that is responsible for this neutralization is a devoicing rule that targets geminate bilabial stops. This rule is formalized in (24). The six word types which surface with [bb] in the corpus can be considered lexical exceptions to this devoicing rule.

(24) *Devoicing of geminate bilabial stops*

$$\begin{bmatrix} \text{+labial} \\ \text{-son} \\ \text{-cont} \\ \text{+long} \end{bmatrix} \rightarrow \text{[-voice]}$$

The effect of this devoicing rule can be seen in the examples in (25). The geminate bilabial stops in these examples are underlying (rather than surface) geminates which result from a non-concatenative morphological process. The words *ʕa**pp**er* and *nṣa**pp**er* are perfect verbs that are generated from triliteral roots by a pattern which geminates the second radical (C_2), which is a bilabial stop (see Section 9.2.1 for further details on how non-concatenative morphological processes create underlying geminates). It can be seen that when the underlying bilabial stop is a geminate, it is realized as voiceless whether it is voiced (e.g., /ʕa**bb**er/) or voiceless (e.g., /n-ṣa**pp**er/) in the underlying representation.

(25) *Examples illustrating the effect of the geminate bilabial stop devoicing rule*

*ʕa**pp**er*	/ʕa**bb**er/	'he is entering'	IV.200
*nṣa**pp**er* [7]	/n-ṣa**pp**er/	'I am (being) patient'	IV.320

The presented analysis may raise the following questions: How can the underlying forms of these geminate bilabial stops be determined? Why is it not possible that both verbs have underlying voiceless geminates that just surface unaltered? These questions can be answered when the perfect verb forms in (25) are compared to other inflectional forms of the same verbs, such as the preterit forms *iʕ**b**er* and

7 It is transcribed as *nṣappar* in the original text.

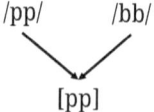

aṣpar in (26). These preterit forms are generated by morphological patterns in which the second radical of the root is not geminated. In these two inflectional forms, the underlying singleton bilabial stops surface unaltered because the conditions for postvocalic voicing (presented in Section 5.2.1) or preconsonantal devoicing (presented in Section 5.2.2) are not met. Since *iʕ**ber*** and *a**ṣpar*** have two different underlying bilabial stops, the related forms *ʕ**apper*** and *nṣ**apper*** which are derived from the same roots must also have two different underlying bilabial stops. It is the devoicing rule that neutralizes the difference between them.

(26) *ʕ**apper***	/ʕa**bb**er/	'he is entering'	IV.200
*iʕ**ber***	/iʕ**b**er/	'he entered'	IV.150
*nṣ**apper*** [8]	/n-ṣa**pp**er/	'I am (being) patient'	IV.320
*a**ṣpar***	/aṣ**p**ar/	'he was patient'	IV.250

The derivation in (27) summarizes the discussion above by illustrating how the surface forms in (26) are derived from their underlying forms.

(27) *A derivation to illustrate the neutralizing effect of the geminate bilabial stop devoicing rule*

/ʕa**bb**er/	/iʕ**b**er/	/n-ṣa**pp**er/	/aṣ**p**ar/	
–	–	–	–	sgl. bilabial stop voicing
ʕa**pp**er	–	–	–	**gem. bilabial stop devoicing**
–	**ʔ**iʕber	–	**ʔ**aṣpar	glottal epenthesis
–	–	–	–	sgl. bilabial stop devoicing
[ʕa**pp**er]	[ʔiʕ**b**er]	[nṣa**pp**er]	[ʔaṣ**p**ar]	

The geminate bilabial stop devoicing rule is a lexical rule which is restricted to the word domain. If the geminates are the result of the concatenation of two voiced bilabial stops across word boundaries, as in ***b-besra*** 'with meat' III.38, the surface geminates will not undergo devoicing (i.e., ****p-pesra***).

The environments in which the geminate bilabial stops occur in the corpus are shown in Table 5.1. As can be seen, the geminate [pp] is most frequent in word-medial position and least frequent in word-initial position. This finding is in line with the cross-linguistic observation that word-medial geminates are in general more common than word-initial geminates (see, e.g., Muller 2001: 17). The table also shows the distribution of the six lexical exceptions.

8 It is transcribed as *nṣappar* in the original text.

Table 5.1: Distribution of the geminate bilabial stops across different environments

Environment	[pp]	[bb]
#__V	4	0
V__V	231	3
V__#	13	3
Total	248	6

The following examples show these two geminates in word-initial, word-medial, and word-final positions. Some of these examples have already been introduced in (2) above.

(28) [pp] *and* [bb] *in word-initial, word-medial, and word-final positions*

(a) [pp] / #__V

***pp**ōfča*	'loaf (of bread)'	III.128
***pp**ōban*	'loaves (EPL)'	III.128

(b) [bb] / #__V (no examples)

(c) [pp] / V__V

*ḥašo**pp**a*	'Sunday'	III.152
*to**pp**a*	'bear'	IV.256

(d) [bb] / V__V

*ra**bb**i*	'big (INDF.M.SG)'	IV.54
*ṭa**bb**i*	'alive (INDF.M.SG)'	IV.300

(e) [pp] / V__#

*li**pp***	'my heart'	IV.170
*ša**pp***	'young men (EPL)'	III.238

(f) [bb] / V__#

*ra**bb***	'big (INDF.M.SG)'	IV.58
*ṭa**bb***	'alive (INDF.M.SG)'	III.306

5.4 Conclusion

In this chapter, I have investigated the distribution of the singleton and geminate bilabial stops, and I have provided and formalized three phonological rules which are responsible for their distribution: bilabial stop voicing (in postvocalic position), bilabial stop devoicing (before a voiceless consonant), and geminate bilabial stop devoicing.

The presented analyses support the theoretical proposals which differentiate between lexical rules and postlexical rules (e.g., Kiparsky 1982; Kaisse & Shaw 1985). "The most obvious diagnostic of a postlexical rule is the ability to apply between words as well as within them" (Kaisse & Shaw 1985: 4). Based on this diagnostic, I have considered bilabial stop voicing and geminate bilabial stop devoicing to be lexical rules because they only apply within words but considered bilabial stop devoicing a postlexical rule because it can apply within and between words.

Another difference between lexical and postlexical rules, according to Kaisse & Shaw (1985: 7), is how native speakers judge the output of these rules: Native speakers differentiate between the different outputs of lexical rules, but they consider the different outputs of postlexical rules to be the same. This can be seen clearly in the teaching materials produced by authors from the Maaloula Aramaic speech community. These authors, who are native speakers of the language, differentiate orthographically between [p] and [b] when bilabial stop voicing (which is a lexical rule) applies, as in (29a). However, they do not differentiate between [p] and [b] in the environment where the postlexical rule of bilabial stop devoicing applies, as in (29b).

(29) *The outputs of lexical and postlexical rules as transcribed by native speakers*

(a) [p] and [b] are contrasted when bilabial stop voicing applies

*rix**p**iṯ*	'I rode'	Rizkallah 2010: 170
*rxī**b**a*	'riding (3F.SG)'	Rizkallah 2010: 185

(b) [p] and [b] are not contrasted when bilabial stop devoicing applies

***b**sōna*	'boy'	Rihan 2017: 16	(cf. ***p**sōna* III.62)
***b**isinō*	'boys'	Rihan 2017: 90	(cf. ***b**isinō* III.282)
*xawka**b**ṯa*	'star'	Rizkallah 2010: 205	(cf. *xawka**p**ṯa* III.114)
*xawk**b**ō*	'stars'	Rizkallah 2010: 87	(cf. *xawk**b**ōṯa* VI.930)

In this chapter, no cross-linguistic reference to the surrounding Arabic dialects has been made because Arabic does not have the phoneme /p/.

6 Morpho-phonological alternations in feminine nouns

6.1 Introduction

In this chapter, I investigate two morpheme-specific alternations that occur in feminine nouns by conducting two corpus-based studies. In the first study, I examine the feminine marker which shows the alternation *-ṯa* ~ *-ča* (e.g., *šaʕ**ṯa*** 'hour' III.302 vs. *frīs**ča*** 'right' IV.82). In the second study, I investigate the plural marker which shows the alternation *-ōṯa* ~ *-yōṯa* (e.g., *ḏukk**ōṯa*** 'places' III.200 vs. *maščuy**ōṯa*** 'weddings' III.374). In each study, I attempt to identify the variables that are responsible for the distribution of the two alternants in question. The investigated variables include the segments which immediately precede the alternant, the templatic pattern of the entire feminine noun, and the length of the base vowels. I also discuss whether the alternation can be considered as allomorphy and present what I consider to be the underlying form for each alternant and provide arguments to support the proposed analyses.

6.2 Feminine marker alternation

The previous literature (e.g., Spitaler 1938: 103–104; Arnold 1990a: 290–298) has shown that many feminine nouns end with a feminine marker which is *-ṯa* in some nouns and *-ča* in other nouns, as in (1).[1]

(1)	(a)	*šaʕ**ṯa***	'hour'	III.302
		*xall**ṯa***	'daughter-in-law'	IV.130
		*ʕaym**ṯa***	'cloud'	IV.64
		*rxopp**ṯa***	'knee'	III.364
		*matras**ṯa***	'school'	III.88
	(b)	*ġūr**ča***	'hole'	III.90
		*ṯinaġel**ča***	'hen'	IV.124
		*ʕžīp**ča***	'miracle'	III.226

1 There are other feminine nouns which do not end with a feminine marker (e.g., *arʕa* 'earth; ground' III.368, *īḏa* 'hand' IV.162) (see Arnold 1990a: sec. 6.2), but these nouns need not concern us here.

https://doi.org/10.1515/9783111447124-006

ḥīrča	'confusion; puzzlement'	IV.8
frīsča	'right'	IV.82

In this work, I divide *-ṯa* and *-ča* further into two affixes: the feminine marker itself *-ṯ* or *-č* and the nominal ending *-a*. This analysis is shown in (2a). I will henceforth use *-ṯ* or *-č* to refer to the feminine marker except when I review the previous accounts where I keep the original notation used in the reviewed references (i.e., *-ṯa* and *-ča*). I use the term *base* to refer to the part of the word which precedes the suffixes. There are two reasons for not considering *-a* as part of the feminine marker. First, the nominal ending *-a* is not restricted to feminine nouns. It also appears in masculine nouns (e.g., ***ṭūra*** 'mountain' IV.334, ***ḏīka*** 'rooster' IV.22). Second, this nominal ending occurs only in the citation form of nouns. When a pronominal suffix is attached to a feminine noun, as in (2b), only the nominal ending *-a* will disappear, but *-ṯ* or *-č* will remain.

(2) (a) *šaʕ-**ṯ**-a* — *ṯinaġel-**č**-a*
hour-F-NE — hen-F-NE
'hour' III.302 — 'hen' IV.124

(b) *soləf-**ṯ**-e* [2] — *ḥōl-**č**-iš*
story-F-3M.SG — uncle-F-2F.SG
'his story' IV.26 — 'your (F.SG) aunt/stepmother' IV.168

6.2.1 Spitaler's account

Spitaler (1938: 103–104) presented a diachronic account that lays out the change which the feminine marker has undergone (i.e., *-ṯā* > *-ṯa* and *-tā* > *-ča*) and connects the distribution of *-ṯa* and *-ča* to the distribution of the historical sounds [ṯ] and [t]. These two sounds used to be two allophones of the ancient phoneme /t/ which was realized as [ṯ] in postvocalic position and as [t] elsewhere at earlier stages of Aramaic. Later, these two allophones developed into two separate phonemes (i.e., [ṯ] > /ṯ/ and [t] > /č/), see Section 5.2 for a brief overview of the historical sound change that the stops /b g d k p t/ underwent. For more details, see Bergsträsser (1928: 80), Spitaler (1938: 12–21), and Arnold (1990a: 12–14, 2008: 171–176).

According to Spitaler, the old environments still, to a great extent, play a decisive role in the current distribution of the feminine alternants. However, he did not

2 It is transcribed as *sōləfṯe* in the original text.

provide further details or examples to illustrate these environments and to show how they may influence the distribution. He did, however, make interesting synchronic observations on the environments in which the feminine alternants occur. For example, he observed that the nouns which have a long vowel usually take -*ča*, as in (3a), but there are certain monosyllabic Arabic loanwords which take -*ṯa* although they have long vowels, as in (3b). The examples are from MASC.

(3)	(a)	***ḏōrča***	'house'	IV.138
		ḥōlča	'maternal aunt; stepmother'	IV.166
	(b)	***sōḥṯa***	'(village) square'	III.178
		ʕōṯṯa	'custom; habit'	III.66

He also pointed out that both -*ṯa* and -*ča* are equally common in the feminine nouns which have the templatic pattern maCCaCCa, as in (4). The examples are from MASC.

(4)	***malʕaḳṯa***	'spoon'	III.72
	maḥkamṯa	'(law) court'	IV.300
	mapxarča	'censer'	III.200
	maṣfarča	'scissors'	III.62

He argued that certain Arabic loanwords are attested with both alternants, as in (5). However, Spitaler's variants *ḳoppča* and *maḥramča* are not attested in more recent data.

(5)	***ḳoppṯa***	~	***ḳoppča***	'dome'	Spitaler 1938: 104
	maḥramṯa	~	***maḥramča***	'handkerchief; tissue'	Spitaler 1938: 104

In general, Spitaler's generalizations are insightful because they shed light on the important role of (a) the phonological environment in which the feminine marker occurs and (b) the templatic pattern of the feminine noun in determining the distribution of the feminine alternants. However, these generalizations leave a number of open questions.

6.2.2 Open questions

First, Spitaler's generalizations do not cover all the environments and templatic patterns. Whereas his generalizations describe the alternation in the feminine nouns which have a long vowel (as in (3) above) and in the feminine nouns which have the templatic pattern maCCaCCa (as in (4) above), he did not investigate other patterns, such as the ones presented in (6).

(6)	CCVCCa	(e.g., *spaʕṯa*	'finger'	IV.10)
	CVCCCa	(e.g., *ʕaymṯa*	'cloud'	IV.64)
	CCVGGCa	(e.g., *mʕarrṯa*	'cave'	III.368)
	CVCVCCa	(e.g., *ḳamesča*	'shirt'	III.272)[3]
	CVCCVCCa	(e.g., *žawharča*	'gem'	IV.84)
	CVCVCVCCa	(e.g., *ṯinaġelča*	'hen'	IV.124)

To address this point, my first research question will be: What are the specific environments and templatic patterns in which each alternant occurs?

Second, one of Spitaler's generalizations shows that although a specific set of feminine nouns share the same templatic pattern maCCaCCa, not all of the nouns in this set have the same feminine marker (e.g., *malʕaḳṯa* 'spoon' vs. *mapxarča* 'censer'). My second research question is: In the cases where the distribution of *-ṯ* and *-č* does not depend on the templatic pattern, what other factors influence this distribution?

Third, according to another generalization of Spitaler's, certain Arabic loanwords are attested with both alternants. However, the examples which he presented to demonstrate this variation are ungrammatical, at least from a modern perspective (e.g., *ḳoppča* 'dome' and *maḥramča* 'handkerchief; tissue'). As a result, it is not clear whether *-ṯ* and *-č* are in free variation indeed, and the examples used are obsolete or ungrammatical, or whether *-ṯ* and *-č* are not in free variation in the first place because the alleged variation is based on false evidence. This lack of clarity does not necessarily imply that this variation does not exist or never existed. It could be the case that the language data available to Spitaler were not large enough to show such a variation. Since larger, more modern, and more easily accessible data are available now, this reported variation can be examined more thoroughly. To do that, I formulate my third research question: Are *-ṯ* and *-č* in free variation (at least in a specific set of words)?

Only when these questions are answered can the morpho-phonological status of *-ṯ* and *-č* be determined (i.e., whether they are phonologically conditioned allomorphs, they are allomorphs in free variation, or they are not allomorphs but rather two different morphemes).

3 It is transcribed as *ḳameṣča* in the original text.

6.2.3 Data and method

I used the data set called “MASC_dataframe.csv”, introduced in Section 3.4.1, to collect as many nouns as possible that have the feminine marker. Since the words in the data set are not provided with part-of-speech annotation, I collected all the words which end with *-ṯa* or *-ča* regardless of their part of speech and of whether they really have the feminine marker or not. As a next step, I went through this word list manually, with the help of my language consultant, to eliminate the unwanted words. The eliminated words included masculine nouns, as in (7a), verbs, as in (7b), and adjectives, as in (7c). I also excluded all feminine plural nouns because the feminine marker in the plural is always *-ṯ* (i.e., no alternation), as in (7d).

(7) *Excluded words exemplified*

(a)	*payṯa*	‘house’	IV.228
	mawṯa	‘death’	III.218
	waḳča	‘time’	III.172
	čaxča	‘bed’	IV.214
(b)	*mōyṯa*	‘she dies’	IV.170
	ayṯa	‘bring (2M.SG)!’	IV.194
	ḥmičča	‘I saw her’	IV.324
	naḥḥīča	‘she (is) going down’	III.224
(c)	*manḥōyṯa*	‘eastern (DEF.F.SG)’	III.224
	kkōmča	‘black (DEF.F.SG)’	III.76
	ḥuwwōrča	‘white (DEF.F.SG)’	IV.16
	ẓʕōrča [4]	‘small (DEF.F.SG)’	III.72
(d)	*bisənyōṯa*	‘girls’	III.376
	samkōṯa	‘fish (PL)’	IV.140
	žawəhrōṯa	‘gems; jewels’	IV.126
	ḏwōṯa	‘hands’	IV.30

After eliminating the unwanted words, a total of 618 unique feminine nouns were included in the final feminine noun data set (hereafter referred to as the FemN data set). I coded the data set by creating a number of variables. For coding, I considered the underlying (rather than the surface) forms of the feminine nouns (i.e., before they undergo phonological processes such as preconsonantal degemination, vowel

4 It is transcribed as *zʕōrča* in the original text.

and glottal epenthesis, and assimilation). In what follows, I briefly present the created variables.

Feminine alternant. I included the variable FEMMARKER to indicate whether the feminine alternant in each word in the data set is ṯ or č.

Phonological environment. I created the variable ENVIRONMENT with the values `vocoid_`, `CC_`, `GG_`, `VVC_`, `VC_`, and `other` to identify the phonological environments in which the feminine marker occurs. `Vocoid` refers to a vowel or a glide, `GG` refers to a geminate, `VV` refers to a long vowel, and `V` refers to a short vowel. The environment labeled as `other` represents the cases in which the feminine marker is an underlying geminate (e.g., *ġbečča* 'cheese' III.34, *ḥḏučča* 'bride' III.60). Since only underlying representations are analyzed, the environment `other` does not include the cases where the feminine marker is a surface geminate which is formed by assimilation (e.g., *freṯṯa* 'grain; (coffee) bean' III.44; *ʕōṯṯa* 'custom; habit' III.66) (for the difference between underlying geminates and surface geminates, see Section 9.2). The environments `CC_`, `GG_`, `VVC_`, and `VC_` do not include the cases where the consonant which immediately precedes the feminine marker is a glide because these cases are already covered by the environment `vocoid_`.

Templatic pattern. I added the variable TEMPLATICPATTERN to examine the underlying templatic patterns of the feminine nouns (e.g., `CVCCCa` for *baḥərṯa* and `CVCCVCCa` for *balbalča*).

Preceding segment. I created the variable PRECEDINGSEGMENT to identify the immediately preceding segment (e.g., `r`, `k`, `ʕ`) and the variable MANNER to classify this preceding segment according to its manner of articulation (e.g., `Rhotic`, `Stop`, `Fricative`).

The FemN data set is illustrated in (8).

(8) *Extract from the FemN data set*

SG FORM	FEM MARKER	ENVIRONMENT	TEMPLATIC PATTERN	PRECEDING SEGMENT	MANNER
baḥərṯa	ṯ	CC__	CVCCCa	r	Rhotic
balbalča	č	VC__	CVCCVCCa	l	Lateral
ballōrča	č	VVC__	CVGGVVCCa	r	Rhotic
barəmṯa	ṯ	CC__	CVCCCa	m	Nasal
baṣṣṯa	ṯ	GG__	CVGGCa	ṣ	Fricative
baṭrakōyṯa	ṯ	vocoid__	CVCCVCVVCCa	y	Glide
baṭraxōnča	č	VVC__	CVCCVCVVCCa	n	Nasal

6.2.4 Results

Table 6.1 shows the distribution of *-ṯ* and *-č* in this data set. It can be noticed that *-ṯ* is nearly twice as frequent as *-č*.

Table 6.1: Distribution of the feminine alternants

-ṯ	-č	Total
407	211	618

A closer examination of the data set shows that the distribution of *-ṯ* and *-č* can be determined based on the environments in which they occur in 59.39% of the cases. Table 6.2 summarizes this distribution. It can be noticed that with the exception of the environments VVC__ and CV__ where both markers occur (251 nouns), either *-ṯ* or *-č* occurs in the other environments (367 nouns).

Table 6.2: Distribution of the feminine alternants across the different environments in which they occur

Environment	-ṯ	-č	Distribution
VVC__	12	158	Mixed in 251 nouns (40.61%)
VC__	33	48	
vocoid__	148	0	Mutually exclusive in 367 nouns (59.39%)
CC__	179	0	
GG__	35	0	
other	0	5	
Total	407	211	

As can be seen in Table 6.2, the distribution of the feminine alternants cannot be determined by the immediately preceding environment in 40.61% of the nouns. These nouns have a clear tendency to take the feminine alternant *-č*, but no further details can be deduced from this table. In order to obtain the needed details, I will investigate the distribution of the feminine alternants across the same phonological environments but with the templatic patterns of the feminine nouns as a grouping factor. This distribution is shown in Table 6.3. The parentheses in the templatic patterns indicate optional constituents, and the symbol X refers to “any number of segments of any type" (after Hayes 2009: 101). The templatic patterns are numbered for ease of reference (i.e., no order is assumed among the different numbers).

Table 6.3: Distribution of the feminine alternants across the different phonological environments with the templatic pattern as a grouping factor

Environment	Templatic pattern		-ṯ	-č	Distribution
VVC___	(C)VVCCa	No. 1	12	28	Mixed in 106 nouns (17.15%)
VC___	(C)CVCCa	No. 2	11	2	
VC___	(C)(C)VCCVCCa	No. 3	21	28	
VC___	(C)(C)VGGVCCa	No. 4	1	3	
VVC___	(X)GGVVCCa	No. 5	0	25	Mutually exclusive in 512 nouns (82.85%)
VVC___	XCVVCCa	No. 6	0	105	
VC___	(X)VCVCCa	No. 7	0	15	
vocoid___	Different patterns	No. 8	148	0	
CC___	(C)(C)VCCCa	No. 9	175	0	
CC___	CVVCCCa	No. 10	4	0	
GG___	(C)(C)VGGCa	No. 11	35	0	
other	XGGa	No. 12	0	5	
Total			407	211	

Table 6.3 describes the distribution of the feminine alternants more accurately than Table 6.2. The number of nouns in the groups which have a mutually exclusive distribution has increased from 367 nouns (59.39%) in Table 6.2 to 512 nouns (82.85%) in Table 6.3.

As Table 6.3 shows, there are four groups of nouns which have a mixed distribution (i.e., the groups in which both alternants occur). These groups are exemplified in (9), (10), (11) and (12).

(9) *Group 1. Environment: VVC___, templatic pattern: (C)VVCCa*

(a)	*sōḥṯa*	CVVCCa	'(village) square'	III.178
	rīḥṯa	CVVCCa	'smell'	III.166
	šōmṯa	CVVCCa	'mole (on the skin)'	IV.106
	ṭōpṯa	CVVCCa	'good(ness); well-being'	IV.178
	ōfṯa	VVCCa	'horned viper'	III.86

(b)	*ḏōrča*	CVVCCa	‘house’	IV.138
	ḥōlča	CVVCCa	‘maternal aunt; stepmother’	IV.166
	sūsča	CVVCCa	‘mare’	IV.156
	šīrča	CVVCCa	‘the rest’	IV.256
	ḥīlča	CVVCCa	‘trick; ruse’	IV.8

(10) *Group 2. Environment: VC___, templatic pattern: (C)CVCCa*

(a)	*spaʕṯa*	CCVCCa	‘finger’	IV.10
	freṯṯa	CCVCCa	‘grain; (coffee) bean’	III.44
	beʕṯa	CVCCa	‘egg’	III.326
	šaʕṯa	CVCCa	‘hour’	III.302
	laxṯa	CVCCa	‘walk(ing); on foot’	IV.286
(b)	*lṭarča* [5]	CCVCCa	‘ratl (a unit of weight)’	IV.338
	berča	CVCCa	‘daughter’	IV.298

(11) *Group 3. Environment: VC___, templatic pattern: (C)(C)VCCVCCa*

(a)	*xawkapṯa*	CVCCVCCa	‘star’	III.114
	žumžomṯa	CVCCVCCa	‘skull’	IV.14
	matrasṯa	CVCCVCCa	‘school’	III.88
	mamlakṯa	CVCCVCCa	‘kingdom’	IV.106
	marfaḳṯa	CVCCVCCa	‘pillow; cushion’	III.184
(b)	*žawharča*	CVCCVCCa	‘gem’	IV.84
	mapxarča	CVCCVCCa	‘censer’	III.200
	maṣfarča	CVCCVCCa	‘scissors’	III.62
	ḳušbarča	CVCCVCCa	‘corn husks’	III.38
	armalča	VCCVCCa	‘widow’	IV.80

(12) *Group 4. Environment: VC___, templatic pattern: (C)(C)VGGVCCa*

(a)	*ḥammešṯa*	CVGGVCCa	‘Thursday’	III.154
(b)	*msažžalča*	CCVGGVCCa	‘tape recorder’	III.298
	msaddasča	CCVGGVCCa	‘six-sided figure’	III.114
	awwalča	VGGVCCa	‘beginning’	IV.182

5 It is transcribed as *ṭarča* in the original text.

The eight groups of nouns, shown in Table 6.3, which have a mutually exclusive distribution of the feminine alternants (i.e., where only one alternant occurs) are exemplified below.

(13) *Group 5. Environment: VVC__, templatic pattern: (X)GGVVCCa*

ḳattēšča	CVGGVVCCa	'female saint'	III.146
xayyōṭča	CVGGVVCCa	'female tailor'	IV.308
šuppōpča	CVGGVVCCa	'(reed) flute'	IV.212
ḳannīnča	CVGGVVCCa	'bottle'	IV.274
ppōfča	GGVVCCa	'loaf (of bread)'	III.128

(14) *Group 6. Environment: VVC__, templatic pattern: XCVVCCa*

maḥōlča [6]	CVCVVCCa	'sieve (with a fine mesh)'	III.38
aġīrča	VCVVCCa	'maid; maidservant'	IV.64
šbōpča	CCVVCCa	'female neighbor'	III.62
ġmōʕča	CCVVCCa	'group of people'	IV.248
frīsča	CCVVCCa	'right'	IV.82

(15) *Group 7. Environment: VC__, templatic pattern: (X)VCVCCa*

ṯinaġelča	CVCVCVCCa	'hen'	IV.124
mṣaraʕča	CCVCVCCa	'wrestling'	IV.232
mẓaharča	CCVCVCCa	'demonstration'	IV.272
msabaḳča	CCVCVCCa	'competition'	III.194
maḏenča	CVCVCCa	'minaret'	IV.252

(16) *Group 8. Environment: vocoid__, different templatic patterns*

bisnīṯa	CVCCVVCa	'girl'	IV.88
šunīṯa	CVCVVCa	'woman'	IV.262
ṣlōṯa	CCVVCa	'prayer; Mass'	III.162
ṯulṯōyṯa	CVCCVVCCa	'(medium-sized) clay jar'	IV.144
ḥḏawṯa	CCVCCa	'joy; wedding (party)'	VI.353

6 It is transcribed as *maḥḥōlča* in the original text.

(17) *Group 9. Environment: CC___, templatic pattern: (C)(C)VCCCa* [7]

ʕaymṯa	CVCCCa	'cloud'	IV.64
berkṯa	CVCCCa	'Saint Thecla'	III.182
fartṯa	CVCCCa	'bundle'	IV.180
šafərṯa	CVCCCa	'razor blade'	III.296
tabəkṯa	CVCCCa	'dabke (a folk dance)'	III.184

(18) *Group 10. Environment: CC___, templatic pattern: CVVCCCa*

bōykṯa	CVVCCCa	'stable (for animals)'	III.366
ṭōyfṯa [8]	CVVCCCa	'(religious) denomination'	III.260
mōyṯṯa	CVVCCCa	'altar table; dining table'	III.234
tōyrṯa [9]	CVVCCCa	'(government) department'	VI.830

(19) *Group 11. Environment: GG___, templatic pattern: (C)(C)VGGCa* [10]

rxoppṯa	CCVGGCa	'knee'	III.364
šoppṯa	CVGGCa	'week'	III.46
xaffṯa	CVGGCa	'shoulder'	IV.228
ṯeffṯa	CVGGCa	'fireplace'	III.32
ḳoppṯa	CVGGCa	'dome'	IV.70

(20) *Group 12. Environment: other, templatic pattern: XGGa*

ġbečča	CCVGGa	'cheese'	III.34
ḥḏučča	CCVGGa	'bride'	III.60
šbičča	CCVGGa	'godmother'	III.200
žičča [11]	CVGGa	'grandmother'	VI.979
ṯēčča	CVVGGa	'Ain Al-Tinah (a nearby village)'	III.272

The fact that the distribution of *-ṯ* and *-č* is not predictable in groups 1, 2, 3, and 4, which constitute 17.15% of the nouns in the data set leads to my second research

7 An epenthetic vowel may be inserted between the two consonants which immediately precede the feminine marker (see Sections 8.2.2 and 8.3.5).
8 It is transcribed as *tōyfṯa* in the original text.
9 It is transcribed as *tōyərṯa* in the original text.
10 At the surface level, these underlying geminates (i.e., /GG/) undergo degemination and surface as singletons (i.e., [C]) because they occur in preconsonantal position. Degemination is presented and discussed in Section 9.3.2.
11 It is transcribed as *žečča* in Arnold's (2019: 979) dictionary.

question: In the cases where the distribution of *-ṯ* and *-č* does not depend on the templatic pattern, what other factors influence this distribution? There was one specific factor which was able to provide the most convincing categorization of the feminine nouns in groups 1, 2, 3, and 4. It is the manner of articulation (or sonority) of the consonant which immediately precedes the feminine marker. Although the distribution of *-ṯ* and *-č* across the different manners of articulation is not mutually exclusive, as Table 6.4 shows, a general tendency can be observed.

Table 6.4: Distribution of *-ṯ* and *-č* in groups 1, 2, 3, and 4 by the manner of articulation of the preceding consonant

Sonority	**Manner of articulation**	**-ṯ**	**-č**	**Proportions**
Obstruents	Stop	14	2	Proportion of *-ṯ* = 76%
	Fricative	24	10	(38 / 50)
Sonorants	Nasal	5	6	Proportion of *-č* = 87.5%
	Lateral	2	11	(49 / 56)
	Rhotic	0	32	
Total		45	61	

If this distribution is plotted, as in Figure 6.1, it can be seen that the likelihood of a feminine noun taking *-č* increases as the sonority of the preceding consonant increases, and vice versa, the likelihood of a feminine noun taking *-ṯ* decreases as the sonority of the preceding consonant increases.

I now turn to my third research question: Are *-ṯ* and *-č* in free variation (at least in a specific set of words)? In contrast to Spitaler's generalization, which states that certain Arabic loanwords are attested with both *-ṯ* and *-č*, the data set contains only one example of such variation (i.e., *ṣīġṯa* IV.154 ~ *ṣīġča* III.60 'jewelry'). This single attestation does not provide enough evidence to prove that this type of variation really exists.

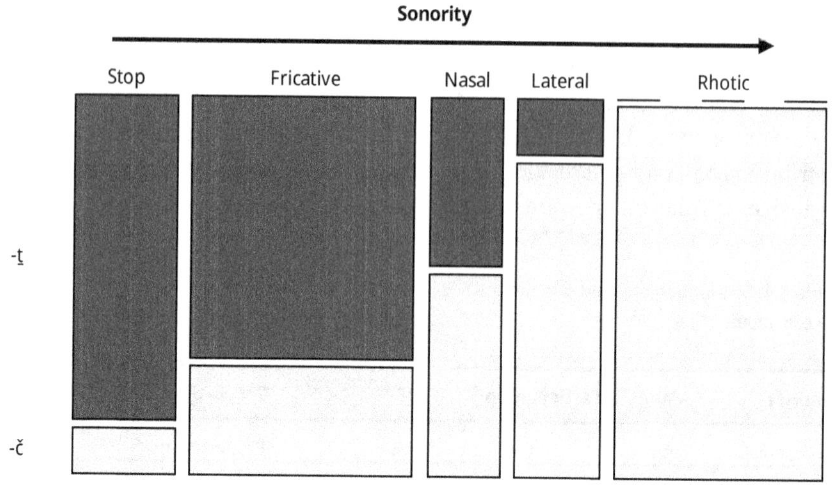

Fig. 6.1: Distribution of *-ṯ* and *-č* in groups 1, 2, 3, and 4 by the manner of articulation of the preceding consonant

6.2.5 Summary of results

The main aim of this corpus-based study was to identify the variables that determine the distribution of the feminine alternants *-ṯ* and *-č*. The study has shown that the distribution of the alternants *-ṯ* and *-č* is predictable in 82.85% of the feminine nouns in the data set. In these nouns, the distribution depends on the phonological environments in which the feminine marker occurs and on the templatic patterns of the nouns which have the feminine marker. In the remaining 17.15%, the distribution of *-ṯ* and *-č* can be described in terms of higher and lower probabilities rather than absolute certainty. In these nouns, the choice between the two alternants depends largely on the manner of articulation (or sonority) of the consonant preceding the feminine marker. In more specific terms, the proportion of *-č* (vs. *-ṯ*) increases from 24% in the nouns whose feminine marker is preceded by an obstruent to 87.5% in the nouns whose feminine marker is preceded by a sonorant, and vice versa, the proportion of *-ṯ* (vs. *-č*) decreases from 76% in the nouns whose feminine marker is preceded by an obstruent to 12.5% in the nouns whose feminine marker is preceded by a sonorant.

In summary, as Table 6.5 shows, the combination of these three variables (i.e., the preceding environment, the templatic pattern, and sonority) can predict the distribution of *-ṯ* and *-č* for the vast majority of nouns (96.9% accuracy).

Table 6.5: Accuracy of predicting the distribution of -*ṯ* and -*č* when all three variables are used

Groups of feminine nouns		Frequency	Accuracy
Groups 1-4	Obstruents	38/50	= 76%
	Sonorants	49/56	= 87.5%
Groups 5-12		512/512	= 100%
Total		599/618	= 96.9%

6.2.6 Formalization

The remaining problem to be solved from Section 6.2.2 is theoretical in nature. It concerns the morpho-phonological status of -*ṯ* and -*č*. I assume that in the environments where the alternation is predictable, there is a {FEMININE} marker which has the two phonologically conditioned allomorphs [ṯ] and [č]. This morpheme is left unspecified as /T/ in underlying representations, as in (21).

(21)	*bisnīṯa*	/bisnī-**T**-a/	'girl'	IV.88
	farwṯa	/farw-**T**-a/	'sheepskin (cloak)'	IV.198
	ʕaymṯa	/ʕaym-**T**-a/	'cloud'	IV.64
	mʕarrṯa	/mʕarr-**T**-a/	'cave'	III.368
	ḳattēšča	/ḳattēš-**T**-a/	'female saint'	III.146
	furrōʕča	/furrāʕ-**T**-a/	'axe'	IV.16
	ġrōrča	/ġrār-**T**-a/	'quern'	IV.110
	ṯinaġelča	/ṯinaġel-**T**-a/	'hen'	IV.124

/T/ represents a voiceless coronal obstruent which is not specified for the features [continuant], [strident], and [anterior] in underlying representation. The values of these features are determined by one of two rules: /T/ spirantization and /T/ palatalization. If /T/ spirantization applies, the allomorph [ṯ] is realized, and if /T/ palatalization applies, the allomorph [č] is realized. In order to formalize these two rules, the environments in which they apply need to be expressed accurately and succinctly. The environments revealed by the analysis presented in Table 6.2, repeated here as Table 6.6, will prove helpful.

Table 6.6: The environments in which the feminine alternants occur

Environment	**-ṯ**	**-č**	**Summary**
VVC__	12	158	(V)VC__ *(where C is not a glide)*
VC__	33	48	
vocoid__	148	0	elsewhere
CC__	179	0	
GG__	35	0	
other	0	5	lexically conditioned
Total	407	211	

The environments VVC__ and VC__ converge into the environment (V)VC__ where the sequence (V)V refers to a short or long vowel and C to any consonant excluding a glide. In this environment, 82.1% of the nouns take *-č* and 17.9% take *-ṯ*. The environments vocoid__, CC__, and GG__ are rearranged as the "elsewhere" environments, in which only *-ṯ* occurs. The five nouns under "other", which have the feminine marker as an underlying geminate, are too few to form a clear pattern. For this reason, I will consider them lexically conditioned and leave them out of the phonological rules.

Benefitting from the converged and rearranged environments, I make the following generalization:

(22) *Deriving the feminine marker allomorphs*

(a) The underlying form of the feminine marker is /T/.
(b) If the feminine marker is preceded by a sequence of an underlying vowel followed by a consonant (which is not a glide), it is realized as [č] through the /T/ palatalization rule (with an accuracy of 82.1%).
(c) Elsewhere, it is realized as [ṯ] through the /T/ spirantization rule.

This generalization is formalized in (23). In this formalization, (23a) and (23b) correspond to (22b) and (22c) respectively.

(23) /T/ *palatalization and* /T/ *spirantization*

(a) $$\begin{bmatrix}\text{-voice}\\ \text{+cor}\\ \text{-son}\end{bmatrix} \rightarrow \begin{bmatrix}\text{-cont}\\ \text{+strid}\\ \text{-ant}\end{bmatrix} \Big/ \begin{bmatrix}\text{+syllabic}\\ \text{-cons}\end{bmatrix}\begin{bmatrix}\text{-syllabic}\\ \text{+cons}\end{bmatrix}\underline{\quad}$$

(b) $$\begin{bmatrix}\text{-voice}\\ \text{+cor}\\ \text{-son}\end{bmatrix} \rightarrow \begin{bmatrix}\text{+cont}\\ \text{-strid}\\ \text{+ant}\end{bmatrix} \Big/ \text{elsewhere}$$

The following derivation illustrates these rules.

(24) *A derivation which illustrates /T/ palatalization and /T/ spirantization*

'female saint'	'girl'	
/ḳattēš-**T**-a/	/bisnī-**T**-a/	
ḳattēš**č**a	–	/T/ palatalization
–	bisnī**ṯ**a	/T/ spirantization
[ḳattēš**č**a]	[bisnī**ṯ**a]	

With regard to the 45 nouns which have the (V)VC__ environment but take -*ṯ* rather than -*č*, I consider them to be lexical exceptions. In these words, the feminine marker is specified underlyingly as /ṯ/, rather than /T/, as in (25).

(25) *rīḥṯa*	/rīḥ-**ṯ**-a/	'smell'	III.166
beʕṯa	/beʕ-**ṯ**-a/	'egg'	III.326
marfaḳṯa	/marfaḳ-**ṯ**-a/	'pillow; cushion'	III.184
xawkapṯa	/xawkab-**ṯ**-a/	'star'	III.114

Now I turn to the second study which investigates the plural marker alternation.

6.3 Plural marker alternation

Most feminine plural nouns end with either -*ōṯa*, as in (26a), or -*yōṯa*, as in (26b), regardless of whether their singular forms have the feminine marker -*ṯ* or -*č* (Spitaler 1938: 108; Arnold 1990a: 292).[12]

(26)	Singular		Plural		
(a)	*ḏokkṯa*	IV.306	*ḏukk**ōṯa***	III.200	'place'
	farwṯa	IV.198	*farw**ōṯa***	IV.198	'sheepskin (cloak)'
	soləfṯa[13]	IV.140	*salf**ōṯa***	IV.234	'story'

12 There are other ways in which feminine plural nouns are formed. These ways include, for example, adding the plural marker -*ō* (e.g., *freṯṯa* '(coffee) bean' III.44; *fritt**ō*** '(coffee) beans' III.72) or suffixing -*wōṯa* (e.g., *ḥōṯa* 'sister' III.264; *ḥaṯa**wōṯa*** 'sisters' IV.248) (see Spitaler 1938: 107–111; Arnold 1990a: 293–298). Since these plural suffix allomorphs are not phonologically conditioned, this allomorphy will not be discussed in this work.

13 It is transcribed as *sōləfṯa* in the original text.

	ṯinaġelča	IV.124	*ṯinaġl**ōṯa***	IV.118	'hen'
	žawharča	IV.84	*žawəhr**ōṯa***	IV.126	'gem; jewel'
(b)	*masčūṯa*	III.362	*masču**yōṯa***	III.374	'wedding'
	htīṯa	IV.262	*hti**yōṯa***	IV.76	'gift'
	ġūrča	III.90	*ġur**yōṯa***	III.90	'hole'
	aġīrča	IV.64	*aġir**yōṯa***	IV.64	'maid; maidservant'
	ḳannīnča	IV.274	*ḳannin**yōṯa***	IV.236	'bottle'

In this work, I divide *-ōṯa* and *-yōṯa* further into three affixes: the plural marker itself *-ō* or *-yō*, the feminine marker which is always *-ṯ* in the plural, and the nominal ending *-a* (see Section 6.2 for the motivation for having separate glosses for the feminine marker and nominal ending). This analysis is shown in (27). I will henceforth use *-ō* or *-yō* to refer to the plural marker except when I review the previous accounts where I keep the original notation.

(27) *ḏukk-**ō-ṯ-a*** *masču-**yō-ṯ-a***
place-PL-F-NE wedding-PL-F-NE
'places' III.200 'weddings' III.374

6.3.1 Previous accounts

Spitaler (1938: 108) shows that the plural alternants have developed from earlier forms (i.e., *āṯā* > *-ōṯa* and *yāṯā* > *-yōṯa*). However, no clear picture of their distribution can be obtained from his account. Although the way he groups his examples, some of which I present below, suggests that a pattern could be drawn, he makes no explicit generalization about the distribution.

(28) *Spitaler's (1938: 108) examples*

	Singular	Plural	
(a)	*samәkṯa*	*samkōṯa*	'fish'
	kelәmṯa	*kilmōṯa*	'word'
	wazzṯa	*wazzōṯa*	'goose'
	ḥeṭṭṯa	*ḥiṭṭōṯa*	'wheat grain'
	maḥramṯa	*maḥәrmōṯa*	'handkerchief; tissue'
(b)	*xarōfča*	*xarufyōṯa*	'sheep'
	ḏōrča	*ḏaryōṯa*	'(house with) courtyard'

(c) *bisnīṯa* *bisənyōṯa* 'girl'
šunīṯa *šunyōṯa* 'woman'

(d) *buntḳōyṯa* *buntaḳyōṯa* 'musket; rifle'
ṭaḳōyṯa *ṭaḳiyōṯa* 'hat; cap'

Arnold (1990a: 292) points out that there is no rule for the distribution of *-ōṯa* and *-yōṯa*. However, he notes that most singular forms which have the sequence VVC before the feminine marker take *-yōṯa* in their plural forms. This observation is supported by the examples in (28b).

Rihan (2017: 87) observes that if the base of the singular form does not have a long vowel, the plural marker is *-ō*, as in (28a); if the base of the singular form has a long vowel, the plural marker is *-yō*, as in (28b,c);[14] and if the base of the singular form ends in *y*, the plural marker is *-ō*, as in (28d).

Rihan's generalization can accurately and economically account for all the data presented in (28), but it poses one theoretical problem. It implies that plural surface forms are generated from singular surface forms, rather than from underlying forms. To address this problem, I consider the singular base and the plural base two phonologically conditioned allomorphs of the same underlying morpheme. For example, I assume that both the singular surface form *xarōfča* 'sheep (SG)' and the plural surface form *xarufyōṯa* 'sheep (PL)' (from (28b) above) have the underlying base /xarōf/. In the singular surface form [xarōfča], the base allomorph [xarōf] surfaces unchanged because it does not undergo any phonological rules. In the plural surface form [xarufyōṯa], the base allomorph [xaruf] surfaces because the underlying /ō/ in /xar**ō**f/ is shortened and raised to [u] since it precedes a stressed syllable (i.e., [xar**u**fˈyōṯa]). The phonological rules that the underlying /ō/ undergoes in this example are called pretonic shortening and pretonic raising, and they will be presented in Section 10.3. The pretonic shortening rule is the reason why surface plural bases never have long vowels even if they have long vowels underlyingly. The plural bases always occur in pretonic position, and their underlying long vowels are therefore shortened. In contrast, the long vowels in singular bases are not shortened because they occur in stressed (rather than pretonic) position (e.g., [xarˈ**ō**fča]).

Based on the assumption that plural surface forms and singular surface forms have the same base underlyingly, Rihan's generalization can be summarized as follows: The plural marker in feminine nouns is *-yō* if the base has an underlyingly long vowel and does not end in /y/, and *-ō* elsewhere. In this generalization (and in

---

14 Maaloula Aramaic words can have no more than one long vowel per word (Arnold 1990a: 22, 2011: 687) (see also Section 10.4.1).

the rest of this chapter), I make reference to the underlying base, rather than to the singular base.

The research questions to be answered are: Can the generalization above account for the plural alternation *-ō* ~ *-yō* in all of the feminine nouns attested in the corpus? Are there any counterexamples or any nouns which occur with both alternants? In addition to these questions, I intend to discuss the morpho-phonological status of these two alternants from a formal perspective.

6.3.2 Data and method

For this study, I used as a starting point the FemN data set which I introduced in Section 6.2.3. This data set contains 618 unique singular feminine nouns which end either with *-ṯ* or *-č*. Each noun in the data set was supplemented with its plural form (if there is one). To obtain the plural forms, I relied on two resources, namely the MASC dataframe (introduced in Section 3.4.1) and my language consultant who provided the majority of the plural forms.

After adding the plural forms, I eliminated the word forms which did not meet these two conditions. (1) The singular form must have a plural form. If a noun does not have a plural form (e.g., *rīḥṯa* 'smell' III.166), it was removed from the data set. (2) The plural form must have the plural marker *-ō* or *-yō* immediately followed by the feminine marker *-ṯ*. If the plural is formed in a different way (e.g., *mʕarr**ō*** 'caves' III.368; *ḥalč**wō**ṯa* 'maternal aunts' IV.72), it was eliminated.

The final subset (of the FemN data set) included 337 unique feminine nouns in their singular and plural forms. Since Rihan (2017: 87) observed that the choice between *-ō* and *-yō* depends on the properties of the singular base (which I interpreted above as the properties of the underlying base), I added the variable Base to the FemN data set with the possible values VV if the underlying base has a long vowel, V if it has no long vowels, and y if it ends in /y/. I also added the variable PLMarker with the values ō if the plural marker is *-ō*, yō if the plural marker is *-yō*, and (y)ō if the plural noun is attested with both plural markers. The added variables are shown in (29).

(29) *The variables added to the FemN data set*

SGForm	...	Base	PLForm	PLMarker
aġīrča	...	VV	aġiryōṯa	yō
akəlṯa	...	V	aklōṯa	ō
amōnča	...	VV	amanyōṯa	yō

SGFORM	...	BASE	PLFORM	PLMARKER
argīlča	...	VV	argilyōṯa	yō
armalča	...	V	armlōṯa	ō
baḥərṯa	...	V	baḥrōṯa	ō
balbalča	...	V	balbalyōṯa	yō
ballōrča	...	VV	ballaryōṯa	yō
binōyṯa	...	y	binayōṯa	ō

6.3.3 Results

Table 6.7 shows the distribution of the plural alternants *-ō* and *-yō* in the data set. Most of the feminine plural nouns have either *-ō* or *-yō*, and only four nouns have both variants.

Table 6.7: Distribution of the plural alternants

-ō	-yō	-ō ~ -yō	Total
191	142	4	337

Grouping the plural forms according to the properties of the underlying bases yielded the following distribution.

Table 6.8: Distribution of the plural alternants with the properties of the underlying bases as the grouping factor

Underlying base properties	-ō	-yō	-ō ~ -yō
base with a long vowel	5	135	4
base with no long vowels	157	7	0
base ending in /y/	29	0	0
Total	191	142	4

These results support Rihan's (2017: 87) generalization. First, if the underlying base has a long vowel and does not end in /y/, the plural marker is *-yō* in the majority of nouns in the data set, as in (30). The presented examples are assumed to have a long vowel in their underlying bases because this long vowel surfaces in the singular bases.

(30) *The plural marker -yō occurring if the underlying base has a long vowel*

Singular		Plural		
*muġərf**ī**ṯa*	III.56	*muġrəf**yō**ṯa*	FW	‘hoe’
*ʕunn**ī**ṯa*	III.190	*ʕunni**yō**ṯa*	FW	‘song’
*xaš**ī**ṯa*	III.28	*xaši**yō**ṯa*	FW	‘pile; heap’
*ḳuṭṭar**ī**ṯa* [15]	IV.284	*ḳuṭṭar**yō**ṯa*	FW	‘quarrel’
*ṣl**ō**ṯa*	III.162	*ṣla**yō**ṯa*	FW	‘prayer; Mass’
*ḳatt**ē**šča*	III.146	*ḳattiš**yō**ṯa*	FW	‘female saint’
*saḥḥ**ō**rča*	III.106	*saḥḥar**yō**ṯa*	III.326	‘crate; box’
*furr**ō**ʕča*	IV.16	*furraʕ**yō**ṯa*	FW	‘axe’
*maḥ**ō**lča* [16]	III.38	*maḥul**yō**ṯa*	FW	‘sieve (with a fine mesh)’
*ġr**ō**rča*	IV.110	*ġrar**yō**ṯa*	FW	‘quern’

However, as Table 6.8 shows, there are few exceptions to this generalization. Five nouns, exemplified in (31a), take the plural marker -*ō*, and four nouns, indicated above and exemplified in (31b), have both variants.

(31) *Exceptions: -ō occurring although the underlying base has a long vowel*

	Singular		Plural					
(a)	*bh**ī**mča*	III.98	*bhim**ō**ṯa*	III.116				‘(draft) animal’
	*ʕ**ō**ṯṯa*	III.66	*ʕat**ō**ṯa*	III.238				‘custom; habit’
	*š**ō**mṯa*	IV.106	*šam**ō**ṯa*	FW				‘mole (on the skin)’
(b)	*rf**ī**ḳča*	IV.96	*rfiḳ**ō**ṯa*	FW	~	*rfiḳ**yō**ṯa*	VI.649	‘female friend’
	*ʕž**ī**pča*	III.226	*ʕžib**ō**ṯa*	III.226	~	*ʕžib**yō**ṯa*	FW	‘miracle’
	*xy**ō**rča*	VI.934	*xyar**ō**ṯa*	IV.238	~	*xyar**yō**ṯa*	FW	‘cucumber’

Second, if the underlying base has no long vowels, the plural marker is -*ō* in the majority of cases in the data set, as in (32).

15 It is transcribed as *ḳuttarīṯa* in the original text.

16 It is transcribed as *maḥḥōlča* in the original text.

(32) *The plural marker -ō occurring if the underlying base has no long vowels*

Singular		Plural		
ḥḏawṯa	VI.353	*ḥḏawōṯa*	III.278	'joy; wedding (party)'
marfaḳṯa	III.184	*marfḳōṯa*	III.302	'pillow; cushion'
matrasṯa	III.88	*matərsōṯa*	FW	'school'
loʕəpṯa	IV.16	*luʕbōṯa*	III.84	'game; toy' [17]
rxoppṯa	III.364	*rxuppōṯa*	FW	'knee'
mapxarča	III.200	*mabəxrōṯa*	FW	'censer'
maṣfarča	III.62	*maṣəfrōṯa*	FW	'scissors'
armalča	IV.80	*arəmlōṯa*	FW	'widow'
msažžalča	III.298	*msažžlōṯa*	FW	'tape recorder'
maḳbarča	III.220	*maḳəbrōṯa*	FW	'cemetery'
manšarča [18]	III.56	*manəšrōṯa*	FW	'carpenter's workshop'

However, there are seven plural nouns which can be regarded as exceptions to this generalization. In these nouns, which are exemplified in (33), the plural marker *-yō* occurs although the underlying base has no long vowels.

(33) *Exceptions: -yō occurring although the underlying base has no long vowels*

Singular		Plural		
mnasapča	III.76	*mnasabyōṯa*	III.76	'occasion'
ḳamesča	III.272	*ḳaməsyōṯa*	III.272	'shirt' [19]
ḥormṯa	III.272	*ḥarəmyōṯa* [20]	III.166	'woman'

Third, if the underlying base ends in /y/ even if it has a long vowel, the plural marker is -*ō*, as in (34).

(34) *The plural marker -ō occurring if the underlying base ends in /y/*

Singular		Plural		
kuppōyṯa	III.80	*kuppayōṯa*	III.346	'cup; glass'
ʕbōyṯa	III.50	*ʕbayōṯa*	III.176	'cloak'

17 The [p] ~ [b] alternation in the examples presented in pairs is due to a devoicing process which bilabial stops undergo before a voiceless consonant (see Section 5.2.2).

18 It is transcribed as *manžarča* in the original text.

19 These two examples are transcribed as *ḳameṣča* and *ḳaməṣyōṯa* in the original text.

20 It is transcribed as *ḥurəmyōṯa* in the original text.

ġallōyṯa	III.74	*ġallayōṯa*	III.72	'(coffee) pot'
ḥkōyṯa	IV.80	*ḥkayōṯa*	FW	'story'
mrōyṯa	IV.252	*mrayōṯa*	FW	'mirror'
buntḳōyṯa	IV.208	*buntaḳyōṯa*	IV.208	'musket; rifle'
ṭulṯōyṯa	IV.144	*ṭulṯyōṯa*	FW	'(medium-sized) clay jar'
ṣunōyṯa	III.66	*ṣunyōṯa*	III.32	'tray'

6.3.4 Formalization

Formulating a phonological rule that can express Rihan's (2017: 87) generalization is not a straightforward task. To account for the *-ō* ~ *-yō* alternation, one may formulate either a /y/ deletion rule or a [y] epenthesis rule, but neither rule is satisfactory. The /y/ deletion analysis, which I present in (35a), proposes that the allomorphs [ō] and [yō] have the underlying form /yā/ which undergoes /y/ deletion if the base has a short vowel or ends in /y/. On the other hand, the [y] epenthesis analysis, presented in (35b), proposes that both allomorphs have the underlying form /ā/, and that an epenthetic [y] is inserted before the /ā/ if the base has an underlyingly long vowel and does not end in /y/. In both analyses, the underlying /ā/ is turned into [ō] through the /ā/ rounding process, which I introduce in Section 7.3.1.

(35) (a) /y/ Deletion analysis

/ġūr-**yā**-T-a/ [21]	→	[ġur'**yō**ṯa]	'holes'	III.90	
/spaʕ-**yā**-T-a/	→	[spa'**ʕō**ṯa]	'fingers'	FW	(/y/ deletion applies)
/ʕbāy-**yā**-T-a/	→	[ʕba'**yō**ṯa]	'cloaks'	III.176	(/y/ deletion applies)

(b) [y] Epenthesis analysis

/ġūr-**ā**-T-a/	→	[ġur'**yō**ṯa]	'holes'	III.90	([y] epenthesis applies)
/spaʕ-**ā**-T-a/	→	[spa'**ʕō**ṯa]	'fingers'	FW	
/ʕbāy-**ā**-T-a/	→	[ʕba'**yō**ṯa]	'cloaks'	III.176	

Both analyses have to be rejected because the proposed rules apply to two environments that have nothing in common with each other (i.e., the base having a vowel of a certain length and ending (or not ending) in /y/), and because there is no independent evidence supporting these analyses.

21 In all of the presented examples, /T/ is realized as [ṯ] through the /T/ spirantization rule (see Section 6.2.6), and /ā/ is realized as [a] through the pretonic shortening rule (see Section 10.3.2) or as [ō] through the /ā/ rounding rule (see Section 7.3.1).

Alternatively, a morphological account can be considered, but a more general question needs to be answered first: In which cases can a morphological account provide a better explanation of the alternation than a phonological account? According to Hayes (2009: 203), a morphological account should be adopted if (1) the alternation is morpheme-specific and (2) the allomorphs are not phonologically similar, e.g., the Yidiɲ ergative suffixes *-du* and *-ŋgu* (Dixon 1977: 50; Hayes 2009: 199–200). With regard to the allomorphs [ō] and [yō] in Maaloula Aramaic, the second condition is not met because although the alternation is morpheme-specific, the two allomorphs are phonologically similar.

Hayes (2009: 201-203) argues that in similar cases where the alternation is morpheme-specific, but the two allomorphs are phonologically similar, the correct analysis cannot be determined. This is, for example, the case for the Lardil accusative future suffixes *-kuṛ* and *-uṛ* (Hale 1973: 423; Hayes 2009: 173–174, 202). According to Hayes (2009: 202), a morphological analysis, here, would have the advantage that complicated phonological rules (like the ones that I presented above) would no longer be needed but the disadvantage that it would not capture the similarities between the allomorphs. Clearly, the Maaloula Aramaic allomorphs [ō] and [yō] are more similar to cases like the Lardil accusative future suffixes, which Hayes (2009: 201) reasonably considers "hard to diagnose", than to straightforward cases like the Yidiɲ ergative suffixes where a morphological account is definitely more adequate.

One way to resolve the uncertainty about the type of analysis to be applied would be to examine whether the phonologically conditioned allomorphy is suppletive or not. According to Kalin (2022), if the allomorphy is suppletive, the choice between the two allomorphs precedes the phonology of the language (see also Paster 2009 and Kalin 2020 for the view that morphology precedes phonology). If I can establish that the allomorphy between [ō] and [yō] is suppletive, I can argue more strongly for adopting a morphological account whereby the choice between the two allomorphs is decided by the morphological component.

Kalin (2022: 646) presents a decision tree that can be used for determining whether the allomorphy is suppletive or not. According to her decision tree, if two allomorphs are not phonologically similar, they are considered suppletive. This condition applies, for example, to the Yidiɲ ergative suffixes *-du* and *-ŋgu*. If the two allomorphs are phonologically similar, the decision tree presents an additional condition: If the alternation is phonologically motivated, the allomorphy is not suppletive, but if the alternation is not phonologically motivated (either cross-linguistically or language-specifically), then the allomorphy is suppletive.

The alternation between [ō] and [yō] does not seem to be phonologically motivated as it does not necessarily repair or avoid phonologically ill-formed sequences or syllables. For example, it cannot be argued on purely phonological grounds that [spaʕ**ō**ṯa] is well-formed but *[spaʕ**yō**ṯa] is ill-formed. The sequence <aʕyō> in *[spaʕyōṯa] is attested in other words from the corpus (e.g., *wa**ʕyō**ṯa* 'clothes' IV.234, *ḳa**ʕyō**la* 'she/it (F) sits' IV.124), and the templatic pattern of *[spaʕyōṯa] (which is CCaCyōṯa) is also attested (e.g., *šhatyōṯa* 'certificates; degrees' IV.270, *ġraryōṯa* 'querns' FW).

Since the alternation between the allomorphs [ō] and [yō] is not phonologically motivated, the allomorphy can be considered suppletive, according to Kalin's (2022) decision tree, in spite of the phonological similarity between the allomorphs. This conclusion calls for an account whereby the morphological component produces the two outputs /ā/ and /yā/: /yā/ if the base has a long vowel and does not end in /y/, and /ā/ elsewhere, as in (36). The outputs of the morphological component will serve as the inputs for the phonological component where /ā/ and /yā/ will be realized as [ō] and [yō] respectively due to /ā/ rounding.

(36) /ā/ *and* /yā/ *as outputs of the morphological component*

Outputs of the morphological component		Outputs of the phonological component	
/yā/	→	[yō]	
/ā/	→	[ō]	
Examples:			
/ġūr-**yā**-T-a/	→	[ġur'**yō**ṯa]	'holes'
/spaʕ-**ā**-T-a/	→	[spa'ʕ**ō**ṯa]	'fingers'
/ʕbāy-**ā**-T-a/	→	[ʕba'**yō**ṯa]	'cloaks'

This analysis seems more plausible than the two phonological analyses presented above, but unless the morphology-phonology interaction is assumed to be cyclic, the presented analysis cannot explain how the phonological component can condition the allomorph choice although this choice is determined in the preceding morphological component. Since the analytical framework which I adopt in this book does not make the assumption that morphology and phonology interact cyclically, the gap in the presented analysis remains unbridged.

6.4 Conclusion

In this chapter, I have reported the results of two corpus-based studies which investigated two morpheme-specific alternations that occur in feminine nouns.

In the first study, I identified the variables that are responsible for the distribution of the two feminine marker alternants *-ṯ* and *-č* in a data set that contains 618 unique feminine nouns. I demonstrated that a combination of three variables can correctly predict the distribution of the two alternants for the vast majority of nouns (96.9% accuracy): the preceding environment (e.g., VC___, CC___), the templatic pattern of the feminine noun, and the sonority of the preceding consonant. From a formal perspective, I have proposed that there is one {FEMININE} marker that has the two phonologically conditioned allomorphs [ṯ] and [č]. This morpheme is left unspecified as /T/ in underlying representations. The surface forms are determined by one of the two rules: /T/ palatalization (i.e., /T/ → [č]) if /T/ is preceded by a sequence of an underlying vowel followed by a consonant (which is not a glide), and /T/ spirantization (i.e., /T/ → [ṯ]) elsewhere. There are exceptions to the /T/ palatalization rule where [ṯ] surfaces instead of [č]. I have considered the feminine marker in these exceptions to be specified underlyingly as /ṯ/ rather than /T/.

In the second study, I investigated the plural alternation *-ō* ~ *-yō*, using 337 feminine nouns in their singular and plural forms. The results showed that the plural marker is *-yō* if the base has an underlyingly long vowel and does not end in /y/, and it is *-ō* elsewhere. The quantitative results support Rihan's (2017: 87) generalization. From a formal perspective, I have considered the *-ō* ~ *-yō* alternation to be a case of phonologically conditioned allomorphy and argued that the morphological (rather than the phonological) component produces the two outputs /ā/ and /yā/ which serve as the inputs for the phonological component where they are realized as [ō] and [yō] respectively due to /ā/ rounding. The presented analysis provides support for the view that when an alternation is not phonologically motivated or optimizing, a morphological account is to be preferred to a phonological account (see, e.g., Kalin 2022).

7 Local and long-distance assimilation

7.1 Introduction

In this chapter, two types of assimilation are presented and discussed: local assimilation and long-distance assimilation. In local assimilation, "the sound undergoing the change is immediately adjacent to the trigger of the change" (Zsiga 2013: 232). I refer to this type simply as *assimilation.* In long-distance assimilation, "vowels affect each other even though consonants intervene" (Zsiga 2013: 232). In accordance with Arnold's (2011: 687) terminology, I use the term *umlaut* to refer to this type of assimilation in Maaloula Aramaic.

7.2 Assimilation

In this section, I review and formalize the individual assimilation processes that have been described in the previous literature. Most assimilation processes in Maaloula Aramaic occur across morphological boundaries (i.e., morpheme or word boundaries). The assimilating consonants may occur in bound bases (e.g., /far**t**-T-a/ → [far**ṯ**ṯa] 'bundle' IV.178, see Section 7.2.2), in affixes (e.g., /yarḥ-**l** čammuz/ → [yarḥi**č** čammuz] 'the month of July' III.32, see Section 7.2.8), in clitics (e.g., /**b**-felk-a/ → [**f**-felka] 'in half' IV.236, see Section 7.2.1), or in free morphemes (e.g., /ma**ʕ** ḥayā-T-l zalm-T-a/ → [ma**ḥ** ḥayōṯəl zaləmṯa] 'about the man's life' III.214, see Section 7.2.6).

For each assimilation process, I begin by providing background information on the morpheme which (or part of which) assimilates to an adjacent segment or which an adjacent segment assimilates to. This background information does not introduce the assimilation process yet. It only sheds light on the form and meaning of the morpheme involved in the assimilation process and where it usually occurs. This is supplemented by glossed examples. After this brief introduction, I introduce, exemplify, and formalize the assimilation process that the morpheme in question undergoes. For the formalization, I give a feature-geometrical representation for each assimilation process.

7.2.1 Assimilation of the preposition *b-*

Maaloula Aramaic has the prepositional clitic *b-* 'in; at' (Arnold 1990a: 383):

https://doi.org/10.1515/9783111447124-007

(1) *The prepositional clitic b-*

b=*ḏayr-a*	***b***=*ḏemseḳ*
in=monastery-NE	in=Damascus
'in the monastery/convent' IV.310	'in Damascus' IV.238

This preposition can be considered as an underlying morpheme /b/ which has three phonologically conditioned allomorphs: [p], [b], and [bə] (see Spitaler 1938: 34; Arnold 1990a: 383). It is realized as [p] before a word-initial voiceless consonant due to the bilabial stop devoicing process (introduced in Section 5.2.2), as in (2a). It is realized as [b] before a word-initial voiced segment, as in (2b). When it occurs before a cluster of two consonants, it is realized as [bə] regardless of the voicing of these consonants, as in (2c). This is because the epenthetic vowel [ə] is inserted between the preposition /b/ and the first consonant in the following noun (for a derivation that shows how bilabial stop devoicing and vowel epenthesis account for the different realizations of this morpheme, see the end of Section 5.2.2; for more on vowel epenthesis, see Sections 8.2.2 and 8.3.5).

(2) *The allomorphs of the morpheme* /b/

(a)	***p***-*felka*	/**b**-felk-a/	'in half'	IV.100
	p-*siryōn*	/**b**-siryān/	'in Aramaic'	III.300
	p-*xarma*	/**b**-xarm-a/	'in the vineyard'	III.98
(b)	***b***-*ġūrča*	/**b**-ġūr-T-a/	'in a hole'	III.90
	b-*imōma*	/**b**-imām-a/	'by day'	III.136
	b-*ḏokkṯa*	/**b**-ḏokk-T-a/	'in a place'	IV.306
(c)	***bə***-*klēsya*	/**b**-klēsy-a/	'in the church'	III.152
	bə-*blōta*	/**b**-blāt-a/	'in the village'	III.260
	bə-*mʕarrṯa*	/**b**-mʕarr-T-a/	'in a cave'	III.368

The morpheme /b/ assimilates completely to the following labial consonants /f/ and /m/ (Spitaler 1938: 34; Arnold 1990a: 381), as in (3).

(3)

f-*felka*	/**b**-felk-a/	'in half'	IV.236
f-*forna*	/**b**-forn-a/	'in the bakery'	III.368
f-*fayylə ḥmōra*	/**b**-fayy-l ḥmār-a/	'in the shade of the donkey'	IV.284
m-*maʕlūla*	/**b**-maʕlūla/	'in Maaloula'	III.116
m-*mōya*	/**b**-m-āy-a/	'in the water'	III.62
m-*mar sarkes*	/**b**-mar sarkes/	'at (the church of) Saint Sergius'	III.194

This process seems to apply optionally as some of the examples presented above can also occur unassimilated:

(4)	***f**-felka*	IV.236	~	***p**-felka*	IV.100	'in half'
	***f**-forna*	III.368	~	***p**-forna*	IV.238	'in the bakery'
	***m**-maʕlūla*	III.116	~	***b**-maʕlūla*[1]	III.224	'in Maaloula'
	***m**-mōya*	III.62	~	***b**-mōya*	III.64	'in the water'

However, this assimilation process is blocked when an epenthetic vowel is inserted between the morpheme /b/ and the following /f/ or /m/, as in (5).

(5)	***bə**-frīsčil muṭrōna*	/**b**-frīs-T-l/	'about the bishop's right'	IV.300
	***bə**-ffōye*	/**b**-ff-āy-e/	'in his face'	IV.80
	***bə**-mšīḥa*	/**b**-mšīḥ-a/	'in Christ'	III.170
	***bə**-mʕarrṯa*	/**b**-mʕarr-T-a/	'in a cave'	III.368

The assimilation of *b-* is formalized in (6).

(6) *Assimilation of the preposition b- (optional)*

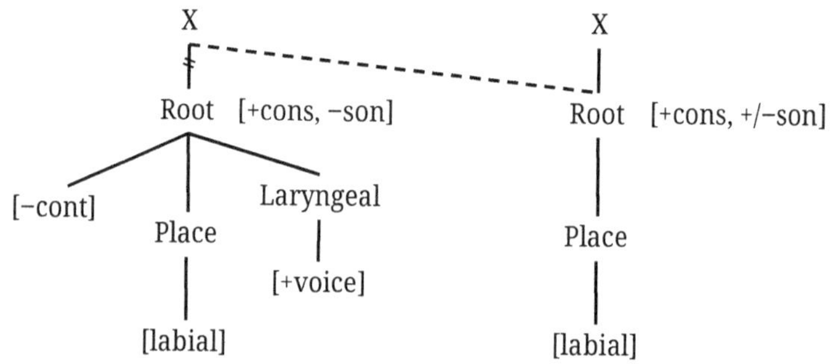

Since the assimilation of *b-* applies across word boundaries, I consider it a postlexical process (see Kaisse & Shaw 1985: 4). I show in the derivation in (7) that in order to account for all the different realizations of the morpheme /b/, the assimilation of *b-* must be ordered after vowel epenthesis (a postlexical rule presented in Section 8.3.5) and before bilabial stop devoicing (a postlexical rule introduced in

1 The right variants of the last two examples are transcribed as ***m**-maʕlūla* and ***m**-mōya* in the original texts although the speakers clearly pronounce them with [b].

Section 5.2.2). The branching arrows in (7) indicate that the assimilation of *b-* is optional. Throughout this book, I use a branching derivation to indicate optionality.

(7) *A derivation which illustrates the assimilation of the preposition b-*

'in half'		'in Maaloula'		'in Christ'	
/**b**-felk-a/		/**b**-maʕlūla/		/**b**-mšīḥ-a/	
–		–		bə-mšīḥa	vowel epenthesis
f-felka	–	**m**-maʕlūla	–	–	**assimilation of *b*-**
–	**p**-felka	–	–	–	bilabial stop devoicing
[**f**-felka]	[**p**-felka]	[**m**-maʕlūla]	[**b**-maʕlūla]	[**bə**-mšīḥa]	

If this ordering is reversed, the output will be either ungrammatical or incomplete. The latter scenario is shown in (8) where the expected variant [**f**-felka] does not surface because bilabial stop devoicing turns /b/ in /**b**-felk-a/ into [p] and therefore bleeds (or blocks) the assimilation of *b-*.

(8) *A derivation that shows the wrong rule ordering*

'in half'	'in Maaloula'		'in Christ'	
/**b**-felk-a/	/**b**-maʕlūla/		/**b**-mšīḥ-a/	
–	–		**bə**-mšīḥa	vowel epenthesis
p-felka	–		–	bilabial stop devoicing
–	**m**-maʕlūla	–	–	assimilation of *b*-
[**p**-felka]	[**m**-maʕlūla]	[**b**-maʕlūla]	[**bə**-mšīḥa]	

7.2.2 Assimilation of base-final /t/

Most feminine nouns are marked by a feminine marker which can be either *-ṯ* or *-č* (Spitaler 1938: 103–104; Arnold 1990a: 290–298). In the examples in (9), this feminine marker occurs between the base and the nominal (and citation form) ending *-a*.

(9) *The feminine marker alternants -ṯ and -č*

*rxopp-**ṯ**-a*	*ġrōr-**č**-a*
knee-F-NE	quern-F-NE
'knee' III.364	'quern' IV.110

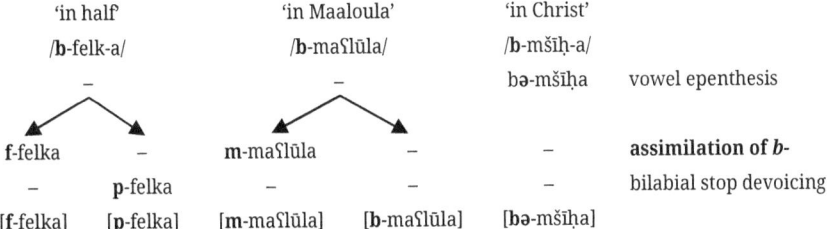

In Section 6.2, I identified the variables that can predict the distribution of the two alternants for the vast majority of nouns. I assumed that there is one {FEMININE} marker that has the two phonologically conditioned allomorphs [ṯ] and [č]. This morpheme is left unspecified as /T/ in underlying representations, as in (10). The surface forms are determined by one of the two rules: /T/ spirantization (i.e., /T/ → [ṯ]) or /T/ palatalization (i.e., /T/ → [č]).

(10)	*rxoppṯa*	/rxopp-**T**-a/	'knee'	III.364
	ġrōrča	/ġrār-**T**-a/	'quern'	IV.110

I also showed that there are exceptions to the /T/ palatalization rule where [ṯ] surfaces instead of [č] and considered the feminine marker in these exceptions to be specified underlyingly as /ṯ/ rather than /T/, as in (11).

(11)	*xawkapṯa*	/xawkab-**ṯ**-a/	'star'	III.114
	marfaḳṯa	/marfaḳ-**ṯ**-a/	'pillow; cushion'	III.184

If the last base consonant in a feminine noun is /t/, it assimilates completely to the immediately following feminine marker allomorph [ṯ] (Spitaler 1938: 37), as in (12).

(12)	*far**ṯ**ṯa* [2]	/far**t**-T-a/	'bundle'	IV.178
	*fre**ṯ**ṯa*	/fre**tt**-T-a/	'grain; (coffee) bean'	III.44
	*ʕō**ṯ**ṯa*	/ʕā**t**-ṯ-a/	'custom; habit'	III.66
	*warə**ṯ**ṯa*	/war**t**-T-a/	'rose; flower'	III.246
	*me**ṯ**ṯa*	/me**tt**-T-a/	'period (of time)'	IV.166
	*ḳaʕə**ṯ**ṯa* [3]	/ḳaʕ**t**-T-a/	'sitting down'	IV.200

This process is optional, as the following examples show:

(13)	*far**ṯ**ṯa*	VI.284	~	*far**t**ṯa*	VI.284	'bundle'
	*warə**ṯ**ṯa*	III.246	~	*warə**t**ṯa*	VI.890	'rose; flower'

The assimilation of base-final /t/ to the feminine marker allomorph [ṯ] is formalized in (14).

2 It is transcribed as *fartṯa* in the original text, but both variants *fartṯa* and *farṯṯa* are listed as valid lemmas in Arnold's (2019: 284) dictionary.

3 This word is misspelled as *ḳaʕṯa* in the original transcription, but it is corrected as *ḳaʕəṯṯa* in Arnold's (2019: 446) dictionary.

(14) *Assimilation of base-final /t/ to the feminine marker allomorph [ṯ] (optional)*

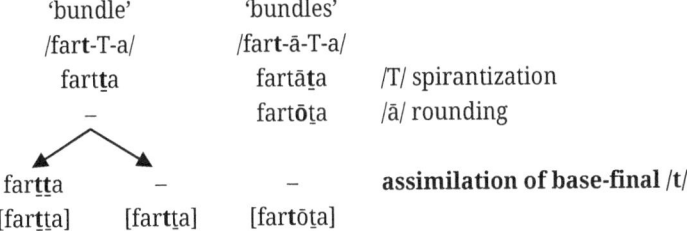

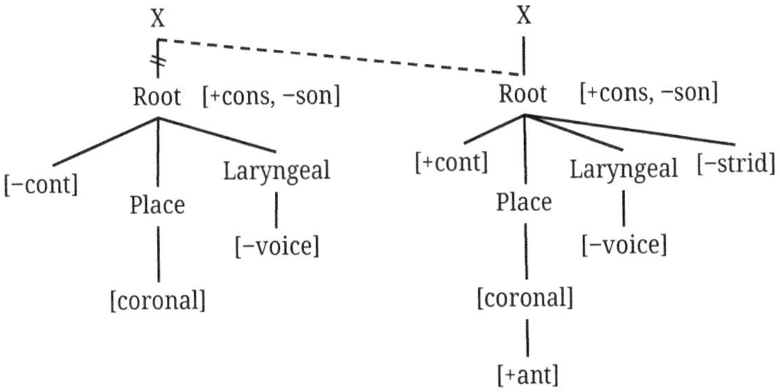

The derivation in (15) illustrates how this assimilation rule applies optionally to the singular noun *fartṯa* ~ *farṯṯa* 'bundle' (from (13) above). It also shows that the assimilation rule does not apply to the plural form of this noun (i.e., *fartōṯa* 'bundles' VI.284) because the base-final /t/ is not adjacent to the feminine marker *-ṯ* but is separated from it by the plural morpheme *-ō* (for /T/ spirantization, see Section 6.2.6, and for /ā/ rounding, see Section 7.3.1).

(15) *A derivation which illustrates the assimilation of base-final /t/*

'bundle'		'bundles'	
/far**t**-T-a/		/far**t**-ā-T-a/	
fart**ṯ**a		fart**ā**ṯa	/T/ spirantization
–		fart**ō**ṯa	/ā/ rounding
far**ṯṯ**a	–	–	**assimilation of base-final /t/**
[farṯṯa]	[fartṯa]	[fartōṯa]	

7.2.3 Assimilation of the prefixes *č-*

There are a few homophonous prefixes that have the underlying form /č/. Here are three examples. First, the second person subject prefix *č-* is attached to subjunctive, present, and perfect verbs (see Arnold 1990a: chap. 4), as in (16).

(16) *mō* *batt-ax* ***č**-išw-Ø?*
what will-2M.SG 2-do.SBJV-SG
'What will you (M.SG) do?' III.302

č-ḏōmx-in *hōxa*
2-sleep.PRS-M.PL here
'you (M.PL) sleep here' III.134

č-yaḏḏīʕ-a
2-know.PRF-F.SG
'you (F.SG) know' IV.282

Second, the third person feminine singular subject prefix *č-* is attached to subjunctive verbs (see Arnold 1990a: chap. 4), as in (17).

(17) *batt-a* *č-rōžaʕ-Ø*
will-3F.SG 3F-return.SBJV-SG
'she will return' III.170

Third, the detransitivizing prefix *č-* is attached to specific verb Forms such as II_2 and III_2, as in (18) (see Arnold 1990a: 63, 89–90 for Forms II_2 and III_2, and see Section 2.4 in this book for a brief introduction to verb Forms in Maaloula Aramaic).

(18) *yi-č-ḳattaš-Ø* *ešm-ax*
3-DTR-hallow.SBJV-M.SG name-2M.SG
'hallowed be thy name' III.144

Arnold (1990a: 18) points out that these prefixes occasionally assimilate to a following /t/, as in (19).

(19) *ttawwar*	/č-tawwar/	'(that) you (SG) look for'	IV.122
ttaffrenna	/č-taffr-enn-a/	'(that) she gets rid of her'	IV.168
ttapprenna	/č-tappr-enn-a/	'(that) you (M.SG) take care of her'	IV.92
ttaxxlennaḥ	/č-taxxl-enn-aḥ/	'(that) you (M.SG) lead us (into)'	III.144

The corpus data show that the homophonous *č-* prefixes assimilate to other segments as well (e.g., /ṭ ṯ ḏ s ṣ z š ž/), as in (20). What these segments have in common is that all of them are coronal stops or fricatives (i.e., coronal obstruents) (for a cross-linguistic comparison, see the assimilation of *t-* of the detransitivizing prefix in Cairene and San'ani Arabic in Watson 2002: 222–224).

(20) *ṭṭallek̩*	/č-ṭallek̩/	'(that) she divorces (her husband)'	IV.288
ṯṯēla	/č-ṯē-l-a/	'(that) it (F) comes'	III.114
ḏḏōyak̩	/č-ḏāyak̩/	'he felt (economically) distressed'	IV.20

ssalleḳ	/**č**-salleḳ/	'you (M.SG) are going up'	IV.76
ṣṣammīča[4]	/**č**-ṣammīč-a/	'you (F.SG) are silent'	IV.126
zzappen	/**č**-zappen/	'(that) you (M.SG) sell'	IV.142
ššōḳel	/**č**-šāḳel/	'you (M.SG) take'	IV.22
žžarrṣinni	/**č**-žarrṣ-inn-i/	'(that) you (F.SG) shame me'	IV.98

This process applies optionally, as the following examples show:

(21) ***ṯṯēla***	III.114	~ ***čṯēla***	III.314	'(that) it (F) comes'
ssalleḳ	IV.76	~ ***čsalleḳ***	III.134	'you (M.SG) are going up'

The assimilation of *č*- to a following coronal obstruent is formalized in (22).

(22) *Complete assimilation of č- to a following coronal obstruent (optional)*

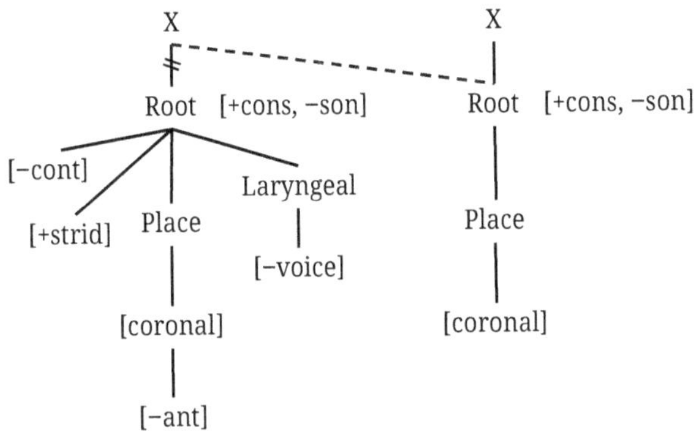

This is not the only assimilation process that the homophonous *č*- prefixes undergo. The previous literature reports that *č*- becomes voiced (i.e., [ğ] or [dʒ] in IPA) when it is adjacent to /z ḏ ž ḍ ẓ/ (Arnold 1990a: 20; see also Spitaler 1938: 12).

(23) ***čzubnenne***[5]	[**ğ**zubnenne]	'(that) you (M.SG) buy it (M)'	IV.18
čḏikkel	[**ğ**ḏikkel]	'(that) you (M.SG) lie'	IV.88

4 The words *ṣṣammīča, zzappen, ššōḳel,* and *žžarrṣinni* are transcribed respectively as *ṣammīča, čzappen, links čšōḳel,* and *čžarrsinni* in the original text.

5 Arnold did not use the symbol <ğ> in his transcripts of the narratives because he adopted a phonemic transcription, and [ğ] is not a Maaloula Aramaic phoneme (Arnold 1990a: 19). We followed this practice while compiling the MASC corpus. As a result, in these examples the assimilating consonant is transcribed as *č* in the normal (phonemic) transcription and as [ğ] in the narrower transcription.

This phonological process can be re-expressed as a voicing assimilation process whereby *č-* becomes voiced before a voiced coronal fricative, and it can be formalized as follows:

(24) *Voicing assimilation of č- to a following voiced coronal fricative*

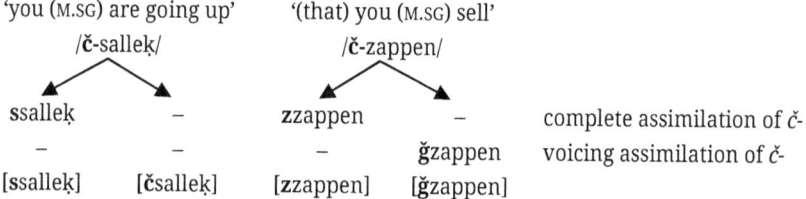

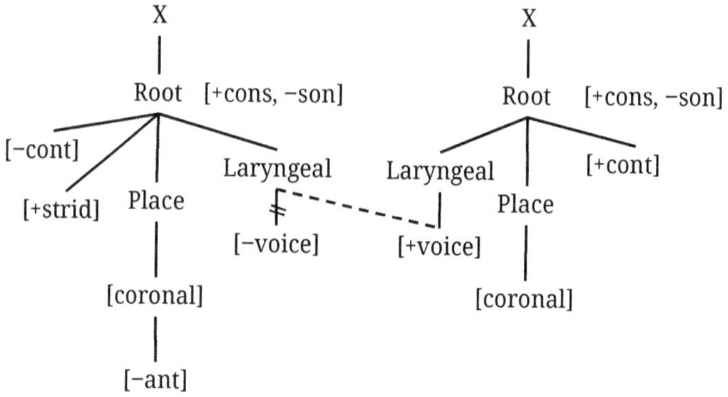

The derivation in (25) illustrates how the complete and voicing assimilation rules apply to *č-* in the verbs /**č**-salleḳ/ and /**č**-zappen/ (from (20) above).

(25) *A derivation which illustrates the two assimilation rules*

'you (M.SG) are going up' /**č**-salleḳ/		'(that) you (M.SG) sell' /**č**-zappen/		
ssalleḳ	–	zzappen	–	complete assimilation of *č-*
–	–	–	ǧzappen	voicing assimilation of *č-*
[ssalleḳ]	[čsalleḳ]	[zzappen]	[ǧzappen]	

7.2.4 Assimilation of suffix-final /ṯ/

The phoneme /ṯ/ occurs in the third person feminine singular inflectional suffix *-aṯ* and in the first person singular inflectional suffix *-iṯ* which are attached to verbs in the preterit tense (Spitaler 1938: 146; Arnold 1990a: 70), as in (26).

(26) (a) The suffix *-a*ṯ (3F.SG)

*zaʕḳ-**aṯ***	*app-**aṯ*** [6]
call.PRET-3F.SG	give.PRET-3F.SG
'she called; she screamed' IV.68	'she gave' III.54

(b) The suffix *-iṯ* (1SG)

*zabn-**iṯ***	*amr-**iṯ***
buy.PRET-1SG	say.PRET-1SG
'I bought' III.52	'I said' III.338

When a preterit verb takes a dative pronominal object, the suffix *-l* is attached to it. If this preterit verb already has the suffix *-aṯ* or *-iṯ*, then the /ṯ/ in the suffix assimilates completely to the immediately following /l/ (Spitaler 1938: 37; Arnold 1990a: 226), as in (27). This assimilation process is obligatory and is confined to the word domain.

(27) (a) Assimilation of /ṯ/ in the suffix *-aṯ* (3F.SG)

zaʕḳalla	/zaʕḳ-aṯ-l-a/	'she called her'	IV.68
appalle	/app-aṯ-l-e/	'she gave him'	IV.152
amralle	/amr-aṯ-l-e/	'she said to him'	III.58

(b) Assimilation of /ṯ/ in the suffix *-iṯ* (1SG)

zabnille	/zabn-iṯ-l-e/	'I bought (for) him'	III.312
amrilla	/amr-iṯ-l-a/	'I said to her'	IV.326
faṯḥilla	/faṯḥ-iṯ-l-a/	'I opened for her'	III.62

The assimilation of suffix-final /ṯ/ is formalized in (28) and illustrated by the derivation in (29). The examples in the derivation are from (26) and (27) above.

6 It is transcribed as *ʕappaṯ* in the original text.

(28) *Assimilation of suffix-final /ṯ/ to the following suffix -l (obligatory)*

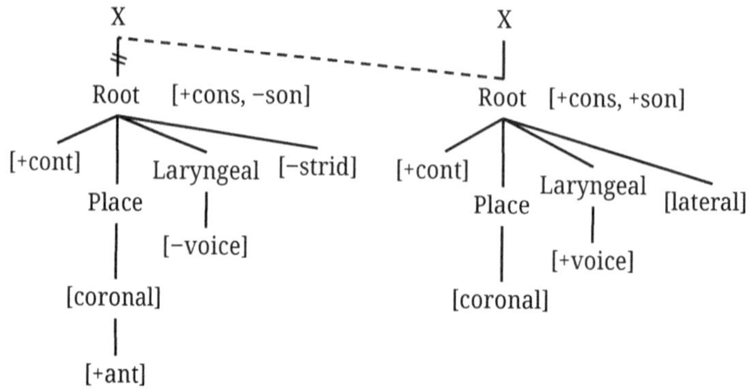

(29) *A derivation which illustrates the assimilation of suffix-final /ṯ/*

'she called'	'she called her'	'I bought'	'I bought for him'	
/zaʕḳ-aṯ/	/zaʕḳ-aṯ-l-a/	/zabn-iṯ/	/zabn-iṯ-l-e/	
–	zaʕḳalla	–	zabnille	assimilation of suffix-final /ṯ/
[zaʕḳaṯ]	[zaʕḳalla]	[zabniṯ]	[zabnille]	

7.2.5 Assimilation of /ḏ/ in *hōḏ*

The feminine singular demonstrative pronoun in Maaloula Aramaic is *hōḏ* 'this (F.SG)' (for demonstrative pronouns see Spitaler 1938: 56–57; Arnold 1990a: 43–44, 2011: 688):

(30) *The demonstrative pronoun hōḏ*

hōḏ *blōt-a*
DEM.F.SG village-NE
'this village' IV.206

hōḏ *arʕ-a*
DEM.F.SG land-NE
'this (piece of) land' IV.302

The phoneme /ḏ/ in *hōḏ* assimilates completely to the following consonant in the immediately following word (Spitaler 1938: 35, 57; Arnold 1990a: 44):

(31)	*hō**b** bisnīṯa*	/hāḏ bisnī-T-a/	'this girl'	IV.246
	*hō**k** klēsya*[7]	/hāḏ klēsy-a/	'this church'	IV.310
	*hō**ḳ** ḳoppṯa*	/hāḏ ḳopp-T-a/	'this dome'	IV.72
	*hō**f** farwṯa*	/hāḏ farw-T-a/	'this sheepskin (cloak)'	IV.198
	*hō**ṯ** ṯinaġelča*	/hāḏ ṯinaġel-T-a/	'this hen'	IV.124
	*hō**z** zaləmṯa*	/hāḏ zalm-T-a/	'this man'	IV.142
	*hō**ġ** ġrōrča*	/hāḏ ġrār-T-a/	'this quern'	IV.110
	*hō**ʕ** ʕaymṯa*	/hāḏ ʕaym-T-a/	'this cloud'	IV.64
	*hō**n** nūra*	/hāḏ nūr-a/	'this fire'	III.172
	*hō**r** rayya*	/hāḏ rayy-a/	'this rain'	IV.64

This process is very common but not obligatory, as the following examples show:

(32)	*hō**b** bisnīṯa*	IV.246	~	*hō**ḏ** bisnīṯa*	IV.170	'this girl'
	*hō**š** šunīṯa*	IV.120	~	*hō**ḏ** šunīṯa*	IV.122	'this woman'
	*hō**ḥ** ḥormṯa*	III.272	~	*hō**ḏ** ḥormṯa*	III.230	'this woman'

The assimilation of /ḏ/ is a postlexical process because it applies across word boundaries. It is formalized in (33) and illustrated by the derivation in (34). The examples in the derivation are from (32).

(33) *Assimilation of /ḏ/ in hōḏ to a following consonant (optional)*

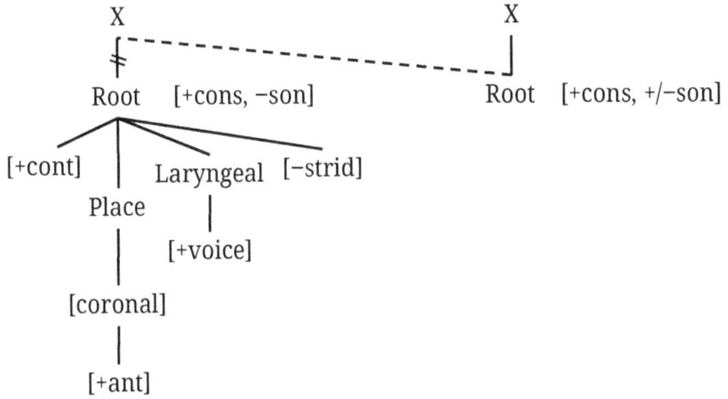

7 *hōk* is not transcribed in the original text.

(34) *A derivation which illustrates the assimilation of /ḏ/ in hōḏ*

'this girl'		'this woman'		
/hā**ḏ** bisnī-T-a/		/hā**ḏ** šunī-T-a/		
hāḏ bisnī**ṯ**a		hāḏ šunī**ṯ**a		/T/ spirantization
h**ō**ḏ bisnīṯa		h**ō**ḏ šunīṯa		/ā/ rounding
hō**b** bisnīṯa	–	hō**š** šunīṯa	–	**assimilation of /ḏ/**
[hō**b** bisnīṯa]	[hō**ḏ** bisnīṯa]	[hō**š** šunīṯa]	[hō**ḏ** šunīṯa]	

7.2.6 Assimilation of preposition-final /ʕ/

There are three prepositions which can or must end in [ʕ] at the surface level. The first one is *maʕ* 'from; about' (see Arnold 1990a: 384):

(35) *The preposition maʕ*

inḥeč-Ø	***maʕ***	*sūs-č-a* [8]
go down.PRET-3M.SG	from	mare-F-NE

'He dismounted from the mare.' IV.156

batt-aḥ	*n-aḥək*	***maʕ***	*ḳahwe*
will-1PL	1-talk.SBJV	about	coffee

'We will talk about coffee.' III.72

The second preposition is *laʕ* 'to'. This preposition has been consistently transcribed as *lʕa* or *l-ʕa* in the (Western) academic literature on Maaloula Aramaic:

(36) *The preposition laʕ as transcribed in the academic literature*

inḥeč ***lʕa*** [sic] *bisnīṯa* [9]	'he went down to the girl'	Bergsträsser 1915: 2
zēx ***lʕa*** [sic] *ḳašīša*	'go to the priest!'	Bergsträsser 1918: 118
niḥčaṯ ***lʕa*** [sic] *šbōpča*	'she went down to her neighbor (F)'	Spitaler 1957: 317
ṯalla ***l-ʕa*** [sic] *šrōġa*	'she came to the (oil) lamp'	Arnold 1991b: 42

8 The preposition *maʕ* in this example is transcribed as *m-ʕa* in the original text.

9 To avoid inconsistency, these examples are uniformly transcribed according to the standards adopted in the corpus and this work. As a result, they may differ from the original transcripts.

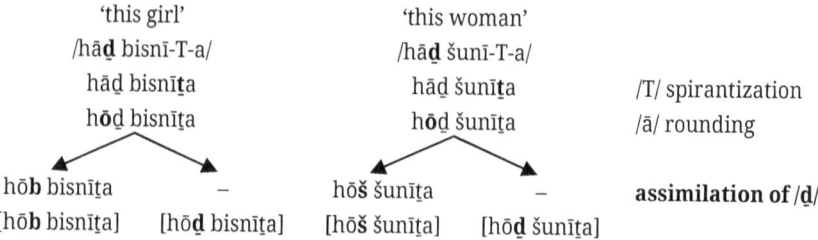

However, in the community-produced materials, such as grammar references and textbooks (e.g., Rizkallah 2010: 171; Rihan 2017: 64), this preposition is transcribed as *laʕ*, which accurately reflects how native speakers of Maaloula Aramaic pronounce it. For this reason, in the corpus and subsequently in this work this preposition is always transcribed as *laʕ*:

(37) *The preposition laʕ*

Ø-ṯ-ē-l-e	***laʕ***	*ḥḏuč-č-a*
3-come.PRS-M.SG-OM-3M.SG	to	bride-F-NE

'He comes to the bride(-to-be).' III.204

zal-l-e	*wzīr-a*	***laʕ***	*malk-a*
go.PRET-OM-3M.SG	vizier-NE	to	king-NE

'The vizier went to the king.' IV.272

The third preposition is *ʕa* 'on; to' (see Arnold 1990a: 384) which, unlike the two previous prepositions, does not end in /ʕ/. However, this preposition can be optionally reduced to *ʕ* when it is followed by a word which begins with one consonant, as in (38). If the following word begins with a consonant cluster (e.g., ***bl**ōta* 'village'), this reduction does not apply (e.g., *ʕa **bl**ōta* but not **ʕ blōta* 'to the village' III.354).

(38) *The preposition ʕa which is optionally realized as ʕ* [10]

Ø-tōḳḳ-a	***ʕ***	*ṯarʕ-a*
3-knock.PRS-F.SG	on	door-NE

'She knocks on the door.' IV.64

Ø-sōlḳ-in	*šapp-ō*	***ʕ***	*rayš-il*	*šenn-a*
3-go up.PRS-M.PL	young-PL	to	head-CST	rock-NE

'The young men go up to the top of the rock.' III.176

The consonant /ʕ/ in the three prepositions *maʕ*, *laʕ*, and *ʕ* assimilates in voicing to an immediately following word-initial /ḥ/ (see Spitaler 1938: 33–34; Arnold 1991a: 214):

10 In these two examples, this preposition is transcribed as *ʕa* rather than *ʕ* in the original text.

(39) *maḥ ḥayōṯəl zaləmṯa*	/maʕ ḥayā-T-l/	'about the man's life'	III.214
laḥ ḥōne [11]	/laʕ ḥōn-e/	'to his brother'	IV.136
laḥ ḥrīṯa	/laʕ ḥrī-T-a/	'to the other one (F)'	IV.164
ḥ ḥaṣṣe [12]	/ʕa ḥaṣṣ-e/	'on his back'	IV.178
ḥ ḥanke	/ʕa ḥank-e/	'on his cheek'	IV.162

This process applies optionally, as the following examples show:

(40) *maḥ ḥayōṯəl zaləmṯa*	~	*maʕ ḥayōṯəl eppay*
'about the man's life' III.214		'about my father's life' III.378
laḥ ḥōne	~	*laʕ ḥunōye*
'to his brother' IV.136		'to his brothers' IV.150

Since the assimilation of preposition-final /ʕ/ applies across word boundaries, I consider it a postlexical process. This process is formalized in (41).

(41) *Assimilation of preposition-final /ʕ/ to word-initial /ḥ/ (optional)*

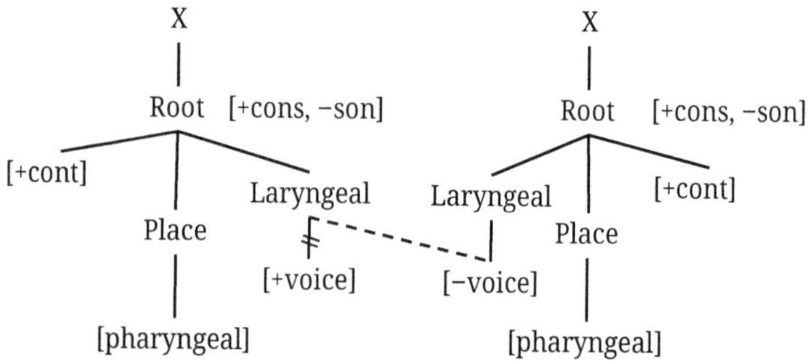

The derivation in (42) illustrates how the assimilation of preposition-final /ʕ/ applies optionally in the example /laʕ ḥōn-e/ 'to his brother' (from (39) above) but not in /laʕ malk-a/ 'to the king' (from (37) above) where the conditions are not met.

11 In the second and third examples, *laḥ* is transcribed as *l-ʕa* and *ʕa* respectively in the original text.

12 In the third and fourth examples, *ḥ* is transcribed as *ʕa* in the original text.

(42) *A derivation which illustrates the assimilation of preposition-final /ʕ/*

'to his brother'		'to the king'	
/laʕ ḥōn-e/		/laʕ malk-a/	
laḥ ḥōne	–	–	assimilation of preposition-final /ʕ/
[laḥ ḥōne]	[laʕ ḥōne]	[laʕ malka]	

7.2.7 Assimilation of /n/

The phoneme /n/ which undergoes the assimilation process to be introduced in this section occurs in two different morphological environments: in plural suffixes and as the final radical of the roots of some verbs. In the first morphological environment, the phoneme /n/ occurs in the masculine plural suffixes *-un* and *-in* and in the feminine plural suffix *-an*. These suffixes attach to verbs in different tenses. For example, *-un* attaches to subjunctive verbs, as in (43a); *-in* attaches to present and perfect verbs, as in (43b); and *-an* attaches to subjunctive and present verbs, as in (43c) (for a detailed account of the different tenses and the inflectional suffixes associated with each tense, see Spitaler 1938 and Arnold 1990a).

(43) (a) The suffix *-un* (M.PL)

*y-išw-**un***
3-do.SBJV-M.PL
'(that) they (M) do' III.212

*y-aḥəšm-**un***
3-have dinner.SBJV-M.PL
'(that) they (M) have dinner' III.258

(b) The suffix *-in* (M.PL)

*ni-m-baššl-**in***
1-PRS-cook-M.PL
'we (M) cook' III.38

*n-assīḳ-**in***
1-take up.PRF-M.PL
'we (M) are taking up' III.90

(c) The suffix *-an* (F.PL)

*y-nufḳ-**an***
3-go out.SBJV-F.PL
'(that) they (F) go out' III.52

*Ø-m-ayṯy-**an***
3-PRS-bring-F.PL
'they (F) bring' IV.156

When the object marking suffix *-l* is attached to a verb which already has the plural suffix *-un*, *-in*, or *-an*, the /n/ in the plural suffix assimilates completely to the suffix *-l*

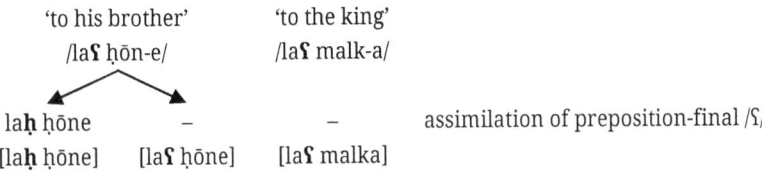

(Spitaler 1938: 37, 221; Arnold 1990a: 216, 221, 227, 232), as in (44). This assimilation process is obligatory.

(44) (a) Assimilation of /n/ in the suffix *-un* (M.PL)

yišwullun	/y-išw-u**n**-l-un/	'(that) they (M) do for them (M)'	III.178
yṣaffull mōya	/y-ṣaff-u**n**-l/	'(that) they (M) drain the water'	III.32

(b) Assimilation of /n/ in the suffix *-in* (M.PL)

mbaššlilla	/m-baššl-i**n**-l-a/	'they (M) cook it (F)'	III.40
assiḳille	/assīḳ-i**n**-l-e/	'they (M) have taken him up'	III.348

(c) Assimilation of /n/ in the suffix *-an* (F.PL)

yimṭall baʕḍinn	/y-imṭ-a**n**-l/	'(that) they (F) reach each other'	IV.64
maffḳallen	/m-affḳ-a**n**-l-en/	'they (F) bring them (F) out'	III.272

In the second morphological environment, the phoneme /n/ occurs as the final radical of the verb, as in (45).

(45) *The phoneme* /n/ *occurring as the final radical of the verb*

Ø-*ṭōʕe***n**-Ø (the root is *ṭʕ***n**)
3-carry.PRS-M.SG
'he carries' III.238

*zab***n**-*iṯ* (the root is *zb***n**)
buy.PRET-1SG
'I bought' III.376

When the object marking suffix *-l* is attached to a verb whose final radical is /n/, the /n/ assimilates completely to the suffix *-l* (Spitaler 1938: 37; Arnold 1990a: 19, 276), as in (46).

(46) *Assimilation of* /n/ *which occurs as the final radical of the verb*

ṭaʕelle	/ṭāʕe**n**-l-e/	'he carries it (M)'	III.200
zabəllaḥle	/zab**n**-laḥ-l-e/	'we bought (for) him'	III.118
mzappella	/m-zappe**n**-l-a/	'he sells it (F)'	IV.72
ṯḳella	/ṯḳe**n**-l-a/	'it's been [a period of time]'	IV.220
mṭammell bōle	/m-ṭamme**n**-l/	'he gets reassured'	III.108
mxammella	/m-xamme**n**-l-a/	'he thinks that she'	IV.74

However, in this environment the /n/ assimilation does not seem to be absolutely obligatory as the corpus data show counterexamples (although such examples are rare):

(47) *ṭaʕ**en**le*	/ṭāʕ**en**-l-e/	'he carries it (M)'	III.284
*mzappe**n**lon*[13]	/m-zappe**n**-l-un/	'he sells them (M)'	IV.108
*mxazze**n**lon*[14]	/m-xazze**n**-l-un/	'he stores them (M)'	IV.200

The assimilation of /n/ in both environments is formalized in (48) and is illustrated by the derivation in (49). The examples are from (43) and (44).

(48) *Assimilation of* /n/ *to the suffix -l*

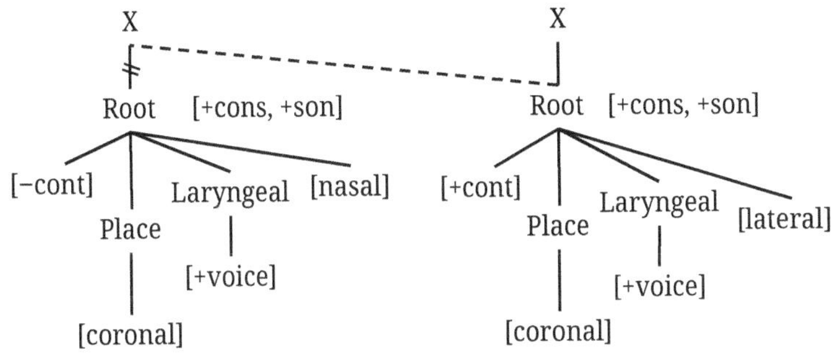

(49) *A derivation which illustrates the assimilation of* /n/

'(that) they (M) do'	'(that) they (M) do for them (M)'	
/y-išw-u**n**/	/y-išw-u**n**-l-un/	
–	yišwu**ll**un	assimilation of /n/
[yišwu**n**]	[yišwu**ll**un]	

7.2.8 Assimilation of /l/

The phoneme /l/ occurs in (and sometimes forms on its own) different unrelated morphemes. For example, it occurs as a geminate in the monomorphemic word ***xull*** 'all', as in (50).

(50) *The geminate /ll/ in **xull***

*xu**ll** ḥun-ō-x*
all brother-PL-2M.SG
'all of your brothers' IV.136

*xu**ll** ḳirš-ō*
all piaster-PL
'all of the money' III.120

13 It is transcribed as *mzappenlun* in the original text.
14 It is transcribed as *mxazzenlun* in the original text.

This geminate assimilates completely to a following coronal across word boundaries (Spitaler 1938: 35), as in (51).

(51) ***xutt** tarba* [15]	/**xull** tarb-a/	'all of the way'	III.202
***xuṭṭ** ṭīma*	/**xull** ṭīm-a/	'its (F) entire price'	IV.262
***xuss** saḥḥaryōṯa*	/**xull** saḥḥār-yā-T-a/	'all crates/boxes'	III.326
***xušš** šappō* [16]	/**xull** šapp-ā/	'all the young people'	III.182
***xurr** rezḳa*	/**xull** rezḳ-a/	'the entire livelihood'	III.106

The assimilation here is optional. This optionality can be seen in the corpus examples which do not undergo assimilation although the conditions are met:

(52) ***xull** tarba*	/**xull** tarb-a/	'all of the way'	IV.94
***xull** ḏwōṯe* [17]	/**xull** ḏw-ā-T-e/	'all of his hands'	IV.68
***xull** sažra*	/**xull** sažr-a/	'all trees'	III.150
***xull** šamʕa*	/**xull** šamʕ-a/	'all candles'	III.156
***xull** rūḥa*	/**xull** rūḥ-a/	'every spirit'	III.198

An example that shows /l/ as a morpheme is the prepositional clitic *l-* 'to; for; until'. This morpheme is shown in the examples in (53).

(53) *The prepositional clitic l-*

***l**=arʕ-a*	***l**=eḥḏ-a*
to=ground-NE	to=one-F
'to the ground/earth' IV.48	'until one [o'clock]' III.188

The prepositional clitic *l-* assimilates completely to an immediately following coronal consonant across word boundaries, as in (54).

(54) ***t**-tiḏōye*	/**l**-tiḏ-āy-e/	'to his parents'	III.198
***č**-čōžra*	/**l**-čāžr-a/	'to the dealer'	III.116
***ṯ**-ṯarʕlə klēsya*	/**l**-ṯarʕ-l klēsy-a/	'to the door of the church'	III.208
***ḏ**-ḏokkṯa*	/**l**-ḏokk-T-a/	'to a place'	IV.242
***ṣ**-ṣarḳōy* [18]	/**l**-ṣarḳ-āy/	'for Muslims'	III.268

15 It is transcribed as *xull tarba* in the original text.
16 It is transcribed as *xull šappō* in the original text.
17 It is transcribed as *xulle ḏwōṯe* in the original text.
18 It is transcribed as *s-sarḳōy* in the original text.

***š**-šaʕṯa eṭšaʕ*	/**l**-šaʕ-ṯ-a eṭšaʕ/	'until nine o'clock'	III.302
***r**-rayša*	/**l**-rayš-a/	'to the head'	IV.44

The assimilation of the prepositional clitic *l-* applies optionally, as the examples in (55) show. Compare, for example, ***t**-tiḏōye* and ***ḏ**-ḏokkṯa* in (54) with ***l**-tiḏōye* and ***l**-ḏokkṯa* in (55).

(55)	***l**-tiḏōye*	/**l**-tiḏ-āy-e/	'to his parents'	IV.156
	***l**-čaʕba*	/**l**-čaʕb-a/	'to tiredness; to trouble'	IV.194
	***l**-ḏokkṯa*	/**l**-ḏokk-T-a/	'to a place'	IV.30
	***l**-sōḥṯa*	/**l**-sāḥ-ṯ-a/	'to the (village) square'	III.178
	***l**-zuppōna*	/**l**-zuppān-a/	'for sale'	IV.58
	***l**-šaʕṯa arpaʕ*	/**l**-šaʕ-ṯ-a arpaʕ/	'until four o'clock'	III.190
	***l**-žappōnča*	/**l**-žappān-T-a/	'to the cemetery'	III.254

Another example that shows /l/ as a morpheme is the suffix *-l* that can be attached to nouns, verbs, and prepositions, connecting them to a following noun (Arnold 1990a: 19). It connects two nouns in the genitive construction (Correll 1978: 6; Arnold 1990a: 301–302), as in (56a); a verb with its definite object (Correll 1978: 12; Arnold 1990a: 300–301), as in (56b); and a preposition with its complement (Correll 1978: 93; Arnold 1990a: 384–386), as in (56c).

(56) (a) *ṯarʕ-**il*** *payṯ-a*
door-CST house-NE
'the house door' III.214

(b) *ḳaṭʕ-Ø-**il*** *xōl-a*
cut.PRET-3M.SG-OM food-NE
'he stopped eating' IV.88

(c) *ʕemm-**il*** *biʕl-iš*
with-OM husband-2F.SG
'with your (F.SG) husband' IV.12

The suffix *-l* assimilates completely to an immediately following coronal consonant (Spitaler 1938: 34–35; Arnold 1990a: 19), as in (57). This assimilation applies across word boundaries. The examples in (57) are given in pairs. The first example in each pair illustrates this assimilation process, whereas the second example shows how assimilation does not apply when the segment following /l/ is not a coronal consonant. For clarity, in each pair of examples the first word is identical. From a cross-linguistic perspective, this process can be compared with the assimilation of /l/ of the Arabic definite article to a following coronal consonant (see, e.g., Wright 1896: 15 for Standard Arabic, Cowell 1964: 493 for Damascus Arabic, Watson 2002: 216–218 for Cairene and San'ani, and Galea 2016: 91 for Maltese).

(57)	*payṯ**it** tiḏōye*	/payṯ-**l** tiḏ-āy-e/	'his parents' house'	IV.46
	*payṯ**il** ġabrōna*	/payṯ-**l** ġabrōn-a/	'the man's house'	IV.8
	*ʕemm**iṭ** ṭiflō*	/ʕemm-**l** ṭefl-ā/	'with the children'	III.362
	*ʕemm**il** ḥōne*	/ʕemm-**l** ḥōn-e/	'with his brother'	III.362
	*yarḥ**ič** čammuz*	/yarḥ-**l** čammuz/	'the month of July'	III.32
	*yarḥ**il** iyyar*	/yarḥ-**l** iyyar/	'the month of May'	III.162
	*faṯḥ**ōṯ** ṯarʕa*	/fāṯḥ-ā-**l** ṯarʕ-a/	'she opens the door'	IV.264
	*faṯḥ**ōl** makčūba* [19]	/fāṯḥ-ā-**l** makčūb-a/	'she opens the letter'	IV.92
	*naġpičč**iḏ** ḏīka*	/naġp-ičč-**l** ḏīk-a/	'I stole the rooster'	IV.22
	*naġpičč**il** xōčma*	/naġp-ičč-**l** xōčm-a/	'I stole the ring'	IV.66
	*berč**is** sōba*	/ber-T-**l** sāb-a/	'the mayor's daughter'	IV.324
	*berč**il** malka*	/ber-T-**l** malk-a/	'the king's daughter'	IV.184
	*axerč**iṣ** ṣawma*	/axer-T-**l** ṣawm-a/	'the end of the fast'	III.334
	*axerč**il** yarḥa*	/axer-T-**l** yarḥ-a/	'the end of the month'	III.162
	*ʕemm**iz** zamra*	/ʕemm-**l** zamr-a/	'with reed pipe music'	III.188
	*ʕemm**il** ḳašīša*	/ʕemm-**l** ḳašīš-a/	'with the priest'	III.156
	*rayš**iš** šenna*	/rayš-**l** šenn-a/	'the top of the rock'	IV.332
	*rayš**il** ʕarḳūba*	/rayš-**l** ʕarḳūb-a/	'the top of the mountain'	IV.10
	*m-ġapp**ir** riḥwyōṯa*	/ġapp-**l** riḥwy-ā-T-a/	'from the mills'	III.122
	*l-ġapp**il** eččṯe*	/ġapp-**l** ečč-T-e/	'to his wife'	IV.246
	*emm**in** nažīb*	/emm-**l** nažīb/	'Mother of Najib'[20]	III.54
	*emm**il** milād*	/emm-**l** milād/	'Mother of Milad'	III.60

Although this assimilation process is very common and well attested in the corpus, it cannot be considered obligatory because the corpus contains examples in which

19 It is transcribed as *faṯḥōll makčūba* in the original text.

20 This unofficial, but very common, naming system is a form of teknonymy according to which a parent is named after their eldest son.

this process does not apply, as in (58). These examples are pronounced in careful speech or with brief pauses between the words. If the same examples were pronounced in rapid speech or without pauses, assimilation would most probably apply.

(58) *ʕomril ṭefla*	/ʕomr-**l** ṭefl-a/	'the child's age'	III.202
eččṯil čōžra	/ečč-T-**l** čāžr-a/	'the merchant's wife'	IV.262
ḳommil ṯarʕa	/ḳomm-**l** ṯarʕ-a/	'in front of the door'	III.156
ġappil ḏōḏax	/ġapp-**l** ḏāḏ-ax/	'at your uncle's (house)'	III.110
rayšil šenna	/rayš-**l** šenn-a/	'the top of the rock'	III.174

The /l/ assimilation process, which I have reviewed using three examples, is formalized in (59).

(59) *Assimilation of /l/ to a following coronal (optional)*

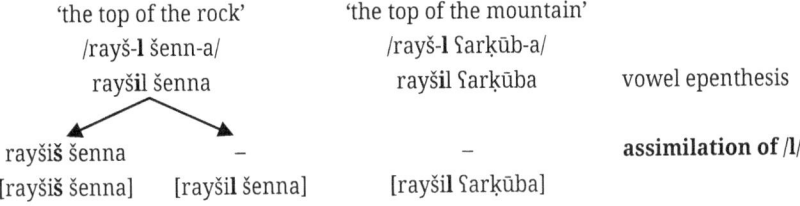

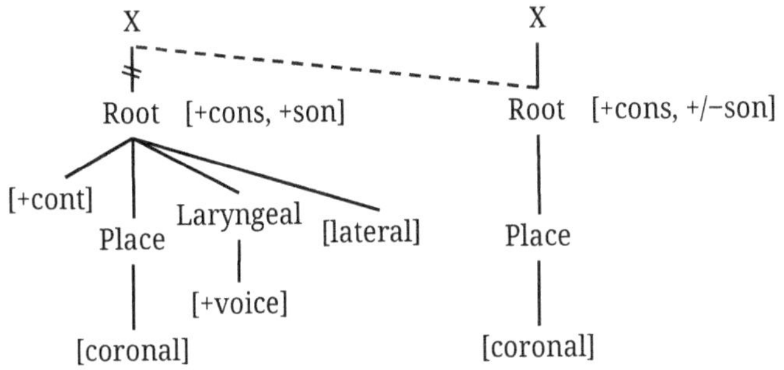

The derivation in (60) shows how /l/ assimilates optionally to a following coronal (i.e., [rayšiš šenna] ~ [rayšil šenna]) but does not assimilate to a non-coronal consonant (i.e., [rayšil ʕarḳūba]).

(60) *A derivation which illustrates the /l/ assimilation rule*

'the top of the rock'		'the top of the mountain'	
/rayš-**l** šenn-a/		/rayš-**l** ʕarḳūb-a/	
rayš**il** šenna		rayš**il** ʕarḳūba	vowel epenthesis
rayši**š** šenna	–	–	**assimilation of /l/**
[rayši**š** šenna]	[rayš**il** šenna]	[rayš**il** ʕarḳūba]	

As can be seen from the derivation in (60), *-l* suffixation may result in a consonant cluster that is usually broken up by a vowel epenthesis process (which I discuss in detail in Sections 8.2.2 and 8.3.5). This vowel epenthesis process interacts with /l/ assimilation in two different ways. If the epenthetic vowel is inserted before the suffix *-l* (as in /rayš-**l** šenn-a/ → [rayš**iš** šenna] in the previous example), assimilation applies because the epenthetic vowel does not separate the suffix *-l* from the following coronal.

However, if the epenthetic vowel is inserted after the suffix *-l*, assimilation will be blocked because the epenthetic vowel will separate the suffix *-l* from the following coronal, as in the examples in (61) and (62).

(61) *yōm**l**ə ṯrō*	/yōm-**l** ṯrō/	'(the day of) Monday'	III.152
*felk**l**ə ḏrōʕa*	/felk-**l** ḏrāʕ-a/	'half a cubit'	IV.150
*ḳatt**l**ə spaʕṯa*	/ḳatt-**l** spaʕ-ṯ-a/	'as small as a finger'	IV.10
*ʕēḏ**l**ə ṣlība*	/ʕēḏ-**l** ṣlīb-a/	'the Feast of the Cross'	IV.316
*berč**l**ə šbabō*	/ber-T-**l** šbāb-ā/	'the neighbors' daughter'	IV.128

(62) *A derivation to illustrate how vowel epenthesis can bleed /l/ assimilation*

'(the day of) Monday'	'the Feast of the Cross'	
/yōm-**l** ṯrō/	/ʕēḏ-**l** ṣlīb-a/	
yōml**ə** ṯrō	ʕēḏl**ə** ṣlība	vowel epenthesis
–	–	assimilation of /l/
[yōm**l**ə ṯrō]	[ʕēḏ**l**ə ṣlība]	

7.2.9 Lexically restricted assimilation

Few lemmas have certain segments which undergo assimilation. For example, the /n/ in the verbs ***infeḳ yinfuḳ*** 'to go out' and ***inḥeč yinḥuč*** 'to go down' assimilates optionally to the following consonant (Spitaler 1938: 36; Arnold 1990a: 115–118), as in (63). The /r/ in the verb ***amar yīmar*** 'to say' assimilates optionally to the suffix *-l* (Spitaler 1938: 37), as in (64). The assimilation in these cases is lexically restricted, and no generalizations can be made beyond these lemmas because the same segments do not undergo assimilation in other lemmas which have the same environments, as the examples below show.

(63) *yi**n**fuḳ*	III.178	~	*yi**f**fuḳ*	IV.134	'(that) he goes out'
*yi**n**ḥuč*	III.330	~	*yi**ḥ**ḥuč*	IV.252	'(that) he goes down'

but no assimilation in:

*yi**n**ġub*	'(that) he steals'	IV.150
*yi**n**kab*	'(that) it (M) dries'	III.100

(64) *amerle*	IV.196	~	*amelle*	IV.292	'he said to him'
amerlon	IV.116	~	*amellon*	III.284	'he said to them (M)'[21]

but no assimilation in:

nimbaḳḳarle	'I know him'	IV.156
mčapparla	'he smashes it (F)'	IV.202

The reason for assimilation in these specific lemmas could be lemma frequency. Cross-linguistic evidence has shown that high frequency words tend to undergo articulatory reduction (see, e.g., Pluymaekers, Ernestus & Baayen 2005; Gahl 2008). It is indeed the case that the lemmas ***infeḳ yinfuḳ*** 'to go out', ***inḥeč yinḥuč*** 'to go down', and ***amar yīmar*** 'to say', which undergo assimilation, have high lemma frequencies of 251, 227, and 1925 occurrences in MASC (respectively). In comparison, the lemmas ***inġab yinġub*** 'to steal', ***inkeb yinkab*** 'to dry', ***baḳḳar ybaḳḳar*** 'to know', and ***čappar yčappar*** 'to smash', which do not undergo assimilation, have lower lemma frequencies of 40, 6, 51, and 11 respectively.

7.3 Umlaut

This section discusses umlaut in Maaloula Aramaic. It is divided into two main subsections. In the first one, I review regressive umlaut, a process whereby the suffix vowel /i/ triggers alternations in the preceding mid vowel across the consonants separating the two vowels. In the second section, I introduce progressive umlaut, a process whereby a mid front vowel triggers alternations in the following suffix vowel /u/ across the consonants between them. To my knowledge, no previous accounts have described progressive umlaut in Maaloula Aramaic.

7.3.1 Regressive umlaut

In Maaloula Aramaic, the vowels /e o ē ō/ are realized as [i u ī ū] respectively when they occur in a base to which a suffix containing /i/ is attached (Spitaler 1938: 39–41; Arnold 1990a: 27–28). In more general terms, the mid vowels in the base alternate to agree in height with the suffix vowel /i/. The examples in (65) illustrate this regressive umlaut process. Some of these examples also appear in Spitaler (1938: 40) and Arnold (1990a: 27–28). The examples are organized into four groups according

21 These examples are transcribed as *amerlun* and *amellun* respectively in the original texts.

to the base vowel. In each group, the examples are given in pairs of word forms which have the same base. In the first word form, the base is attached to a suffix containing /i/ such as *-i* (1SG), *-iš* (2F.SG), or *-in* (M.PL). This is the word form that undergoes umlaut. In the second word form, the base is attached to a suffix which does not contain the vowel /i/. In this word form, umlaut does not apply, and therefore the underlying and surface representations of the base vowel are identical.

(65) (a) /e/ → [i]

*l**i**ppi*	/l**e**pp-i/	'my heart'	IV.328
*l**e**ppe*	/l**e**pp-e/	'his heart'	IV.84
*ʕ**i**mmiš*	/ʕ**e**mm-iš/	'with you (F.SG)'	IV.246
*ʕ**e**mma*	/ʕ**e**mm-a/	'with her'	IV.330
*yaff**i**nniš*	/y-aff-**e**nn-iš/	'may He [God] protect you (F.SG)'	IV.170
*yaff**e**nnax*	/y-aff-**e**nn-ax/	'may He [God] protect you (M.SG)'	IV.174
*ṯ**i**mmiš*	/ṯ**e**mm-iš/	'your (F.SG) mouth'	IV.130
*ṯ**e**mma*	/ṯ**e**mm-a/	'her mouth'	III.282

(b) /o/ → [u]

*b**u**ġti*	/b**o**ġt-i/	'my rug'	IV.38
*b**o**ġtax*	/b**o**ġt-ax/	'your (M.SG) rug'	IV.38
*ʕ**u**mriš*	/ʕ**o**mr-iš/	'your (F.SG) life/age'	IV.28
*ʕ**o**mrax*	/ʕ**o**mr-ax/	'your (M.SG) life/age'	IV.46
*ḳ**u**mmi*	/ḳ**o**mm-i/	'in front of me'	IV.330
*ḳ**o**mma*	/ḳ**o**mm-a/	'in front of her'	IV.18
*š**u**ġliš*	/š**o**ġl-iš/	'your (F.SG) business/work'	IV.50
*š**o**ġlax*	/š**o**ġl-ax/	'your (M.SG) business/work'	IV.50

(c) /ē/ → [ī]

*ayṯ**ī**li*	/ayṯ-**ē**-l-i/	'he brought me (sthg.)'	III.50
*ayṯ**ē**le*	/ayṯ-**ē**-l-e/	'he brought him (sthg.)'	IV.226
*app**ī**li*	/app-**ē**-l-i/	'he gave me'	IV.300
*app**ē**la*	/app-**ē**-l-a/	'he gave her'	IV.130
*nčḳ**ī**li*	/nčḳ-**ē**-l-i/	'he encountered me'	III.344
*nčḳ**ē**la*	/nčḳ-**ē**-l-a/	'he encountered her'	III.122

*ḥam**ī**li*	/ḥām-**ē**-l-i/	'he sees me'	FW
*ḥam**ē**la*	/ḥām-**ē**-l-a/	'he sees her'	III.124

(d) /ō/ → [ū]

*balḥ**ū**ḏiš*	/balḥ**ō**ḏ-iš/	'alone (2F.SG)'	IV.68
*balḥ**ō**ḏe*	/balḥ**ō**ḏ-e/	'alone (3M.SG)'	III.240
*ġabr**ū**ni*	/ġabr**ō**n-i/	'my man'	IV.252
*ġabr**ō**na*	/ġabr**ō**n-a/	'her man'	IV.250
*summ**ū**ḳin*	/summ**ō**ḳ-in/	'red (INDF.M.PL)'	III.354
*summ**ō**ḳan*	/summ**ō**ḳ-an/	'red (INDF.F.PL)'	III.174
*ḥuww**ū**rin*	/ḥuww**ō**r-in/	'white (INDF.M.PL)'	III.202
*ḥuww**ō**ran*	/ḥuww**ō**r-an/	'white (INDF.F.PL)'	IV.78

This umlaut process can be formalized in (66) as the spreading of the feature [+high] of the suffix vowel /i/ to the left (hence the term *regressive*). This representation shows how umlaut applies in spite of the presence of one or more intervening consonants, distinguished by the feature [+cons], between the base vowel and suffix vowel. These intervening consonants do not interfere with umlaut because none of the Maaloula Aramaic consonants is characterized by the feature [high].

(66) *Regressive umlaut*

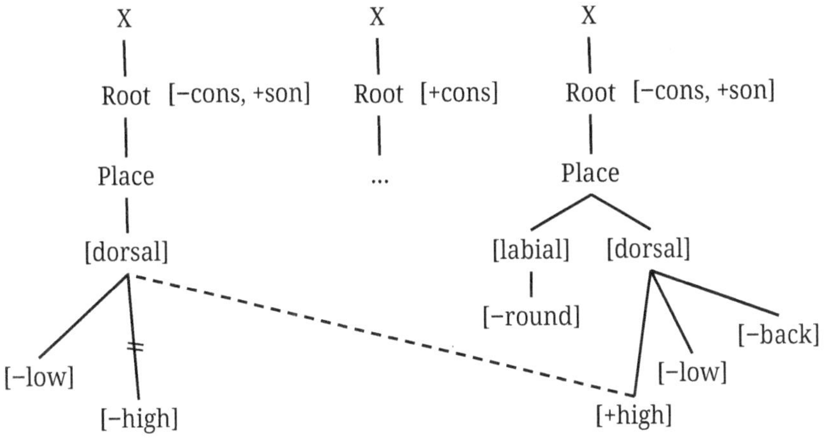

The derivation in (67) illustrates this regressive umlaut process.

(67) *A derivation to illustrate regressive umlaut*

'behind him'	'behind me'	'her husband'	'my husband'	
IV.40	IV.40	IV.266	IV.100	
/r**o**ḥl-e/	/r**o**ḥl-i/	/b**e**ʕl-a/	/b**e**ʕl-i/	
–	r**u**ḥli	–	b**i**ʕli	regressive umlaut
[r**o**ḥle]	[r**u**ḥli]	[b**e**ʕla]	[b**i**ʕli]	

Exceptional cases

There is an exceptional case where regressive umlaut does not apply. This case consists of the words whose base vowel *ō* is not raised to *ū* when attached to a suffix containing *i*, as in (68) (cf. (65d) above).

(68) *xṯ**ō**bi*	**xṯ**ū**bi*	'my book'	IV.40
*bl**ō**ti*	**bl**ū**ti*	'my village'	IV.208
*ḥ**ō**ṯiš*	**ḥ**ū**ṯiš*	'your (F.SG) sister'	IV.68
*ḥ**ō**lčiš*	**ḥ**ū**lčiš*	'your (F.SG) aunt/stepmother'	IV.168
liššōni	**lišš**ū**ni*	'my tongue'	IV.338
*x**ō**čmiš*	**x**ū**čmiš*	'your (F.SG) ring'	IV.92

This case has already been observed and described in the previous literature (see Spitaler 1938: 40; Arnold 1990a: 27). According to these two accounts, the *ō* in the words which do not undergo umlaut has developed from the old vowel *ā* (see also Spitaler 1938: 7 and Arnold 1990a: 22 where a full picture of this diachronic sound change is presented whereby the old long vowels *ō* and *ā* merged into the long vowel *ō*). In order to account for this case from a synchronic perspective, I make three assumptions. First, the Maaloula Aramaic words that have a surface [ō] may have either /ō/ or /ā/ in their underlying forms. This can be considered a case of neutralization whereby the contrast between /ō/ and /ā/ is neutralized to [ō], as in (69) and (70).

(69) *Neutralization of* /ō/ *and* /ā/

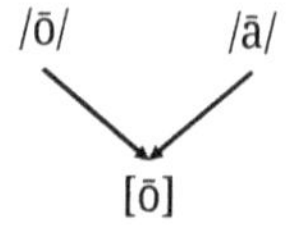

(70) (a) /ō/ → [ō]

ḥōna	/ḥōn-a/	‘brother’	III.300
ġabrōna	/ġabrōn-a/	‘man’	IV.8
ʕaḳōna	/ʕaḳōn-a/	‘crow; raven’	IV.312
yōma	/yōm-a/	‘day’	III.62
naḳōsa	/naḳōs-a/	‘bell’	III.152
xarōfa	/xarōf-a/	‘sheep (SG)’	III.308

(b) /ā/ → [ō]

xṯōba	/xṯāb-a/	‘book’	IV.36
blōta	/blāt-a/	‘village’	IV.12
ḥōṯa	/ḥāṯ-a/	‘sister’	III.264
ḥōlča	/ḥāl-T-a/	‘maternal aunt; stepmother’	IV.166
ḏōḏa	/ḏāḏ-a/	‘paternal uncle’	III.220
ḥmōra	/ḥmār-a/	‘donkey’	IV.284

Second, I assume that the underlying /ā/ in the words in (70b) is realized as [ō] due to a phonological rule formalized in (71).

(71) /ā/ *Rounding*

$$\begin{bmatrix} \text{+syllabic} \\ \text{+long} \\ \text{+back} \\ \text{-high} \\ \text{+low} \\ \text{-round} \end{bmatrix} \rightarrow \begin{bmatrix} \text{-low} \\ \text{+round} \end{bmatrix}$$

This rule is illustrated in (72) which presents a derivation of two words, one from (70a) and one from (70b). These examples show how the distinction between /ō/ and /ā/ is neutralized in the surface forms.

(72) *A derivation to illustrate the /ā/ rounding process*

‘brother’	‘book’	
/ḥōn-a/	/xṯāb-a/	
–	xṯōba	/ā/ rounding
[ḥōna]	[xṯōba]	

Third, I assume that regressive umlaut is ordered before /ā/ rounding. The derivation in (73) illustrates this assumption and gives the correct output.

(73) *A derivation to illustrate the interaction between regressive umlaut and /ā/ rounding*

'brother'	'my brother'	'book'	'my book'	
/ḥōn-a/	/ḥōn-i/	/xṯāb-a/	/xṯāb-i/	
–	ḥūni	–	–	regressive umlaut
–	–	xṯōba	xṯōbi	/ā/ rounding
[ḥōna]	[ḥūni]	[xṯōba]	[xṯōbi]	

If /ā/ rounding were ordered before regressive umlaut, the wrong output would be produced, as in (74).

(74) *A derivation that gives the wrong output*

'brother'	'my brother'	'book'	'my book'	
/ḥōn-a/	/ḥōn-i/	/xṯāb-a/	/xṯāb-i/	
–	–	xṯōba	xṯōbi	/ā/ rounding
–	ḥūni	–	xṯūbi	regressive umlaut
[ḥōna]	[ḥūni]	[xṯōba]	*[xṯūbi]	

Although the proposed analysis accounts for the exceptional cases presented above, it raises two questions. First, is there any independent evidence for the underlying /ā/? Second, the /ā/ rounding rule predicts that no word should surface with an [ā]. Is that really the case?

The independent evidence for the underlying /ā/ is provided by the pretonic shortening and raising processes, which I discuss in detail in Section 10.3 (see Arnold 1990a: 22 for a similar argument). When the singular nouns presented in (70) above are turned into the plural form, the base vowel will surface as [u] in the nouns in (70a) (e.g., *ḥōna* 'brother', *ḥunō* 'brothers') but as [a] in the nouns in (70b) (e.g., *xṯōba* 'book', *xṯabō* 'books'). This difference in the realization of the base vowels happens because the two groups of nouns indeed have different underlying base vowels. The underlying vowel in the group in (70a) is /ō/. When the plural is formed, the /ō/ will occur in pretonic position and will therefore be shortened and raised to [u] (i.e., /ḥōn-ā/ → [ḥuˈnō]). In contrast, the underlying vowel in the group in (70b) is /ā/. When the plural is formed, the /ā/ will occur in pretonic position and will therefore be shortened to [a] (i.e., /xṯāb-ā/ → [xṯaˈbō]). In summary, proposing an underlying /ā/ vowel is well motivated because it can have two different realizations. It either undergoes shortening and surfaces as an [a] when it occurs in pretonic position (e.g., [xṯaˈbō]) or surfaces as an [ō] elsewhere due the /ā/ rounding rule (e.g., [xṯōba]).

With regard to the second question, there are words which surface with an [ā] (e.g., *ṯāx* 'come (2M.SG)!' III.52 and *ḥmāy* 'look (2F.SG)!' IV.124). However, it is unclear whether these words have an underlying /ā/ which avoids /ā/ rounding or whether they have an underlying /a/ which undergoes lengthening. These analyses will be presented and discussed in detail in Section 10.4.1.

Opaque and problematic cases

There are cases reported in the previous literature where umlaut is believed to apply although no [i] is attached to the base words. The following examples, collected from Spitaler (1938: 40–41) and Arnold (1990a: 27–28), illustrate these cases. I divided the examples into three sets for reasons that will be explained below.

(75) Set 1:	*minn*	'from me'	vs.	*menne*	'from him'
	ḥūn	'my brother'	vs.	*ḥōnax*	'your (M.SG) brother'
	ġabrūn	'my man'	vs.	*ġabrōna*	'man'
Set 2:	*ḳirš*	'piasters (EPL)'	vs.	*ḳerša*	'piaster'
	ibər	'sons (EPL)'	vs.	*ebra*	'son'
	yūm	'days (EPL)'	vs.	*yōma*	'day'
Set 3:	*aḥrīf*	'answer (2F.SG)!'	vs.	*aḥrēf*	'answer (2M.SG)!'
	šḳūl	'take (2F.SG)!'	vs.	*šḳōl*	'take (2M.SG)!'
	ḳūm	'get up (2F.SG)!'	vs.	*ḳōm*	'get up (2M.SG)!'

Set 1 consists of words which have the pronominal suffix *-i* (1SG) in their underlying representations (i.e., /menn-i/, /ḥōn-i/, and /ġabrōn-i/). However, this suffix does not surface in these examples due to a word-final /i/ deletion process (that I will discuss and formalize later in this section). To account for the opacity in Set 1, I assume that word-final /i/ deletion is ordered after regressive umlaut. This rule ordering is shown in the derivation in (76).

(76) *A derivation to illustrate the interaction between regressive umlaut and word-final /i/ deletion*

'your (M.SG) brother'	'my brother'		
/ḥōn-ax/	/ḥōn-i/		
–	ḥūni		regressive umlaut
–	– ↙	↘ ḥūn	word-final /i/ deletion
[ḥōnax]	[ḥūni]	[ḥūn]	

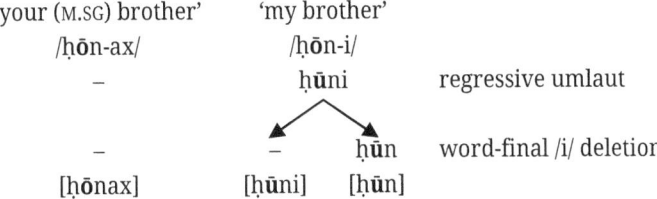

As indicated by the arrows in the branching derivation, word-final /i/ deletion applies optionally. This optionality is exemplified by the following words which are attested in the corpus with and without the suffix *-i*. It can be noticed that regressive umlaut applies in both variants.

(77)	*lippi*	IV.328	~	*lipp*	IV.320	'my heart'
	ḳummi	IV.330	~	*ḳumm*	III.86	'in front of me'
	ġabrūni	IV.252	~	*ġabrūn*	IV.252	'my man'
	aytīli	III.50	~	*aytīl*	III.50	'he brought me (sthg.)'
	ʕimmi	IV.330	~	*ʕimm*	III.134	'with me'
	birči	IV.70	~	*birč*	IV.264	'my daughter'

If word-final /i/ deletion were ordered before regressive umlaut, the wrong output would be produced, as in (78).

(78) *A derivation that gives the wrong output*

'your (M.SG) brother'	'my brother'		
/ḥōn-ax/	/ḥōn-i/		
–	–	ḥōn	word-final /i/ deletion
–	ḥūni	–	regressive umlaut
[ḥōnax]	[ḥūni]	*[ḥōn]	

This analysis raises a question about the status of the word-final /i/ deletion rule in the phonology of Maaloula Aramaic. Is this phonological rule well motivated and attested in other contexts not related to umlaut, or is it a rule of very limited scope that is needed only to explain the opacity in Set 1? The word-final /i/ deletion rule is attested in different contexts that are not necessarily related to umlaut. For example, this process targets:

(i) the words which end with the first person singular pronominal suffix *-i* (see Spitaler 1938: 5; Arnold 1990a: 43):

(79)	*xṯōbi*	IV.40	~	*xṯōb*	IV.36	'my book'
	liššōni	IV.338	~	*liššōn*	IV.136	'my tongue'

(ii) the verbs whose third radical is /y/ and which are inflected for the third person masculine singular (see Spitaler 1938: 5; Arnold 1990a: sec. 4.7):

(80) *ḳōr***i**	IV.302	~ *ḳōr*	IV.36	'he reads'	(the root is *ḳr***y**)
*mʕann***i**	IV.162	~ *mʕann*	IV.164	'he sings'	(the root is *ʕn***y**)

(iii) nouns in the enumerative plural form (see Spitaler 1938: 5, 104–105; Arnold 1990a: sec. 6.1):

(81) *ʕizz***i**	III.374	~ *ʕizz* [22]	Rizkallah 2010: 150	'goats (EPL)'
*mutt***i**	III.36	~ *mutt*	IV.228	'mudds (EPL) (a measure of capacity for grain)'

(iv) miscellaneous words which end with /i/:

(82) *ṯēn***i**	IV.158	~ *ṯēn*	IV.112	'second; next'
*balk***i**	IV.44	~ *balk*	IV.224	'maybe'

The word-final /i/ deletion rule is formalized in (83).

(83) *Word-final* /i/ *deletion*

i → Ø /__ # (optional)

The vowel /i/ *is deleted in word-final position.*

This rule is illustrated in the derivation in (84). The used example is from (79) above and does not involve regressive umlaut.

(84) *A derivation to illustrate the word-final* /i/ *deletion rule*

'my book'		
/xṯāb-**i**/		
–		regressive umlaut
xṯ**ō**bi		/ā/ rounding
↙	↘	
xṯōb	–	**word-final /i/ deletion**
[xṯōb]	[xṯōb**i**]	

22 It is transcribed as *ʕiz* in the original text.

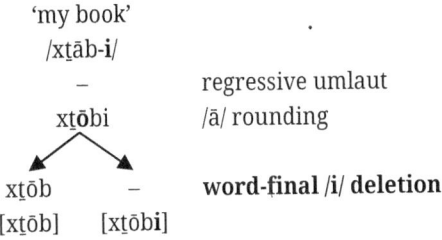

However, there are a few lexical exceptions to this rule, as in (85).

(85)	*ti*	**t*	'who; which; that'	IV.190
	misti	**mist*	'in the middle of'	IV.52
	žurži	**žurž*	'George'	III.130

In addition to these lexical exceptions, there are non-random cases in which word-final /i/ deletion does not apply if /i/ is preceded by an underlying CCC sequence. In these cases, word-final /i/ deletion will be blocked, so that a CCC# sequence would neither surface nor be repaired by vowel epenthesis, as in (86).[23]

(86)	-C(ə)CCi#	*-CCC#	*-CCəC#		
	*šaġəl**ṯi***	**šaġlṯ*	**šaġləṯ*	'my profession'	IV.30
	*aḏəm**xi***	**aḏmx*	**aḏməx*	'he let me sleep'	III.50
	*ḳaʕp**ri***	**ḳaʕpr*	**ḳaʕpər*	'mice (EPL)'	III.332
	*mufč**ḥi***	**mufčḥ*	**mufčəḥ*	'keys (EPL)'	IV.54

It is not clear how this blocking can be motivated in a rule-based approach. It remains for future research to identify the rules or constraints that can account for it.

In summary, with regard to the question about the status of the word-final /i/ deletion rule in the phonology of Maaloula Aramaic, it has become clear that this phonological rule can adequately account not only for the opacity in Set 1 but also for alternations which do not necessarily involve umlaut.

Set 2 in (75) above consists of nouns in the enumerative plural form. They are repeated here for convenience:

(87) Set 2:	***ḳirš***	'piasters (EPL)'	vs.	*ḳerša*	'piaster'
	ibər	'sons (EPL)'	vs.	***ebra***	'son'
	yūm	'days (EPL)'	vs.	*yōma*	'day'

The enumerative plural is the plural form used after numerals and is formally distinguishable from the general plural, which is not preceded by a numeral (e.g., compare *bōṯar ṯlōṯa* ***yūm*** 'after three days (EPL)' III.258 with *bann* ***yumō*** 'in these days (PL)'

23 To my knowledge, neither Spitaler (1938) nor Arnold (1990a) noticed or addressed this deletion-blocking problem. For example, there are words, such as *šimʕin* [sic] 'he heard me' (Arnold's 1990a: 202), which are assumed to occur without the word-final /i/. However, according to my native language consultant, these variants are not grammatical, and only the variant with the suffix *-i* is possible (e.g., *šiməʕni*).

III.44) (see Spitaler 1938: 104–105; Arnold 1990a: 289). Spitaler (1938: 5, 104–105) observed that the nouns in the enumerative plural form have a word-final *-i* which can be dropped optionally, as in the following examples which are attested in the transcriptions published in the first half of the twentieth century:

(88) *ḳirši*	~	*ḳirš*	'piasters (EPL)'	Bergsträsser 1915: 13~72
ibri	~	*ibər*	'sons (EPL)'	Bergsträsser 1915: 12~47
yūmi	~	*yūm*	'days (EPL)'	Bergsträsser 1915: 20~5
išni	~	*išən*	'years (EPL)'	Bergsträsser 1915: 92~14
mutti	~	*mutt*	'mudds (EPL) (a measure of capacity for grain)'	Bergsträsser 1915: 91~1933: 8

Given the occurrence of *-i* at the end of enumerative plural nouns, Spitaler (1938: 39–40) reasonably assumed that these nouns undergo umlaut, a case similar to Set 1. However, the situation has changed since Spitaler's grammar was written. The variant with *-i* is rarely attested in more recent transcripts, which suggests that this variant has almost fallen out of use. For example, searching for the same five words from (88) in the corpus yields the results shown in (89). The word frequency is given in parentheses. This corpus-based evidence is further supported by my language consultant who confirms that he does not use the variants with *-i*, and he does not remember hearing them from speakers his age.

(89) *ḳirši*	(0)	~	*ḳir(ə)š*	(4)	'piasters (EPL)'
ibri	(0)	~	*ibər*	(5)	'sons (EPL)'
yūmi	(0)	~	*yūm*	(82)	'days (EPL)'
išni	(0)	~	*išən*	(58)	'years (EPL)'
mutti	(2)	~	*mutt*	(2)	'mudds (EPL)'

From a synchronic perspective, two analyses can be proposed: a phonological analysis and a morphological analysis. From a phonological perspective, the same analysis that I proposed to account for the opacity in Set 1 can be proposed for Set 2. However, this analysis has some limitations here. The following derivation demonstrates that if it is assumed that the word meaning 'days (EPL)' has the underlying form /yōm-i/, then both [yūmi] and [yūm] will have to surface because word-final /i/ deletion applies optionally. However, this is not the case as [yūmi] is not attested anymore.

(90) *A derivation that illustrates the problem with the phonological account*

'days (EPL)'		
/yōm-i/		
yūmi		regressive umlaut
–	yūm	word-final /i/ deletion
?[yūmi]	[yūm]	

In order to provide a solution to this problem, I will have to assume that optionality is a gradient concept, and that the degree of optionality is higher for Set 1 (where both variants occur commonly) than for Set 2 (where the variant with [i] is rarely or never attested).

From a morphological perspective, it could be proposed that the base vowel alternation in Set 2 (e.g., *ḳirš* vs. *ḳerša*, *ibər* vs. *ebra*, and *yūm* vs. *yōma*) represents a case of base allomorphy that is morphologically conditioned. For example, it can be assumed that the morpheme /yōm/ 'day' has the allomorph [yūm] when the enumerative plural zero-suffix *-Ø* is attached to it, and the allomorph [yōm] elsewhere (e.g., when the nominal ending *-a* or the pronominal suffixes such as *-ax* '2M.SG' and *-aḥ* 1PL are attached to it). Forms like [yūm-Ø] 'days (EPL)', [yōm-a] 'day', and [yōm-ax] 'your (2M.SG) day' are therefore the output of the morphological, rather than the phonological, component. They, then, serve as the underlying form (or the input) of the phonological component where the phonological rules apply.

I now turn to Set 3 which I repeat here for convenience:

(91) Set 3:	*aḥrīf*	'answer (2F.SG)!'	vs.	*aḥrēf*	'answer (2M.SG)!'
	šḳūl	'take (2F.SG)!'	vs.	*šḳōl*	'take (2M.SG)!'
	ḳūm	'get up (2F.SG)!'	vs.	*ḳōm*	'get up (2M.SG)!'

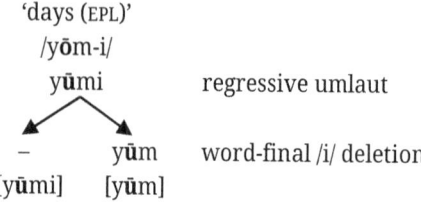

This set consists of verbs in the imperative form. The high vowels in the second person feminine singular forms (on the left) correspond to the mid vowels in the second person masculine singular forms (on the right). According to Spitaler (1938: 40–41) and Arnold (1990a: 27), the vowel change in the feminine forms can only be due to the influence of a feminine ending (i.e., *-i*) which must have existed in the past but disappeared a long time ago. From a synchronic perspective, however, it cannot be assumed that the raising of the mid vowels in Set 3 is the result of a phonological umlaut process. There is no phonological evidence to support that an underlying /i/ is responsible for triggering this regressive umlaut. For this reason, I will adopt a morphological analysis, similar to the one proposed for Set 2, and consider the pairs in Set 3 as a case of morphological umlaut, a case similar to the German umlaut (e.g., *Mantel* ~ *Mäntel* 'coat ~ coats').

7.3.2 Progressive umlaut

The two pronominal suffixes *-un* (3M.PL) and *-xun* (2M.PL) can, like all the other pronominal suffixes, be attached to bases of different parts of speech (see Arnold 1990a: 43 for the pronominal suffixes). The following examples show these suffixes attached to nominal and verbal bases.

(92) (a) The suffixes *-un* and *-xun* attached to nominal bases

*ṯarʕ-**un***	*īḏ-**xun***
door-3M.PL	hand-2M.PL
'their (M) door' IV.26	'your (M.PL) hand' III.296

(b) The suffixes *-un* and *-xun* attached to verbal bases

*ġarrb-ičč-**un***	*n-m-app-ō-l-**xun***
try.PRET-1SG-3M.PL	1-PRS-give-F.SG-OM-2M.PL
'I tried them (M)' III.80	'I (F) give you (M.PL)' III.276

When listening carefully to the audio recordings of the narratives, which make up the corpus (see Chapter 3), one can notice an alternation in the pronunciation of these suffixes: between [**u**n] and [**o**n] and between [x**u**n] and [x**o**n]. This alternation is triggered by a preceding vowel across the consonants between them. The suffixes /un/ (3M.PL) and /xun/ (2M.PL) are realized as [on] and [xon] respectively if they are preceded by /e/ or /ē/ and as [un] and [xun] elsewhere, as in (93).[24] Interestingly, this alternation is absent from the original transcriptions of these recordings and also from the previous grammars which only have the variants [un] and [xun] regardless of the preceding vowel (e.g., *šwēl**un*** [sic] 'he made them (something)' in both Spitaler 1938: 222 and Arnold 1990a: 282). Consequently, the words in (93) reflect our (rather than the original) transcription. To show that this alternation is not idiosyncratic, I collected the examples from different speakers.

24 I am grateful to my language consultant who first drew my attention to this alternation.

(93) (a) The allomorphs [on] and [xon]

*lepp***on**	/lepp-**un**/	'their (M) heart'	IV.210
*ebr***on**	/ebr-**un**/	'their (M) son'	IV.116
*amell***on**	/amer-l-**un**/	'he said to them (M)'	III.284
*mappēl***on**	/m-app-ē-l-**un**/	'he gives them (M)'	III.352
*ebər***xon**	/ebr-**xun**/	'your (M.PL) son'	III.354
*berč***xon**	/ber-T-**xun**/	'your (M.PL) daughter'	III.204
*nṭumren***xon**	/n-ṭumr-en-**xun**/	'(that) I hide you (M.PL)'	IV.306
*nayṯēl***xon**	/n-ayṯ-ē-l-**xun**/	'(that) I bring you (M.PL) (sthg.)'	III.104

(b) The allomorphs [un] and [xun]

*payṯ***un**	/payṯ-**un**/	'their (M) house'	III.222
*blōt***un**	/blāt-**un**/	'their (M) village'	IV.118
*mšattarl***un**	/m-šattar-l-**un**/	'he sends them (M)'	III.206
*mamrōl***un**	/m-āmr-ā-l-**un**/	'she says to them (M)'	IV.104
*payṯ***xun**	/payṯ-**xun**/	'your (M.PL) house'	III.312
*īḏ***xun**	/īḏ-**xun**/	'your (M.PL) hand'	III.296
*nmall***xun**	/n-mar-l-**xun**/	'(that) I tell you (M.PL)'	III.188
*nmappōl***xun**	/n-m-app-ā-l-**xun**/	'I (F) give you (M.PL)'	III.276

I assume that this alternation is the result of an umlaut process, which can be formalized in (95) as the spreading of the feature [−high] of the vowels /e ē/ to the right (hence the term *progressive*). As I have shown in Section 7.3.1, umlaut skips the intervening consonants because none of the Maaloula Aramaic consonants is characterized by the feature [high]. The derivation in (94) illustrates this progressive umlaut process.

(94) *A derivation to illustrate progressive umlaut*

'their (M) house'	'their (M) heart'	'your (M.PL) hand'	'(that) I hide you (M.PL)'	
/payṯ-**un**/	/lepp-**un**/	/īḏ-**xun**/	/n-ṭumr-en-**xun**/	
–	lepp**o**n	–	nṭumrenx**o**n	progressive umlaut
[payṯun]	[lepp**o**n]	[īḏxun]	[nṭumrenx**o**n]	

(95) *Progressive umlaut*

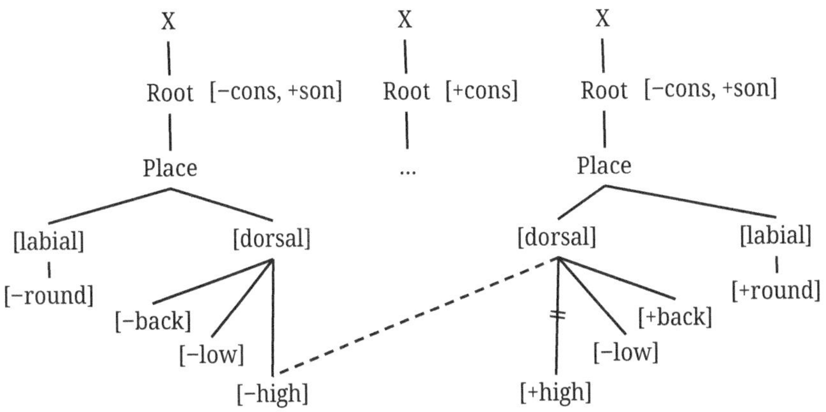

7.4 Conclusion

In this chapter, I have presented two types of assimilation in Maaloula Aramaic: local assimilation and long-distance assimilation (or umlaut). The local assimilation processes have been described in the previous grammars (i.e., Spitaler 1938 and Arnold 1990a). I have reviewed them, shown where they apply and where they cannot apply (using data from the corpus), and formalized a synchronic phonological rule for each assimilation process by giving feature-geometrical representations. With the exception of the voicing assimilation of *č*- (presented in Section 7.2.3), all of the assimilation processes presented in this chapter result in geminates. In Section 9.2.2, I refer to these geminates as *surface geminates* because they consist of underlyingly different segments which have become identical at the surface level through assimilation.

I have divided long-distance assimilation (or umlaut) into two types: regressive umlaut and progressive umlaut. Regressive umlaut has been known and described since Spitaler's (1938) grammar, but some opaque and problematic cases had to be presented and discussed from a synchronic perspective. On the other hand, progressive umlaut had not been described before this work, nor was it captured by the published transcripts (although the alternation which it causes can be heard in the original audio files).

8 Syllable structure and syllabification

8.1 Introduction

One of the intricate topics in the phonology of the Semitic languages is their syllabification and epenthesis processes. Much attention has been given to this topic in the different Arabic dialects (e.g., Selkirk 1981; Itô 1989; Broselow 1992, 2017; Watson 2002, 2007; Kiparsky 2003). This topic, however, has received significantly less attention in the neighboring Neo-Aramaic dialects although they present similarly intricate problems.

Syllable structure and syllabification in Maaloula Aramaic are described in two reference grammars: Spitaler (1938) and Arnold (1990a). These accounts provide a good starting point but leave a number of open questions about the syllable inventory and syllable-related processes such as syllabification, vowel epenthesis, and glottal epenthesis.

In order to deal with these open questions, I propose an alternative inventory of syllable types and provide an analysis of syllable structure and epenthesis inspired by studies on Arabic. The Aramaic facts have repercussions for the typology of epenthesis in varieties of Semitic, which needs to be enriched in order to cover the full range of variability.[1]

8.2 Previous accounts

8.2.1 Syllable structure and syllabification

According to Arnold (1990a: 37–38), the syllable inventory of Maaloula Aramaic contains the following syllable types which are presented here in three lines in order of decreasing frequency:

1 An earlier version of this chapter was published in Eid & Plag (2024). Some individual paragraphs from this previously published paper have also been included in Chapter 1, Sections 2.2, 2.5, 9.3, 10.2, and Chapter 11.

https://doi.org/10.1515/9783111447124-008

(1) *Syllable inventory*

CV	CVC	CVCC	CVV	CVVC	CVVCC
CCV	CCVC	CCVCC	CCVV	CCVVC	CCVVCC
CCCV	CCCVC	CCCVCC	CCCVV	CCCVVC	CCCVVCC[2]

Arnold (1990a: 39) proposes the following rule for the syllabification of word-medial consonant clusters in disyllabic and polysyllabic words.

(2) *Syllabification of word-medial consonant clusters*

The syllable boundary is placed between the two consonants in a two-consonant cluster (i.e., -C.C-) and after the second consonant in a three-consonant cluster (i.e., -CC.C-).

The following examples illustrate this rule:

(3)	**-C.C-**			**-CC.C-**		
	ṯel.ka	'snow'	V.37	*nošəḳ.ṯa*	'kiss'	V.37
	ġbeč.ča	'cheese'	V.38	*frīsč.xun*	'your (M.PL) right'	V.38

Arnold (1990a: 39) also shows that syllabification applies not only within word boundaries, as in (3), but also across word boundaries, as in (4).

(4) *loġəṯlə mšīḥa* [loġəṯ.ləm.šī.ḥa] 'the language of Christ' V.39

The principles which determine this syllabification, however, are not given. These principles would have to explain the tendency to have more consonants in the syllable coda than in the onset of the following syllable as the examples in (3) under -CC.C- show. In the absence of these principles, one can argue that an alternative syllabification, such as -.CCC- or -C.CC- (e.g., *frī.sčxun* or *frīs.čxun* instead of *frīsč.xun*), is also plausible. This alternative syllabification might also have consequences for the syllable inventory shown in (1).

In Section 8.3, I will propose a different syllabification approach which will significantly reduce the syllable types listed in (1).

2 All of these shapes will be illustrated in different examples in this chapter, except for CCCVVCC which seems to be restricted to words which start with CCVVCC and are preceded by a one-consonant clitic (e.g., *lə-frīsčxun* 'for your (M.PL) right' V.39).

8.2.2 Vowel epenthesis

In Maaloula Aramaic, an epenthetic vowel is inserted to break up a consonant cluster. Arnold's (1990a: 20, 40, 2011: 686) main points on this topic can be summarized as follows:

- The epenthetic vowel does not have a phonemic status.
- The epenthetic vowel does not play any role in the syllabification process (i.e., it cannot be a syllable nucleus). For example, Arnold syllabifies the word *nošəḳṯa* 'kiss' V.37 which contains the epenthetic vowel [ə] as *nošəḳ.ṯa.*
- In terms of vowel quality, Arnold (1990a: 40) states rather vaguely that its realization can range between [e] and [i]. With regard to transcription, it is predominantly transcribed as [ə]. However, there are instances where it is variably transcribed as [ə] and [i] in Arnold's (1991a, 1991b) transcripts. This variable transcription is illustrated in (5). The epenthetic vowel is transcribed as [ə] in (5a) and as [i] in (5b). In these examples, the epenthetic vowel is inserted before the suffix *-l* which connects two nouns in the genitive construction (see Correll 1978: 6; Arnold 1990a: 301–302).[3]

(5)	(a)	*mōrəl ġamla*	'the owner of the camel'	IV.230
		maḳōməl berəkṯa	'the shrine of Saint Thecla'	IV.222
		bnōṯəl ḥōnax	'the daughters of your brother'	IV.68
		marōyəl ḏemseḳ	'the people of Damascus'	IV.228
		ffōyəl ṭefla	'the child's face'	III.198
	(b)	*payṯil ġabrōna*	'the man's house'	IV.8
		yarḥil iyyar	'the month of May'	III.162
		berčil malka	'the king's daughter'	IV.184
		axerčil yarḥa	'the end of the month'	III.162
		rayšil ʕarḳūba	'the top of the mountain'	IV.10

Arnold (1990a: 40) presents an algorithm which indicates the place of vowel epenthesis in Maaloula Aramaic:

3 However, it is unclear whether this variation reflects the actual pronunciation of these vowels, or whether it is based on transcription conventions rather than auditory facts. In any case, this variation does not fall within the scope of this work. Future research can investigate the acoustic quality of the epenthetic vowel and verify whether this variation truly exists.

(6) (a) Count the consonants in a consonant cluster from right to left.
(b) Insert an epenthetic vowel after every second consonant.
(c) In the case of two word-final consonants, the right word boundary is counted as a consonant.

This algorithm works word-internally and across word boundaries, as can be seen from the examples in (7). For the sake of clarity, I underline the epenthetic vowels throughout this chapter.

(7) (a)	-Cə̲C#	*iṯə̲r*	'two (M)'	V.40
		xuṯə̲p	'write (2M.SG) me!'	III.374
(b)	-Cə̲CC-	*taxə̲lṯa*	'passageway'	V.40
		šabə̲kṯa	'net'	IV.58
(c)	-CCə̲CC-	*sōblə̲ blōta*	'the mayor of the village'	V.40
(d)	-Cə̲CCə̲CC-	*loġə̲tlə̲ mšīḥa*	'the language of Christ'	V.40

This algorithm can be expressed as a phonological rule:

(8) *Vowel epenthesis in Maaloula Aramaic*

$$\emptyset \rightarrow \text{ə} \, / \, C\_\_C \begin{Bmatrix} \# \\ C \end{Bmatrix}$$

Although this rule predicts accurately where the epenthetic vowel is expected to occur, it leaves four open questions.

First, what do the two environments CCC and CC# have in common where vowel epenthesis occurs? A number of phonologists (e.g., Kahn 1976: 23; Blevins 1995: 209; Hayes 2009: 259, 264) have expressed their dissatisfaction with environments such as /C_C{#, C} because word boundaries (#) do not form a natural class with consonants (C).

Second, how can this vowel epenthesis rule be explained from a perspective which takes syllable structure into account? According to the epenthesis algorithm in (6), the insertion of the epenthetic vowel does not seem to be governed or affected by syllable structure. The following examples show that epenthesis can occur in onsets (9a) as well as codas (9b) if Arnold's syllabification scheme (explained in (2)) is applied.

(9) (a)	*bə̲-spaʕ.ṯa*	'with a finger'	V.39
(b)	*nošə̲ḳ.ṯa*	'kiss'	V.37

Third, in Arnold's words, this epenthetic vowel is "functionally non-syllabic" (2011: 686), which can be interpreted as not being able to form a syllable nucleus. For example, this can be seen in the word *nošə̱ḳṯa* 'kiss' in (9b), which Arnold considers disyllabic [nošə̱ḳ.ṯa], rather than trisyllabic [no.šə̱ḳ.ṯa], although it has the three potential nuclei [o], [ə], and [a]. This tendency to disregard the epenthetic schwa in syllabification is most probably due to the problem of syllable-stress interaction.

In Maaloula Aramaic, word stress falls on the final CVV(C_0) or CVCC syllable.[4] Otherwise, it falls on the penultimate syllable (Bergsträsser 1915: xxi; Spitaler 1938: 46; Arnold 1990a: 40) (this stress algorithm is revised in Section 10.2). The epenthetic schwa seems to be considered non-syllabic because it is not visible to stress (see Bergsträsser 1915: xix). For example, if, contrary to Arnold's syllabification, the epenthetic vowel in *nošəḳṯa* were considered syllabic (i.e., [no.šə̱ḳ.ṯa]), then the penultimate syllable [šə̱ḳ]$_\sigma$ would receive stress (see (10a)). Since in *nošə̱ḳṯa* the first syllable receives stress, this would not be the right analysis. Arnold's syllabification avoids the problem posed by this opaque interaction between the epenthetic vowel and stress. By disregarding the epenthetic vowel, [nošə̱ḳ] would be considered the penultimate syllable that duly receives stress (see (10b)). However, such a solution which considers a sequence like [nošə̱ḳ] as monosyllabic, rather than disyllabic, is not fully convincing either. An account is needed which can generate a syllabification such as ['no.šə̱ḳ.ṯa] where [šə̱ḳ]$_\sigma$ is a syllable that does not interact with stress (see (10c)):

(10) (a)	*nošə̱ḳṯa*	→	*[no.'šə̱ḳ.ṯa]	The wrong account: [šə̱ḳ]$_\sigma$ is visible to stress
(b)	*nošə̱ḳṯa*	→	['nošə̱ḳ.ṯa]	Arnold's account: [šə̱ḳ] is not a syllable
(c)	*nošə̱ḳṯa*	→	['no.šə̱ḳ.ṯa]	The desired account: [šə̱ḳ]$_\sigma$ is not visible to stress

Fourth, why does Maaloula Aramaic seem to tolerate certain word-initial and word-medial CCC clusters where epenthesis is surprisingly ruled out? In the following examples, vowel epenthesis is not possible, contra Arnold's algorithm:

(11) (a) word-initial CCC clusters (i.e., #CCC-)

sčfī.tič	(and not **sə̱čfī.tič*)	'you (M.SG) benefitted'	V.39
sčfēt	(and not **sə̱čfēt*)	'benefit!'	V.39

(b) word-medial CCC clusters (i.e., -CCC-)

sūsč.xen	(and not **sūsə̱č.xen*)	'your (F.PL) horse'	V.38
frīsč.xun	(and not **frīsə̱č.xun*)	'your (M.PL) right'	V.38

4 C_0 refers to any number of consonants including zero.

If the epenthesis algorithm presented in (6) applies to all CCC clusters, then why does it not apply to these cases? If these are exceptional cases, are there other exceptions, and is there anything in common among them? In order to answer these questions, I will present in Section 8.3 an alternative syllabification scheme which accounts for epenthesis from a syllable-based perspective.

Before doing so, a word on the variation in the application of vowel epenthesis and on the phonological status of this vowel is in order. It seems that vowel epenthesis is obligatory in some environments and optional in other environments. For example, the same words in (12) are attested with and without the epenthetic vowel although in all these words the conditions for vowel epenthesis are met.

(12) variant with no epenthetic vowel			variant with an epenthetic vowel		
berkṯa	III.182	~	*berə̱kṯa*	III.180	'Saint Thecla'
aḳtriṯ	III.48	~	*aḳə̱triṯ*	III.56	'I was able (to)'
loʕpṯa	III.164	~	*loʕə̱pṯa*	IV.16	'game; toy'
mofčḥa[5]	IV.56	~	*mofə̱čḥa*	IV.70	'key'
ṯarč	IV.64	~	*ṯarə̱č*	III.104	'two (F)'
imṭ	III.172	~	*imə̱ṭ*	IV.116	'he/they arrived'

In addition to the words above, which can appear with and without the epenthetic vowel, there are words that are always attested with an epenthetic vowel. For example, there are a total of 58 tokens of the word type *išə̱n* 'years (EPL)' in the corpus. In all these instances, *išə̱n* appears epenthesized. I am using the term 'optionality' to refer to all these cases where epenthesis can apply. Optionality does not refer to the cases in which epenthesis cannot apply, such as in the words *sčfītič* (**sə̱čfītič*) and *frīsčxun* (**frīsə̱čxun*) in (11).

I do not know the reasons for the optionality in the application of epenthesis. The literature on Maaloula Aramaic makes no reference to it. However, a number of studies on the surrounding Arabic dialects have shown that optionality may be dependent on sonority. Hall (2011: 1576), for example, generalizes that "epenthesis [in Lebanese Arabic] is more or less obligatory in coda clusters of an obstruent followed by a sonorant […], and optional in most other clusters". Optionality might also be attributed to other factors. For example, Watson (2007: 345) argues that the epenthesized and non-epenthesized word forms in Libyan Tripoli Arabic "may well be stylistic variants".

5 It appears as *mufčḥa* rather than *mofčḥa* in the original text, but my language consultant dismisses *mufčḥa* as incorrect.

Throughout this chapter, whenever I refer to vowel epenthesis, I mean the cases where epenthesis *can* (or, in some cases, *must*) apply. The cases where epenthesis *cannot* apply, even if there is a consonant cluster, are dealt with in Section 8.4.2.

With regard to the phonological status of this vowel, I have considered it to be an epenthetic vowel although two alternative analyses may seem plausible at first sight. The first analysis would be to consider this vowel a lexical (or underlying) vowel that undergoes deletion in a set of words. In order to compare the deletion analysis with the epenthesis analysis, I present two data sets, one in (13) and one in (14). In each data set, the surface forms are accounted for first by the epenthesis analysis and then by the deletion analysis.

The first data set, shown in (13), presents Ø ~ ə alternations in pairs of words. Each pair represents the singular and plural forms of the same lexeme. This is why they have the same base. Analysis (13a) represents the epenthesis option, and analysis (13b) represents the deletion option. Analysis (13a) is more plausible because it assumes that a vowel is inserted to break up a CCC cluster, which is a marked structure cross-linguistically. In the word forms which do not have consonant clusters, epenthesis does not apply. By contrast, analysis (13b) is less convincing because the application of vowel deletion to some word forms (but not to other word forms) does not seem to be phonologically motivated (i.e., it does not repair an illicit structure of any type).

(13) *First data set: Two competing analyses to account for the same surface forms*

(a) [ə] Epenthesis analysis

/samk-T-a/ [6]	→	[samə̲kt̲a]	'fish (SG)'	III.278	(epenthesis applies)
/samk-ā-T-a/ [7]	→	[samkōt̲a]	'fish (PL)'	IV.140	
/šabk-T-a/	→	[šabə̲kt̲a]	'net'	IV.58	(epenthesis applies)
/šabk-ā-T-a/ [8]	→	[šapkōt̲a]	'nets'	FW	

(b) /ə/ Deletion analysis

/samə̲k-T-a/	→	[samə̲kt̲a]	'fish (SG)'	III.278	
/samə̲k-ā-T-a/	→	[samkōt̲a]	'fish (PL)'	IV.140	(deletion applies)
/šabə̲k-T-a/	→	[šabə̲kt̲a]	'net'	IV.58	
/šabə̲k-ā-T-a/	→	[šapkōt̲a]	'nets'	FW	(deletion applies)

6 /T/ indicates the {FEMININE} marker that I intend to leave unspecified in underlying representations. At the surface level, this morpheme has the two allomorphs [č] and [t̲] (see Section 6.2.6).

7 /ā/ is realized as [ō] in all examples through the /ā/ rounding process (see Section 7.3.1).

8 /b/ undergoes devoicing and is realized as [p] before a voiceless consonant (see Section 5.2.2).

The second data set, shown in (14), presents variation in the position of [ə] with respect to the suffix *-l*. The vowel [ə] occurs before-*l* in some examples and after it in other examples. In each of the examples presented in (14), two nouns are connected in the genitive construction by the suffix *-l* (for the genitive construction in Maaloula Aramaic, see Correll 1978: 6; Arnold 1990a: 301–302). Analysis (14a) proposes that in each example there is an underlying consonant cluster across word boundaries (i.e., CCCC and CCC), and [ə] is epenthesized to break up that cluster. The noticeable variation in the position of the epenthetic vowel is dependent on the cluster (i.e., CCə̱CC and Cə̱CC), regardless of the position of the suffix *-l*. This is why the same underlying structure /mār-l/ 'owner of' surfaces as [mōrlə̱] if the cluster is CCCC and as [mōrə̱l] if the cluster is CCC (the same can be said about /ʕēḏ-l/ 'feast of').

Analysis (14b) proposes that there are two underlying schwas, one before and one after the suffix *-l*, and that one of them is deleted. This analysis has to be ruled out because it does not explain why only one schwa is deleted and one is left, and why the first schwa is deleted in some examples and the second is deleted in other examples.

(14) *Second data set: Two competing analyses to account for the same surface forms*

(a) [ə] Epenthesis analysis

/mār-l xṯāb-a/	→ [mōrlə̱ xṯōba]	'the owner of the book'	IV.40
/mār-l ġaml-a/	→ [mōrə̱l ġamla]	'the owner of the camel'	IV.230
/ʕēḏ-l ṣlīb-a/	→ [ʕēḏlə̱ ṣlība]	'the Feast of the Cross'	IV.316
/ʕēḏ-l ʕanṣar-T-a/	→ [ʕēḏə̱l ʕanṣarča]	'(the Feast of the) Pentecost'	III.162

(b) /ə/ Deletion analysis

/mār-ə̱lə̱ xṯāb-a/	→ [mōrlə̱ xṯōba]	'the owner of the book'	IV.40
/mār-ə̱lə̱ ġaml-a/	→ [mōrə̱l ġamla]	'the owner of the camel'	IV.230
/ʕēḏ-ə̱lə̱ ṣlīb-a/	→ [ʕēḏlə̱ ṣlība]	'the Feast of the Cross'	IV.316
/ʕēḏ-ə̱lə̱ ʕanṣar-T-a/	→ [ʕēḏə̱l ʕanṣarča]	'(the Feast of the) Pentecost'	III.162

In defense of the deletion account, one could still argue that there might be a constraint on word size which militates against having more than three syllables in a word. As a result of this constraint, the underlying /ə/ is deleted in the offending words so that the number of syllables is reduced to three. However, the fact that the schwa is retained (not deleted) in the words in (15) shows that the deletion account is not the correct one.

(15)

matə̱rsōṯa	'schools'	FW
bisə̱nyōṯa	'girls'	III.376
muġə̱rfīṯa	'hoe'	III.56
žawə̱hrōṯa	'gems'	IV.126
ḳamə̱syōṯa [9]	'shirts'	III.272

Based on the discussion above, the deletion analysis has to be rejected.

The second alternative analysis would be to consider the Maaloula Aramaic schwa an intrusive (or excrescent) vowel, rather than an epenthetic vowel. Intrusive vowels "are actually phonetic transitions between consonants" (Hall 2006: 387). To determine whether this vowel is intrusive or not, I will use Hall's (2006: 391) diagnostics for intrusive vowels. The Maaloula Aramaic vowel in question has two of the properties of intrusive vowels. Its quality is schwa, and it is inserted optionally. However, it differs from intrusive vowels in two important aspects.

First, whereas an intrusive vowel "generally occurs in heterorganic clusters" (Hall 2006: 391), the Maaloula Aramaic schwa occurs freely in homorganic clusters. In the examples in (16), the vowel [ə] occurs between alveolar consonants.

(16) *The vowel* [ə] *occurring in homorganic clusters*

matə̱rsōṯa	'schools'	FW
bisə̱nyōṯa	'girls'	III.376
ʕisə̱r	'twenty'	III.304
irə̱ṣ	'he/they accepted'	IV.226
warə̱ṯṯa	'rose; flower'	VI.890

Second, whereas the intrusive vowel "does not seem to have the function of repairing illicit structures" (Hall 2006: 391), the Maaloula Aramaic schwa clearly has the function of repairing illicit or marked structures, such as consonant clusters. Notice that in the examples in (13) and (14) above, the schwa is inserted only when a consonant cluster is formed. This ability to repair a marked structure is a property of epenthetic (rather than intrusive) vowels, according to Hall (2006: 391). Based on these diagnostics, the intrusive (or excrescent) vowel analysis has to be ruled out.

9 It is transcribed as *ḳaməṣyōṯa* in the original text.

8.2.3 Glottal epenthesis

According to Spitaler (1938: 25) (see also Arnold 1990a: 12), a glottal stop occurs at the beginning of a vowel-initial word in a number of phonological environments. Based on the analysis of these environments, using data extracted from MASC and data elicited from my native speaker consultant, I propose that a glottal stop is epenthesized in three prosodically defined positions: after a pause (obligatorily), as in (17), in a hiatus context (i.e., V#_V) (obligatorily), as in (18), and when the preceding word ends in a consonant (i.e., C#_V) (optionally and less commonly), as in (19). These three environments are not restricted to Maaloula Aramaic. For example, these are the same environments where glottal epenthesis applies in Cairene Arabic (see Watson 2002: 232–233). Although the glottal stop occurs and can be heard at the beginning of the examples presented in (17), (18), and (19), the glottal stop is not marked in the original transcription of the examples (see my comment on the adopted transcription system in Section 2.2.2). For this reason, I write the glottal stop between square brackets whenever it is pronounced but not written in the original text.

(17) *Glottal epenthesis after a pause (obligatory)*

[ʔ]*ana*	‘I’	III.28
[ʔ]*anaḥ*	‘we’	III.260
[ʔ]*orḥa*	‘once’	III.294
[ʔ]*ōṯ*	‘there is’	IV.282

(18) *Glottal epenthesis in a hiatus context (i.e., V#_V) (obligatory)*

ḥmačče [ʔ]*eččṯe*	‘his wife saw him’	IV.58
ti [ʔ]*ixšen*	‘which is coarse-grained’	III.38
mō [ʔ]*ešma*	‘what is it (F) called?’	IV.138
mō [ʔ]*ōṯ*	‘what is there/the matter?’	III.226

(19) *Glottal epenthesis when the preceding word ends in a consonant (i.e., C#_V) (optional and less common)*

*l-**ʔ**eḥḏa*	III.160	~	*l-eḥḏa*	III.188	‘until one [o’clock]’
*l-**ʔ**ommṯa*	IV.294	~	*ʕal‿ommṯa* [10]	III.152	‘to/on (the) people’
*hōʔ **ʔ**orḥa*	IV.196	~	*hōḏ‿orḥa*	IV.188	‘this time’
*ʕal-ōʔ **ʔ**arʕa*	III.28	~	*ʕal-ōḏ‿arʕa*	IV.186	‘on this earth/ground’

10 The linking symbol “‿” is used to indicate the absence of a break or a glottal stop between two words.

What unites the three environments presented in (17), (18), and (19) is that the vowel-initial words, which undergo glottal epenthesis, begin with an onsetless syllable. In Maaloula Aramaic, onsetless syllables are disallowed. This can be seen in Arnold's (1990a: 37–38) syllable inventory which contains no onsetless syllables (see Section 8.2.1 above). In order to avoid these illicit onsetless syllables, a glottal stop is inserted to serve as their onsets (see Watson 2002: 233; Hayes 2009: 257–258; Zsiga 2013: 280). This glottal stop is inserted through a glottal epenthesis rule which can be formalized as follows (following Hayes 2009: 258):

(20) *Glottal epenthesis*

Ø → ʔ / $[_{\sigma}$__V

The open question is: Why does glottal epenthesis apply obligatorily after a pause and in a hiatus context (as in (17) and (18) above) but optionally when the preceding word ends in a consonant (as in (19) above)? This question will be dealt with in Section 8.3.6.

8.3 Syllable-based analysis

In this section, I put forward an alternative syllable inventory that differs completely from the one presented by Arnold (in Section 8.2.1). I propose that Maaloula Aramaic allows only three syllable types: CV, CVV, and CVC. This proposal is inspired by the classification of syllable types in the Arabic dialects (Watson 2002; Kiparsky 2003).

The various Arabic dialects can be said to fall into three major groups primarily based on the position of the epenthetic vowel in a word-medial CCC cluster. Adopting Kiparsky's (2003) terminology, I refer to these groups as VC-dialects, CV-dialects, and C-dialects.[11] I use the oft-cited example 'I/you (M.SG) said to him' to show the position of the epenthetic vowel in each of these groups (see, e.g., Selkirk 1981: 228–231; Itô 1989: 241–251; Broselow 1992: 23–24; Kiparsky 2003: 150). VC-dialects, such as Iraqi Arabic, epenthesize the vowel as CV̲CC (e.g., ***gíli̲tla***). CV-dialects, such as

11 However, this is not the only available typology. Watson (2007) identified a fourth group which displays mixed epenthesis patterns (e.g., Central Urban Sudanese). She named this group *Cv-dialects*. Lindsay-Smith (2021) presented a different phonological typology, incorporating the variation across the Arabic dialects into two axes, namely TOLERANCE and REPAIR. TOLERANCE refers to the type of syllables that these dialects tolerate, and REPAIR refers to how these dialects deal with violations of syllable structure.

Cairene Arabic, epenthesize the vowel as CC<u>V</u>C (e.g., *ʔultí̱lu*). C-dialects, such as Moroccan Arabic, tolerate CCC sequences (e.g., *qəltlu*). The difference between these dialect groups is schematized in (21).

(21) *Vowel epenthesis in a CCC cluster in different Arabic dialect groups*

VC-dialects	**CV-dialects**	**C-dialects**	
(e.g. Iraqi)	(e.g. Cairene)	(e.g. Moroccan)	
/gi**l**-**t**-**l**-a/	/ʔu**l**-**t**-**l**-u/	/qə**l**-**t**-**l**-u/	underlying forms
CVCC	CCVC	CCC	
[gí**l** i̱ **t** **l**a]	[ʔu**l** **t** í̱ **l**u]	[qə**l** **t** **l**u]	surface forms

In addition to the difference in the position of the epenthetic vowel in a CCC cluster, these three Arabic dialect groups differ in a number of other properties pointed out in Kiparsky (2003: 149–150) (see also Watson 2007). These properties include (among other things not directly related to my research questions) the tolerance of phrase-final CC clusters, phrase-initial onset CC clusters, word-initial geminates, and non-final CVVC syllables as well as the interaction between epenthesis and stress. These properties are summarized in (22).

(22) *Some properties of the Arabic dialect groups (based on Kiparsky 2003: 149–150)*

	Arabic VC-dialects	Arabic CV-dialects	Arabic C-dialects
Phrase-final CC	not permitted/permitted (only with falling sonority)	permitted	permitted
Phrase-initial CC	permitted (but may be broken up by a prosthetic vowel)	not permitted	permitted
Initial geminates	permitted (but may be broken up by a prosthetic vowel)	not permitted	permitted
Non-final CVVC	permitted	shortened	permitted
Epenthesis/stress interaction	opaque	not opaque	no epenthesis

The model of classification of Arabic dialects can be applied to other Semitic languages, such as Aramaic. The analysis presented in this chapter will reveal that Maaloula Aramaic shows features of both VC- and C-dialects (see Section 8.3.7).

Following Kiparsky's (2003) analysis of syllable-related processes in these three Arabic dialect groups, I argue that in Maaloula Aramaic, syllabification and stress assignment take place at the lexical level, whereas epenthesis and resyllabification apply at the postlexical level.

8.3.1 Data and method

In order to test my syllabification scheme empirically on as many words as possible, I compiled a word list from the data set called "MASC_dataframe.csv" (this data set has been introduced in Section 3.4.1). The compiled word list consists of around 12,000 word forms. Using a spreadsheet (like the one shown in (23)), I syllabified all the word forms in the list according to the predefined syllables: CV, CVC, and CVV. The syllabification column represents syllabification at the lexical level, so if a word contains a schwa in its surface representation, this epenthetic vowel is ignored and not represented by a V.

(23) *Extract from the syllabification spreadsheet*

Root	Lemma	Word form	Syllabification
ḏwḏ	ḏōḏa	ḏaḏō	#CV.CVV#
ḏwḏ	ḏōḏa	ḏaḏōye	#CV.CVV.CV#
ḏḥḳ	ḏaḥaḳōna	ḏaḥaḳōna	#CV.CV.CVV.CV#
ḏhb	ḏahba	ḏahba	#CVC.CV#
ḏhb	ḏahba	ḏahbō	#CVC.CVV#

In addition to this word list, I conducted several elicitation sessions with my native speaker consultant. These sessions had the aim of generating inflectional forms which were not attested in Arnold's texts (see, e.g., the inflectional forms in Section 8.4.2) and of verifying whether the consultant will consider the variant with an epenthetic vowel to be acceptable or not.

8.3.2 Syllable weight

Like in Arabic, the weight of a syllable in Maaloula Aramaic plays an important role in determining the position of stress. The unit of syllable weight that I use is the mora (represented by μ). I adopt Hayes's (1989) version of moraic theory, according to which CV is considered a light syllable: its short vowel receives one mora (24a).

CVV is heavy: its long vowel receives two moras (24b). CVC is heavy in a non-final position: its vowel receives one mora, and its coda consonant receives one mora through Weight-by-Position (24c). The Weight-by-Position rule is language-specific whereby CVC syllables are heavy in some languages and light in other languages (Hayes 1989: 258). In word-final position, however, I follow Hayes (1995: 125) in assuming that CVC is light (24d). The reason for this assumption is that word-final CVC syllables would attract stress if phonologically heavy, which they don't (see Section 10.2 for details on stress assignment).[12]

(24) (a) (b) (c) (d)

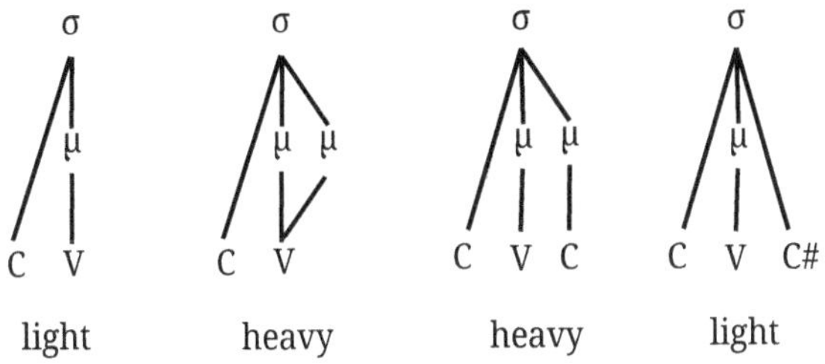

These three syllable types are shown in the two disyllabic words in (25). The word in (25b) consists of two CVC syllables, the first of which is heavy through Weight-by-Position while the second syllable is light because it is word-final.

(25) (a) (b)

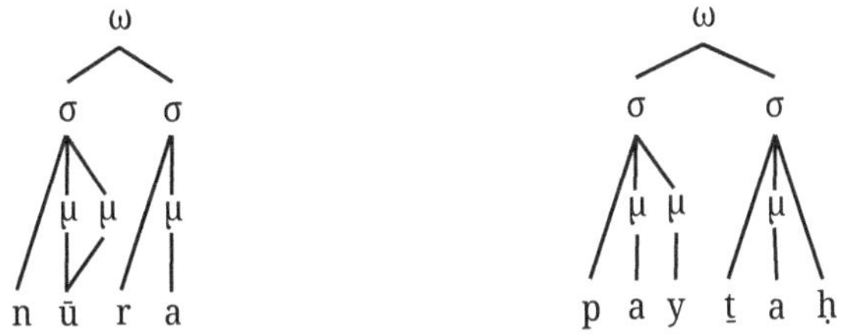

/nūr-a/→['nū.ra] 'fire' III.80 /payṯ-aḥ/→['pay.ṯaḥ] 'our home' III.60

12 Hayes (1995: 125-129) assumes that word-final consonants are extrametrical in Palestinian Arabic. As a result of this consonant extrametricality, the coda consonant in a word-final CVC syllable is not assigned a mora. This renders word-final CVC syllables monomoraic or light.

8.3.3 Syllabification

Syllables in Maaloula Aramaic are formed according to the syllabification scheme in (26) which borrows elements from a number of interrelated analyses including Kahn (1976: 37–38), Clements (1990: 299), and Watson (2002: 63).

(26) *Syllabification scheme*

(a) **Nucleus formation:** Associate each [+syllabic] segment to a syllable node.
(b) **Onset formation:** Given P (an unsyllabified segment) preceding Q (a nucleus), adjoin P to the syllable containing Q.
(c) **Coda formation:** Given Q (a nucleus) followed by R (an unsyllabified segment), adjoin R to the syllable containing Q if Q is monomoraic.

The coda formation process (26c) is conditional in order to allow the formation of CVC syllables but block the formation of CVVC syllables.

These three steps are illustrated in the syllabification of the two words *nūra* and *payṯaḥ* already introduced in (25):

(27) *Syllabification scheme exemplified*

/nūr-a/	→	[ˈnū.ra]	‘fire’	III.80
/payṯ-aḥ/	→	[ˈpay.ṯaḥ]	‘our home’	III.60

(a) Nucleus formation

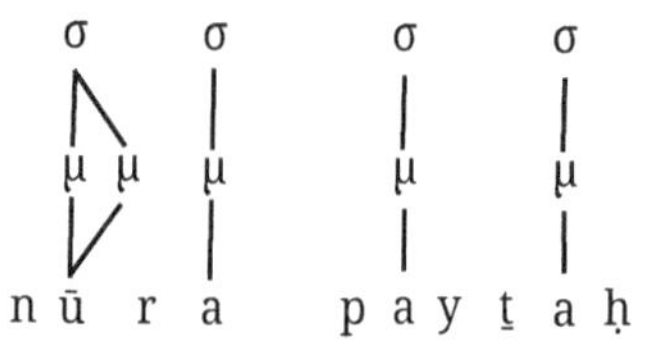

(b) Onset formation

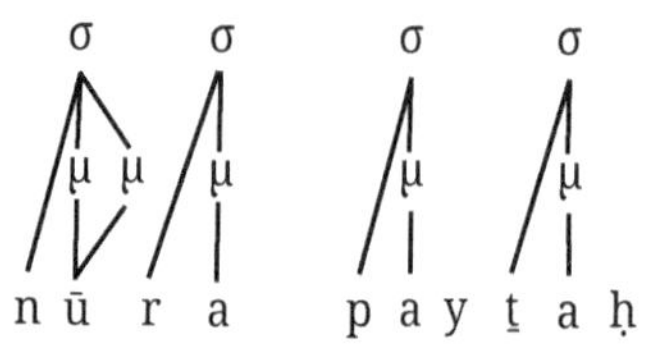

(c) Coda formation

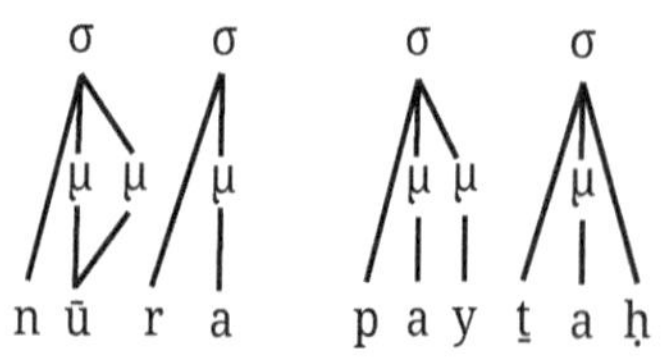

8.3.4 Stray consonants

When the syllabification scheme applies, some consonants remain unsyllabified. As they are not part of syllables, they are called ‘stray consonants’ (e.g., Selkirk 1981; Itô 1989; Archangeli 1991; Broselow 1992). In Maaloula Aramaic, individual stray consonants are tolerated at the lexical level. The corpus data shows that these stray consonants can occur word-initially, word-medially, and word-finally as can be seen in (28). The stray consonants are given in angled brackets:

(28) *Stray consonants resulting from the application of the syllabification scheme*

(a) Word-initial stray consonants

underlying forms		lexical level		
/xṯāb-a/	→	[⟨x⟩.ˈṯō.ba]	‘book’	IV.36
/ʕṣofr-a/	→	[⟨ʕ⟩.ˈṣof.ra]	‘morning’	IV.256
/blāt-a/	→	[⟨b⟩.ˈlō.ta]	‘village’	IV.12
/mšīḥ-a/	→	[⟨m⟩.ˈšī.ḥa]	‘Christ’	III.154
/xšūr-a/	→	[⟨x⟩.ˈšū.ra]	‘wood’	IV.334

(b) Word-medial stray consonants

underlying forms		lexical level		
/nošḳ-T-a/	→	[ˈnoš.⟨ḳ⟩.ṯa]	‘kiss’	V.37
/berk-T-a/	→	[ˈber.⟨k⟩.ṯa]	‘Saint Thecla’	III.180
/ġabrn-ā/	→	[ġab.⟨r⟩.ˈnō]	‘men’	III.364
/ḥāl-T-a/	→	[ˈḥō.⟨l⟩.ča]	‘maternal aunt; stepmother’	IV.166
/ḳāḏ̣y-a/	→	[ˈḳō.⟨ḏ̣⟩.ya]	‘judge’	IV.146

(c) Word-final stray consonants

underlying forms		lexical level		
/ṯarč/	→	[ˈṯar.⟨č⟩]	‘two (F)’	III.274
/ʕisr/	→	[ˈʕis.⟨r⟩]	‘twenty’	III.304
/yarḥ/	→	[ˈyar.⟨ḥ⟩]	‘months (EPL)’	IV.142
/mōn/	→	[ˈmō.⟨n⟩]	‘who’	IV.296
/lōb/	→	[ˈlō.⟨b⟩]	‘if’	III.120

(d) Stray consonants in more than one position

underlying forms		lexical level		
/klēsy-a/	→	[⟨k⟩.ˈlē.⟨s⟩.ya]	'church'	III.166
/ṯlēṯ/	→	[⟨ṯ⟩.ˈlē.⟨ṯ⟩]	'thirty'	IV.262
/sčafḳt-e/	→	[⟨s⟩.ˈčaf.⟨ḳ⟩.te]	'he checked up on him'	IV.214

In terms of moraic analysis, I follow Kiparsky (2003) in assuming that a stray consonant is associated with one mora which is adjoined not to a syllable node but to the node of a higher phonological domain (usually the phonological word).[13] This assumption is exemplified in the syllabification of four words (taken from (28)) in which the stray consonants occur in word-initial, word-medial, and word-final positions:

(29) *Syllabification scheme: stray consonants involved*

(a) Nucleus formation

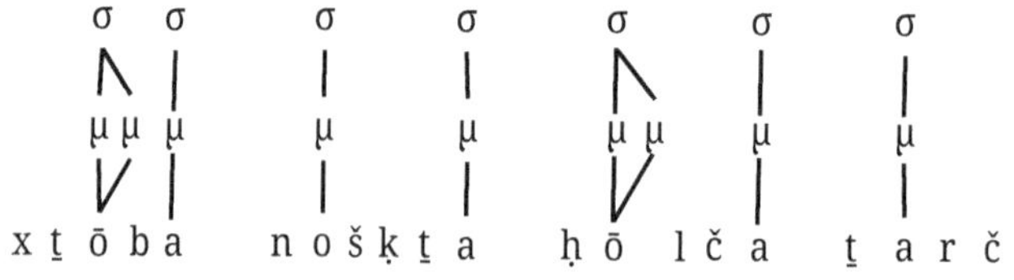

(b) Onset formation

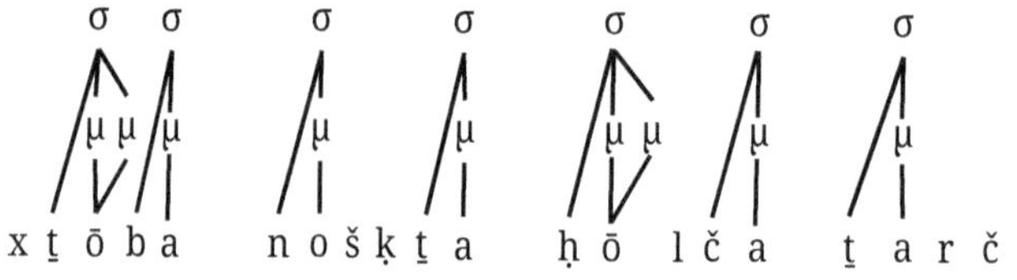

13 Kiparsky refers to the consonants directly adjoined to the word node as 'semisyllables'. However, I will keep referring to them as 'stray consonants' throughout this book.

(c) Coda formation: the remaining segments are stray consonants

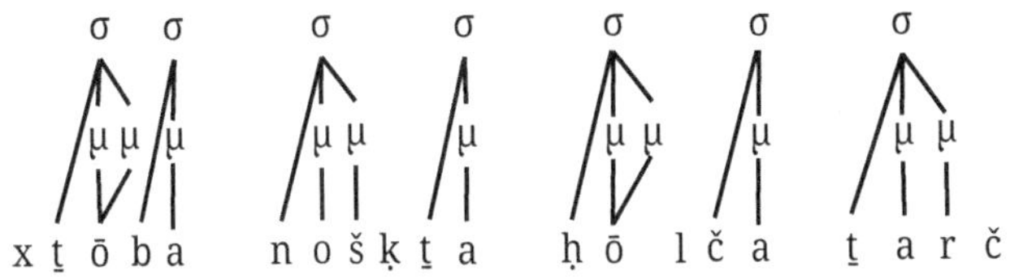

(d) Association of stray consonants to word nodes

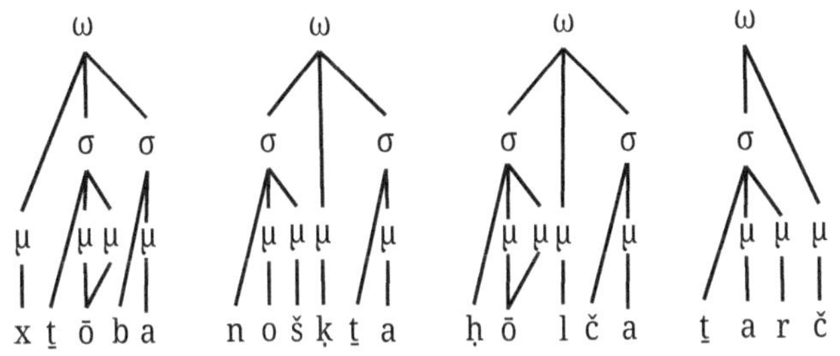

8.3.5 Vowel epenthesis and resyllabification

Inspired by Kiparsky's (2003: 156–157) analysis, I propose the following account of vowel epenthesis in Maaloula Aramaic. Vowel epenthesis

(i) occurs between a syllabified consonant and a following stray consonant,
(ii) is a postlexical process,
(iii) and occurs within and across word boundaries.

(i) Vowel epenthesis occurs between a syllabified consonant and a following stray consonant.

I showed in Section 8.3.4 that some consonants remain extrasyllabic or stray. At the postlexical level, an epenthetic [ə] is inserted between a syllabified consonant (represented by $C]_\sigma$) and a following stray consonant (represented by C′). In (30), I show the difference between the rule based on consonant counting ((30a) originally introduced in (8)) and the alternative rule based on syllable structure (30b) (for a similar evaluation of Yawelmani epenthesis rules, see Hayes 2009: 264–266).

(30) *Vowel epenthesis in Maaloula Aramaic*

(a) consonant-based rule: Ø → ə / C__C$\left\{\begin{matrix}\#\\ C\end{matrix}\right\}$

(b) syllable-based rule: Ø → ə / C]$_{\sigma}$__C′

Rule (30b) has many advantages over (30a), one of which is that it answers the question of what the two environments CCC and CC# have in common (the first question in Section 8.2.2). Rule (30b) does not consider word boundaries and focuses instead on the syllable boundary and the stray consonants remaining outside it. This also means that (30b) provides an adequate answer to the second question, which problematized the role of the syllable in the epenthesis process.

Vowel epenthesis triggers a resyllabification process in which the coda of the previous syllable becomes the onset of a new syllable whose nucleus is the epenthetic vowel and whose coda is the stray consonant. In (31), I show how epenthesis and resyllabification apply, using the same examples from (28). It can be noticed that in many words in (31) (e.g., (31a)) epenthesis does not apply even when there is a stray consonant in the word. This is because the existence of a stray consonant is not the only component of the environment C]$_{\sigma}$__C′. For epenthesis to take place, the stray consonant has to be preceded by a syllabified consonant.

(31) *Epenthesis and resyllabification in the environment C]$_{\sigma}$__C′*

(a) Word-initial stray consonants

underlying forms	lexical level	postlexical level		
/xṯāb-a/	→ [⟨x⟩.ˈṯō.ba]	→ [⟨x⟩.ˈṯō.ba]	‘book’	IV.36
/ʕṣofr-a/	→ [⟨ʕ⟩.ˈṣof.ra]	→ [⟨ʕ⟩.ˈṣof.ra]	‘morning’	IV.256
/blāt-a/	→ [⟨b⟩.ˈlō.ta]	→ [⟨b⟩.ˈlō.ta]	‘village’	IV.12
/mšīḥ-a/	→ [⟨m⟩.ˈšī.ḥa]	→ [⟨m⟩.ˈšī.ḥa]	‘Christ’	III.154
/xšūr-a/	→ [⟨x⟩.ˈšū.ra]	→ [⟨x⟩.ˈšū.ra]	‘wood’	IV.334

(b) Word-medial stray consonants

underlying forms	lexical level	postlexical level		
/nošḳ-T-a/	→ [ˈnoš.⟨ḳ⟩.ṯa]	→ [ˈno.šə̱ḳ.ṯa]	‘kiss’	V.37
/berk-T-a/	→ [ˈber.⟨k⟩.ṯa]	→ [ˈbe.rə̱k.ṯa]	‘Saint Thecla’	III.180
/ġabrn-ā/	→ [ġab.⟨r⟩.ˈnō]	→ [ġa.bə̱r.ˈnō]	‘men’	III.364
/ḥāl-T-a/	→ [ˈḥō.⟨l⟩.ča]	→ [ˈḥō.⟨l⟩.ča]	‘maternal aunt’	IV.166
/ḳāḏ̣y-a/	→ [ˈḳō.⟨ḏ̣⟩.ya]	→ [ˈḳō.⟨ḏ̣⟩.ya]	‘judge’	IV.146

(c) Word-final stray consonants

underlying forms	lexical level	postlexical level		
/ṯarč/	→ [ˈṯar.⟨č⟩]	→ [ˈṯa.rə̱č]	'two (F)'	III.274
/ʕisr/	→ [ˈʕis.⟨r⟩]	→ [ˈʕi.sə̱r]	'twenty'	III.304
/yarḥ/	→ [ˈyar.⟨ḥ⟩]	→ [ˈya.rə̱ḥ]	'months (EPL)'	IV.142
/mōn/	→ [ˈmō.⟨n⟩]	→ [ˈmō.⟨n⟩]	'who'	IV.296
/lōb/	→ [ˈlō.⟨b⟩]	→ [ˈlō.⟨b⟩]	'if'	III.120

(d) Stray consonants in more than one position

underlying forms	lexical level	postlexical level		
/klēsy-a/	→ [⟨k⟩.ˈlē.⟨s⟩.ya]	→ [⟨k⟩.ˈlē.⟨s⟩.ya]	'church'	III.166
/ṯlēṯ/	→ [⟨ṯ⟩.ˈlē.⟨ṯ⟩]	→ [⟨ṯ⟩.ˈlē.⟨ṯ⟩]	'thirty'	IV.262
/sčafḳt-e/	→ [⟨s⟩.ˈčaf.⟨ḳ⟩.te]	→ [⟨s⟩.ˈča.fə̱ḳ.te]	'he checked up on him'	IV.214

The account of epenthesis I propose is illustrated in (32) by showing the resyllabification of the same four words whose lexical syllabification has been shown in (29). In these words, the stray consonants occur in word-initial, word-medial, and word-final positions:

(32) *Epenthesis and resyllabification illustrated*

(a) Input (lexical level)

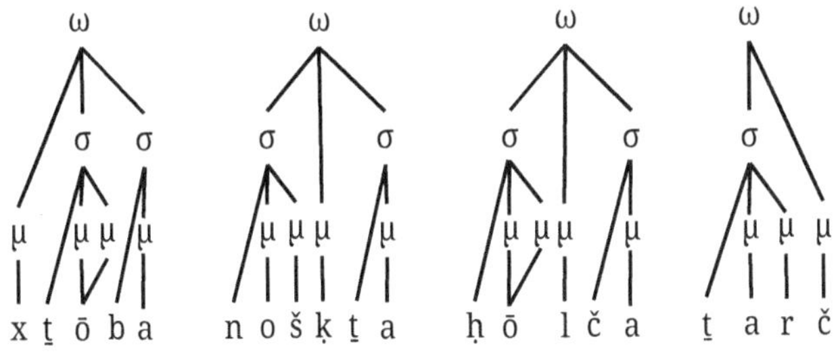

(b) Vowel epenthesis

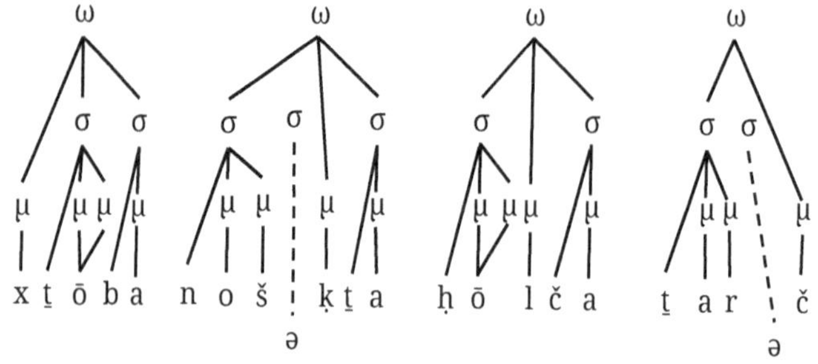

(c) Resyllabification

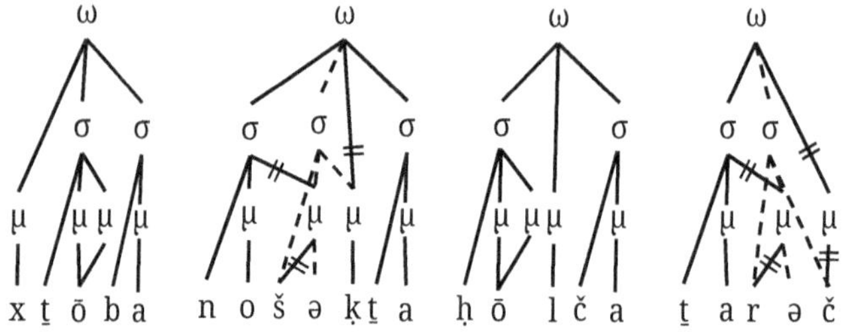

(d) Output (postlexical level)

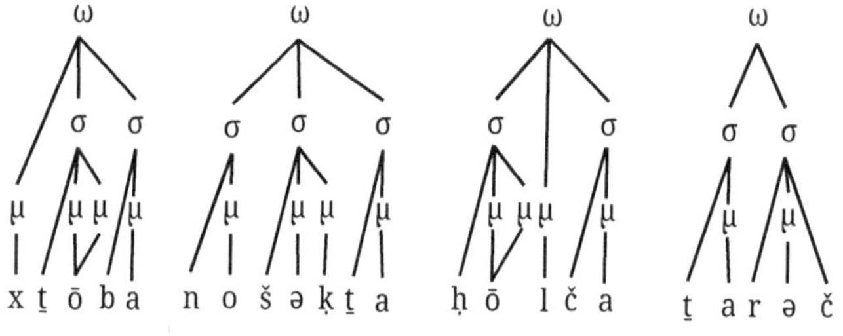

(ii) Vowel epenthesis is a postlexical process.

The assumption that syllabification and stress assignment are lexical processes while epenthesis and resyllabification are postlexical processes solves the problem posed by the opaque relation between epenthesis and stress (the third question in Section 8.2.2). The postlexically formed syllables, whose nuclei are the epenthetic vowel [ə], are not visible to stress because stress assignment applies earlier, taking only the available lexical syllables into account. In (33), for example, the postlexical syllable [šə̱ḳ]$_\sigma$ is formed too late to interact with stress.

(33) *A derivation to illustrate the interaction between vowel epenthesis and stress*

'kiss' V.37	
/nošḳ-T-a/	
nošḳṯa	/T/ spirantization
noš.⟨ḳ⟩.ṯa	syllabification
ˈ**noš**.⟨ḳ⟩.ṯa	**stress assignment**
ˈnoš.⟨ḳ⟩.ṯa	lexical form
ˈnoš.**ə̱**⟨ḳ⟩.ṯa	**vowel epenthesis**
ˈno.**šə̱ḳ**.ṯa	**resyllabification**
[ˈno.šə̱ḳ.ṯa]	postlexical form

If epenthesis and resyllabification were to apply lexically (as in (34)), then the penultimate syllable [šə̱ḳ]$_\sigma$ would be eligible for stress, and the resulting word would be *[no.ˈšə̱ḳ.ṯa].

(34) *A derivation that gives the wrong output*

/nošḳ-T-a/	
nošḳṯa	/T/ spirantization
noš.⟨ḳ⟩.ṯa	syllabification
noš.**ə̱**⟨ḳ⟩.ṯa	**vowel epenthesis**
no.**šə̱ḳ**.ṯa	**resyllabification**
*no.ˈ**šə̱ḳ**.ṯa	**stress assignment**
*[no.ˈšə̱ḳ.ṯa]	surface form

This syllable-based analysis provides deeper insight into word stress in Maaloula Aramaic. On the one hand, it comprehensively explains the interaction between stress and syllabification, and on the other hand, it is capable of providing a stress algorithm for the language in moraic terms. This moraic version of the stress algorithm is presented in Section 10.2.

(iii) Vowel epenthesis occurs within as well as across word boundaries.

The domain of postlexical resyllabification is the phonological phrase, rather than the phonological word. Therefore, epenthesis applies whenever a stray consonant is preceded by a coda consonant even when they are separated by a word boundary, as the examples below show.

(35) underlying form	lexical level	postlexical level	
/ex ḥmīr-a/	→ [ˈʔex#⟨ḥ⟩.ˈmī.ra]	→ [ˈʔe.xə̱ḥ.ˈmī.ra]	‘like dough’ III.28
/ḳalles d̠lūḳ-a/	→ [ˈḳal.les#⟨d̠⟩.ˈlū.ḳa]	→ [ˈḳal.le.sə̱d̠.ˈlū.ḳa]	‘some firewood’ IV.108
/balleš ṣyūḥ-a/	→ [ˈbal.leš#⟨ṣ⟩.ˈyū.ḥa]	→ [ˈbal.le.šə̱ṣ.ˈyū.ḥa]	‘he started shouting’ III.354

This assumption is also in line with the available literature on both Maaloula Aramaic and Arabic which clearly shows that word boundaries and syllable boundaries do not necessarily match (see Arnold 1990a: 39 for Maaloula Aramaic and Broselow 2017: 36 for Arabic).

8.3.6 Glottal epenthesis and resyllabification

In Section 8.2.3, I showed that glottal epenthesis in Maaloula Aramaic applies at the beginning of word-initial onsetless syllables (i.e., Ø → ʔ / [$_\sigma$__V). The question that has remained open from Section 8.2.3 is: Why does this glottal epenthesis rule apply obligatorily after a pause, as in (36a), and obligatorily in a hiatus context (i.e., V#__V), as in (36b), but optionally when the preceding word ends in a consonant (i.e., C#__V), as in (36c)? In other words, why does glottal epenthesis seem to apply obligatorily in one environment and optionally in another?

(36) (a) [ʔ]***orḥa*** *nōb p-xarmō* ‘once I was in the vineyards’ III.338
(b) *ʕa payt̠il mīt̠a* [ʔ]***orḥa*** *ḥrīt̠a* ‘to the dead person’s house again’ III.216
(c) *hōd̠‿**orḥa*** IV.188 ~ *hōʔ* ***ʔorḥa*** IV.196 ‘this time’

I argue that glottal epenthesis does not apply obligatorily in one environment and optionally in another as the examples in (36) may suggest. Glottal epenthesis always applies obligatorily. However, it is the interaction between postlexical resyllabification and glottal epenthesis that is responsible for this inconsistency in the application of glottal epenthesis.

Resyllabification applies across word boundaries in the C#V environment, turning the final consonant in the preceding word into an onset for the onsetless syllable in the following word (e.g., *hōd̠‿orḥa* [hō.**d̠**or.ḥa] in (36c)). Why does resyllabification (rather than glottal epenthesis) apply here although the conditions for glottal epenthesis are met? Resyllabification is ordered before glottal epenthesis.

When resyllabification applies, it bleeds (or blocks) glottal epenthesis because the environment [$_\sigma$__V is no longer present.

However, resyllabification is an optional process. It does not apply if hesitations interrupt the flow of connected speech or if the words are spoken in isolation. In these cases where resyllabification does not apply, glottal epenthesis applies because the conditions are met (i.e., the environment [$_\sigma$__V is present) (e.g., *hōʔ ʔorḥa* in (36c)) (a similar analysis of the interaction between glottal epenthesis and resyllabification in Cairene Arabic is presented in Watson 2002: 232–233).

To illustrate this interaction between resyllabification and glottal epenthesis, I provide a derivation for the three examples shown in (36) above (for the other phonological rules involved in this derivation, see Section 7.3.1 for /ā/ rounding, and Section 7.2.5 for the assimilation of /ḏ/ in the demonstrative pronoun *hōḏ*).

(37) *A derivation to illustrate the interaction between resyllabification and glottal epenthesis*

/orḥ-a/	/mīṯ-a orḥ-a/	/hāḏ orḥ-a/		
or.ḥa	mī.ṯa or.ḥa	hā.⟨ḏ⟩ or.ḥa		syllabification
–	–	h**ō**.⟨ḏ⟩ or.ḥa		/ā/ rounding
–	–	hō.**ḏor**.ḥa	–	**resyllabification**
ʔor.ḥa	mī.ṯa **ʔ**or.ḥa	–	hō.⟨ḏ⟩ **ʔ**or.ḥa	**glottal epenthesis**
–	–	–	hō.⟨**ʔ**⟩ **ʔ**or.ḥa	/ḏ/ assimilation
[**ʔ**or.ḥa]	[mī.ṯa **ʔ**or.ḥa]	[hō.**ḏ**or.ḥa]	[hō.⟨ʔ⟩ **ʔ**or.ḥa]	

This derivation shows that glottal epenthesis applies obligatorily whenever there is an onsetless syllable. However, if resyllabification applies before it (e.g., in [hō.**ḏor**.ḥa]), resyllabification bleeds glottal epenthesis. If resyllabification does not apply (as it is an optional rule), then glottal epenthesis applies (e.g., in [hō.⟨ʔ⟩ **ʔ**or.ḥa]). Resyllabification and glottal epenthesis have the same aim here. Both provide onsets for illegal onsetless syllables, but they do it in different ways. Resyllabification turns the final consonant in the preceding word into an onset for the onsetless syllable, and glottal epenthesis inserts a glottal stop in the empty onset slot.

8.3.7 A cross-linguistic perspective

Although Maaloula Aramaic is not a variety of Arabic, it bears similarities with the surrounding Arabic dialects. This should come as no surprise, given the fact that they are all Semitic varieties, and given that Aramaic has been in contact with Arabic over many centuries. Maaloula Aramaic is more similar to VC-dialects than to CV-dialects. For example, in both Maaloula Aramaic and Damascus Arabic, the epenthetic vowel is inserted before the stray consonant (see (38)). Moreover, the relation between stress and vowel epenthesis is opaque in both varieties because vowel epenthesis applies postlexically (see Kiparsky 2003: 150, 156–157).

(38)

	underlying forms	lexical level	postlexical level	
Maaloula Aramaic	/ṯarč/	→ [ˈṯar.⟨č⟩]	→ [ˈṯa.ra̱č]	'two (F)' III.274
Damascus Arabic	/daras-t/	→ [da.ˈras.⟨t⟩]	→ [da.ˈra.sa̱t]	'I studied' Cowell 1964: 19

However, in Cairene Arabic, according to Kiparsky (2003: 157) and as example (39) shows, the epenthetic vowel [i] is inserted at the lexical level immediately after the consonant that would otherwise be left unsyllabified. This is because stray consonants are not allowed to surface either lexically or postlexically. That epenthesis applies lexically makes all syllables, including the one which contains the epenthetic vowel, equally visible to stress.

(39) *Epenthesis and syllabification in Cairene Arabic (a CV-dialect)*

underlying form	surface form (lexical and postlexical)		
/bint-na/	→ [bin.ˈti̱.na]	'our daughter'	(Kiparsky 2003: 150)

On the other hand, the ability of Maaloula Aramaic to tolerate CCC sequences word-medially and word-initially (as seen in (11) above) makes it similar to the C-dialects of Arabic (see Hellmuth 2013: 56). Since Maaloula Aramaic shows features of both VC- and C-dialects (as illustrated in (40)), I propose to call it a vC-dialect to distinguish it from VC- and C-dialects. Future research will have to determine whether further Semitic varieties belong to this category.

(40) *Maaloula Aramaic compared to the different Arabic dialect groups*

	Maaloula Aramaic	**Arabic VC-dialects**	**Arabic CV-dialects**	**Arabic C-dialects**
Medial CCC	surfaces as CV̲CC / CCC	surfaces as CV̲CC	surfaces as CCV̲C	surfaces as CCC
Phrase-final CC	variation in the application of vowel epenthesis	not permitted/ permitted (only with falling sonority)	permitted	permitted
Phrase-initial CC	permitted	permitted (but may be broken up by a prosthetic vowel)	not permitted	permitted
Initial geminates	permitted	permitted (but may be broken up by a prosthetic vowel)	not permitted	permitted
Non-final CVVC	permitted	permitted	shortened	permitted
Epenthesis/stress interaction	opaque	opaque	not opaque	no epenthesis

8.4 Two adjacent stray consonants

So far, I have investigated the words which contain single stray consonants. In this section, I turn to the words which contain two adjacent stray consonants (hereafter C′C′).

Most of the words containing C′C′ in my word list are the result of morphosyntactic processes. Nearly all of the attested words are word forms (or morphosyntactic words) rather than lexemes that can be listed as dictionary entries. This can be easily verified by checking Arnold's (2019) dictionary, in which only three of the attested words appear as lemmas. These three words are shown in (41).

(41) underlying forms surface forms (lexical and postlexical)

/bāyk-T-a/	→	[ˈbō.⟨y⟩⟨k⟩.ṯa]	‘stable (for animals)’	III.366
/ṭāyf-T-a/	→	[ˈṭō.⟨y⟩⟨f⟩.ṯa][14]	‘(religious) denomination’	III.260
/māyt-T-a/	→	[ˈmō.⟨y⟩⟨ṯ⟩.ṯa][15]	‘altar table; dining table’	III.234

14 In the original text, it is spelled as *tōyfṯa*.

15 This word appears as *mōyṯṯa* in Arnold’s transcription of the narrative (III.234) but as *mayṯṯa* ~ *mayṯṯa* in Arnold's (2019: 582) dictionary. In the example above, I cite the former. The underlying /t/ assimilates to the following [ṯ].

Apart from these three words, all the other attested words are word forms that result from morphosyntactic processes, such as suffixation (42a-b), formation of the enumerative plural (42c), root-and-pattern morphology (e.g., inflected verbs which belong to specific verb Forms, such as Form I_8 (see Arnold 1990a: 93) and Form I_{10} (see Arnold 1990a: 96)) (42d), and the concatenation of words in connected speech (42e).

(42) *Morphosyntactic processes leading to C′C′*

(a) C′C′ resulting from the suffixation of *-l* [16]

mōr-l	*ḥaḳl-a*	[ˈmō.⟨**r**⟩⟨**l**⟩# ˈḥaḳ.la] → [ˈmō.rə̲l.ˈḥaḳ.la]
owner-CST	field-NE	
'owner of the field'		III.94

(b) C′C′ resulting from the suffixation of *-xun* 'your (M.PL)'

bawwōp-č-xun	[baw.ˈwō.⟨**p**⟩⟨**č**⟩.xun]
gate-F-2M.PL	
'your (M.PL) gate'	III.306

(c) C′C′ resulting from enumerative plural formation[17]

šōht-Ø	[ˈšō.⟨**h**⟩⟨**t**⟩] → [ˈšō.hə̲t]
witness-EPL	
'witnesses (EPL)'	III.372

(d) C′C′ resulting from root-and-pattern morphology[18]

nčḳ-al-l-e	[⟨**n**⟩⟨**č**⟩.ˈḳal.le]
meet.PRET-3F.SG-OM-3M.SG	
'she met him'	IV.154

16 The suffix *-l* connects two nouns in the genitive construction (see Correll 1978: 6; Arnold 1990a: 301–302).

17 The enumerative plural is the plural form used after numerals (Arnold 1990a: 289).

18 As I have shown in Section 2.4, Arnold (1990a: 53–54) classifies Maaloula Aramaic verbs into eleven Forms: I, II, III, IV, I_2, II_2, III_2, IV_2, I_7, I_8, and I_{10}. In the verbal Form I_8, the infix *-č-* is inserted after the first radical (Arnold 1990a: 65). In certain inflectional forms, however, such as *nčḳalle* 'she met him' (whose root is *nḳy* Arnold 2019: 617), the infix *-č-* is inserted after the first radical *n* and immediately before the second radical *ḳ*, resulting in a #CCC sequence. From a cross-linguistic perspective, the Maaloula Aramaic verbal Form I_8 corresponds to the Arabic verbal Form VIII, and the Maaloula Aramaic infix *-č-* corresponds to the Arabic infix *-t-* (see, e.g., Watson 2002: 134).

(e) C′C′ resulting from the concatenation of words in connected speech

ṯarč	*ḏrōʕ-Ø*	[ˈṯar.⟨**č**⟩#⟨**ḏ**⟩.ˈrō.⟨ʕ⟩] → [ˈṯar.čə̱ḏ.ˈrō.⟨ʕ⟩]
two.F	cubit-EPL	
‘two cubits’		III.110

8.4.1 Epenthesis in the case of C′C′

As can be seen from examples (42a, c, e) above, these C′C′ clusters rarely surface because an epenthetic vowel is usually inserted between them. This generalization can be expressed as a phonological rule:

(43) *Vowel epenthesis in case of C′C′*

Ø → ə / C′__C′

The following words provide further examples of this rule:

(44) *Epenthesis in the environment C′__C′*

ṭaššr-īš-n-Ø	[ṭaš.ˈrī.⟨š⟩⟨n⟩] → [ṭaš.ˈrī.šə̱n][19]
leave.PRET-2F.SG-LM-1SG	
‘you (F.SG) left me’	IV.320
ẓx-īč-n-Ø	[⟨ẓ⟩.ˈxī.⟨č⟩⟨n⟩] → [⟨ẓ⟩.ˈxī.čə̱n]
defeat.PRET-2M.SG-LM-1SG	
‘you (M.SG) defeated me’	IV.138
līṭr-Ø[20]	[ˈlī.⟨ṭ⟩⟨r⟩] → [ˈlī.ṭə̱r]
rotl-EPL	
‘rotls (EPL)’	III.274
ḥōl-č-Ø	[ˈḥō.⟨l⟩⟨č⟩] → [ˈḥō.lə̱č]
uncle-F-1SG	
‘my maternal aunt’	IV.130

19 The underlying geminate /šš/ surfaces as [š] because geminates are realized as singletons in preconsonantal position (see Section 9.3.2 as well as Arnold 1990a: 17).

20 *līṭər* in the original text.

Epenthesis in the environment C′__C′ can also apply across word boundaries. This can be seen in example (42e) which is repeated below for convenience:

(45) *ṯarč* *ḏrōʕ-Ø* [ˈṯar.⟨č⟩#⟨ḏ⟩.ˈrō.⟨ʕ⟩] → [ˈṯar.čəḏ.ˈrō.⟨ʕ⟩]
two.F cubit-EPL
'two cubits' III.110

Example (45) reveals another similarity between Maaloula Aramaic and Damascus Arabic. In both varieties, if the C′C′ sequence results from the concatenation of two words in connected speech, an epenthetic vowel is inserted between them, and the two stray consonants are resyllabified around the epenthetic vowel at the postlexical level (see (46) for a Damascus Arabic example).

(46) *bənt* *ẓġīr-e* [ˈbən.⟨t⟩#⟨ẓ⟩.ˈġī.re] → [ˈbən.təẓ.ˈġī.re]
girl little-F
'a little girl' Cowell 1964: 29

Not only is the phrase *ṯarč ḏrōʕ*, given in (45), an example of epenthesis that applies across word boundaries, but it is also an interesting case that would meet the conditions of both epenthesis rules which have been introduced in (30b) (i.e., Ø → ə / C]$_σ$__C′) and (43) (i.e., Ø → ə / C′__C′). This raises the question of why (43) is applied, and not (30b). I propose that directionality is responsible for this. According to Itô's (1989) notion of directionality, syllabification can go either from left to right in some languages (e.g., Cairene Arabic) or from right to left in other languages (e.g., Iraqi Arabic).

In Maaloula Aramaic, I clearly distinguish between lexical syllabification and postlexical resyllabification. In Section 8.3.3, I showed that in lexical syllabification, the nucleus is formed first, then the onset, and then the coda. In other words, lexical syllabification seems to spread from the center (the nucleus) to the left (the onset) and then to the right (the coda). This means that it goes neither exclusively from left to right, nor exclusively from right to left.

In contrast, postlexical epenthesis and resyllabification have a clear direction: right-to-left. As can be seen in (47b), the epenthetic vowel is inserted before the right stray consonant [ḏ] and not before the left stray consonant [č]. The resyllabification, shown in (47c), preempts (or bleeds) the epenthesis rule in the C]$_σ$__C′ environment because [č] is no longer a stray consonant. Thus, (43) bleeds (30b).

(47) *Right-to-left resyllabification in Maaloula Aramaic*

(a) Input (lexical level)

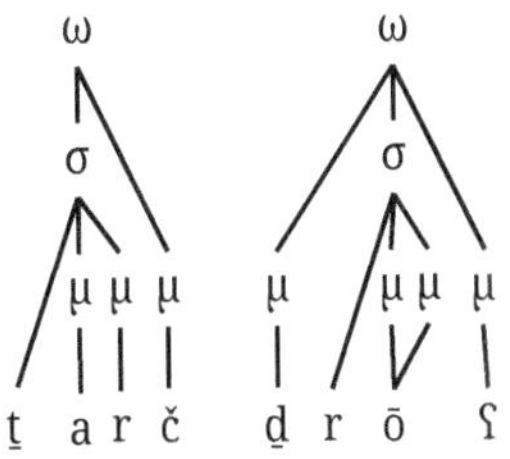

(b) Vowel epenthesis

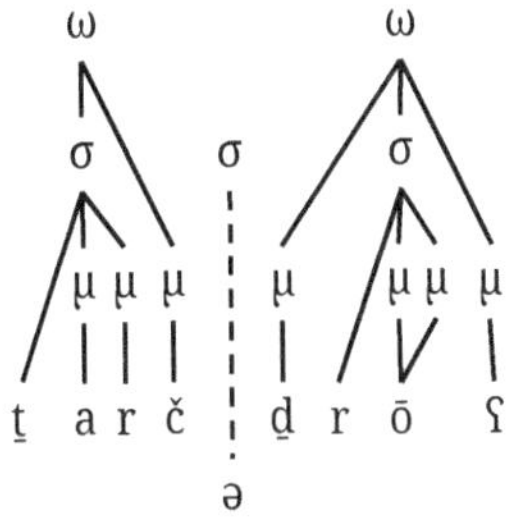

(c) Resyllabification

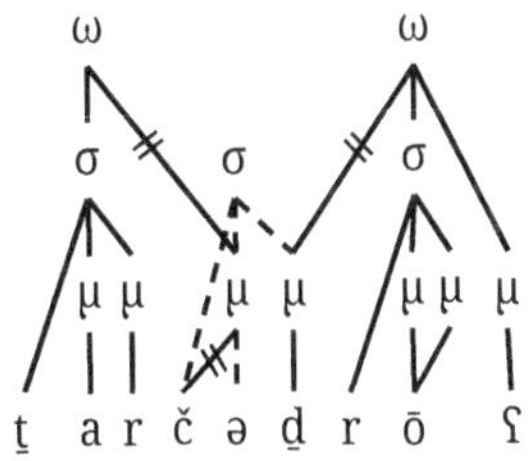

(d) Output (postlexical level)

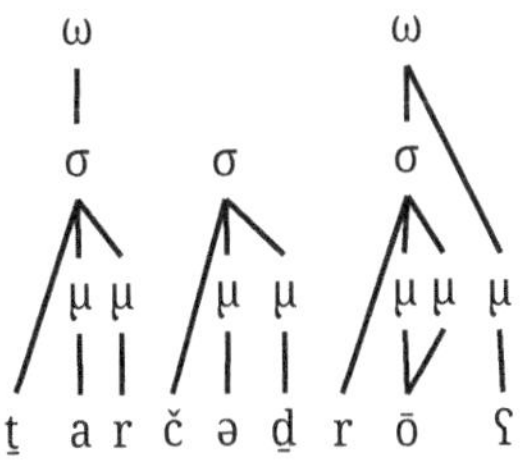

8.4.2 C′C′ yet no epenthesis

The rule Ø → ə / C′__C′ applies to many words in Maaloula Aramaic, as the examples in the previous section show. However, this rule is blocked in certain words in which C′C′ are immediately followed by an onset consonant within the same word (i.e., #..C′C′σ..#). It is this specific environment that the four attested words in (11), repeated here as (48), have in common. These data had prompted the question as to why epenthesis is not permissible even though there is a consonant cluster (the fourth question in Section 8.2.2):

(48) (a) word-initial CCC clusters (i.e., #CCC-)

sčfītič	(and not **sə̲čfītič*)	'you (M.SG) benefitted'	V.39
sčfēt	(and not **sə̲čfēt*)	'benefit!'	V.39

(b) word-medial CCC clusters (i.e., -CCC-)

sūsčxen	(and not **sūsə̲čxen*)	'your (F.PL) horse'	V.38
frīsčxun	(and not **frīsə̲čxun*)	'your (M.PL) right'	V.38

By applying the syllabification scheme presented in this chapter to the words in (48), one can notice the presence of the #..C′C′σ..# environment (see (49)). In these CCC clusters, C_1 and C_2 are two adjacent stray consonants, and C_3 is an onset consonant of the following syllable:

(49) *Syllabification of the words in (48)*

(a) word-initial CCC clusters (i.e., #CCC-)

underlying forms		lexical and postlexical forms	ungrammatical forms
/sčfīt-ič/	→	[⟨s⟩⟨č⟩.ˈfī.tič]	*[sə̱č.ˈfī.tič]
/sčfēt/	→	[⟨s⟩⟨č⟩.ˈfēt]	*[sə̱č.ˈfēt]

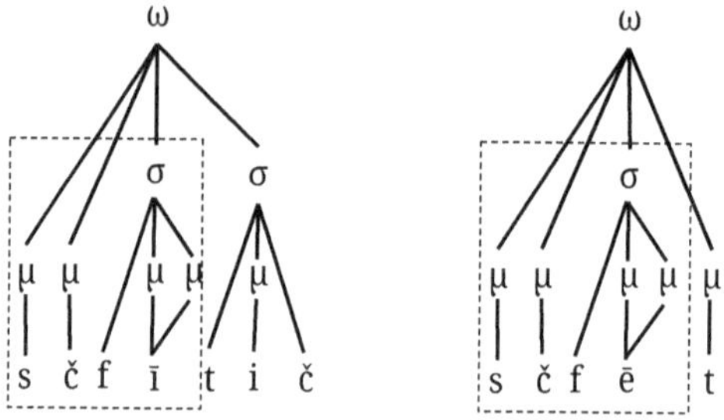

(b) word-medial CCC clusters (i.e., -CCC-)

underlying forms		lexical and postlexical forms	ungrammatical forms
/sūs-T-xen/	→	[ˈsū.⟨s⟩⟨č⟩.xen]	*[ˈsū.sə̱č.xen]
/frīs-T-xun/	→	[⟨f⟩.ˈrī.⟨s⟩⟨č⟩.xun]	*[⟨f⟩.ˈrī.sə̱č.xun]

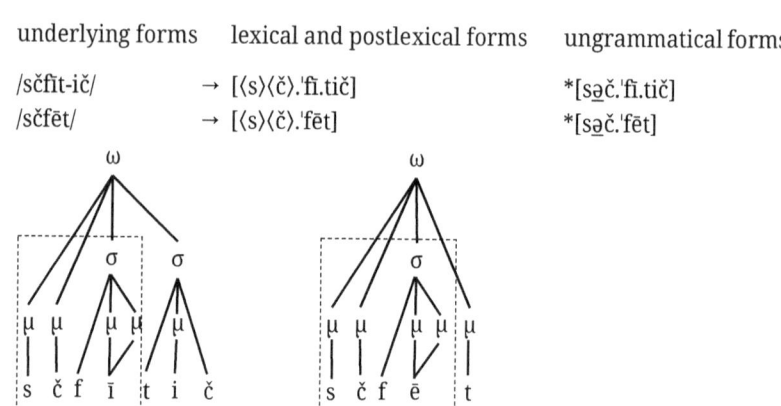

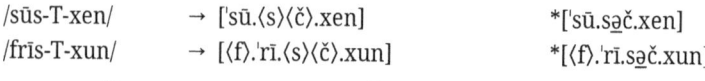

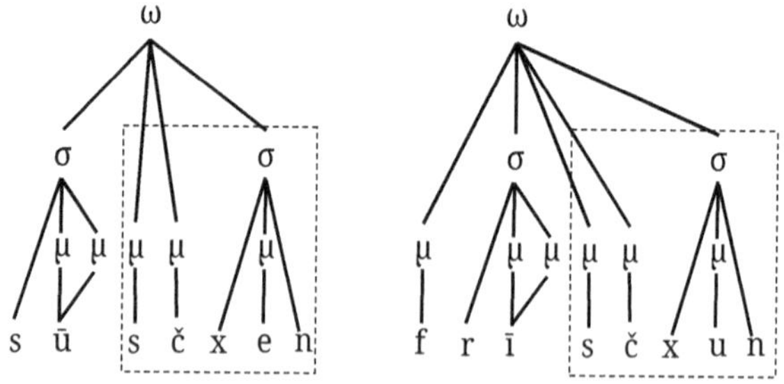

These four examples are not the only words with the environment #..C′C′σ..# in Maaloula Aramaic. The data set contains further examples of this epenthesis-blocking environment. A careful examination of these examples shows that they are not random exceptions as they share interesting structural properties. To lay out these properties, I will classify these words into two groups according to the position of C′C′ inside them (i.e., words with initial C′C′ and words with medial C′C′).

Words with initial C′C′

The corpus and elicited data include 24 words with initial C′C′, in all of which C'_2 = [č]. These words are inflected forms of only seven different verbs. The words in (50) represent one example from each verb.

(50) *Structural analysis of the words with initial C′C′*

(a) *nčḳ-al-l-e* [⟨n⟩⟨**č**⟩.ˈḳal.le] (*[nə̱č.ˈḳal.le])
meet.PRET-3F.SG-OM-3M.SG
'she met him' IV.154

(b) *sčfēt* [⟨s⟩⟨**č**⟩.ˈfē⟨t⟩] (*[sə̱č.ˈfēt])
benefit.IMP.2M.SG
'benefit!' V.39

(c) *sčliḳ-Ø-n-e* [21] [⟨s⟩⟨**č**⟩.ˈliḳ.ne] (*[sə̱č.ˈliḳ.ne])
catch.PRET-3M.SG-LM-3M.SG
'he caught it/him' IV.240

(d) *ščḥ-ačč-e* [⟨š⟩⟨**č**⟩.ˈḥač.če] (*[šə̱č.ˈḥač.če])
find.PRET-3F.SG-3M.SG
'she found him' IV.252

(e) *ščġel-l-ax* [⟨š⟩⟨**č**⟩.ˈġel.lax] (*[šə̱č.ˈġel.lax])
work.IMP-OM-2M.SG
'work!' IV.108

(f) *xčlīf-in* [⟨x⟩⟨**č**⟩.ˈlī.fin] (*[xə̱č.ˈlī.fin])
argue.PRF-M.PL
'they [were/have been] arguing' IV.86

(g) *žčmīʕ-in* [⟨ž⟩⟨**č**⟩.ˈmī.ʕin] (*[žə̱č.ˈmī.ʕin])
gather.PRF-M.PL
'gathered together' III.252

The templates in (51) represent the syllable structure of these words.

21 Incorrectly written as *sčlīḳle* in the original text.

(51) *Templates of words with initial C'C'*

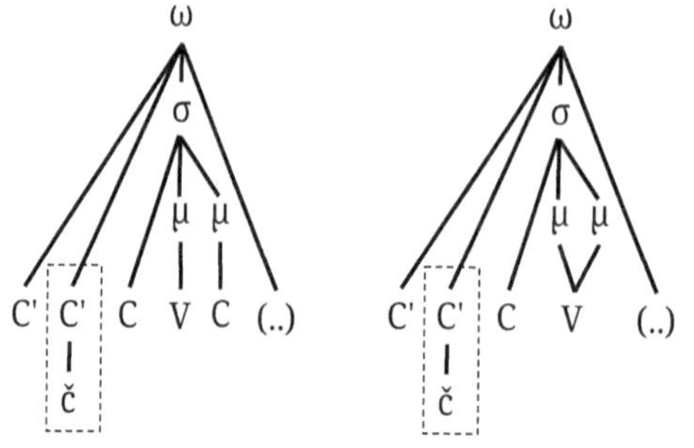

If this generalization is compared with what the literature says about Damascus Arabic, another similarity can be drawn. Cowell (1964: 25) indicates that word-initial CCC clusters are attested in Damascus Arabic but only in few words beginning with [st] (see (52)).

(52) underlying forms		surface forms (lexical and postlexical)		
/strīḥ/	→	[⟨s⟩⟨t⟩.ˈrīḥ]	'rest!'	Cowell 1964: 25
/stfīd/	→	[⟨s⟩⟨t⟩.ˈfīd]	'benefit!'	Cowell 1964: 25

It seems that the words that begin in #C'C' are not many in either variety, and that the segments filling the C'_2 slot are strictly limited to one specific consonant in each variety ([č] in Maaloula Aramaic and [t] in Damascus Arabic). With regard to the segments filling the C'_1 slot, they are more varied in Maaloula Aramaic than in Damascus Arabic.

Words with medial C'C'

The attested words with medial C'C' are more numerous and can be further divided into two groups. The first group is the result of a productive suffixation process whereby the suffixes *-xun* 'your (M.PL)' and *-xen* 'your (F.PL)' are attached to base words of a specific structure. These base words are feminine nouns marked by the feminine morpheme /T/, and they have a long vowel (e.g., [ī], [ō], [ū]) in the last syllable of the base. The suffixation process concatenates C'C' between the long vowel of the base and the consonant-initial suffix *-xun* or *-xen*. The C'_2 position is always occupied by an allomorph of the feminine morpheme /T/ (either [č] or [ṯ]). The words in (53) exemplify this group.[22]

(53) underlying forms surface forms (lexical and postlexical)

/sūs-T-xen/	→	[ˈsū.⟨s⟩⟨č⟩.xen]	'your (F.PL) horse'	V.38
/frīs-T-xun/	→	[⟨f⟩.ˈrī.⟨s⟩⟨č⟩.xun]	'your (M.PL) right'	V.38
/bawwāb-T-xun/	→	[baw.ˈwō.⟨p⟩⟨č⟩.xun][23]	'your (M.PL) gate'	III.306
/ḥāl-T-xen/	→	[ˈḥō.⟨l⟩⟨č⟩.xen]	'your (F.PL) aunt'	FW
/ġmāʕ-T-xun/	→	[ˈ⟨ġ⟩.mō.⟨ʕ⟩⟨č⟩.xun]	'your (M.PL) group'	FW
/ḏār-T-xun/	→	[ˈḏō.⟨r⟩⟨č⟩.xun]	'your (M.PL) house'	FW
/mḏīn-T-xun/	→	[⟨m⟩.ˈḏī.⟨n⟩⟨č⟩.xun]	'your (M.PL) city'	FW
/mrāy-T-xen/	→	[⟨m⟩.ˈrō.⟨y⟩⟨ṯ⟩.xen]	'your (F.PL) mirror'	FW
/ṯulṯōy-T-xun/	→	[ṯul.ˈṯō.⟨y⟩⟨ṯ⟩.xun]	'your (M.PL) jar'	FW
/šičwōy-T-xun/	→	[šič.ˈwō.⟨y⟩⟨ṯ⟩.xun]	'your (M.PL) winter'	FW
/ṣayfōy-T-xun/	→	[ṣay.ˈfō.⟨y⟩⟨ṯ⟩.xun]	'your (M.PL) summer'	FW

The reason why one only finds inflectional forms with the suffixes *-xun* and *-xen*, and not with other suffixes, is that *-xun* and *-xen* are the only pronominal suffixes which begin with a consonant (see Arnold 1990a: 43 for a complete list of the pronominal suffixes). The suffixation to any other personal pronouns would not concatenate word-medial C′C′ as is shown in (54).

(54) underlying forms surface forms (lexical and postlexical)

/frīs-T-e/	→	[⟨f⟩.ˈrī.⟨s⟩.če]	'his right'	FW
/frīs-T-a/	→	[⟨f⟩.ˈrī.⟨s⟩.ča]	'her right'	FW
/frīs-T-un/	→	[⟨f⟩.ˈrī.⟨s⟩.čun]	'their (M) right'	FW
/frīs-T-en/	→	[⟨f⟩.ˈrī.⟨s⟩.čen]	'their (F) right'	FW
/frīs-T-ax/	→	[⟨f⟩.ˈrī.⟨s⟩.čax]	'your (M.SG) right'	FW
/frīs-T-iš/	→	[⟨f⟩.ˈrī.⟨s⟩.čiš]	'your (F.SG) right'	FW
/frīs-T-i/	→	[⟨f⟩.ˈrī.⟨s⟩.či]	'my right'	FW
/frīs-T-aḥ/	→	[⟨f⟩.ˈrī.⟨s⟩.čaḥ]	'our right'	FW
but				
/frīs-T-xun/	→	[⟨f⟩.ˈrī.⟨s⟩⟨č⟩.xun]	'your (M.PL) right'	V.38
/frīs-T-xen/	→	[⟨f⟩.ˈrī.⟨s⟩⟨č⟩.xen]	'your (F.PL) right'	FW

22 Only three examples are attested in the corpus and in Arnold's (1990a) grammar. The rest were elicited from my language consultant. Since this is a productive suffixation process, more word forms can still be generated.

23 /b/ is realized as [p] because it occurs before a voiceless consonant.

The second group of words with medial C′C′ includes three feminine nouns that were originally introduced in (41) and are repeated here as (55). Unlike the words in the first group, these words are lexemes (i.e., no inflectional processes are involved in their formation). All three words are structurally similar in that they have the long vowel [ō], C'_1 = [y], and the feminine marker occupies the position of the onset consonant following C'_2.

(55) underlying forms surface forms (lexical and postlexical)

/bāyk-T-a/	→	[ˈbō.⟨y⟩⟨k⟩.ṯa]	‘stable (for animals)’	III.366
/ṭāyf-T-a/	→	[ˈṭō.⟨y⟩⟨f⟩.ṯa]	‘(religious) denomination’	III.260
/māyt-T-a/	→	[ˈmō.⟨y⟩⟨ṯ⟩.ṯa]	‘altar table; dining table’	III.234

The structure of these two groups can be summarized by the template shown in (56).

(56) *Template of words with medial C′C′*

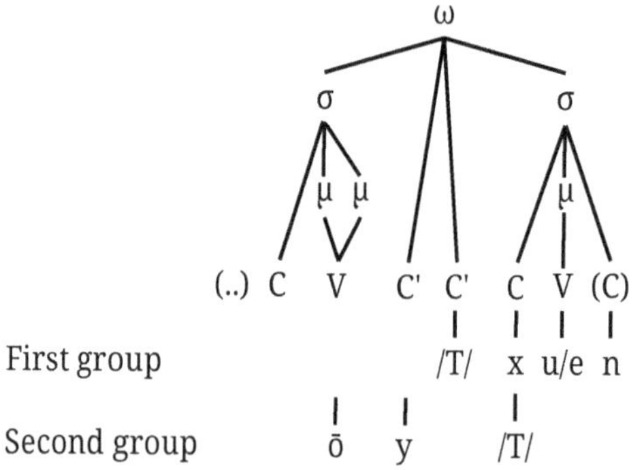

From a comparative perspective, this is where Maaloula Aramaic differs completely from Damascus Arabic (see the examples in (57)). In Damascus Arabic, an epenthetic vowel is inserted between two potential word-medial stray consonants (e.g. between [t] and [l] in [ka.tab.ˈtə̱l.ha] and in [⟨f⟩.ḍī.ˈtə̱l.kon]). The first example (i.e. [ka.tab.ˈtə̱l.ha]) is from Broselow (1992: 41) and Kiparsky (2003: 164), and the second example (i.e. [⟨f⟩.ḍī.ˈtə̱l.kon]) is from the author. As Kiparsky (2003: 163) explains, this epenthesis must apply lexically, which explains why in these examples the syllable [tə̱l]$_\sigma$ receives primary stress. If epenthesis applied postlexically (as it does in the case of single stray consonants), then this syllable would be invisible to stress, but this is obviously not the case. Maaloula Aramaic, however, does not seem to allow lexical epenthesis, which also means that it does not allow any interaction between epenthesis and stress. Nor does it allow postlexical epenthesis in the #..C′C′σ..# environment. Therefore, /frīs-T-xun/ surfaces as [⟨f⟩.ˈrī.⟨s⟩⟨č⟩.xun] at the lexical and postlexical levels.

(57)	underlying forms		surface forms (lexical and postlexical)	
Damascus Arabic	/katab-t-l-ha/	→	[ka.tab.ˈtə̲l.ha] 'I wrote to her'	*[ka.tab.⟨t⟩⟨l⟩.ha]
	/fḍī-t-l-kon/	→	[⟨f⟩.ḍī.ˈtə̲l.kon] '(now) I have time for you (PL)'[24]	*[⟨f⟩.ḍī.⟨t⟩⟨l⟩.kon]
Maaloula Aramaic	/frīs-T-xun/	→	[⟨f⟩.ˈrī.⟨s⟩⟨č⟩.xun] 'your (M.PL) right' V.38	*[⟨f⟩.rī.ˈsə̲č.xun]

8.5 Summary and discussion

The main goal of this chapter was to examine syllable structure and syllabification in Maaloula Aramaic from a cross-linguistic perspective. I have proposed a syllable-based analysis that draws on previous analyses of similar phonological processes in Arabic. The presented analysis successfully addresses most of the gaps and shortcomings of previous analyses. It highlights the role of the syllable and syllabic structure, rather than that of the segment or of the word boundary, in the vowel epenthesis process and also accounts for the opaque relation between epenthesis and stress.

The proposed approach can be summarized as follows. Maaloula Aramaic allows only three syllable types: CV, CVV, and CVC. These three syllable types are the result of a syllabification process which takes place at the lexical level. However, there are two types of marked structures that this syllabification process cannot repair: the onsetless syllables that are formed at the beginning of vowel-initial words and the unsyllabified (or stray) consonants. These marked structures are repaired at the postlexical level.

The word-initial onsetless syllables are repaired either by the resyllabification process which turns the final consonant in the preceding word into an onset for the onsetless syllable or by the glottal epenthesis process which inserts a glottal stop in the empty onset slot.

The stray consonants are repaired by the vowel epenthesis and resyllabification processes. An epenthetic vowel [ə ~ i] is inserted between a stray consonant (C′) and the preceding coda consonant. Epenthesis triggers a resyllabification process in which the coda of the preceding syllable becomes the onset of a new syllable, the

24 Literally: 'I've become free (of my obligations) to deal with you / attend to you.'

epenthetic vowel becomes the nucleus, and the stray consonant becomes the coda. These postlexically formed syllables are not visible to stress because stress rules are lexical.

If a morphosyntactic process leads to the concatenation of two stray consonants (C′C′), an epenthetic vowel is usually inserted between them. This epenthesis is blocked, however, in words with specific structural properties in which C′C′ are followed by an onset consonant within the same word (i.e., when the C′C′ sequence is in non-final position).

In summary, vowel epenthesis in Maaloula Aramaic applies according to the following rules:

Ø → ə / C]$_{\sigma}$__C′
Ø → ə / C′__C′ (exceptions are attested, but they are not random)
Insert an epenthetic vowel between a stray consonant and a preceding coda consonant, or between two stray consonants, except in words with specific structural properties in which the C′C′ sequence is in non-final position.

These rules are exemplified in (58) (for the other rules involved in this derivation, see Section 6.2.6 for /T/ palatalization and /T/ spirantization, and Section 7.3.1 for /ā/ rounding).

(58) *Syllabification, epenthesis, and resyllabification exemplified*

‘kiss’	‘two cubits’	‘your right’	
/nošḳ-T-a/	/ṯarč # ḏrāʕ/	/frīs-T-xun/	
–	–	frīs**č**xun	/T/ palatalization
nošḳ**ṯ**a	–	–	/T/ spirantization
noš.⟨ḳ⟩.ṯa	ṯar.⟨č⟩#⟨ḏ⟩.rā.⟨ʕ⟩	⟨f⟩.rī.⟨s⟩⟨č⟩.xun	syllabification
ˈ**noš**.⟨ḳ⟩.ṯa	ˈ**ṯar**.⟨č⟩#⟨ḏ⟩.ˈ**rā**.⟨ʕ⟩	⟨f⟩.ˈ**rī**.⟨s⟩⟨č⟩.xun	stress assignment
–	ˈṯar.⟨č⟩#⟨ḏ⟩.ˈr**ō**.⟨ʕ⟩	–	/ā/ rounding
ˈnoš.⟨ḳ⟩.ṯa	ˈṯar.⟨č⟩#⟨ḏ⟩.ˈrō.⟨ʕ⟩	⟨f⟩.ˈrī.⟨s⟩⟨č⟩.xun	lexical forms
ˈnoš.**ə̠**⟨ḳ⟩.ṯa	ˈṯar.⟨č⟩#**ə̠**⟨ḏ⟩.ˈrō.⟨ʕ⟩	–	vowel epenthesis
ˈno.**šə̠ḳ**.ṯa	ˈṯar.**čə̠ḏ**.ˈrō.⟨ʕ⟩	–	resyllabification
[ˈno.šə̠ḳ.ṯa]	[ˈṯar.čə̠ḏ.ˈrō.⟨ʕ⟩]	[⟨f⟩.ˈrī.⟨s⟩⟨č⟩.xun]	postlexical forms

This derivation shows that a word-medial CCC sequence can either undergo epenthesis, or not. For instance, in the word /nošḳ-T-a/ ‘kiss’ epenthesis applies, while in /frīs-T-xun/ ‘your right’ epenthesis is blocked. What is responsible for this variation? In both words, C_3 is syllabified as an onset and C_2 remains unsyllabified (i.e., a stray consonant). However, the two words differ in the syllabification of C_1, which is a coda in [no**š**.⟨ḳ⟩.t̠a] and a stray consonant in [⟨f⟩.rī.⟨**s**⟩⟨č⟩.xun]. In [noš.⟨ḳ⟩.t̠a], since C_2 is a stray consonants preceded by a coda consonant, epenthesis can apply. In [⟨f⟩.rī.⟨s⟩⟨č⟩.xun], C_1 and C_2 are stray consonants, but since both of them are in non-final position, epenthesis is blocked.

There is another interesting problem concerning the status of [č] as C'_2. The examples presented so far in which epenthesis is blocked may suggest that it is enough to have a $C'C'$ sequence in which C'_2 is [č] to block epenthesis. But this is not true. Rather, even if C'_2 is [č], epenthesis is blocked only in the #..$C'_1C'_2$σ..# environment. In other words, for epenthesis to be blocked, neither C'_1 nor C'_2 may occur in word-final position. For example, epenthesis is not blocked in the examples in (59) although they have the sequence $C'_1C'_2$ and C'_2 is [č]. It is not blocked because C'_1 is in word-final position in (59a), and because C'_2 is in word-final position in (59b). Note that clitic groups (i.e., clitics and their hosts, such as the first example) are treated as two separate words in this work (see the rationale in Section 2.5).

(59) *Vowel epenthesis although C'_2 is* [č]

(a) C'_1 in word-final position

b=čbōr-t̠ *t̠arʕ-a* [⟨**b**⟩#⟨**č**⟩.ˈbō.⟨r⟩⟨l⟩# ˈt̠ar.ʕa] → [**bə̠č**.ˈbō.ri̠t̠ ˈt̠ar.ʕa][25]
with=breaking-CST door-NE
'by breaking the door' Arnold 2002: 32

y-īb-Ø *č-naḥḥeč-Ø* [ˈyī.⟨**b**⟩#⟨**č**⟩.ˈnaḥ.ḥeč] → [ˈyī.**bə̠č**.ˈnaḥ.ḥeč]
3-be.SBJV-M.SG 2-go down.PRF-M.SG
'then you (M.SG) must be going down' IV.250

(b) C'_2 in word-final position

ḥōl-č-Ø [ˈḥō.⟨**l**⟩⟨**č**⟩] → [ˈḥō.**lə̠č**]
uncle-F-1SG
'my maternal aunt' IV.130

frīs-č-Ø [⟨f⟩ˈrī.⟨**s**⟩⟨**č**⟩] → [⟨f⟩ˈrī.**sə̠č**]
right-F-1SG
'my right' FW

25 The suffix *-l* in /čbōr-l/ assimilates completely to the following coronal consonant /t̠/ in /t̠arʕ-a/ (see Section 7.2.8 as well as Spitaler 1938: 34–35 and Arnold 1990a: 19).

8.6 Implications

From a typological perspective, it can be said that Maaloula Aramaic and Damascus Arabic (a VC-dialect of Arabic) are similar in their treatment of single C's, of two adjacent C′C′ resulting from the concatenation of words in connected speech, and (to some extent) of word-initial C′C′. They are also similar with respect to the relation between epenthesis and stress. However, in the words containing word-medial C′C′, Maaloula Aramaic and Damascus Arabic exhibit major dissimilarities in terms of epenthesis and epenthesis-stress interaction.

This study has implications for the areas of syllable structure and vowel epenthesis in phonological theory. The presented results support syllable-based accounts of epenthesis (e.g., Selkirk 1981; Itô 1989; Broselow 1992; Watson 2002, 2007; Kiparsky 2003), and they challenge accounts which claim that epenthesis can be accounted for purely by sequential constraints (e.g., Côté 2000) or by segmental constraints. For example, vowel epenthesis, in Maaloula Aramaic, does not apply to prohibit two identical or similar segments from being adjacent, which would be expected according to the Obligatory Contour Principle (OCP) (see Goldsmith 1976; Leben 1973; McCarthy 1979, 1986). If this were the case, then the epenthetic vowel would be inserted whenever any two similar segments are adjacent (regardless of their position in the syllable) and not strictly in the $C]_\sigma$__C′ and C′__C′ environments. For instance, the epenthetic vowel would be inserted in the C′__$[_\sigma C$ environment if the conditions were met, but this is clearly not the case. Having said that, I am not arguing that segmental effects do not exist or do not play any role in vowel epenthesis. Their effect has been shown on two occasions in this chapter. First, I have noted in Section 8.2.2 that segmental constraints (especially sonority) may be responsible for the optionality in the application of vowel epenthesis. Second, I have shown that the words which resist epenthesis share structural and segmental properties.

The presented study also calls into question two cross-linguistic assumptions about stray (or extrasyllabic) consonants by Kiparsky (2003: 156). Kiparsky claimed that stray consonants (or "semisyllables" in his terms) have a "restricted segmental inventory" (Kiparsky 2003: 156). Although this may be true for a number of languages, such as English (see, e.g., Giegerich 1992: chap. 6) and German (see, e.g., Wiese 1992), this is not a property of Maaloula Aramaic stray consonants. In Maaloula Aramaic, the segments that may occur as stray consonants do not belong to a specific subset of consonants, as the examples in (60) illustrate.

(60) *Some of the segments that may occur as stray consonants in Maaloula Aramaic*

(a) Labials:

*loʕə̱**p**ṯa*	'game; toy'	IV.16
*solə̱**f**ṯa* [26]	'story'	IV.140
*zalə̱**m**ṯa*	'man'	IV.142

(b) Coronals:

*aḳə̱**t**riṯ*	'I was able (to)'	III.56
*imə̱**ṭ***	'he arrived'	IV.116
*irə̱**ṣ***	'he accepted'	IV.226
*mofə̱**č**ḥa*	'key'	IV.70
*bisə̱**n**yōṯa*	'girls'	III.376
*ʕisə̱**r***	'twenty'	III.304

(c) Dorsals:

*šabə̱**k**ṯa*	'net'	IV.58
*sčafə̱**ḳ**te*	'he checked up on him'	IV.214

(d) Pharyngeals:

*yarə̱**ḥ***	'months (EPL)'	IV.142
*ačə̱**ʕ**baṯ*	'she felt tired'[27]	IV.24

(e) Glottals:

*iṣə̱**h***	'he felt thirsty'	III.360
*žawə̱**h**rōṯa*	'gems; jewels'	IV.126

The other cross-linguistic assumption made by Kiparsky states that stray consonants are "sometimes restricted to peripheral position (typically word edges)" (Kiparsky 2003: 156). Although many of the stray consonants in the data set can be analyzed as domain-peripheral (i.e., word-peripheral or morpheme-peripheral), there are many other examples of words with word-internal or even morpheme-internal stray consonants, as the ones shown in (61). I believe that stray consonants in Maaloula Aramaic are the result of syllabification and not the result of any

26 It is transcribed as *sōləfṯa* in the original text.
27 This is the literal meaning. In the narrative, the intended (figurative) meaning was that the situation 'has become bad'.

alignment constraint which would align stray consonants with word or morpheme edges (for such constraints see, e.g., Cho & King 2003).

(61) *Words with morpheme-internal stray consonants*

y-aḥšm-un ['yaḥ.⟨**š**⟩.mun] → ['ya.ḥə̲**š**.mun]
3-have dinner.SBJV-M.PL
'(that) they (M) have dinner' III.258

Ø-m-ašph-ō-š ['maš.⟨**p**⟩.hō.⟨š⟩] → ['ma.šə̲**p**.hō.⟨š⟩]
3-PRS-resemble-F.SG-2F.SG
'she looks like you (F.SG)' IV.176

In addition to these typological and theoretical aspects, the present study represents a detailed case study of an under-researched language using corpus data, empirical methodology, and universal frameworks, such as moraic phonology. Such theoretically informed case studies involving large amounts of data are necessary to enhance our typological and theoretical understanding of vowel epenthesis cross-linguistically.

9 Gemination

9.1 Introduction

Geminates are traditionally defined as double consonants which are distinguished from the corresponding singleton consonants by their longer period of articulation (see, e.g., Bussmann 1996: 451; Davis 2011: 873; Galea 2016: 6; Ben Hedia & Plag 2017: 34; Ben Hedia 2019: 5). However, previous research has shown that geminates are marked not only by their longer duration but also by other phonological and phonetic properties, such as their interaction with syllable weight, syllabification, word stress, and the duration of the preceding vowels. These properties are discussed in this chapter for Maaloula Aramaic.

Gemination is contrastive in some languages, as the examples in (1) show.

(1) *Geminate versus singleton consonants in different languages*

(a) Italian (Bussmann 1996: 451)

fato 'fate'
fatto 'done'

(b) Buginese (Cohn, Ham & Podesva 1999: 587)

lapa 'lava'
lappa 'joint'

(c) (Cairene) Arabic (Davis & Ragheb 2014: 4)

kasar 'he broke'
kassar 'he smashed'

(d) Maltese (Galea 2016: 6)

papa 'pope'
pappa 'food'

This contrast between geminate and singleton consonants is also attested in Maaloula Aramaic, as the examples in (2) show.

https://doi.org/10.1515/9783111447124-009

(2) *Geminate versus singleton consonants in Maaloula Aramaic* [1]

(a)	***n**ōfeḳ*	'he goes out'	IV.22
	***nn**ōfeḳ*	'I go out'	III.228
	***s**alleḳ*	'he is going up'	IV.248
	***ss**alleḳ* [2]	'you (M.SG) are going up'	IV.76
(b)	*i**r**ex*	'it (M) became longer'	Rizkallah 2010: 198
	*i**rr**ex*	'long; tall (INDF.M.SG)'	III.316
	*ḳa**t**em* [3]	'of old; in/from/since the past'	IV.208
	*ḳa**tt**em*	'he came forward/closer'	IV.148
	*la**ḳ**eṭle*	'he holds him/it (M)'	III.68
	*la**ḳḳ**eṭle* [4]	'he chose for him'	IV.118
(c)	*yiḥmu**n***	'(that) they (M) see'	IV.188
	*yiḥmu**nn***	'(that) they (M) see them'	IV.84
	*taḳḳa**n***	'knocks (EPL)'	III.158
	*taḳḳa**nn*** [5]	'he hammered them'	IV.152

As can be seen from the examples above, Maaloula Aramaic geminates can occur in word-initial position, as in (2a), in word-medial position, as in (2b), and in word-final position, as in (2c) (Arnold 1990a: 17). In addition, geminates may occur across word boundaries due to the concatenation of identical singleton consonants across word boundaries, as in (3a), or due to assimilation, as in (3b) (for details, see Section 9.2.2).

(3) *Gemination across word boundaries in Maaloula Aramaic*

(a)	*e**x** **x**ifō*	'like stones'	III.192
	***b**-**b**esra*	'with meat'	III.38
	*awwa**l** **l**ēlya*	'the first night'	III.206

1 The pairs in (2c) differ not only in the final consonant being a singleton or a geminate but also in their stress patterns (i.e., *yíḥmun* vs. *yiḥmúnn* and *táḳḳan* vs. *taḳḳánn*). However, this difference in their stress patterns is due to the interaction between word-final gemination and stress. This is explained in detail in Section 9.3.3.

2 *ssalleḳ* is a variant of *čsalleḳ*, in which the word-initial [č] assimilates to the following [s].

3 It is transcribed as *ḳatim* in the original text.

4 It is transcribed as *ḷaḳḳeṭle* in the original text.

5 It is transcribed as *taḳḳan* in the original text.

(b) *hōʕ ʕaymṯa*	'this cloud'	IV.64
rayšiš šenna	'the top of the rock'	IV.332
maḥ ḥayōṯəl zaləmṯa	'about the person's life'	III.214

9.2 Underlying and surface geminates

Previous research (e.g., Hayes 1986; Galea 2016; Ben Hedia 2019) has differentiated between two types of geminates. The first type consists of the geminate consonants which can be contrasted with the corresponding singleton consonants in their underlying and surface representations. These geminates are not the result of processes that concatenate identical segments or assimilate underlyingly different segments. These geminates are referred to with different terms, such as *true geminates* (Hayes 1986: 327), *underlying lexical geminates* (Galea 2016: 6), *phonological geminates* (Ben Hedia & Plag 2017: 34), and *lexical geminates* (Ben Hedia 2019: 5). In this work, I refer to these geminates as *underlying geminates*. I assume that underlying geminates in Maaloula Aramaic can be further divided into two sub-types: (non-concatenative) morphological geminates and lexical geminates (see the schematic representation in (5) as well as Section 9.2.1).

The second type of geminates arises when two consonants are concatenated across a morphological boundary (i.e., a morpheme or word boundary) (Hayes 1986: 326–327; Galea 2016: 6; Ben Hedia 2019: 5). These two adjacent consonants may be underlyingly identical, as in (4a), or they may be underlyingly different but have become identical at the surface level through assimilation (Galea 2016: 6), such as the assimilation of /l/ in the definite article in (4b).

(4) *Geminates arising from the concatenation of two consonants*

(a) *u**nn**atural*		(English, Ben Hedia 2019: 5)
*fu**n n**ame*		(English, Ben Hedia 2019: 5)
*To**m m**ar jgħum*	'Tom went swimming'	(Maltese, Galea 2016: 7)
(b) *i**r-r**as*	'the head'	(Maltese, Galea 2016: 92)
*i**n-n**ar*	'the fire'	(Maltese, Galea 2016: 92)
*i**s-s**itt*	'the woman'	(Cairene Arabic, Watson 2002: 217)
*i**š-š**ams*	'the sun'	(Cairene Arabic, Watson 2002: 217)

This second type of geminates has been labeled as *fake geminates* (Hayes 1986: 327), *surface geminates* (Galea 2016: 6), and *morphological geminates* (Ben Hedia & Plag 2017: 34; Ben Hedia 2019: 5) (see Ben Hedia 2019: 5 for a review of the terms which have been given to these geminates and for the literature in which each term has been used). In this work, I refer to them as *surface geminates* (see the schematic representation in (5) as well as Section 9.2.2). I will not refer to them by the term *morphological geminates* because morphology is involved in the formation of both types of geminates in Maaloula Aramaic: non-concatenative morphology in the first type (i.e., underlying geminates) and concatenative morphology in the second type (i.e., surface geminates).

(5) *Types of geminates in Maaloula Aramaic*

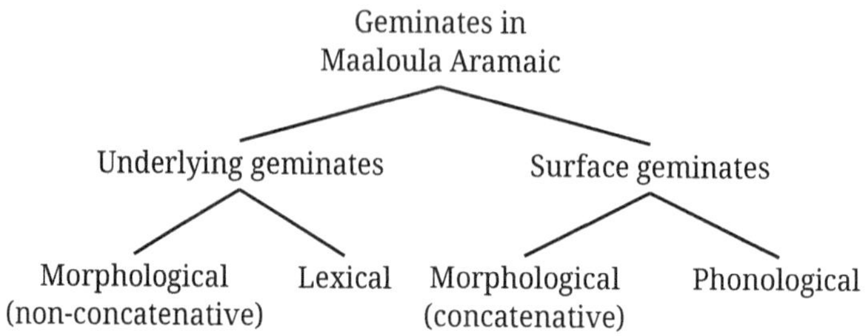

9.2.1 Underlying geminates

As already introduced in the previous section, underlying geminates are part of the underlying representation of words and are not the result of any synchronic phonological processes. Nor are they the result of the concatenation of identical phonemes across morphological boundaries. I propose that underlying geminates in Maaloula Aramaic are either morphological or lexical. The main difference between them is whether or not there is an alternation between singletons and geminates when different words are derived from the same root. When this morphologically motivated alternation occurs, the geminates in question are considered morphological. When there is no alternation, the geminates are considered lexical.

Morphological underlying geminates

Morphological underlying geminates are the result of non-concatenative morphological processes. They are created when the pattern by which a word is generated requires one of the root consonants (also called radicals) to geminate. For example, when the noun *ṭaḥḥōna* 'miller' IV.250 is derived from the consonantal roots *ṭḥn* (C_1= *ṭ*, C_2= *ḥ*, C_3= *n*), the second radical is geminated in the morphology because the pattern by which this noun is derived has the form C_1a$\mathbf{G_2G_2}$ōC_3a. It is not within the scope of this chapter to describe the numerous patterns that contain a geminated radical. I will show only four examples of these patterns. The presented examples will be contrasted with words derived from the same root but by a pattern which does not require any radical to geminate. The aim of these comparisons is to illustrate that it is morphology that is responsible for turning the same radical into a geminate in some words and into a singleton in other words.

As discussed in Section 2.4, Arnold (1990a: 53–54) classifies Maaloula Aramaic verbs into eleven Forms: I, II, III, IV, I_2, II_2, III_2, IV_2, I_7, I_8, and I_{10}. The perfect forms of many Form I verbs are generated from triliteral roots by a pattern which geminates the second radical (C_2). However, the other forms of the same verbs (e.g., preterit, subjunctive, and present forms) are generated by patterns in which the second radical is not geminated. The examples in (6), which are inflected for the third person masculine singular, illustrate this alternation. The roots provided in all of the examples in this section are taken from Arnold's (2019) dictionary, and the inflected forms are taken from Arnold's (1990a) grammar, Arnold's (2019) dictionary, and my native language consultant (see also Arnold 1990a: 55–59, 67–78 for Form I verbs).

(6) *Singleton-geminate alternation in Form I verbs*

Root		Preterit	Subjunctive	Present	Perfect
$C_1C_2C_3$		$iC_1C_2eC_3$/ $iC_1C_2aC_3$	$yiC_1C_2aC_3$/ $yiC_1C_2uC_3$	$C_1\bar{o}C_2eC_3$/ $C_1\bar{o}C_2aC_3$	$C_1aG_2G_2eC_3$
ṯḳn	'to become'	*iṯḳen*	*yiṯḳan*	*ṯōḳen*	*ṯaḳḳen*
nfḳ	'to go out'	*infeḳ*	*yinfuḳ*	*nōfeḳ*	*naffeḳ*
nḥč	'to go down'	*inḥeč*	*yinḥuč*	*nōḥeč*	*naḥḥeč*
slḳ	'to go up'	*isleḳ*	*yislaḳ*	*sōleḳ*	*salleḳ*
ʕbr	'to come in'	*iʕber*	*yiʕbar*	*ʕōbar*	*ʕapper* [6]
šmʕ	'to listen'	*išmeʕ*	*yišmaʕ*	*šōmaʕ*	*šammeʕ*
bhč	'to be ashamed'	*ibheč*	*yibhač*	*bōheč*	*bahheč*
sḳṭ	'to fall'	*isḳaṭ*	*yisḳaṭ*	*sōḳeṭ*	*saḳḳeṭ*
šmṭ	'to escape'	*išmaṭ*	*yišmuṭ*	*šōmeṭ*	*šammeṭ*

Form II verbs have the second radical geminated. The examples in (7) consist of Form I and Form II preterit verbs inflected for the third person masculine singular. In contrast to Form II verbs, Form I verbs have a second radical that is not geminated. Semantically, Form II verbs are the causative version of Form I verbs (for

6 /bb/ is realized as [pp] in *ʕapper* by a devoicing process that targets geminate bilabial stops (see Section 5.3).

more details on Form II verbs, see Arnold 1990a: 59–60, 78–82; to compare with Arabic, see Watson 2002: 125–126, 134).

(7) *Singleton-geminate alternation in Form I and Form II verbs derived from the same root*

xṯb	Form I:	*ixṯab*	'he wrote'	$iC_1C_2aC_3$
	Form II:	*xaṯṯeb*	'he made someone write'	$C_1aG_2G_2eC_3$
sḳṭ	Form I:	*isḳaṭ*	'he fell'	$iC_1C_2aC_3$
	Form II:	*saḳḳeṭ*	'he made someone fall'	$C_1aG_2G_2eC_3$
ṣmč	Form I:	*iṣmeč*	'he remained silent'	$iC_1C_2eC_3$
	Form II:	*ṣammeč*	'he silenced someone'	$C_1aG_2G_2eC_3$
rḳḏ	Form I:	*irḳaḏ*	'he danced'	$iC_1C_2aC_3$
	Form II:	*raḳḳeḏ*	'he made someone dance'	$C_1aG_2G_2eC_3$
nkb	Form I:	*inkeb*	'it (M) dried'	$iC_1C_2eC_3$
	Form II:	*nakkeb*	'he dried something (in the sun)'	$C_1aG_2G_2eC_3$

The subjunctive forms of Form I verbs whose second and third radicals are identical are generated by a pattern which geminates the first radical when they are inflected for the singular and for the first person plural (see Arnold 1990a: 59, 133–135). In the following examples, these subjunctive forms are contrasted with their preterit and present counterparts. All verbs are inflected for the third person masculine singular. The first verb is from Arnold's (1990a: 59) grammar.

(8) *Singleton-geminate alternation in Form I verbs whose second and third radicals are identical*

Root		Preterit	Subjunctive	Present
$C_1C_2C_3$ (C_2= C_3)		aC_1aC_2	$yiG_1G_1uC_2$	$C_1\bar{o}C_2eC_3$
lmm	'to collect'	*alam*	*yillum*	*lōmem*
tḳḳ	'to knock'	*ataḳ*	*yittuḳ*	*tōḳeḳ*
sbb	'to swear at'	*asab*	*yissub*	*sōbeb*
tll	'to show/indicate'	*atal*	*yittul*	*tōlel*
ršš	'to sprinkle'	*araš*	*yirruš*	*rōšeš*
zčč	'to throw'	*azač*	*yizzuč*	*zōčeč*
ṭbb	'to topple/overturn'	*aṭab*	*yiṭṭub*	*ṭōbeb*

Some nouns are derived by a pattern in which the second radical is geminated (see Arnold 1990a: 334–338). For example, some of the nouns which indicate a male person who has a certain profession or does something professionally or intensively are of the pattern $C_1aG_2G_2\bar{o}C_3a$, as in (9) (cf. the similar pattern $C_1aG_2G_2\bar{a}C_3$ in Arabic). These nouns are contrasted with Form I preterit verbs which are derived from the same root.

(9) *Singleton-geminate alternation in the derivation of verbs and nouns from the same root*

*ṭ**ḥ**n*	verb:	*iṭ**ḥ**an*	'he ground into flour'	$iC_1C_2aC_3$
	noun:	*ṭa**ḥḥ**ōna*	'miller'	$C_1aG_2G_2\bar{o}C_3a$
*s**b**ḥ*	verb:	*is**b**aḥ*	'he swam'	$iC_1C_2aC_3$
	noun:	*sa**pp**ōḥa* [7]	'swimmer'	$C_1aG_2G_2\bar{o}C_3a$
*ḥ**l**ḳ*	verb:	*iḥ**l**aḳ*	'he cut hair/shaved'	$iC_1C_2aC_3$
	noun:	*ḥa**ll**ōḳa*	'barber'	$C_1aG_2G_2\bar{o}C_3a$
*ẓ**r**ʕ* [8]	verb:	*iẓ**r**aʕ*	'he sowed/planted'	$iC_1C_2aC_3$
	noun:	*ẓa**rr**ōʕa*	'sower; farmer'	$C_1aG_2G_2\bar{o}C_3a$
*ḥ**l**b*	verb:	*iḥ**l**ab*	'he milked'	$iC_1C_2aC_3$
	noun:	*ḥa**ll**ōba*	'milker'	$C_1aG_2G_2\bar{o}C_3a$

Lexical geminates

There are cases where there is no morphologically motivated alternation between a singleton and a geminate. For example, although every word in (10) has a geminate, there are no other derivatives with the same root where the geminate radical alternates with the corresponding singleton radical. I refer to this subcategory of underlying geminates as lexical geminates.

(10) *Lexical geminates*

***pp**ōfča*	'loaf (of bread)'	III.128
***ff**ō*	'face; surface'	III.34
*ḥlu**ff**ašīṯa*	'(dung) beetle'	VI.363
*nawe**ll**a*	'(weaving) loom'	III.310

7 /bb/ is realized as [pp] in *sappōḥa* by the same devoicing process indicated by the previous footnote.

8 The root is *zrʕ* in Arnold's (2019: 966) dictionary.

*ḥašo**pp**a*	'Sunday'	III.152
*ʕa**kk**ōra*	'roof'	IV.288
*ḥa**ṣṣ**a*	'back'	IV.200
*ʕe**zz**a*	'goat'	III.124
*to**pp**a*	'bear'	IV.256
*i**yy**ar*	'May'	III.162

Some of these lexical geminates are the result of historical processes. For example, the geminates in (11) are the result of historical assimilation. However, they have become lexicalized in Maaloula Aramaic, and the historical segments which have undergone the change no longer surface.

(11) *Geminates resulting from historical assimilation (examples collected from Spitaler 1938: 37)*

*ha**nn**a*	'this (M.SG)'	<	**hā**ḏn**ā* [9]		
*e**rr**aʕ*	'down; below; under'	<	**e**lr**aʕ*	<	***lr**aʕ*
*ḥḏu**čč**a*	'bride'	<	**ḥḏu**tt**a*	<	**ḥḏū**ṯt**ā*

9.2.2 Surface geminates

Surface geminates are created through morphosyntactic and phonological processes, and are therefore classified (in this work) as morphological geminates and phonological geminates.

Morphological surface geminates

Morphological surface geminates arise through morphosyntactic processes when two identical consonants are concatenated across morpheme boundaries, as in (12a), or across word boundaries, as in (12b) (see Hayes 1986: 326–327; Galea 2016: 6; Ben Hedia 2019: 5).

(12) (a) ***n-n**ōfeḳ-Ø*
1-go out.PRS-M.SG
'I (M) go out.' III.228

9 The asterisks in these examples do not indicate ungrammaticality. They indicate that the words are hypothetical or reconstructed, rather than attested.

lā *č-čubʕ-unn-Ø*
not 2-follow.SBJV-M.PL-3M.PL
'Do not follow (M.PL) them!' Rizkallah & Saadi 2016: Luke 21:8

*ni-**m-m**ass-ī-š* *p=xayr-a*
1-PRS-greet in the evening-M.SG-2F.SG in=good-NE
'Good evening. / I wish you (F.SG) a good evening!' IV.28

(b) ***ex*** *xif-ō*
like stone-PL
'like stones' III.192

***b**=**b**esr-a*
in=meat-NE
'with meat' III.38

*awwa**l*** ***l**ēly-a*
first night-NE
'the first night' III.206

Phonological geminates

Phonological geminates arise through phonological processes, such as assimilation and devoicing, when two underlyingly different consonants become identical at the surface level. For example, the surface geminates in (13) are the result of assimilation which applies within and across word boundaries (see Section 7.2).

(13)	***tt**awwar*	/**č-t**awwar/	'(that) you (SG) look for'	IV.122
	*zaʕḳa**ll**a*	/zaʕḳ-a**ṯ-l**-a/	'she called her'	IV.68
	*mbaššli**ll**a*	/m-baššl-i**n-l**-a/	'they (M) cook it (F)'	III.40
	***f-f**elka*	/**b-f**elk-a/	'in half'	IV.236
	*hō**r r**ayya*	/hā**ḏ r**ayy-a/	'this rain'	IV.64
	*yarḥi**č č**ammuz*	/yarḥ-**l č**ammuz/	'the month of July'	III.32

Having clarified the provenance of geminates in Maaloula Aramaic as being either underlying or surface geminates and shown how they can be formed in each of these two types and their sub-types, I now turn to the analysis of the phonological and phonetic properties of geminates.

9.3 The phonological and phonetic properties of Maaloula Aramaic geminates

Not much is known about the phonological and phonetic properties of geminates in Maaloula Aramaic. In this section, I will investigate these properties in the three positions: word-initial, word-medial, and word-final.

While analyzing the phonological properties, I focus on the representation of geminates and the interaction between gemination and other processes (e.g., stress and vowel epenthesis). I adopt the widely accepted moraic representation of geminates as proposed by Hayes (1989) (see Davis 2011 for general discussion, and Davis & Ragheb 2014 for an analysis of Arabic in these terms). This moraic representation is a continuation of the moraic analysis proposed in Chapter 8.

While analyzing the phonetic properties, I focus on two acoustic correlates of gemination: the duration of the consonant itself and the duration of the preceding vowel. Previous studies have shown that consonant duration is the primary acoustic correlate of gemination. Although the singleton-to-geminate duration ratios reported in these studies vary, the results collectively show that geminates are longer than singletons (see, e.g., Cohn, Ham & Podesva 1999; Payne 2005; Khattab & Al-Tamimi 2014; Galea 2016). In addition to consonant duration, the duration of the surrounding vowels, especially the preceding vowel, has been proposed to be a correlate of gemination (see, e.g., Maddieson 1985; Lahiri & Hankamer 1988; Cohn, Ham & Podesva 1999).

Although there are other less prominent acoustic correlates, such as voice onset time (VOT) for stops and the amplitude of the surrounding vowels, the different empirical studies which have investigated these correlates in different languages and in different positions varied in their findings. For this reason, I have decided not to include these acoustic correlates in the present study (for an overview of the acoustic correlates of gemination see, e.g., Khattab & Al-Tamimi 2014: 232–233; Galea 2016: sec. 3.1.5, 3.2.6, 3.3.7).

The general aim of the present study is to examine the phonetic reality of the phonological difference between a geminate and a singleton and to illustrate how phonetics and phonology are connected. More concretely, the presented study aims to answer the following research questions:

1. How can geminates be phonologically represented in word-initial, word-medial, and word-final positions?
2. How does gemination interact with other phonological processes (e.g., stress and vowel epenthesis)?
3. What are the singleton-to-geminate duration ratios in word-initial, word-medial, and word-final positions?

4. Does the duration of the preceding vowel differ depending on whether the following consonant is a singleton or a geminate?

9.3.1 Methodology

To my knowledge, no previous acoustic analyses of any type have been conducted on Maaloula Aramaic. The creation of MASC (Eid et al. 2022) (see Chapter 3) has made it possible to run such analyses, using time-aligned phonetic transcriptions. In this study, I examine the acoustic correlates of gemination, using data from MASC.

Data

Using MASC, I compiled a list of all of the Maaloula Aramaic consonants (of both types: singletons and geminates), and then for each consonant I extracted a list of all word tokens which contain this consonant. This process resulted in a word list which contained 164,907 tokens. I coded the data by creating the following variables:

Consonant status and position. I included the variable GEMINATION to code whether the consonant in question was a singleton (`sgl`) or a geminate (`gem`). I also included the variable POSITION with the values `initial`, `medial`, and `final` to indicate the position of the consonant in the word.

Environment. I included the variable ENVIRONMENT to indicate the phonological environment in which the consonant (i.e., the singleton or geminate) occurs (e.g., #_C, #_V, C_#, C_C, C_V, V_#, V_C, V_V). The symbol # refers to a word boundary, C refers to any consonant (including glides), and V refers to any short or long vowel except the epenthetic schwa.

Consonant duration. To measure the duration of singletons and geminates, I created the variable SEGMENTDURATION. Cross-linguistic evidence has shown that consonant duration is the primary correlate of gemination (see, e.g., Galea 2016: chap. 3 for a comprehensive cross-linguistic review). For example, the singleton-to-geminate duration ratio has been reported to be 1:1.65 in Buginese, 1:1.55 in Madurese, 1:2.2 in Toba Batak (Cohn, Ham & Podesva 1999: 589), 1:1.9 in Italian (Payne 2005: 168), and 1:2.15 and 1:1.82 in Lebanese Arabic, depending on whether the previous vowel is phonologically short or long respectively (Khattab & Al-Tamimi 2014: 251).

Manner of articulation. The variable MANNER was added to indicate the manner of articulation of the consonant. It had the values `stop`, `affricate`, `fricative`, `nasal`, `lateral`, `rhotic`, and `glide`. This variable was created because even within the same language, the singleton-to-geminate duration ratio has been found to vary depending on the manner of articulation of the consonant (Khattab & Al-Tamimi 2014: 232; Galea 2016: 48; Ben Hedia 2019: 6).

Preceding vowel. I added the variable PrecedingSegment to identify the preceding vowel, and the variable PrecedingVowel to indicate whether the preceding vowel was phonologically `short` or `long` (see Section 4.3 for vowel length). I also created the variable PrecedingSegmentDuration to measure the duration of the preceding vowel. These variables were included because the duration of the preceding vowel has been proposed as a correlate of gemination and has been investigated in a number of languages. Nevertheless, no clear picture of its interaction with gemination emerges from the previous accounts. For example, Maddieson (1985: 208) reports the results of previous studies which found that in certain languages, such as Kannada, Italian, Arabic, and Amharic, the vowel which precedes a geminate is shorter than the vowel which precedes a singleton. Similar results have been found in other languages, such as Bengali (Lahiri & Hankamer 1988: 335), Buginese, Madurese, and Toba Batak (Cohn, Ham & Podesva 1999: 589). However, no significant difference in duration was found in other languages, such as Turkish (Lahiri & Hankamer 1988: 332). Lebanese Arabic (Khattab & Al-Tamimi 2014) is an interesting case because (like Maaloula Aramaic) it has phonologically short and phonologically long vowels and both types can precede a geminate or a singleton. When the preceding vowels are short, there is no significant difference in their duration, but when the preceding vowels are long, their duration differs significantly (i.e., they are longer before a singleton) (Khattab & Al-Tamimi 2014: 250).

In addition to these variables, I added the variable Word to indicate the word token which has the consonant in question, and the variable Speaker to identify the speaker who produced the word token.

To obtain durations from the TextGrid files in MASC, a Python script was used.[10] The Python script successfully read the durations in 167 (out of 176) TextGrid files and transferred them into the data set. The nine TextGrid files which were not accessible to the script were not included in the final data set. No manual correction of the automatically aligned boundaries was made due to the large number of tokens.

The environments in which only singletons can occur were removed so that singletons and geminates can be measured and compared in identical environments. These removed environments included #__# (e.g., ***b*** 'in; with' III.38), #__C (e.g., ***ġ****bečča* 'cheese' III.34), C__# (e.g., *bal****k*** 'maybe' IV.224), and C__C (e.g., *aḳ****t****riṯ* 'I was able (to)' III.48). Additionally, I removed the environment C__V because only 14 geminates occur in it (compared to 28,742 singletons) (e.g., *far****ṯṯ****a* 'bundle' VI.284). I also removed the environment V__C because the underlying geminates which occur in this environment undergo preconsonantal degemination and surface as singletons (e.g., *xa****ff****ṯa* [xa**f**ṯa] 'shoulder' IV.228) (see Section 9.3.2 and Arnold 1990a: 17).

10 I am grateful to Simon David Stein for his help with the Python scripts.

The remaining environments which I included are the vocalic environments shown in (14).

(14) *The environments included in the study*

Environment	Example			
#__V	*forna*	'oven'	III.44	(singleton)
	ffō	'face; surface'	III.34	(geminate)
V__V	*baḥar*	'a lot; very'	III.146	(singleton)
	aḥḥaḏ	'someone (M)'	III.350	(geminate)
V__#	*hōš*	'now'	III.48	(singleton)
	hašš	'you (F.SG)'	IV.66	(geminate)

I also excluded the tokens in which the consonant in question is at word edges and the preceding or following word ends or begins with an identical consonant (e.g., *iṣʕe**b** **b**aḥar* 'very difficult' IV.166). I excluded these tokens because in many cases the two identical consonants at word edges are pronounced as one consonant in connected speech.

Descriptive overview of the data

The final data set consisted of 78,971 observations. In this data set, all consonants occur as singletons and geminates except the two marginal phonemes /ʔ/ and /g/ which occur only as singletons. Table 9.1 shows the distribution of the singletons and geminates in the data set across the three positions: word-initial, word-medial, and word-final. It is noticeable that word-medial geminates are the most frequent and word-initial geminates are the least frequent. This observation is in line with the cross-linguistic observation that word-initial geminates are less common than word-medial geminates (see, e.g., Muller 2001: 17).

Table 9.1: Distribution of singletons and geminates

Position	Singleton	Geminate
Word-initial	32,570	225
Word-medial	14,358	12,732
Word-final	16,086	3,000
Total	63,014	15,957

Table 9.2 shows the distribution of phonologically short and long vowels before word-medial and word-final singletons and geminates in the data set. As can be seen from the table, phonologically long vowels occur considerably less commonly before geminates than before singletons.

Table 9.2: Distribution of short and long vowels before medial and final consonants

Vowels	Before medial singletons	Before medial geminates	Before final singletons	Before final geminates
Short vowels	6,641	12,613	12,512	2,984
Long vowels	7,717	119	3,574	16
Total	14,358	12,732	16,086	3,000

Statistical analysis

To measure the significance of the durational differences between singletons and geminates on the one hand and between the vowels preceding them on the other hand, I used standard statistical tests (i.e., the *t*-test and the Wilcoxon test). The *t*-test was used when the data were normally distributed, and the Wilcoxon test was used when the distribution was skewed (see Baayen 2008: 76). To test the normality of the distribution, I made quantile–quantile plots (see, e.g., Baayen 2008: 72; Crawley 2015: 79) and also used the Shapiro-Wilk test for normality (see, e.g., Baayen 2008: 73).

In addition, I fitted a mixed-effects regression model for each of the three positions (word-initial, word-medial, and word-final), using the package `lme4` (Bates et al. 2015). The variable SEGMENTDURATION was included as the response variable. The variables GEMINATION, MANNER, PRECEDINGVOWEL, and PRECEDINGSEGMENTDURATION were included as the fixed effects, and the variables SPEAKER and WORD were included as the random effects. The *p*-values generated by the mixed-effects models were in line with the *p*-values obtained by the Wilcoxon test in word-initial and word-medial position.

In what follows, I will present the phonological and phonetic properties of geminates in the three positions: word-initial, word-medial, and word-final. I will start with word-medial geminates because they are the most common geminates. After that, I will move on to word-final geminates and then to word-initial geminates.

9.3.2 Word-medial geminates

At the phonological level, a geminate consonant always receives a mora underlyingly (Hayes 1989: 256–257). In (15), the moraic representation of the word *irrex* 'long; tall (INDF.M.SG)', which has the word-medial geminate /rr/, is contrasted with the moraic representation of the word *irex* 'it (M) became longer', which has the word-medial singleton /r/. The examples are from (2) above.

(15) *Moraic representation of word-medial geminates*

(a) The geminate /rr/
irrex [ˈʔir.rex]
'long; tall (INDF.M.SG)'

(b) The singleton /r/
irex [ˈʔi.rex]
'it (M) became longer'

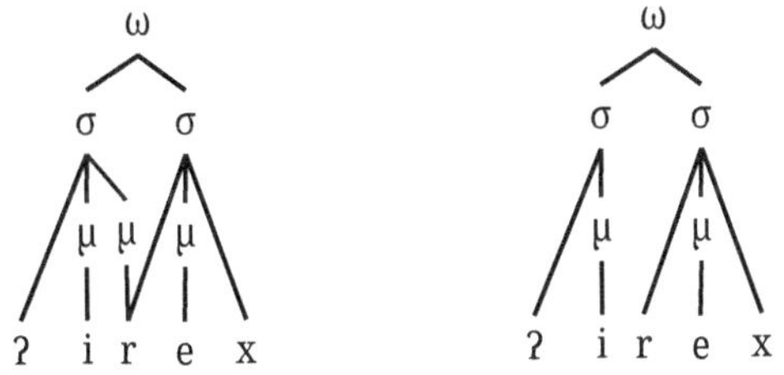

It can be seen that /rr/ in *irrex* receives a mora and serves as the coda of the penultimate syllable and as the onset of the final syllable. However, /r/ in *irex* does not receive a mora because onsets do not receive moras (see Section 8.3.2 for syllable structure and syllable weight, Section 8.3.3 for syllabification, and Sections 8.2.3 and 8.3.6 for glottal epenthesis).

One important property of geminates is that they cannot be split by an epenthetic vowel. This property is called "integrity" by Hayes (1986). When an underlying geminate is followed by a consonant, the sequence /GGC/ does not undergo vowel epenthesis (i.e., *[GəGC]), in contrast to the sequence /CCC/ which usually surfaces as [CəCC] (see Section 8.2.2). What happens instead, in Maaloula Aramaic, is that the geminate consonant /GG/ is degeminated (i.e., is realized as [C]) when it occurs in preconsonantal position (Arnold 1990a: 17), as in (16). This phenomenon is also known in other Semitic languages (see, e.g., Cowell 1964: 27 for Damascus Arabic; Jastrow 1993: 17 for Turoyo; Watson 2002: 210 for San'ani Arabic).

(16) *Preconsonantal degemination* [11]

ḏokkṯa	/ḏo**kk**-T-a/	→	[ḏo**k**.ṯa]	'place'	IV.306
mʕarrṯa	/mʕa**rr**-T-a/	→	[⟨m⟩.ʕa**r**.ṯa]	'cave'	III.368
xaffṯa	/xa**ff**-T-a/	→	[xa**f**.ṯa]	'shoulder'	IV.228
šattre	/ša**tt**r-e/	→	[ša**t**.re]	'he sent him'	IV.104
ġarrbiččun	/ġa**rr**b-ičč-un/	→	[ġa**r**.bič.čun]	'I tried them (M)'	III.80
nimbaššlin	/ni-m-ba**šš**l-in/	→	[nim.ba**š**.lin]	'we (M) cook'	III.38

The degemination process is formalized in (17) and illustrated in the derivation in (18) which shows how /kk/ degeminates in preconsonantal position in *ḏokkṯa* 'place' IV.306 but does not degeminate in prevocalic position in *ḏukkōṯa* 'places' III.200. For the other phonological rules involved in this derivation, see Section 6.2.6 for /T/ spirantization, Section 8.3.3 for syllabification, Section 10.2 for stress assignment, Section 10.3.1 for pretonic raising, and Section 7.3.1 for /ā/ rounding.

(17) *Preconsonantal degemination*

$$\begin{bmatrix}\text{-syllabic}\\ \text{+long}\end{bmatrix} \rightarrow [\text{-long}] \,/\, \_\_[\text{-syllabic}]$$

Geminates are realized as singletons in preconsonantal position.

(18) *A derivation which illustrates the preconsonantal degemination rule*

'place'	'places'	
/ḏo**kk**-T-a/	/ḏo**kk**-ā-T-a/	
ḏokkṯa	ḏokkāṯa	/T/ spirantization
ḏokṯa	–	**preconsonantal degemination**
ḏok.ṯa	ḏok.kā.ṯa	syllabification
ˈ**ḏok**.ṯa	ḏok.ˈ**kā**.ṯa	stress assignment
–	ḏ**u**k.ˈkā.ṯa	pretonic raising
–	ḏuk.ˈk**ō**.ṯa	/ā/ rounding
[ˈḏo**k**.ṯa]	[ḏ**uk**.ˈ**k**ō.ṯa]	

11 Although the adopted transcription system represents surface forms, the degeminated consonants are transcribed as geminates, rather than the expected singletons (e.g., *ḏokkṯa* rather than *ḏokṯa*) (see Section 2.2.2). This exceptional treatment of degeminated consonants is not restricted to Arnold's (1990a, 1991a; 1991b) volumes, which I have adopted the transcription system from. It is also present in other textbooks on Maaloula Aramaic and other Semitic languages (e.g., Spitaler 1938; Cowell 1964; Jastrow 1993).

At the phonetic level, word-medial geminates are significantly longer than word-medial singletons. This can be seen in Figure 9.1 and Table 9.3. Figure 9.1 shows the distributions of consonant duration in word-medial position. The x-axis indicates whether the consonant is a singleton (`sgl`) or a geminate (`gem`), and the y-axis displays its duration in milliseconds (ms). Boxplots are used to show the distributions. The lower and upper ends of each box mark the first and third quartiles respectively, and the dot inside the box marks the median.

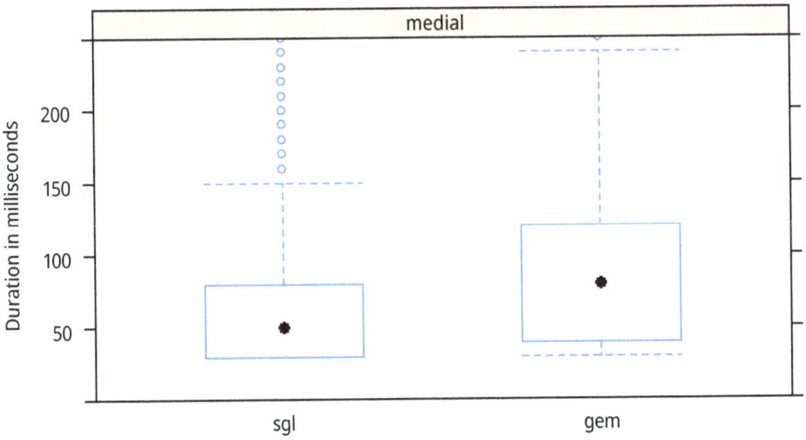

Fig. 9.1: Distributions of consonant duration in word-medial position

In Table 9.3 (as well as in the following tables), *SD* refers to standard deviation, *ratio* to the singleton-to-geminate duration ratio, and *P* to the *p*-value as calculated by the Wilcoxon test.

Table 9.3: Duration of word-medial consonants in milliseconds

Singleton			Geminate			Ratio	*P*
Median	Mean	SD	Median	Mean	SD		
50.00	65.06	51.96	80.00	88.42	59.64	1:1.36	<0.001

Word-medial geminates are consistently longer than word-medial singletons across all manners of articulation. The ranking of singleton-to-geminate duration ratio is: fricative (1:1.62) > rhotic (1:1.60) > stop (1:1.42) > nasal (1:1.34) > glide (1:1.32) > lateral (1:1.31) > affricate (1:1.27).

To investigate the durations of the preceding vowels, it is useful to divide these vowels into phonologically short vowels and phonologically long vowels. Figure 9.2 shows the distributions of vowel duration (in ms) before word-medial singletons (sgl) and before word-medial geminates (gem). The phonologically short vowels are shown in the first panel, the phonologically long vowels in the second.

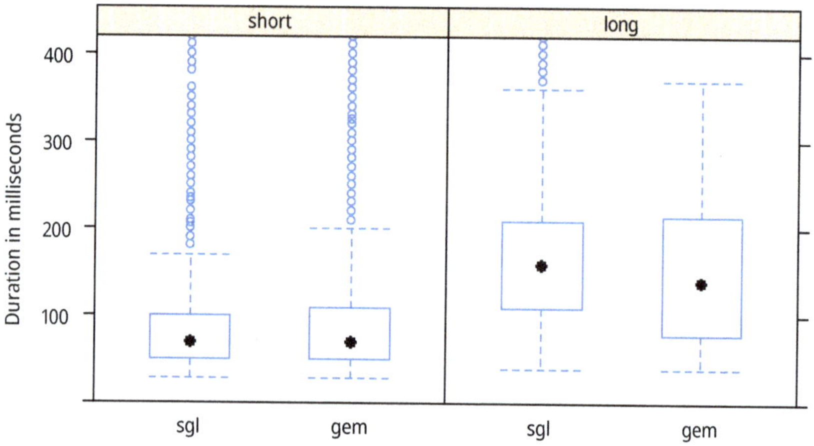

Fig. 9.2: Distributions of the duration of short and long vowels (in ms) before word-medial singletons (sgl) and word-medial geminates (gem)

As Table 9.4 shows, the short vowels which precede a geminate are significantly longer than the short vowels which precede a singleton (in spite of what the medians suggest). In contrast, the long vowels which precede a geminate are shorter than the long vowels which precede a singleton, but the difference in duration is not statistically significant. *Ratio*, here, refers to the ratio of the duration of the vowel which precedes a singleton to the vowel which precedes a geminate.

Table 9.4: Duration of vowels (in ms) before word-medial consonants

	Before singletons			Before geminates			Ratio	P
	Median	Mean	SD	Median	Mean	SD		
Short	70.00	82.75	48.75	70.00	89.56	67.45	1:1.08	<0.001
Long	160.00	168.16	98.94	140.00	159.08	97.65	1:0.95	0.157

In general, the differences in preceding vowel duration are not as large as the difference in consonant duration (compare the ratios 1:1.08 and 1:0.95 in Table 9.4 with the ratio 1:1.36 in Table 9.3). As a result, we can safely say that consonant duration is the primary correlate of word-medial gemination.

9.3.3 Word-final geminates

The durations of geminates and singletons in word-final position turned out to be nearly identical, with a slight difference between their means that is not statistically significant (see Figure 9.3 and Table 9.5).

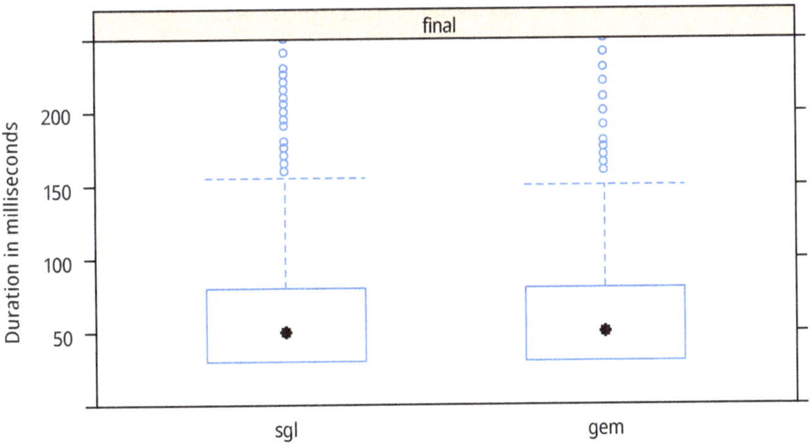

Fig. 9.3: Distributions of consonant duration in word-final position

Table 9.5: Duration of word-final consonants in milliseconds

Singleton			Geminate			Ratio	P
Median	Mean	SD	Median	Mean	SD		
50.00	71.13	69.03	50.00	70.93	62.11	1:0.99	0.321

What these results show is that word-final geminates and word-final singletons are not distinguished by their durations. This may explain why in the available community-produced textbooks (e.g., Rizkallah 2010; Rihan 2017), no distinction is made in the transcription of C# and GG#. Both are transcribed as a single consonant, as the examples in (19) show. It may be the case that native speakers do not consider these word-final segments to be geminates. In contrast, they clearly consider word-initial and word-medial geminates as geminates because they transcribe them as two identical letters.

(19) *Word-final geminates and word-final singletons transcribed identically by native speakers*

(a) Word-final geminates

xul	'every; all of'	Rihan 2017: 90	(cf. ***xull***	III.198)
šič	'sixty'	Rizkallah 2010: 156	(cf. *ši**čč***	IV.54)
haš	'you (F.SG)'	Rizkallah 2010: 160	(cf. *ha**šš***	IV.66)

(b) Word-final singletons

hōš	'now'	Rihan 2017: 90	(cf. *hō**š***	III.48)
emmat	'when'	Rizkallah 2010: 33	(cf. *emma**t***	III.310)
aḥref	'he replied'	Rihan 2017: 96	(cf. *aḥre**f***	IV.84)

If word-final geminates are not longer than word-final singletons, and if native speakers do not seem to distinguish between word-final geminates and word-final singletons (at least orthographically), what arguments are still there to support the claims made in previous research that word-final geminates exist? There are three main arguments, two phonological and one phonetic: first, the interaction between word-final gemination and stress; second, the interaction between word-final gemination and resyllabification; third, the duration of the preceding vowel.

According to the Maaloula Aramaic stress algorithm, if a final syllable is heavy (or bimoraic) it receives word stress (see Section 10.2; see also Bergsträsser 1915: xxi; Spitaler 1938: 46; Arnold 1990a: 40). The opposite is also true. If a final syllable is stressed, it must be heavy, as in the examples in (20) which are stressed on the final syllable. The question is: What makes the final syllable heavy (and therefore eligible for stress) in these examples? It must be the word-final geminate that makes the final syllable heavy because the geminate (i.e., the coda of the syllable) is underlyingly moraic (according to Hayes 1989: 256–257) and the preceding vowel (i.e., the nucleus) is also moraic. A bimoraic syllable is heavy.

(20) ***yiḥmunn*** [yiḥ.'mu**n͡n**] ***taḳḳann***[12] [taḳ.'ḳa**n͡n**]
'(that) they (M) see them' IV.84 'he hammered them' IV.152

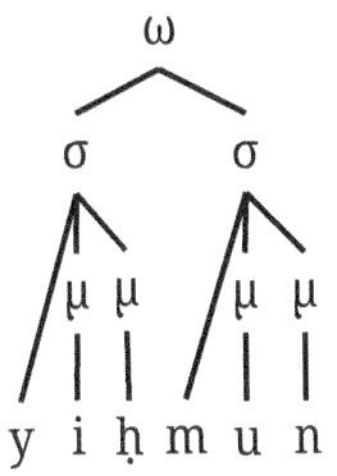

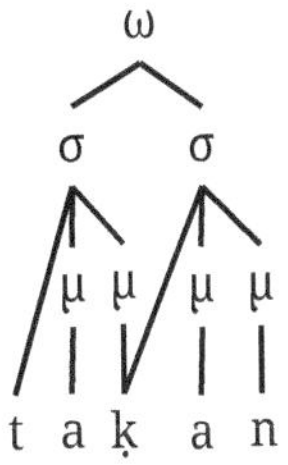

In contrast, if a final syllable is unstressed, it must be light, as in the examples in (21). The final syllables in these two examples are light because they end in singletons which are moraless coda consonants (see Section 8.3.2 for the weight of a final CVC syllable).

(21) *yiḥmun* ['yiḥ.mu**n**] *taḳḳan* ['taḳ.ḳa**n**]
'(that) they (M) see' IV.188 'knocks (EPL)' III.158

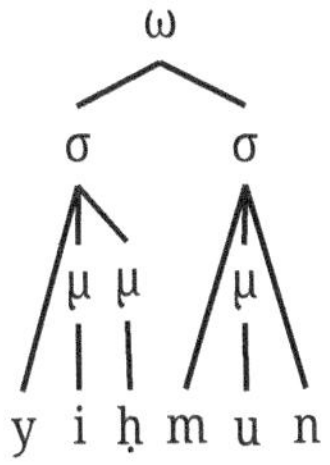

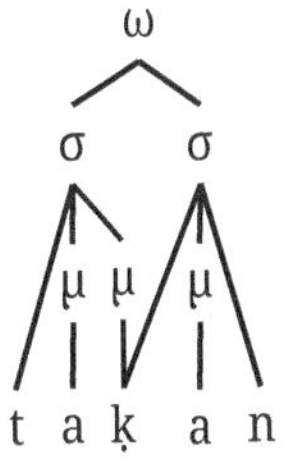

The examples in (20) and (21) above have shown that word-final geminates and word-final singletons contribute differently to the weight of the final syllable. This difference in syllable weight is what accounts for the difference in the stress pattern in pairs like *yiḥmunn* [yiḥ.'mun͡n] and *yiḥmun* ['yiḥ.mun], and *taḳḳann* [taḳ.'ḳan͡n]

---

12 It is transcribed as *taḳḳan* in the original text.

and *taḳḳan* [ˈtaḳ.ḳan]. In summary, word-final singletons and word-final geminates interact differently with word stress.

Second, word-final geminates and word-final singletons interact differently with the resyllabification process which applies (following vowel epenthesis) across word boundaries. If resyllabification applies across word boundaries, a word-final geminate will play the dual role of being the coda of the word-final syllable and at the same time the onset of the newly formed syllable (in a way similar to what a word-medial geminate does word-medially). This dual role cannot be played by a word-final singleton. For example, in the following derivation of ***xull*** *əblatō* 'all villages' III.172, when the word final geminate [l͡l] undergoes resyllabification, it serves as the coda for [xul]$_\sigma$ and as the onset for [**l**əb]$_\sigma$. However, in *ḳalle***s** *əd̲lūḳa* 'some firewood' IV.108, the word-final singleton [s] is resyllabified as the onset of the syllable [**s**əd̲]$_\sigma$ and is no longer the coda of the previous syllable (for vowel epenthesis and resyllabification across word boundaries, see Section 8.3.5).

(22) *A derivation to illustrate how word-final geminates and word-final singletons interact differently with resyllabification*

/**xull** blāt-ā/	/ḳalle**s** d̲lūḳ-a/	
xul͡l ⟨b⟩.lā.tā	ḳal.les ⟨d̲⟩.lū.ḳa	syllabification
ˈxul͡l ⟨b⟩.lā.**ˈtā**	**ˈḳal**.les ⟨d̲⟩.**ˈlū**.ḳa	stress assignment
ˈxul͡l ⟨b⟩.**la**.ˈtā	–	pretonic shortening
ˈxul͡l ⟨b⟩.la.ˈ**tō**	–	/ā/ rounding
ˈxul͡l **ə**⟨b⟩.la.ˈtō	ˈḳal.les **ə**⟨d̲⟩.ˈlū.ḳa	vowel epenthesis
ˈxul.**l**əb.la.ˈtō	ˈḳal.le.**s**əd̲.ˈlū.ḳa	**resyllabification**
[ˈxu**l**.**l**əb.la.ˈtō]	[ˈḳal.le.**s**əd̲.ˈlū.ḳa]	

The third argument for a distinction between geminates and singletons in word-final position concerns phonetic duration: The vowels which precede word-final singletons differ in duration from the vowels which precede word-final geminates. Figure 9.4 shows the distributions of the duration of short and long vowels (in ms) before word-final singletons (sgl) and word-final geminates (gem). The short vowels are shown in the first panel, the long vowels in the second.

As can be seen from Figure 9.4 and Table 9.6, the short vowels which precede a geminate are significantly longer than the short vowels which precede a singleton in word-final position (ratio 1:1.26). This difference is larger than the difference in word-medial position (ratio 1:1.08). The large difference in word-final position may be due to stress assignment. As argued above, a word-final CVC is light and is therefore unstressed, whereas a word-final CVGG is heavy and is therefore stressed. The assignment of stress on the final syllable may correlate with (or result in) a longer vowel duration.

In contrast, there is no statistically significant durational difference between the long vowels which precede a geminate and the long vowels which precede a singleton (according to the Wilcoxon test). However, this result is based on a small sample as not many Maaloula Aramaic words end in the sequence VVGG#. The data set contains only 16 tokens which have this sequence.

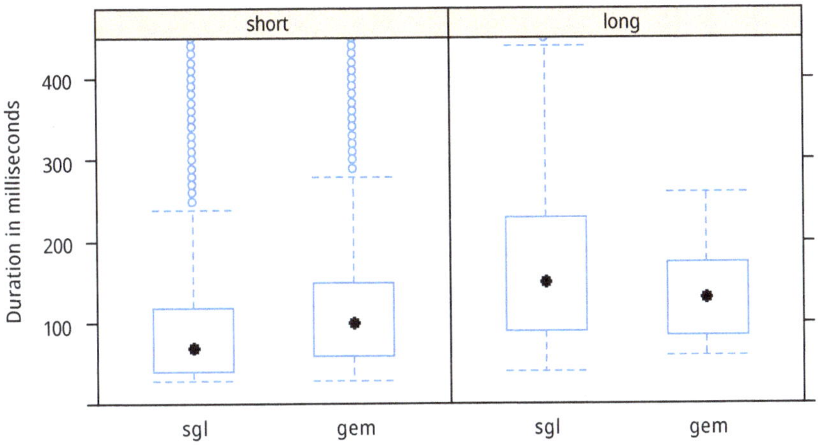

Fig. 9.4: Distributions of the duration of short and long vowels (in ms) before word-final singletons (sgl) and word-final geminates (gem)

Table 9.6: Duration of vowels (in ms) before word-final consonants

	Before singletons			**Before geminates**			**Ratio**	***P***
	Median	**Mean**	**SD**	**Median**	**Mean**	**SD**		
Short	70.00	97.58	80.32	100.00	123.15	91.61	1:1.26	<0.001
Long	150.00	180.79	129.36	130.00	137.50	59.39	1:0.76	0.262

The three arguments presented above provide support for a distinction between geminates and singletons in word-final position. We have seen how these geminates and singletons interact differently with word stress, resyllabification, and the duration of the preceding vowel. However, these arguments do not explain why word-final geminates have the same duration as word-final singletons, and why native speakers do not differentiate between word-final geminates and word-final singletons.

I propose that a degemination process is at work here. Word-final degemination is known in other Semitic languages (see, e.g., Cowell 1964: 27 for Damascus Arabic; Jastrow 1993: 17 for Turoyo). I argue that the domain of the degemination process in Maaloula Aramaic is the phonological phrase, rather than the phonological word. This phrase-final degemination rule is formalized in (23).

(23) *Phrase-final degemination*

$$\begin{bmatrix}\text{-syllabic}\\ \text{+long}\end{bmatrix} \rightarrow [\text{-long}] \;/\; \_\_\,]_{\text{Phrase}}$$

Geminates are realized as singletons in phrase-final position.

The phrase-final degemination rule is a postlexical rule that is ordered after stress assignment and resyllabification. This rule ordering explains why underlying word-final geminates interact with stress assignment and resyllabification before they degeminate if they occur in phrase-final position. The phrase-final degemination rule is illustrated in the derivation in (24) which shows how the word-final geminate /bb/ degeminates in phrase-final position in *ti ʕomre ra**bb*** 'who is old' III.122 but does not degeminate in phrase-medial position in *ra**bb** əb-ʕomra* 'old' III.242.

(24) *A derivation which illustrates the phrase-final degemination rule*

'who is old'	'old'	
/ti ʕomr-e ra**bb**/	/ra**bb** b-ʕomr-a/	
ti ʕom.re rab͡b	rab͡b ⟨b⟩.ʕom.ra	syllabification
ti '**ʕom**.re '**rab͡b**	'**rab͡b** ⟨b⟩.'**ʕom**.ra	stress assignment
–	'rab͡b ə⟨b⟩.'ʕom.ra	vowel epenthesis
–	'rab.**bəb**.'ʕom.ra	resyllabification
ti 'ʕom.re 'ra**b**	–	**phrase-final degemination**
[ti 'ʕom.re 'ra**b**]	['ra**b**.**b**əb.'ʕom.ra]	

9.3.4 Word-initial geminates

Moraic phonology does not provide a straightforward representation for word-initial (or rather syllable-initial) geminates. Hayes (1989: 302–303) provides and discusses a number of possibilities, one of which is to consider the mora of the word-initial consonant as a stray or extrasyllabic mora. This is the account which Davis

(1999: 98) adopts for representing word-initial geminates in Trukese, which Kiparsky (2003: 164–165) adopts for representing word-initial geminates in the Arabic varieties with initial geminates (e.g., Moroccan and Levantine Arabic), and which I adopt in this work for representing word-initial geminates in Maaloula Aramaic. This analysis is shown in (25) where the word-initial geminates /kk/ in ***kkōm*** 'black (INDF.F.SG)' III.356 is contrasted with the word-initial singleton /k/ in ***kōsa*** '(drinking) glass/cup' VI.443.

(25) *Moraic representation of word-initial geminates*

(a) The geminate /kk/
kkōm [ˈ**k͡k**ō.⟨m⟩]
'black (INDF.F.SG)'

(b) The singleton /k/
kōsa [ˈ**k**ō.sa]
'(drinking) glass/cup'

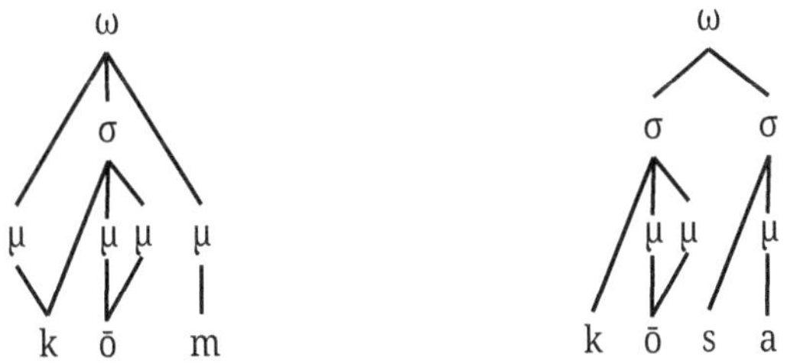

There seems to be no agreement among phonologists on whether a word-initial geminate should receive this stray (or extrasyllabic) mora even when they discuss the same language or dialect. For example, I mentioned above that Kiparsky (2003: 164–165) adopts the view that word-initial geminates are moraic in the Arabic dialects which have initial geminates. In contrast with Kiparsky, Davis & Ragheb (2014: 17) "suspect that in those [Arabic] dialects that have initial geminates, there is an asymmetry in that final geminates are underlyingly moraic while initial geminates are not." This discussion can also be extended to stray consonants in these dialects: Are they moraic (as Kiparsky 2003 represents them) or are they moraless (as Hayes 1995: 126–129 and Davis & Ragheb 2014: 10 represent them)? With regard to Maaloula Aramaic, I follow Kiparsky in assuming that word-initial geminates and stray consonants are moraic (see Section 8.3.4 for stray consonants), but that does not mean that I consider the other account less plausible. In fact, neither account would interfere with stress or stress-related processes because these stray moras occur outside syllables and therefore do not affect syllable weight. Whether one account can provide a more solid theoretical ground for the phonological processes in Maaloula Aramaic is a question which future research can investigate.

At the acoustic level, geminates are slightly longer than singletons in word-initial position, but this difference in duration is not statistically significant (see Figure 9.5 and Table 9.7).

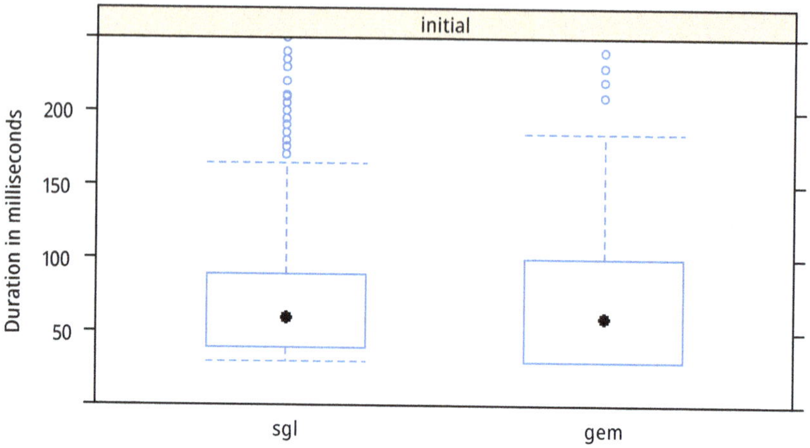

Fig. 9.5: Distributions of consonant duration in word-initial position

Table 9.7: Duration of word-initial consonants in milliseconds

Singleton			Geminate			Ratio	*P*
Median	**Mean**	**SD**	**Median**	**Mean**	**SD**		
60.00	74.70	79.07	60.00	81.53	98.14	1:1.09	0.597

This statistically insignificant difference in duration is surprising for the following reasons. First, the distinction between a word-initial singleton and a word-initial geminate can be heard and has long been marked in the transcripts produced by academic scholars and by members of the local community. Second, word-initial geminates interact with resyllabification, which applies across word boundaries, in a way that is different from how word-initial singletons interact with it. When resyllabification applies, a word-initial geminate will play the dual role of being the coda of the newly formed syllable and at the same time the onset of the word-initial syllable (e.g., the word-initial geminate [p͡p] in *ṯarč* ***əppōban*** 'two loaves (EPL)' III.128 in (26)). In contrast, this dual role cannot be played by a word-initial singleton (e.g., the word-initial singleton [ḏ] in *ṯarč* ***əḏrōʕ*** 'two cubits (EPL)' III.110 in (26)).

(26) *A derivation to illustrate the interaction between word-initial gemination and resyllabification*

‘two loaves (EPL)’	‘two cubits (EPL)’	
/t̠arč **pp**āb-an/	/t̠arč **d̠**rāʕ/	
t̠ar.⟨č⟩ p͡pā.ban	t̠ar.⟨č⟩ ⟨d̠⟩.rā.⟨ʕ⟩	syllabification
ˈ**t̠ar**.⟨č⟩ ˈ**p͡pā**.ban	ˈ**t̠ar**.⟨č⟩ ⟨d̠⟩.ˈ**rā**.⟨ʕ⟩	stress assignment
ˈt̠ar.⟨č⟩ ˈp͡p**ō**.ban	ˈt̠ar.⟨č⟩ ⟨d̠⟩.ˈr**ō**.⟨ʕ⟩	/ā/ rounding
ˈt̠ar.⟨č⟩ **ə**ˈp͡pō.ban	ˈt̠ar.⟨č⟩ **ə**⟨d̠⟩.ˈrō.⟨ʕ⟩	vowel epenthesis
ˈt̠ar.**čəp**.ˈpō.ban	ˈt̠ar.**čəd̠**.ˈrō.⟨ʕ⟩	resyllabification
[ˈt̠ar.čə**p**.ˈ**p**ō.ban]	[ˈt̠ar.čə**d̠**.ˈrō.⟨ʕ⟩]	

Third, some of the word-initial geminates are surface geminates, which are the result of the concatenation of two morphemes (e.g., ***nnōfeḳ*** /**n-n**āfeḳ/ → [ˈ**n͡n**ō.feḳ] ‘I (M) go out’ III.228) (see Section 9.2.2). This concatenation of consonants makes one expect a longer duration.

The unexpected result shown in Figure 9.5 and Table 9.7 may be due to the relatively small number of observations (225 tokens with word-initial geminates compared to 32,570 tokens with word-initial singletons). It may also be due to errors in the automatic segmentation of the TextGrid files (see Section 3.3.5). For example, the duration of the word-initial geminate in ***zzappen*** ‘sell (SBJV.2M.SG)’ IV.142 is 50 ms according to the automatic segmentation (shown in Figure 9.6 on the left). However, if the boundaries were set manually, as in Figure 9.6 on the right, the duration would be 82 ms.

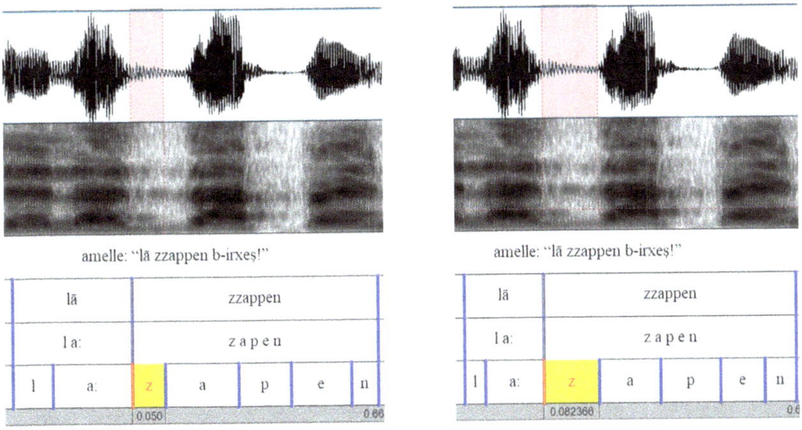

Fig. 9.6: Automatic segmentation of a TextGrid file (on the left) compared to manual segmentation (on the right)

Although these errors may have also occurred in the automatic segmentation of word-medial and word-final consonants, the large number of those observations could have reduced the effect of these errors. Future research will have to determine whether there is a durational difference and will have to identify the variables which influence it.

9.4 Conclusion

In this chapter, I have investigated geminates in Maaloula Aramaic by grouping them according to two principles of classification: provenance and position. According to their provenance, geminates are classified as either underlying geminates or surface geminates. Underlying geminates can be morphological (i.e., as a result of non-concatenative morphological processes) or lexical (e.g., as a result of historical assimilation). Surface geminates are created either through morphosyntactic processes when two identical consonants are concatenated across morpheme or word boundaries, or through phonological processes such as assimilation (see Hayes 1986; Galea 2016; Ben Hedia 2019).

According to their position in the word, geminates are classified as word-initial, word-medial, and word-final (Arnold 1990a: 17). Although previous accounts have reported that word-initial geminates are attested in Maaloula Aramaic, and although it can be argued that these geminates exist on the basis of phonological, morphological, and auditory grounds, the acoustic results have shown that geminates in this position are only slightly longer than singletons. The singleton-to-geminate duration ratio is 1:1.09, and the difference between their means is not statistically significant. This unexpected result may be due to the small number of words which start with a geminate or to errors in the automatic segmentation of the TextGrid files. In any case, this issue remains unsolved and is worthy of future research because word-initial geminates are not as common cross-linguistically and are not as widely investigated as word-medial geminates (Muller 2001: 17; Davis 2011: 5; Galea 2016: 48, 55).

In word-medial position, geminates are significantly longer than singletons (the singleton-to-geminate duration ratio is 1:1.36). The duration of the preceding vowel was also measured, but the differences in vowel duration did not turn out to be as large as the difference in consonant duration. This result has shown that consonant duration is the primary correlate of word-medial gemination, supporting the cross-linguistic evidence reported by previous research (e.g., Cohn, Ham & Podesva 1999; Payne 2005; Khattab & Al-Tamimi 2014; Galea 2016).

In word-final position, the durations of geminates and singletons were nearly identical (the singleton-to-geminate duration ratio is 1:0.99). These nearly identical durations have been argued to be due to the neutralizing effect of a phrase-final degemination rule. Word-final degemination is known in other Semitic languages (see, e.g., Cowell 1964: 27 for Damascus Arabic; Jastrow 1993: 17 for Turoyo). The application of this rule after the other phonological processes explains why word-final singletons and word-final geminates interact differently with word stress, re-syllabification, and the duration of the preceding vowel.

10 Stress

10.1 Introduction

In this chapter, I describe word stress in Maaloula Aramaic. I will begin by reviewing and revising the word-stress algorithm which has been known since Bergsträsser (1915). I will then review and formalize the two stress-dependent processes: pretonic raising of short mid vowels and pretonic shortening of long vowels. Lastly, I will review and evaluate the restrictions (described in Arnold 1990a) on the distribution of vowels in stressed, pretonic, and post-tonic positions.

10.2 Stress algorithm

The word-stress algorithm, as put forward in the available literature on Maaloula Aramaic (e.g., Bergsträsser 1915: xxi; Spitaler 1938: 46; Arnold 1990a: 40), is given in (1). For clarity, the stressed syllables are indicated by an acute accent, and the syllable boundaries are set according to Arnold's (1990a: 39) syllabification scheme.

(1) *Maaloula Aramaic stress algorithm (according to the available literature)*

(a) Stress the final syllable if it has a long vowel or ends with two consonants or a geminate:

mal.kṓ	'kings'	IV.46
i.mṓḏ	'today'	III.196
ray.šáyn	'their heads'	III.350
ʕan.mášḳ	'I am watering'	III.346
min.náyy	'from them'	III.136
riḥ.máčč [1]	'she loved me'	III.132

(b) Otherwise stress the penultimate syllable:

ṯár.ʕa	'door'	IV.68
čám.muz	'July'	III.32
šḗ.ḏa	'devil'	IV.266
ḥaẓ.ẓū́.ra	'apple'	III.204
ṯi.na.ġél.ča	'hen'	IV.124
saḥ.ḥar.yṓ.ṯa	'crates; boxes'	III.326

1 It is transcribed as *raḥmačč* in the original text.

https://doi.org/10.1515/9783111447124-010

Arnold (1990a: 40–41, 328) points out that there is an exception to this algorithm. The loanwords which have the pattern CVCVCa receive stress on the antepenultimate syllable, as in (2). The examples are from Arnold's grammar (syllabification added).

(2)	*sá.la.ṭa*	'salad'	V.328
	má.ka.na	'car'	V.328
	sí.na.ma	'cinema'	V.328

The corpus data show that the vast majority of words are stressed on the final or penultimate syllable (as predicted by the stress algorithm). A small minority of words (around 70 word forms) do not conform to what the algorithm predicts. However, these words are not restricted to the specific category described by Arnold (i.e., only loanwords which have the pattern [CV́.CV.Ca]). These words belong to different templatic patterns, as the examples in (3) show, and not all of them are necessarily loanwords.

(3)	*ʕá.ly.ṭa*	'leaf'	III.154	[CV́.CV.CV]
	ʕá.ra.beṭ	'Arabic'	III.184	[CV́.CV.CVC]
	mḳá.rw.šin	'they talk noisily'	III.310	[CCV́.CV.CVC]
	mḥát.ti.tin	'they set/make certain'	III.202	[CCV́G.GV.CVC]
	mit.tá.rw.šin	'they dress as dervishes'	IV.164	[CVG.GV́.CV.CVC]
	mič.rát.ti.tin	'they visit frequently'	III.260	[CVC.CV́G.GV.CVC]

Although these words have different templatic patterns, they have two things in common. First, they have the same stress pattern. In all of the found examples, stress falls on the antepenultimate syllable even if the word still has preantepenultimate syllables (e.g., *mittárwšin* [CVG.GV́.CV.CVC] and *mičráttitin* [CVC.CV́G.GV.CVC]). Second, these words have light final and light penultimate syllables (i.e., the final syllable is CV or CVC, and the penultimate syllable is CV, see Section 8.3.2). Given these similarities, I suggest that these polysyllabic words be integrated into the stress algorithm. In (4) I present a revised stress algorithm in order to accommodate these words. I present the stress algorithm from a moraic perspective, which is in line with the analysis presented in Chapter 8. In the presented examples, the syllable boundaries are set according to the syllabification scheme described in Section 8.3.

(4) *Maaloula Aramaic stress algorithm (revised moraic version)*

(a) Stress the final syllable if it is bimoraic:

malkō	μμ μμ [mal.ˈkō]	‘kings’	IV.46
rayšayn	μμ μμ μ [ray. ˈšay.⟨n⟩]	‘their heads’	III.350

(b) Otherwise stress the penultimate syllable if it is bimoraic:

ṯarʕa	μμ μ [ˈṯar.ʕa]	‘door’	IV.68
ḥaẓẓūra	μμ μμ μ [ḥaẓ.ˈẓū. ra]	‘apple’	III.204
ṯinaġelča	μ μ μμ μ [ṯi.na.ˈġel.ča]	‘hen’	IV.124

(c) Otherwise stress the penultimate syllable in disyllabic words and stress the antepenultimate syllable in polysyllabic words:

Penultimate stress in disyllabic words:

baḥar	μ μ [ˈba.ḥar]	‘a lot; very’	III.146
aḏab	μ μ [ˈʔa.ḏab]	‘it (M) melted’	III.32

Antepenultimate stress in polysyllabic words:

ʕalyṯa	μ μ μ [ˈʕa.li.ṯa]	‘leaf’	III.154
ʕarabeṯ	μ μ μ [ˈʕa.ra.beṯ]	‘Arabic’	III.184
mičrattitin	μμ μμ μ μ [mič.ˈrat.ti.tin]	‘they visit frequently’	III.260

This algorithm shows that Maaloula Aramaic has a three-syllable window at the right word edge, which means that stress must fall on the final, penultimate, or antepenultimate syllable of the word. Maaloula Aramaic shows a strong tendency to place stress on one of the last two syllables. It is only when the final and penultimate syllables are light (i.e., monomoraic) in polysyllabic words that stress can be placed on the antepenultimate syllable, regardless of its weight.

10.3 Stress-dependent processes

Sometimes, different inflectional forms of the same lemma have different stress patterns. For example, in the singular noun *malka* 'king', in (5), stress falls on the penultimate syllable $[\text{mal}]_\sigma$ because (a) it is bimoraic, and (b) the final syllable $[\text{ka}]_\sigma$ is monomoraic. In the plural form *malkō* 'kings', which is formed by attaching the plural morpheme *-ō*, the final syllable $[\text{kō}]_\sigma$ receives stress because it is bimoraic (see Spitaler 1938: 104–107 and Arnold 1990a: 289–290, 2006: 8 for plural formation).

(5) Singular form — Plural form

malk-a ['mal.ka]	*malk-ō* [mal.'kō]
king-NE	king-PL
'king' IV.14	'kings' IV.46

This example shows the alternation which the syllable $[\text{mal}]_\sigma$ undergoes. It is stressed in ['mal.ka] but pretonic in [mal.'kō]. The alternation between stressed and pretonic did not change the quality of the vowel in this syllable. However, if the vowel were a mid or a long vowel, then the quality and length of the vowel would change as the syllable stress changes. It is to these changes that I turn in the following sections.

10.3.1 Pretonic raising of short mid vowels

The mid vowels /e o/ are realized as [i u] respectively when they occur in a pretonic syllable (Spitaler 1938: 4–5, 9; Arnold 1990a: 26). These stress-induced vowel alternations can be considered the result of a pretonic vowel raising process that targets mid vowels. This process is exemplified in (6). Some of the presented examples are also found in Spitaler (1938: 5) and Arnold (1990a: 26). The examples are given in pairs of word forms which share the same lemma. In the first word form of each pair, the mid vowel occurs in a stressed syllable. In the second word form, the underlyingly mid vowel occurs in a pretonic syllable, and therefore undergoes pretonic raising.

(6) (a) /e/ → [i] in pretonic position

ġerma	/ġerm-a/	→	['ġer.ma]	'bone'	IV.54
ġirmō	/ġerm-ā/	→	[ġir.'mō]	'bones'	IV.54

*ġ**e**šra*	/ġ**e**šr-a/	→	[ˈġ**e**š.ra]	'(roof) beam'	IV.230
*ġ**i**šrō*	/ġ**e**šr-ā/	→	[ġ**i**š.ˈrō]	'(roof) beams'	IV.230
*ġ**e**lta*	/ġ**e**lt-a/	→	[ˈġ**e**l.ta]	'skin'	III.102
*ġ**i**ltō*	/ġ**e**lt-ā/	→	[ġ**i**l.ˈtō]	'skins'	III.102
***e**šna*	/**e**šn-a/	→	[ˈʔ**e**š.na]	'year'	III.98
***i**šnō*	/**e**šn-ā/	→	[ʔ**i**š.ˈnō]	'years'	III.376
*ḳ**e**lfa*	/ḳ**e**lf-a/	→	[ˈḳ**e**l.fa]	'(fruit) skin'	VI.463
*ḳ**i**lfō*	/ḳ**e**lf-ā/	→	[ḳ**i**l.ˈfō]	'(fruit) skins'	III.328

(b) /o/ → [u] in pretonic position

*k**o**rsa*	/k**o**rs-a/	→	[ˈk**o**r.sa]	'chair'	IV.78
*k**u**rsō*	/k**o**rs-ā/	→	[k**u**r.ˈsō]	'chairs'	III.160
*x**o**ṯla*	/x**o**ṯl-a/	→	[ˈx**o**ṯ.la]	'wall'	III.232
*x**u**ṯlō*	/x**o**ṯl-ā/	→	[x**u**ṯ.ˈlō]	'walls'	IV.182
*b**o**ġta*	/b**o**ġt-a/	→	[ˈb**o**ġ.ta]	'rug'	III.110
*b**u**ġtō*	/b**o**ġt-ā/	→	[b**u**ġ.ˈtō]	'rugs'	III.112
*f**o**rna*	/f**o**rn-a/	→	[ˈf**o**r.na]	'oven'	III.44
*f**u**rnō*	/f**o**rn-ā/	→	[f**u**r.ˈnō]	'ovens'	III.42
***o**rḥa*	/**o**rḥ-a/	→	[ˈʔ**o**r.ḥa]	'time; once'	IV.188
***u**rḥō*	/**o**rḥ-ā/	→	[ʔ**u**r.ˈḥō]	'times'	III.80

This process is formalized in (7) and illustrated in the derivation in (8). In this derivation, I present two pairs of nouns from the examples given in (6).

(7) *Pretonic raising of short mid vowels*

$$\begin{bmatrix} \text{+syllabic} \\ \text{-long} \\ \text{-high} \\ \text{-low} \end{bmatrix} \rightarrow [\text{+high}] \;/\; \_\_\; C_0 \begin{bmatrix} \text{+syllabic} \\ \text{+stress} \end{bmatrix}$$ [2]

The mid vowels /e/ *and* /o/ *are realized as* [i] *and* [u] *respectively in pretonic position.*

2 C_0 refers to any number of consonants.

(8) *A derivation to illustrate the pretonic raising rule*

'bone'	'bones'	'chair'	'chairs'	
/ġ**e**rm-a/	/ġ**e**rm-ā/	/k**o**rs-a/	/k**o**rs-ā/	
ġer.ma	ġer.mā	kor.sa	kor.sā	syllabification
ˈ**ġer**.ma	ġer.ˈ**mā**	ˈ**kor**.sa	kor.ˈ**sā**	stress assignment
–	ġ**i**r.ˈmā	–	k**u**r.ˈsā	**pretonic raising**
–	ġir.ˈm**ō**	–	kur.ˈs**ō**	/ā/ rounding
[ˈġ**e**r.ma]	[ġ**i**r.ˈmō]	[ˈk**o**r.sa]	[k**u**r.ˈsō]	

10.3.2 Pretonic shortening of long vowels

The previous studies (e.g., Spitaler 1938: 4–5, 9; Arnold 1990a: 22–23, 26) have also observed that all long vowels undergo sound changes when they occur in pretonic position. The long high vowels /ī/ and /ū/ are shortened to [i] and [u] respectively, as in (9a, b). The long mid vowels /ē/ and /ō/ are shortened and raised to [i] and [u] respectively, as in (9c, d). The long low vowel /ā/ is shortened to [a], as in (9e). Some of the examples below are also found in Spitaler (1938: 4, 7, 9) and Arnold (1990a: 23, 26, 2011: 687).

(9) (a) /ī/ → [i] in pretonic position

*ḏ**ī**ka*	/ḏ**ī**k-a/	→ [ˈḏ**ī**.ka]	'rooster'	IV.22
*ḏ**i**kō*	/ḏ**ī**k-ā/	→ [ḏ**i**.ˈkō]	'roosters'	IV.216
*ḳ**ī**sa*	/ḳ**ī**s-a/	→ [ˈḳ**ī**.sa]	'stick'	III.346
*ḳ**i**sō*	/ḳ**ī**s-ā/	→ [ḳ**i**.ˈsō]	'sticks'	III.348
*b**ī**ra*	/b**ī**r-a/	→ [ˈb**ī**.ra]	'well'	IV.218
*b**i**rō*	/b**ī**r-ā/	→ [b**i**.ˈrō]	'wells'	IV.322
*ġb**ī**na*	/ġb**ī**n-a/	→ [⟨ġ⟩.ˈb**ī**.na]	'eyebrow'	VI.301
*ġb**i**nō*	/ġb**ī**n-ā/	→ [⟨ġ⟩.b**i**.ˈnō]	'eyebrows'	IV.252
*čilm**ī**ḏa*	/čilm**ī**ḏ-a/	→ [čil.ˈm**ī**.ḏa]	'disciple'	VI.533
*čilm**i**ḏō*	/čilm**ī**ḏ-ā/	→ [čil.m**i**.ˈḏō]	'disciples'	III.154

(b) /ū/ → [u] in pretonic position

*ʕarḳ**ū**ba*	/ʕarḳ**ū**b-a/	→ [ʕar.ˈḳ**ū**.ba]	'mountain'	IV.10
*ʕarḳ**u**bō*	/ʕarḳ**ū**b-ā/	→ [ʕar.ḳ**u**.ˈbō]	'mountains'	IV.214

*ḥaẓẓ**ū**ra*	/ḥaẓẓ**ū**r-a/	→	[ḥaẓ.ˈ**ẓū**.ra]	‘apple’	III.204
*ḥaẓẓ**u**rō*	/ḥaẓẓ**ū**r-ā/	→	[ḥaẓ.**ẓu**.ˈrō]	‘apples’	III.126
*ṭ**ū**ra*	/ṭ**ū**r-a/	→	[ˈ**ṭū**.ra]	‘mountain’	IV.334
*ṭ**u**rō*	/ṭ**ū**r-ā/	→	[**ṭu**.ˈrō]	‘mountains’	VI.870
*ḥ**ū**ṭa*	/ḥ**ū**ṭ-a/	→	[ˈ**ḥū**.ṭa]	‘thread’	III.62
*ḥ**u**ṭō*	/ḥ**ū**ṭ-ā/	→	[**ḥu**.ˈṭō]	‘threads’	III.112
*ḥ**ū**ya*	/ḥ**ū**y-a/	→	[ˈ**ḥū**.ya]	‘snake’	IV.116
*ḥ**u**yō*	/ḥ**ū**y-ā/	→	[**ḥu**.ˈyō]	‘snakes’	IV.218

(c) /ē/ → [i] in pretonic position

*ḏ**ē**ba*	/ḏ**ē**b-a/	→	[ˈ**ḏē**.ba]	‘wolf’	IV.194
*ḏ**i**bō*	/ḏ**ē**b-ā/	→	[**ḏi**.ˈbō]	‘wolves’	IV.194
*x**ē**fa*	/x**ē**f-a/	→	[ˈ**xē**.fa]	‘stone’	IV.188
*x**i**fō*	/x**ē**f-ā/	→	[**xi**.ˈfō]	‘stones’	III.192
*ʕ**ē**ḏa*	/ʕ**ē**ḏ-a/	→	[ˈ**ʕē**.ḏa]	‘feast day’	IV.308
*ʕ**i**ḏō*	/ʕ**ē**ḏ-ā/	→	[**ʕi**.ˈḏō]	‘feast days’	III.76
*ḳatt**ē**ša*	/ḳatt**ē**š-a/	→	[ḳat.ˈ**tē**.ša]	‘saint’	III.278
*ḳatt**i**šō*	/ḳatt**ē**š-ā/	→	[ḳat.**ti**.ˈšō]	‘saints’	VI.491
*ḳatt**ē**la*	/ḳatt**ē**l-a/	→	[ḳat.ˈ**tē**.la]	‘(oil) lamp’	VI.486
*ḳatt**i**lō*	/ḳatt**ē**l-ā/	→	[ḳat.**ti**.ˈlō]	‘(oil) lamps’	Rizkallah 2010: 56

(d) /ō/ → [u] in pretonic position

*ḥ**ō**na*	/ḥ**ō**n-a/	→	[ˈ**ḥō**.na]	‘brother’	III.300
*ḥ**u**nō*	/ḥ**ō**n-ā/	→	[**ḥu**.ˈnō]	‘brothers’	III.262
*ʕaḳ**ō**na*	/ʕaḳ**ō**n-a/	→	[ʕa.ˈ**ḳō**.na]	‘crow’	IV.312
*ʕaḳ**u**nō*	/ʕaḳ**ō**n-ā/	→	[ʕa.**ḳu**.ˈnō]	‘crows’	IV.312
*naḳ**ō**sa*	/naḳ**ō**s-a/	→	[na.ˈ**ḳō**.sa]	‘bell’	III.152
*naḳ**u**sō*	/naḳ**ō**s-ā/	→	[na.**ḳu**.ˈsō]	‘bells’	III.174
*y**ō**ma*	/y**ō**m-a/	→	[ˈ**yō**.ma]	‘day’	III.62
*y**u**mō*	/y**ō**m-ā/	→	[**yu**.ˈmō]	‘days’	III.44
*xar**ō**fa*	/xar**ō**f-a/	→	[xa.ˈ**rō**.fa]	‘sheep (SG)’	III.308
*xar**u**fō*	/xar**ō**f-ā/	→	[xa.**ru**.ˈfō]	‘sheep (PL)’	III.148

(e) /ā/ → [a] in pretonic position

xṯōba	/xṯ**ā**b-a/	→ [⟨x⟩.ˈṯ**ō**.ba]	'book'	IV.36
xṯabō	/xṯ**ā**b-ā/	→ [⟨x⟩.ṯ**a**.ˈbō]	'books'	IV.38
blōta	/bl**ā**t-a/	→ [⟨b⟩.ˈl**ō**.ta]	'village'	IV.12
blatō	/bl**ā**t-ā/	→ [⟨b⟩.l**a**.ˈtō]	'villages'	III.80
ḥmōra	/ḥm**ā**r-a/	→ [⟨ḥ⟩.ˈm**ō**.ra]	'donkey'	IV.284
ḥmarō	/ḥm**ā**r-ā/	→ [⟨ḥ⟩.m**a**.ˈrō]	'donkeys'	III.98
ḏōḏa	/ḏ**ā**ḏ-a/	→ [ˈḏ**ō**.ḏa]	'paternal uncle'	III.220
ḏaḏō	/ḏ**ā**ḏ-ā/	→ [ḏ**a**.ˈḏō]	'paternal uncles'	IV.36
milōxa	/mil**ā**x-a/	→ [mi.ˈl**ō**.xa]	'angel'	III.220
milaxō	/mil**ā**x-ā/	→ [mi.l**a**.ˈxō]	'angels'	III.164

I argue that these complicated alternations are the result of the interaction of different phonological processes. The first process at work is pretonic shortening:

(10) *Pretonic shortening of long vowels*

$$\begin{bmatrix}\text{+syllabic}\\ \text{+long}\end{bmatrix} \rightarrow \text{[-long]} \;/\; \_\_\ C_0 \begin{bmatrix}\text{+syllabic}\\ \text{+stress}\end{bmatrix}$$

The long vowels are realized as short vowels in pretonic position.

This process can account for the alternations in (9a, b) (i.e., /ī/ → [i] and /ū/ → [u]) as the following derivation shows. In this derivation, I present a pair of nouns (in the singular and plural) from each of the first two groups in (9) above.

(11) *A derivation to illustrate the pretonic shortening rule*

'rooster'	'roosters'	'mountain'	'mountains'	
/ḏ**ī**k-a/	/ḏ**ī**k-ā/	/ʕarḳ**ū**b-a/	/ʕarḳ**ū**b-ā/	
ḏī.ka	ḏī.kā	ʕar.ḳū.ba	ʕar.ḳū.bā	syllabification
ˈ**ḏī**.ka	ḏī.ˈ**kā**	ʕar.ˈ**ḳū**.ba	ʕar.ḳū.ˈ**bā**	stress assignment
–	**ḏi**.ˈkā	–	ʕar.**ḳu**.ˈbā	**pretonic shortening**
–	ḏi.ˈ**kō**	–	ʕar.ḳu.ˈ**bō**	/ā/ rounding
[ˈḏ**ī**.ka]	[ḏ**i**.ˈkō]	[ʕar.ˈḳ**ū**.ba]	[ʕar.ḳ**u**.ˈbō]	

However, the pretonic shortening process alone cannot account for the alternations in (9c, d) (i.e., /ē/ → [i] and /ō/ → [u]). It is the interaction of pretonic shortening and pretonic raising that can fully account for these alternations, as the derivation in

(12) shows. In this derivation, I assume that pretonic shortening is ordered before pretonic raising.

(12) *A derivation to illustrate the interaction of pretonic shortening and pretonic raising*

‘wolf’	‘wolves’	‘brother’	‘brothers’	
/ḏ**ē**b-a/	/ḏ**ē**b-ā/	/ḥ**ō**n-a/	/ḥ**ō**n-ā/	
ḏē.ba	ḏē.bā	ḥō.na	ḥō.nā	syllabification
ˈ**ḏē**.ba	ḏē.ˈ**bā**	ˈ**ḥō**.na	ḥō.ˈ**nā**	stress assignment
–	ḏ**e**.ˈbā	–	ḥ**o**.ˈnā	**pretonic shortening**
–	ḏ**i**.ˈbā	–	ḥ**u**.ˈnā	**pretonic raising**
–	ḏi.ˈb**ō**	–	ḥu.ˈn**ō**	/ā/ rounding
[ˈḏ**ē**.ba]	[ḏ**i**.ˈbō]	[ˈḥ**ō**.na]	[ḥ**u**.ˈnō]	

If pretonic raising (which targets only short mid vowels) were ordered before pretonic shortening, the wrong output would be produced, as in (13).

(13) *A derivation that gives the wrong output*

‘wolf’	‘wolves’	‘brother’	‘brothers’	
/ḏ**ē**b-a/	/ḏ**ē**b-ā/	/ḥ**ō**n-a/	/ḥ**ō**n-ā/	
ḏē.ba	ḏē.bā	ḥō.na	ḥō.nā	syllabification
ˈ**ḏē**.ba	ḏē.ˈ**bā**	ˈ**ḥō**.na	ḥō.ˈ**nā**	stress assignment
–	–	–	–	**pretonic raising**
–	ḏ**e**.ˈbā	–	ḥ**o**.ˈnā	**pretonic shortening**
–	ḏe.ˈb**ō**	–	ḥo.ˈn**ō**	/ā/ rounding
[ˈḏ**ē**.ba]	*[ḏ**e**.ˈbō]	[ˈḥ**ō**.na]	*[ḥ**o**.ˈnō]	

As for (9e), the pretonic shortening process is responsible for the alternations in the pretonic syllable (i.e., /ā/ → [a]), and the /ā/ rounding process is responsible for the alternations in the stressed syllable (i.e., /ā/ → [ō]). This is shown in the following derivation, in which I assume that pretonic shortening is ordered before /ā/ rounding.

(14) *A derivation to illustrate the interaction of pretonic shortening and /ā/ rounding*

'book'	'books'	'village'	'villages'	
/xṯ**ā**b-a/	/xṯ**ā**b-ā/	/bl**ā**t-a/	/bl**ā**t-ā/	
⟨x⟩.ṯā.ba	⟨x⟩.ṯā.bā	⟨b⟩.lā.ta	⟨b⟩.lā.tā	syllabification
⟨x⟩.ˈ**ṯā**.ba	⟨x⟩.ṯā.ˈ**bā**	⟨b⟩.ˈ**lā**.ta	⟨b⟩.lā.ˈ**tā**	stress assignment
–	⟨x⟩.**ṯa**.ˈbā	–	⟨b⟩.**la**.ˈtā	**pretonic shortening**
–	–	–	–	pretonic raising
⟨x⟩.ˈṯ**ō**.ba	⟨x⟩.ṯa.ˈb**ō**	⟨b⟩.ˈl**ō**.ta	⟨b⟩.la.ˈt**ō**	**/ā/ rounding**
[⟨x⟩.ˈṯ**ō**.ba]	[⟨x⟩.**ṯa**.ˈbō]	[⟨b⟩.ˈl**ō**.ta]	[⟨b⟩.**la**.ˈtō]	

If /ā/ rounding were ordered before pretonic shortening, the wrong output would be produced, as in (15).

(15) *A derivation that gives the wrong output*

'book'	'books'	'village'	'villages'	
/xṯ**ā**b-a/	/xṯ**ā**b-ā/	/bl**ā**t-a/	/bl**ā**t-ā/	
⟨x⟩.ṯā.ba	⟨x⟩.ṯā.bā	⟨b⟩.lā.ta	⟨b⟩.lā.tā	syllabification
⟨x⟩.ˈ**ṯā**.ba	⟨x⟩.ṯā.ˈ**bā**	⟨b⟩.ˈ**lā**.ta	⟨b⟩.lā.ˈ**tā**	stress assignment
⟨x⟩.ˈṯ**ō**.ba	⟨x⟩.ṯ**ō**.ˈb**ō**	⟨b⟩.ˈl**ō**.ta	⟨b⟩.l**ō**.ˈt**ō**	**/ā/ rounding**
–	⟨x⟩.**ṯo**.ˈbō	–	⟨b⟩.**lo**.ˈtō	**pretonic shortening**
–	⟨x⟩.**ṯu**.ˈbō	–	⟨b⟩.**lu**.ˈtō	pretonic raising
[⟨x⟩.ˈṯ**ō**.ba]	*[⟨x⟩.**ṯu**.ˈbō]	[⟨b⟩.ˈl**ō**.ta]	*[⟨b⟩.**lu**.ˈtō]	

The assumption that the word forms in (9e) have an underlying /ā/ (e.g., /xṯ**ā**b-a/ 'book'), whereas the word forms in (9d) have an underlying /ō/ (e.g., /ḥ**ō**n-a/ 'brother') although in their citation forms all of them have [ō] (e.g., *xṯ**ō**ba* 'book' and *ḥ**ō**na* 'brother') has already been made in Section 7.3.1. In that section, I assumed that the words which have a surface [ō] (e.g., *xṯōba* and *ḥōna*) may have either /ō/ or /ā/ in their underlying forms (i.e., /xṯ**ā**b-a/ vs. /ḥ**ō**n-a/) (see Spitaler 1938: 7, 40 and Arnold 1990a: 22, 27 for the historical perspective). This assumption has proven helpful in Section 7.3.1 as it explained why words, such as *xṯ**ō**ba*, do not undergo regressive umlaut when attached to the affix *-i* (i.e., *xṯ**ō**bi* and not **xṯ**ū**bi* 'my book'), whereas words, such as *ḥ**ō**na*, undergo regressive umlaut (i.e., *ḥ**ū**ni* 'my brother') (see the first two columns in (16)). This same assumption has also proven helpful in this section as it has explained why word forms which have the same surface vowel in a stressed syllable, such as *xṯ**ō**ba* [⟨x⟩.ˈṯ**ō**.ba] and *ḥ**ō**na* [ˈḥ**ō**.na], have different vowels in a pretonic syllable (e.g., *xṯ**a**bō* [⟨x⟩.**ṯa**.ˈbō] 'books' vs. *ḥ**u**nō* [**ḥu**.ˈnō] 'brothers') (see the third and fourth columns in (16)).

(16) *A derivation that gives the correct output because the words in (9e) and in (9d) are assumed to have different underlying vowels*

'my book'	'my brother'	'books'	'brothers'	
/xṯ**ā**b-i/	/ḥ**ō**n-i/	/xṯ**ā**b-ā/	/ḥ**ō**n-ā/	
⟨x⟩.ṯā.bi	ḥō.ni	⟨x⟩.ṯā.bā	ḥō.nā	syllabification
⟨x⟩.ˈ**ṯā**.bi	ˈ**ḥō**.ni	⟨x⟩.ṯā.ˈ**bā**	ḥō.ˈ**nā**	stress assignment
–	ˈḥ**ū**.ni	–	–	regressive umlaut
–	–	⟨x⟩.ṯ**a**.ˈbā	ḥ**o**.ˈnā	pretonic shortening
–	–	–	ḥ**u**.ˈnā	pretonic raising
⟨x⟩.ˈṯ**ō**.bi	–	⟨x⟩.ṯa.ˈb**ō**	ḥu.ˈn**ō**	/ā/ rounding
[⟨x⟩.ˈṯō.bi]	[ˈḥū.ni]	[⟨x⟩.ṯ**a**.ˈbō]	[ḥ**u**.ˈnō]	

10.4 The distribution of vowels

There are restrictions on the distribution of Maaloula Aramaic vowels. For example, a long vowel does not occur in the antepenultimate syllable (see Arnold 1990a: 22). These restrictions apply depending on the position of the vowels in relation to word stress.

10.4.1 Positional restrictions on the distribution of long vowels

This section reviews and discusses two generalizations made by Arnold (1990a: 22). The first generalization predicts the maximum number of long vowels that a word can have, and the second generalization specifies the syllables in which long vowels can occur. In this section, I also present and discuss possible options for accounting for the words which have a surface [ā].

The number of long vowels in a word

According to Arnold (1990a: 22, 2011: 687), a word can have no more than one long vowel, and the syllable that contains this long vowel is the stress-bearing syllable. This generalization is supported by the corpus data. Each of the examples shown in (17) has only one long vowel, and the syllable that contains the long vowel receives stress because long vowels are bimoraic (see Section 10.2).

(17)	*ʕēḏa*	[ˈʕ**ē**.ḏa]	'feast (day)'	IV.308
	nīṣa	[ˈn**ī**.ṣa]	'porcupine'	III.350
	ḳašīša	[ḳa.ˈš**ī**.ša]	'priest'	III.156

ʕurpōla	[ʕur.ˈpō.la]	'sieve'	III.44
ḳawwōm	[ḳaw.ˈwō.⟨m⟩]	'immediately; quickly'	IV.296
ʕannelē	[ʕan.ne.ˈlē]	'sing (2M.SG) for him!'	III.56
buġtō	[buġ.ˈtō]	'rugs'	III.112

A word can have no more than one long vowel because of the pretonic shortening rule (see Section 10.3.2). If a word has two long vowels in the underlying representation, only the stressed one will surface as a long vowel, whereas the pretonic one will surface as a short vowel, as the following derivation shows. The presented examples are taken from Section 10.3.2.

(18) *A derivation which shows why a word can have no more than one long vowel*

'roosters'	'mountains'	'wolves'	'crows'	
/ḏīk-**ā**/	/ʕarḳūb-**ā**/	/ḏēb-**ā**/	/ʕaḳōn-**ā**/	
ḏī.kā	ʕar.ḳū.bā	ḏē.bā	ʕa.ḳō.nā	syllabification
ḏī.ˈ**kā**	ʕar.ḳū.ˈ**bā**	ḏē.ˈ**bā**	ʕa.ḳō.ˈ**nā**	stress assignment
ḏ**i**.ˈkā	ʕar.ḳ**u**.ˈbā	ḏ**e**.ˈbā	ʕa.ḳ**o**.ˈnā	**pretonic shortening**
–	–	ḏi.ˈbā	ʕa.ḳ**u**.ˈnā	pretonic raising
ḏi.ˈk**ō**	ʕar.ḳu.ˈb**ō**	ḏi.ˈb**ō**	ʕa.ḳu.ˈn**ō**	/ā/ rounding
[ḏ**i**.ˈkō]	[ʕar.ḳ**u**.ˈbō]	[ḏ**i**.ˈbō]	[ʕa.ḳ**u**.ˈnō]	

The position of long vowels

A long vowel can occur either in the final or in the penultimate syllable (Arnold 1990a: 22). This generalization is also supported by the corpus data. The examples below show the long vowels in the final syllable (19a) and in the penultimate syllable (19b).

(19) *Long vowels in final and penultimate syllables*

(a)	*ḳroḥī*	[⟨ḳ⟩.ro.ˈḥ**ī**]	'read (2M.SG) to us!'	IV.40
	xussūy	[xus.ˈs**ū**.⟨y⟩]	'my clothes/clothing'	IV.116
	kursō	[kur.ˈs**ō**]	'chairs'	III.160
	ayṯāy	[ʔay.ˈṯ**ā**.⟨y⟩]	'bring (2F.SG)!'	IV.308
(b)	*īḏa*	[ˈʔ**ī**.ḏa]	'hand'	IV.162
	šunīṯa	[šu.ˈn**ī**.ṯa]	'woman'	IV.262
	maščūṯa	[maš.ˈč**ū**.ṯa]	'wedding'	III.362
	ġabrōna	[ġab.ˈr**ō**.na]	'man'	IV.8

The following derivation illustrates what happens if a word has an underlyingly long vowel in the antepenultimate syllable. In the word form /assīḳ-in-l-e/, the bimoraic penultimate syllable [ḳin]σ receives stress, so the antepenultimate syllable [sī]σ becomes pretonic. As a result, the long vowel [ī] in it undergoes pretonic shortening and surfaces as the short vowel [i]. In contrast to /assīḳ-in-l-e/, the long vowel [ī] in the word form /assīḳ-in/ is not shortened because it occurs in the stressed penultimate syllable [sī]σ (see Arnold 2011: 687 for another example).

(20) *A derivation which shows what happens if a word has an underlyingly long vowel in the antepenultimate syllable*

'they (M) have taken/are taking up' III.324[3]	'they (M) have taken him up' III.348	
/as**sī**ḳ-in/	/as**sī**ḳ-in-l-e/	
–	assīḳille	/n/ assimilation
as.sī.ḳin	as.sī.ḳil.le	syllabification
as.ˈ**sī**.ḳin	as.sī.ˈ**ḳil**.le	stress assignment
–	as.**si**.ˈḳil.le	pretonic shortening
ʔas.ˈsī.ḳin	**ʔ**as.si.ˈḳil.le	glottal epenthesis
[ʔas.ˈsī.ḳin]	[ʔas.**si**.ˈḳil.le]	

Words with a surface [ā]

In Section 7.3.1, I introduced the /ā/ rounding rule which turns /ā/ into [ō]. Although the /ā/ rounding rule predicts that no word should surface with an [ā], the corpus contains a number of words with a surface [ā]. However, these words are not numerous: 219 word types including loanwords and proper nouns, compared to 2,562 word types which have a surface [ō]. If the loanwords and proper nouns are excluded, the number of types plummets to 67. Most of these word types (i.e., 51 types) are imperative verbs, such as the examples in (21a, b). The rest are miscellaneous words, as in (21c).

(21) *Words with a surface* [ā]

(a)	*ḥmā*	'look (2M.SG)!'	III.330
	ḥmāy	'look (2F.SG)!'	IV.124
	ṯāx	'come (2M.SG)!'	III.52
	ṯāš	'come (2F.SG)!'	IV.18

3 It is transcribed as *nassīḳin* 'we (M) have taken/are taking up' in the original text.

(b)	*ayṯā*	'bring (2M.SG)!'	III.312
	ayṯāy	'bring (2F.SG)!'	IV.308
	šḳollāx	'take (2M.SG)!'	IV.262
(c)	*bā*	'in it (F)'	IV.114
	bāḥ	'in us'	III.324
	lā	'no'	IV.198

One possible approach for dealing with these words would be to consider their long [ā] underlyingly short (i.e., /a/). This short /a/ undergoes vowel lengthening (as proposed by Arnold 1990a: 22) and surfaces as [ā] when it occurs in the final syllable. However, this analysis raises two questions: First, what triggers /a/ lengthening? Second, when an /a/ is lengthened to an [ā], why does it not undergo /ā/ rounding and surface as an [ō]?

In the case of monosyllabic words, as in (21a, c), it is possible to answer these two questions adequately. With regard to the first question, it could be argued that the reason for /a/ lengthening is the minimal word constraint which is "the cross-linguistically common requirement that content words be at least bimoraic" (Davis 2011: 876). As a result of this constraint, monosyllabic content words which have a short /a/, such as /ḥm-a/, /ḥm-ay/, /ṯa-x/, and /ṯa-š/ (from (21a) above), cannot surface as *[ḥma], *[ḥmay], *[ṯax], and *[ṯaš] because these forms are monomoraic. When the short /a/ in these words is lengthened, the long vowel will become bimoraic, and the minimal word constraint will be fulfilled. For this reason, these words surface as [ḥm**ā**], [ḥm**ā**y], [ṯ**ā**x], and [ṯ**ā**š].

As for the second question, the fact that [ā] does not undergo /ā/ rounding could be due to rule ordering. It could be proposed that /ā/ rounding applies first, turning /ā/ into [ō] (if there is one) but not affecting /a/. After that, /a/ lengthening applies, turning /a/ into [ā]. The derivation in (22) illustrates this rule ordering. The examples are from (21a, c) above.

(22) *A derivation to illustrate the ordering of /ā/ rounding and /a/ lengthening*

'look (2M.SG)!'	'come (2F.SG)!'	'in it (F)'	
/ḥm-**a**/	/ṯ**a**-š/	/b-**a**/	
⟨ḥ⟩.ma	ṯaš	ba	syllabification
–	–	–	**/ā/ rounding**
⟨ḥ⟩.mā	ṯāš	bā	**/a/ lengthening**
[⟨ḥ⟩.mā]	[ṯāš]	[bā]	

However, in the case of polysyllabic words, such as the words presented in (21b), the /a/ lengthening account cannot adequately answer the two questions posed above. With regard to the first question, what triggers /a/ lengthening is not clear. If /a/ lengthening applies solely to satisfy the minimal word constraint, why does it apply to the words in (21b)? These words already have more than one mora (since they are disyllabic) and would not violate the minimal word constraint even if their [ā] was short. For this reason, the minimal word constraint cannot be considered responsible for triggering /a/ lengthening in these polysyllabic imperative verbs.

If, in contrast to what I assumed above, /a/ lengthening does not aim to satisfy the minimal word constraint and can apply to any word regardless of its weight, then why does it not apply to the many words in the corpus which surface with an [a], rather than an [ā] (e.g., *arʕ**a*** and not **arʕ**ā*** 'earth; ground' III.368, *yarḥ**a*** and not **yarḥ**ā*** 'month' III.162)? There is no clear answer to this question. It could be proposed that /a/ lengthening is restricted to imperative verbs regardless of their weight, but this proposal would not account for the long [ā] in the words in (21c).

We may now turn to the second question: When an /a/ is lengthened to an [ā], why does it not undergo /ā/ rounding and surface as an [ō]? Although the rule ordering proposed above (i.e., /ā/ rounding > /a/ lengthening) can answer this question and predict the correct output for monosyllabic words, this rule ordering predicts surface forms with the wrong stress pattern in the case of polysyllabic words, as the derivation in (23) shows. The surface forms *[ˈʔay.ṯā] and *[⟨š⟩.ˈḳol.lāx] predicted by the derivation are ungrammatical because they are stressed on the penultimate syllable whereas the stress in the actual surface forms falls on the final syllable (i.e., [ʔay.ˈṯā] and [⟨š⟩.ḳol.ˈlāx]).

(23) *A derivation to illustrate that ordering /a/ lengthening after /ā/ rounding predicts the wrong stress pattern in polysyllabic imperative verbs*

'bring (2M.SG)!'	'take (2M.SG)!'	
/ayṯ-**a**/	/šḳol-l-**ax**/	
ay.ṯa	⟨š⟩.ḳol.lax	syllabification
ˈ**ay**.ṯa	⟨š⟩.ˈ**ḳol**.lax	stress assignment
–	–	**/ā/ rounding**
ˈay.ṯ**ā**	⟨š⟩.ˈḳol.l**āx**	**/a/ lengthening**
ˈ**ʔ**ay.ṯā	–	glottal epenthesis
*[ˈʔay.ṯ**ā**]	*[⟨š⟩.ˈḳol.l**āx**]	

Reversing the rule order (i.e., by ordering /a/ lengthening before /ā/ rounding and stress assignment) would solve the stress pattern problem but would lead to other problems shown in the derivation in (24).

(24) *A derivation to illustrate that reversing the rule ordering predicts ungrammatical surface forms*

'bring (2M.SG)!'	'take (2M.SG)!'	
/ayṯ-**a**/	/šḳol-l-**ax**/	
ay.ṯa	⟨š⟩.ḳol.lax	syllabification
ay.ṯ**ā**	⟨š⟩.ḳol.l**ā**x	**/a/ lengthening**
ay.ˈ**ṯā**	⟨š⟩.ḳol.ˈ**lāx**	**stress assignment**
–	⟨š⟩.**ḳul**.ˈlāx	pretonic raising
ay.ˈṯ**ō**	⟨š⟩.ḳul.ˈl**ō**x	**/ā/ rounding**
ʔay.ˈṯō	–	glottal epenthesis
*[ʔay.ˈṯō]	*[⟨š⟩.ḳul.ˈlōx]	

One possible solution to the wrongly predicted stress pattern problem would be to propose that stress assignment applies cyclically (i.e., stress assignment > /ā/ rounding > /a/ lengthening > stress assignment), as in the derivation in (25). However, this assumption would lead to complicated problems related to other areas of the phonology of Maaloula Aramaic, such as the relation between stress and vowel epenthesis (notice that in Section 8.3.5, I assumed that stress does not apply cyclically).

(25) *A derivation that assumes that stress assignment applies cyclically*

'bring (2M.SG)!'	'take (2M.SG)!'	
/ayṯ-**a**/	/šḳol-l-**ax**/	
ay.ṯa	⟨š⟩.ḳol.lax	syllabification
ˈ**ay**.ṯa	⟨š⟩.ˈ**ḳol**.lax	**stress assignment**
–	–	**/ā/ rounding**
ˈay.ṯ**ā**	⟨š⟩.ˈḳol.l**ā**x	**/a/ lengthening**
ay.ˈ**ṯā**	⟨š⟩.ḳol.ˈ**lāx**	**stress assignment (cyclic)**
ˈ**ʔ**ay.ṯā	–	glottal epenthesis
[ʔay.ˈṯā]	[⟨š⟩.ḳol.ˈlāx]	

In summary, the /a/ lengthening proposal can account for the surface [ā] in monosyllabic words but poses a number of challenges when it is adopted to account for the surface [ā] in polysyllabic imperative verbs. An alternative option would be to assume that the words with a surface [ā] have an underlying /ā/ which does not undergo /ā/ rounding. Given the relatively small number of word types which have a surface [ā], these words can be considered lexical exceptions to the /ā/ rounding rule. It is left for future research to determine which analysis can account for these words.

10.4.2 Positional restrictions on the distribution of short vowels

According to Arnold (1990a: 23), there are restrictions on the distribution of certain short vowels. Arnold's generalizations are summarized in (26).

(26) *The distribution of short vowels (according to Arnold 1990a: 23)*

	Stressed	Pretonic	Post-tonic
[i]	✓	✓	✓
[u]	✓	✓	✓
[a]	✓	✓	✓
[e]	✓	(✓)	✓
[o]	✓	(✓)	×

The symbol ✓ indicates that the vowel can occur in this position, the symbol × indicates that it cannot occur in this position, and the parentheses show that there are restrictions on the occurrence of the vowel in this position.

I will present Arnold's generalizations gradually and will examine each generalization individually using corpus data. The analysis of corpus data will validate Arnold's generalizations on the distribution of short vowels in stressed and pretonic positions but will refute his assumption that [o] does not occur in post-tonic position.

Short vowels in stressed syllables

As can be seen from (26), there are no restrictions on the distribution of short vowels in stressed syllables. All five short vowels can occur in stressed syllables (Arnold 1990a: 23). This generalization is supported by the corpus data, as in (27), and it does not pose any theoretical or empirical problems.

(27) *Short vowels in stressed syllables*

***i**ḳḏum*	[ˈʔ**i**ḳ.ḏum]	'before'	IV.134
*ḥḏ**u**čča*	[⟨ḥ⟩.ˈḏ**u**č.ča]	'bride'	III.60
*ġ**a**mla*	[ˈġ**a**m.la]	'camel'	IV.228
*b**e**rča*	[ˈb**e**r.ča]	'daughter'	IV.298
*f**o**rna*	[ˈf**o**r.na]	'oven'	III.44

Short vowels in pretonic position

In pretonic position, [i], [u], and [a] can occur freely (Arnold 1990a: 23). The corpus provides plenty of examples of [i], [u], and [a] occurring freely in pretonic syllables, as in (28).

(28) *The short vowels* [i], [u], *and* [a] *in pretonic syllables*

imōḏ	[**ʔi**.ˈmō.⟨ḏ⟩]	'today'	III.196
čilmīḏa	[**čil**.ˈmī.ḏa]	'disciple'	VI.533
šunīṯa	[**šu**.ˈnī.ṯa]	'woman'	IV.262
furrōʕča	[**fur**.ˈrō.⟨ʕ⟩.ča]	'axe'	IV.16
ʕaḳōna	[**ʕa**.ˈḳō.na]	'crow'	IV.312
maṣfarča	[**maṣ**.ˈfar.ča]	'scissors'	III.62

However, there are restrictions on the occurrence of [e] and [o] in pretonic position. In this position, the underlying /e/ and /o/ will surface as [i] and [u] due to the pretonic raising rule (discussed earlier in Section 10.3.1). In spite of this rule, pretonic [e] and [o] can occur in the imperative verbs which are stressed on the final syllable (Arnold 1990a: 23). This is illustrated in (29).

(29) *Pretonic* [e] *and* [o] *in imperative verbs (Arnold 1990a: 23 – syllabification added)*

ḳirlelā	[ḳir.**le**.ˈlā]	'read (2M.SG) (it/them) to her!'
fṯoḥlā	[⟨f⟩.ṯ**oḥ**.ˈlā]	'open (2M.SG) for her!'

The corpus contains a few further examples of these verbs, such as the ones shown in (30).

(30) *Pretonic* [e] *and* [o] *in imperative verbs (corpus examples)*

ʕannelē	[ʕan.**ne**.ˈlē]	'sing (2M.SG) for him!'	III.56
aḥkeḥī	[ʔaḥ.**ke**.ˈḥī]	'tell (2M.SG) us!'	IV.36
ḥmeḥī	[⟨ḥ⟩.**me**.ˈḥī]	'have (2M.SG) a look (at sthg.) for us!'	III.284
šḳollāx	[⟨š⟩.**ḳol**.ˈlāx]	'take (2M.SG)!'	IV.262
ḳroḥī	[⟨ḳ⟩.**ro**.ˈḥī]	'read (2M.SG) to us!'	IV.40

It seems that these polysyllabic imperative verbs are problematic in general because they represent an exception not only to the pretonic raising rule (as the examples above show) but also to the /ā/ rounding rule (as the examples presented in Section 10.4.1 show). It could be assumed that a vowel lengthening rule is at work here, but this account would have the same problems that the /a/ lengthening account has (see Section 10.4.1).

Short vowels in post-tonic position

According to Arnold (1990a: 23), all short vowels can occur in post-tonic position, except for [o]. The corpus data show that [i], [u], [a], and [e] can occur freely in post-tonic position, providing support for the first part of the generalization. This is illustrated in (31).

(31) [i], [u], [a], *and* [e] *in post-tonic position*

*ḳaʕ**pri***	[ˈḳaʕ.⟨p⟩.**ri**]	'mice (EPL)'	III.332
*ṯarʕ**un***	[ˈṯar.ʕ**un**]	'their door'	IV.26
*xalp**a***	[ˈxal.p**a**]	'dog'	IV.278
*rayš**e***	[ˈray.š**e**]	'his head'	III.334

However, the second part of Arnold's generalization, which states that [o] does not occur in post-tonic position, poses a complicated problem that has to be dealt with. This generalization seems to be based on another generalization of Arnold's in which he states that [o] changes to [u] in post-tonic position (Arnold 1990a: 26), as in (32).

(32) [o] *in stressed position, but* [u] *in post-tonic position (Arnold 1990a: 26 - syllabification added)*

Stressed [o]:	*yixṯ**o**ble*	[yix.ˈṯ**o**b.le]	'(that) he writes to him'
Post-tonic [u]:	*yixṯ**u**b*	[ˈyix.ṯ**u**b]	'(that) he writes'

Taken together, these two generalizations can be restated as: Post-tonic [o] does not exist in Maaloula Aramaic because /o/ is realized as [u] in post-tonic position. In order to validate this assumption, corpus data need to be collected and examined. If Arnold's (1991a, 1991b) original transcriptions were the only factor to be taken into account while looking for words with post-tonic [o], then this assumption would hold true. In all of these transcriptions, there is no single occurrence of post-tonic [o] (apart from a few loanwords and proper nouns).

This means that Arnold's generalizations and transcriptions are consistent with each other. However, when my language consultant proofread and corrected these transcriptions during the process of creating the corpus, he consistently replaced post-tonic [u] with [o] in four specific sets of words, exemplified in (33). He applied this correction based on both the way he heard these words being pronounced by the original speakers and the way he would pronounce them himself. The examples in (33) reflect our (rather than the original) transcriptions. In the original texts, all of these words are transcribed with [u].

(33) *Words with post-tonic* [o] *(but not according to the original transcriptions)*

Set 1:	*išḳ**o**l*	[ˈʔiš.ḳ**o**l]	‘take (2M.SG)!’	III.118
	*ax**o**l*	[ˈʔa.x**o**l]	‘eat (2M.SG)!’	IV.88
	*aḳ**o***	[ˈʔa.ḳ**o**]	‘get up (2M.SG)!’	IV.88
	*aḏ**o**ḳ*	[ˈʔa.ḏ**o**ḳ]	‘taste (2M.SG)!’	III.46
Set 2:	*zlallx**o**n*	[⟨z⟩.ˈlal.x**o**n]	‘go (2M.PL)!’	III.324
	*ṯallx**o**n*	[ˈṯal.x**o**n]	‘come (2M.PL)!’	IV.316
	*ayṯ**o**n*	[ˈʔay.ṯ**o**n]	‘bring (2M.PL)!’	III.276
	*iḥm**o**n*	[ˈʔiḥ.m**o**n]	‘look (2M.PL)!’	III.306
Set 3:	*lepp**o**n*	[ˈlep.p**o**n]	‘their (M) heart’	IV.210
	*ebr**o**n*	[ˈʔeb.r**o**n]	‘their (M) son’	IV.116
	*ebərx**o**n*	[ˈʔe.bər.x**o**n]	‘your (M.PL) son’	III.354
	*berčx**o**n*	[ˈber.⟨č⟩.x**o**n]	‘your (M.PL) daughter’	III.204
Set 4:	*elġ**o**l*	[ˈʔel.ġ**o**l]	‘inside’	III.150
	*laʔinn**o***	[la.ˈʔin.n**o**]	‘because’	III.70
	*inn**o***	[ˈʔin.n**o**]	‘that’	III.170
	*lawandy**o**s*	[la.ˈwan.⟨d⟩.y**o**s]	‘Lawandios’ (proper noun)	III.294

Set 1 consists of imperative verbs in the second person masculine singular. In this set, if [o] is replaced with [u] (as in the original transcriptions), the resulting word forms will still be well-formed imperative verbs but will have a different meaning. Spelling these words with [u] (rather than [o]) will inflect the imperative verbs for the second person feminine singular (rather than the masculine). In other words, not only does post-tonic [o] exist in this set, but it is also contrastive (i.e., it changes the meaning of the verb). In (34) I show that [o] and [u] are contrastive in post-tonic position by presenting two minimal pairs from the corpus, which would not have been distinguished if the original transcriptions had not been corrected.

(34) *Contrastive post-tonic* [o] *and* [u]

*išḳ**o**l*	[ˈʔiš.ḳ**o**l]	‘take (2M.SG)!’	III.118
*išḳ**u**l*	[ˈʔiš.ḳ**u**l]	‘take (2F.SG)!’	IV.126
*ax**o**l*	[ˈʔa.x**o**l]	‘eat (2M.SG)!’	IV.88
*ax**u**l*	[ˈʔa.x**u**l]	‘eat (2F.SG)!’	IV.18

The previous Maaloula Aramaic grammars do not give a unified account on the existence or non-existence of this contrast between post-tonic [o] and [u] in imperative verbs. For example, Spitaler (1938) apparently observes this contrast in some verbs (e.g., *aḳom* 'get up (2M.SG)!' vs. *aḳum* 'get up (2F.SG)!' 1938: 161) but not in other verbs (e.g., *axul* 'eat (2M.SG)!' vs. *axul* 'eat (2F.SG)!' 1938: 177). Arnold (1990a) is consistent in not considering the contrast to exist (e.g., *iḳṭul* 'kill (2M.SG)!' vs. *iḳṭul* 'kill (2F.SG)!' 1990a: 74; *axul* 'eat (2M.SG)!' vs. *axul* 'eat (2F.SG)!' 1990a: 111).

Set 2 consists of imperative verbs in the second person masculine plural. According to Spitaler (1938) and Arnold's (1990a) grammars, imperative verbs take the second person masculine plural suffix *-un* (e.g., *ayṯun* 'bring (2M.PL)!' Spitaler 1938: 168; Arnold 1990a: 161).[4] However, my language consultant and I believe that *-on*, rather than *-un*, is the second person masculine plural suffix that attaches to imperative verbs. By introducing the suffix *-on*, we are not denying that *-un* exists. For example, we do agree that *-un* is the masculine plural suffix that attaches to verbs in the subjunctive (e.g., *yzubnun* '(that) they (M) buy' Spitaler 1938: 153; Arnold 1990a: 72). Our disagreement, however, is limited to imperative verbs. These verbs, we believe, take *-on* and not *-un*.

The words in Set 3 are the result of the progressive umlaut process whereby the underlying suffixes /un/ and /xun/ are realized as [on] and [xon] respectively if [e] or [ē] occurs in a preceding syllable (see Section 7.3.2 for a detailed discussion of this process). This type of umlaut is neither captured by the original transcriptions nor described in the previous grammars.

Set 4 consists of a few miscellaneous words which are not the result of any morphological or phonological processes. We believe that these words have a post-tonic [o] although they were transcribed with a post-tonic [u] in the original transcriptions and in the grammars (e.g., *elġul* 'inside' Spitaler 1938: 118; Arnold 1990a: 395).

So far, I have presented four sets of words which provide clear counterevidence to Arnold's generalization that [o] does not occur in post-tonic position. The remaining issue to be addressed concerns the cases presented in (32) above, repeated here as (35) for convenience, which exemplify Arnold's (1990a: 26) generalization that [o] is raised to [u] in post-tonic position.

4 Alternatively, the imperative verbs can take the second person masculine plural suffix *-ōn* (e.g., *ayṯōn* 'bring (2M.PL)!' Spitaler 1938: 168; Arnold 1990a: 161). However, the stress-attracting suffix *-ōn* is not relevant to the discussion of post-tonic [o], and besides does not constitute a point of disagreement.

(35) [o] *in stressed position, but* [u] *in post-tonic position (Arnold 1990a: 26 - syllabification added)*

Stressed [o]:	*yixṯ**o**ble*	[yix.ˈṯ**o**b.le]	‘(that) he writes to him’
Post-tonic [u]:	*yixṯ**u**b*	[ˈyix.ṯ**u**b]	‘(that) he writes’

These two examples, as well as other similar examples attested in the corpus, show that the alternation between stressed [o] and post-tonic [u] does exist but is most probably specific to subjunctive verbs undergoing dative object suffixation (see Arnold 1990a: 232–235 for more details on this suffixation process). I did not find other cases where this alternation takes place.

Since this alternation is most probably restricted to one specific morphological process, it is difficult to determine, with any degree of certainty, what processes are responsible for it. Two analyses may be plausible. The first one would be to propose that these verbs have an underlying /o/ which is realized as [u] in post-tonic position and as [o] elsewhere (e.g., /yi-xṯ**o**b/→ [ˈyix.ṯ**u**b], /yi-xṯ**o**b-l-e/→ [yix.ˈṯ**o**b.le]). This analysis is in line with Arnold's (1990a: 26) generalization, but it differs from it in that it restricts this phonological process to subjunctive verbs undergoing dative object suffixation, rather than consider it a general phonological rule that applies across the board. The other plausible analysis would be to consider this [o] ~ [u] alternation the result of a morphologically-conditioned base allomorphy whereby bases like /yi-xṯub/ have different allomorphs such as [yixṯub] and [yixṯob]. The choice between these allomorphs depends on whether these bases are suffixed or not and on the type of suffixation (i.e., accusative or dative object suffixation).

10.5 Summary and conclusion

In this chapter, I have presented a revised moraic version of the word-stress algorithm. This version accommodates a set of polysyllabic words, stressed on the antepenultimate syllable, which do not conform to the algorithm described in the available literature.

I have also reviewed and formalized two stress-dependent processes (i.e., pretonic raising of short mid vowels and pretonic shortening of long vowels) and shown that the ordering of these (and other interrelated) processes produces the correct output. The diagram presented in (36) illustrates this ordering.

(36) *The ordering of different rules reviewed in this chapter*

syllabification
↓
stress assignment
↓
pretonic shortening
↓
pretonic raising
↓
/ā/ rounding

In addition, I have reviewed and examined Arnold's (1990a: 22–23) generalizations which describe the distribution of long and short vowels. With regard to long vowels, the corpus data have validated Arnold's generalizations, which I summarize in (37).

(37) *Distribution of long vowels (a summary of Arnold's generalizations)*

(a) A word can have no more than one long vowel.
(b) Long vowels occur either in the final or in the penultimate syllable.
(c) The syllable that contains a long vowel is the stress-bearing syllable.

As for short vowels, the corpus data have provided support for Arnold's generalizations on the distribution of short vowels in stressed and pretonic positions but have provided counterevidence to his assumption that [o] does not occur in post-tonic position. The corpus-based analysis presented in this chapter has shown that post-tonic [o] does occur in four sets of words. The revised distribution of short vowels is shown in (38).

(38) *Distribution of short vowels (a revised version of Arnold's generalizations)*

(a) In stressed syllables all short vowels are attested.
(b) In pretonic syllables [i], [u], and [a] can occur freely, but [e] and [o] are attested only in polysyllabic imperative verbs which are stressed on the final syllable. Apart from these imperative verbs, the words with underlying /e/ and /o/ will surface with [i] and [u] respectively due to the pretonic raising rule (which is introduced in Section 10.3.1).
(c) In post-tonic syllables all short vowels are attested.

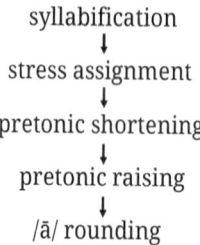

The different phonological processes which were introduced in this chapter (and also in Chapter 7) can account for the different vowel allophones, which are attested in the corpus. The following summary illustrates the underlying form of each vowel, its different realizations, the environments in which each allophone is realized, examples which illustrate the different allophones, and a reference to the sections where the phonological rules responsible for these realizations are discussed. The surface form [ā] is preceded by a question mark because it is not clear whether this surface vowel has an underlying short vowel (i.e., /a/) which undergoes lengthening, or this [ā] has an underlying long vowel (i.e., /ā/) which (for unclear reasons) avoids /ā/ rounding (see Section 10.4.1 for a discussion of these options).

(39) *Summary of the vowel phonemes and their different allophones*

Realization		Environment	Example		Section
/ī/ →	[i]	in pretonic position	/ḏ**ī**k-ā/	→ [ḏ**i**kō]	10.3.2
	[ī]	elsewhere	/ḏ**ī**k-a/	→ [ḏ**ī**ka]	–
/ū/ →	[u]	in pretonic position	/ṭ**ū**r-ā/	→ [ṭ**u**rō]	10.3.2
	[ū]	elsewhere	/ṭ**ū**r-a/	→ [ṭ**ū**ra]	–
/ē/ →	[i]	in pretonic position	/ḏ**ē**b-ā/	→ [ḏ**i**bō]	10.3.2
	[ī]	before a suffix containing /i/	/nčḳ-**ē**-l-i/	→ [nčḳ**ī**li]	7.3.1
	[ē]	elsewhere	/ḏ**ē**b-a/	→ [ḏ**ē**ba]	–
/ō/ →	[u]	in pretonic position	/ḥ**ō**n-ā/	→ [ḥ**u**nō]	10.3.2
	[ū]	before a suffix containing /i/	/ḥ**ō**n-i/	→ [ḥ**ū**ni]	7.3.1
	[ō]	elsewhere	/ḥ**ō**n-a/	→ [ḥ**ō**na]	–
/ā/ →	[a]	in pretonic position	/xṯ**ā**b-ā/	→ [xṯ**a**bō]	10.3.2
	[ō]	elsewhere (due to /ā/ rounding)	/xṯ**ā**b-a/	→ [xṯ**ō**ba]	7.3.1
/i/ →	Ø	in word-final position (optional)	/xṯāb-**i**/	→ [xṯōb]	7.3.1
	[i]	elsewhere	/š**i**mš-a/	→ [š**i**mša]	–
/u/ →	[u]	–	/r**u**miš/	→ [r**u**miš]	–
/e/ →	[i]	in pretonic position	/ġ**e**rm-ā/	→ [ġ**i**rmō]	10.3.1
		before a suffix containing /i/	/l**e**pp-i/	→ [l**i**ppi]	7.3.1
	[e]	elsewhere	/ġ**e**rm-a/	→ [ġ**e**rma]	–
/o/ →	[u]	in pretonic position	/b**o**ġt-ā/	→ [b**u**ġtō]	10.3.1
		before a suffix containing /i/	/b**o**ġt-i/	→ [b**u**ġti]	7.3.1
	[o]	elsewhere	/b**o**ġt-a/	→ [b**o**ġta]	–
/a/ →	?[ā]	(unclear environments)	?/ḥm-**a**/	→ [ḥm**ā**]	10.4.1
	[a]	elsewhere	/y**a**rḥ-**a**/	→ [y**a**rḥ**a**]	–

I want to conclude this chapter with a diagram, shown in (40), which summarizes all the phonological rules presented in this book. The arrows in the diagram indicate rule ordering. The absence of arrows between rules indicates that these rules cannot be ordered with respect to one another on the basis of the phonological and morpho-phonological alternations discussed in this work.

(40) *Summary of the phonological rules presented in this book*

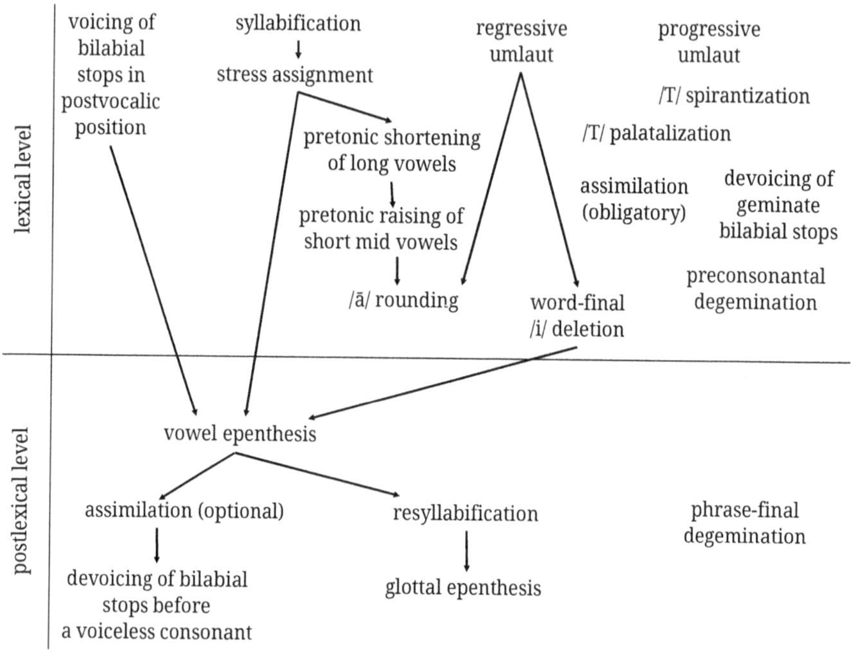

11 Conclusion and outlook

This book provided a phonology of Maaloula Aramaic, an under-researched and endangered variety of Neo-Aramaic. The presented work gave a detailed corpus-based account of the phonological and morpho-phonological processes and provided solutions to previously unaddressed problems at the descriptive, methodological, and theoretical levels.

At the descriptive level, this work revisited the content and presentation of the descriptive generalizations made in previous accounts. In terms of content, many of the previously published generalizations are accurate, but some of them turned out to be either inaccurate or incomplete. This book critically reviewed and reformulated the accurate generalizations and completed and corrected the incomplete and inaccurate generalizations. In terms of presentation, most of the previous accounts were written in German, and many of the generalizations presented in them seem to have been written for a reader specialized in Aramaic or Semitic languages. These facts may explain why the phonology of Maaloula Aramaic is unknown to or has not caught the attention of the larger linguistic community although this Aramaic variety has intricate phonological processes and problems. To my knowledge, these phonological processes and problems have not been featured in the phonological literature either for scholarly discussions (in handbooks and articles) or for pedagogical purposes (in introductory textbooks). This book sheds the needed light on this issue by presenting all of the generalizations in a way accessible to linguists who may or may not be familiar with Semitic languages.

At the methodological level, this work addressed the absence of quantitative research from the previous literature on Maaloula Aramaic by making two main contributions. First, the first electronic speech corpus of this variety, named the Maaloula Aramaic Speech Corpus (MASC, Eid et al. 2022), was published and made available to the scientific community in four formats: (1) transcriptions, (2) lemmatized transcriptions, (3) audio files and time-aligned phonetic transcriptions, and (4) an SQLite database (see Chapter 3). Second, quantitative corpus-based studies were conducted in almost every chapter of this book in order to empirically investigate and validate the descriptive generalizations found in previous research.

In spite of these methodological contributions, quantitative empirical research on Maaloula Aramaic is still in its infancy and can be largely developed in the future. For instance, MASC can be further enlarged and developed to facilitate empirical studies that are not possible now. For example, adding part-of-speech tags (i.e., POS tagging) would make the corpus even more suitable for morphosyntactic

https://doi.org/10.1515/9783111447124-011

analyses. Creating a semantic vector space would make running distributional semantic analyses possible.

At the theoretical level, this book presented a synchronic phonological analysis of Maaloula Aramaic. Some of the obtained results are relevant to a number of disputable issues in phonological theory. For example, the results of the vowel epenthesis analysis (presented in Sections 8.3 and 8.4) support syllable-based accounts of vowel epenthesis (e.g., Selkirk 1981; Itô 1989; Broselow 1992; Watson 2002, 2007; Kiparsky 2003) and challenge accounts which claim that epenthesis can be accounted for purely by sequential constraints (see, e.g., Côté 2000) or by segmental constraints (e.g., the Obligatory Contour Principle). The analysis of the plural marker alternation in feminine nouns (presented in Section 6.3) provides support for the view that when a morpheme-specific alternation is not phonologically motivated or optimizing, a morphological account is to be preferred to a phonological account (see, e.g., Kalin 2022).

Although this work contributed to these contentious issues in phonological theory, these issues were not the main focus of the work. In other words, this work was not intended to be a case study of Maaloula Aramaic that aimed to provide evidence for (or against) particular theoretical arguments. This type of case studies can be conducted more easily in the future due to the data sets and analyses presented in this work and also due to the availability of the electronic speech corpus. The other type of studies that can benefit from this work is the typological research that investigates a specific phonological problem in a range of languages. I hope that this book will contribute to these future studies and to our cross-linguistic understanding of phonology.

I also hope that this book and the speech corpus (MASC) will be helpful at the level of language documentation and revitalization. For example, the generalizations made in the book and the authentic speech data provided by MASC can help course designers, lexicographers, and language teachers design community-friendly language materials (e.g., reference grammars, dictionaries, course books, reading materials, and listening materials) which reflect how people speak the language naturally.

References

Anthony, Laurence. 2020. AntConc [Computer program]. Tokyo, Japan: Waseda University. Version 3.5.9. https://www.laurenceanthony.net/software. (June 23, 2021).

Archangeli, Diana. 1991. Syllabification and prosodic templates in Yawelmani. *Natural Language & Linguistic Theory* 9(2). 231–283. https://doi.org/10.1007/BF00134677.

Arnold, Werner. 1990a. *Das Neuwestaramäische: V. Grammatik.* Wiesbaden: Otto Harrassowitz.

Arnold, Werner. 1990b. New materials on Western Neo-Aramaic. In Wolfhart Heinrichs (ed.), *Studies in Neo-Aramaic*, 131–149. Atlanta, Georgia: Scholars Press. https://doi.org/10.1163/9789004369535_011.

Arnold, Werner. 1991a. *Das Neuwestaramäische: III. Volkskundliche Texte aus Maʿlūla.* Wiesbaden: Otto Harrassowitz.

Arnold, Werner. 1991b. *Das Neuwestaramäische: IV. Orale Literatur aus Maʿlūla.* Wiesbaden: Otto Harrassowitz.

Arnold, Werner. 2002. Neue Lieder aus Maʿlūla. In Werner Arnold & Hartmut Bobzin (eds.), *„Sprich doch mit deinen Knechten aramäisch, wir verstehen es!" 60 Beiträge zur Semitistik. Festschrift für Otto Jastrow zum 60. Geburtstag.*, 31–52. Wiesbaden: Harrassowitz.

Arnold, Werner. 2003. Semitisches Tonarchiv (SemArch). Heidelberg University. http://semarch.ub.uni-heidelberg.de/. (April 19, 2024).

Arnold, Werner. 2006. *Lehrbuch des Neuwestaramäischen* (Semitica Viva: Series Didactica; Band 1). 2nd edn. Wiesbaden: Harrassowitz.

Arnold, Werner. 2008. The begadkephat in Western Neo-Aramaic. In Geoffrey Khan (ed.), *Neo-Aramaic dialect studies*, 171–176. Piscataway, NJ: Gorgias Press. https://doi.org/10.31826/9781463211615-011.

Arnold, Werner. 2011. Western Neo-Aramaic. In Stefan Weninger, Geoffrey Khan, Michael P. Streck & Janet C. E. Watson (eds.), *The Semitic languages. An international handbook*, 685–696. Berlin, Boston: De Gruyter Mouton. https://doi.org/10.1515/9783110251586.685.

Arnold, Werner. 2019. *Das Neuwestaramäische: VI. Wörterbuch.* Wiesbaden: Harrassowitz.

Baayen, R. Harald. 2008. *Analyzing linguistic data: A practical introduction to statistics using R.* Cambridge: Cambridge University Press. https://doi.org/10.1017/CBO9780511801686.

Bates, Douglas, Martin Mächler, Ben Bolker & Steve Walker. 2015. Fitting linear mixed-effects models using lme4. *Journal of Statistical Software* 67(1). 1–48. https://doi.org/10.18637/jss.v067.i01.

Ben Hedia, Sonia. 2019. *Gemination and degemination in English affixation: Investigating the interplay between morphology, phonology and phonetics* (Studies in Laboratory Phonology 8). Berlin: Language Science Press. https://doi.org/10.5281/zenodo.3232849.

Ben Hedia, Sonia & Ingo Plag. 2017. Gemination and degemination in English prefixation: Phonetic evidence for morphological organization. *Journal of Phonetics* 62. 34–49. https://doi.org/10.1016/j.wocn.2017.02.002.

Bergsträsser, Gotthelf. 1915. *Neuaramäische Märchen und andere Texte aus Maʿlūla.* Leipzig: F.A. Brockhaus. https://menadoc.bibliothek.uni-halle.de/publicdomain/content/titleinfo/857071. (April 21, 2024).

Bergsträsser, Gotthelf. 1918. Neue Texte im aramäischen Dialekt von Maʿlula. In *Zeitschrift für Assyriologie und verwandte Gebiete*, vol. 32, 103–163. https://menadoc.bibliothek.uni-halle.de/dmg/periodical/titleinfo/118493. (April 21, 2024).

https://doi.org/10.1515/9783111447124-012

Bergsträsser, Gotthelf. 1928. *Einführung in die semitischen Sprachen. Sprachproben und grammatische Skizzen.* Munich: Max Hueber. https://menadoc.bibliothek.uni-halle.de/publicdomain/content/titleinfo/597992. (April 21, 2024).

Bergsträsser, Gotthelf. 1933. *Phonogramme im neuaramäischen Dialekt von Malula. Satzdruck und Satzmelodie.* Munich: Verlag der Bayerischen Akademie der Wissenschaften. https://menadoc.bibliothek.uni-halle.de/publicdomain/content/titleinfo/857197. (April 21, 2024).

Blevins, Juliette. 1995. The syllable in phonological theory. In John A. Goldsmith (ed.), *The handbook of phonological theory*, 206–244. Oxford: Blackwell.

Boersma, Paul & David J. Weenink. 2021. Praat. Doing phonetics by computer [Computer program]. Version 6.1.49. http://www.praat.org/.

Broselow, Ellen. 1992. Parametric variation in Arabic dialect phonology. In Ellen Broselow, Mushira Eid & John McCarthy (eds.), *Perspectives on Arabic linguistics IV*, 7–45. Amsterdam: John Benjamins. https://doi.org/10.1075/cilt.85.04bro.

Broselow, Ellen. 2017. Syllable structure in the dialects of Arabic. In Elabbas Benmamoun & Reem Bassiouney (eds.), *The Routledge handbook of Arabic linguistics*, 32–47. Abingdon: Routledge.

Bussmann, Hadumod. 1996. *Routledge dictionary of language and linguistics*. (Translated by) Gregory Trauth & Kerstin Kazzazi. London: Routledge.

Cho, Young-mee Yu & Tracy Holloway King. 2003. Semisyllables and universal syllabification. In Caroline Féry & Ruben van de Vijver (eds.), *The syllable in Optimality Theory*, 183–212. Cambridge: Cambridge University Press. https://doi.org/10.1017/CBO9780511497926.008.

Clements, G. N. & Elizabeth Hume. 1995. The internal organization of speech sounds. In John A. Goldsmith (ed.), *The handbook of phonological theory*, 245–306. Oxford: Blackwell.

Clements, George N. 1990. The role of the sonority cycle in core syllabification. In John Kingston & Mary E. Beckman (eds.), *Papers in laboratory phonology 1: Between the grammar and physics of speech*, 283–333. Cambridge: Cambridge University Press. https://doi.org/10.1017/CBO9780511627736.017.

Cohn, Abigail C., William H. Ham & Robert J. Podesva. 1999. The phonetic realization of singleton-geminate contrasts in three languages of Indonesia. In *Proceedings of the 14th International Congress of Phonetic Sciences (ICPhS-14)*, 587–590. San Francisco, CA.

Correll, Christoph. 1978. *Untersuchungen zur Syntax der neuwestaramäischen Dialekte des Antilibanon: (Maʿlūla, Baḫʿa, Ǧubbʿadīn); mit besonderer Berücksichtigung der Auswirkungen arabischen Adstrateinflusses; nebst zwei Anhängen zum neuaramäischen Dialekt von Ǧubbʿadīn.* (Abhandlungen Für Die Kunde Des Morgenlandes 44/4). Wiesbaden: Steiner.

Côté, Marie-Hélène. 2000. *Consonant cluster phonotactics: A perceptual approach.* Cambridge, Massachusetts: MIT Doctoral dissertation. https://doi.org/doi:10.7282/T3HD7TGR.

Cowell, Mark W. 1964. *A reference grammar of Syrian Arabic.* Washington, DC: Georgetown University Press.

Crawley, Michael J. 2015. *Statistics: An introduction using R.* 2nd edn. Chichester: Wiley.

Davis, Stuart. 1999. On the representation of initial geminates. *Phonology* 16. 93–104. https://doi.org/10.1017/S0952675799003711.

Davis, Stuart. 2011. Geminates. In Marc van Oostendorp, Colin J. Ewen, Elizabeth Hume & Keren Rice (eds.), *The Blackwell companion to phonology*, vol. 2, 873–897. Malden, MA & Oxford: Wiley-Blackwell. https://doi.org/10.1002/9781444335262.wbctp0037.

Davis, Stuart & Marwa Ragheb. 2014. Geminate representation in Arabic. In Samira Farwaneh & Hamid Ouali (eds.), *Perspectives on Arabic Linguistics XXIV-XXV*, 3–19. Amsterdam: John Benjamins. https://doi.org/10.1075/sal.1.04dav.

Dixon, Robert M. W. 1977. *A Grammar of Yidiɲ.* Cambridge: Cambridge University Press.

Duntsov, Alexey, Charles Häberl & Sergey Loesov. 2022. A Modern Western Aramaic account of the Syrian Civil War. *WORD* 68(4). 359–394. https://doi.org/10.1080/00437956.2022.2084663.

Eberhard, David M., Gary F. Simons & Charles D. Fennig (eds.). 2023. *Ethnologue: Languages of the world*. 26th edn. Dallas, Texas: SIL International. https://www.ethnologue.com/language/amw/. (July 16, 2023).

Eid, Ghattas & Ingo Plag. 2024. Syllable structure and syllabification in Maaloula Aramaic. *Lingua* 297. 1–31. https://doi.org/10.1016/j.lingua.2023.103612.

Eid, Ghattas, Esther Seyffarth & Ingo Plag. 2022. The Maaloula Aramaic Speech Corpus (MASC): From printed material to a lemmatized and time-aligned corpus. In *Proceedings of the 13th Conference on Language Resources and Evaluation (LREC 2022)*, 6513–6520. Marseille. http://www.lrec-conf.org/proceedings/lrec2022/pdf/2022.lrec-1.699.pdf. (April 21, 2024).

Eid, Ghattas, Esther Seyffarth, Emad Rihan, Werner Arnold & Ingo Plag. 2022. The Maaloula Aramaic Speech Corpus (MASC). Düsseldorf: Heinrich-Heine-Universität Düsseldorf. Zenodo. https://doi.org/10.5281/zenodo.6496714.

Gahl, Susanne. 2008. Time and thyme are not homophones: The effect of lemma frequency on word durations in spontaneous speech. *Language* 84(3). 474–496. https://doi.org/10.1353/lan.0.0035.

Galea, Luke. 2016. *Syllable structure and gemination in Maltese*. Cologne: University of Cologne Doctoral dissertation. http://kups.ub.uni-koeln.de/id/eprint/6934. (April 19, 2024).

Garofolo, John S., Lori F. Lamel, William M. Fisher, Jonathan G. Fiscus, David S. Pallett, Nancy L. Dahlgren & Victor Zue. 1993. *TIMIT Acoustic-Phonetic Continuous Speech Corpus LDC93S1*. Philadelphia: Linguistic Data Consortium. https://doi.org/10.35111/17gk-bn40.

Gensler, Orin D. 2011. Morphological typology of Semitic. In Stefan Weninger, Geoffrey Khan, Michael P. Streck & Janet C. E. Watson (eds.), *The Semitic languages. An international handbook*, 279–302. Berlin, Boston: De Gruyter Mouton. https://doi.org/10.1515/9783110251586.279.

Giegerich, Heinz J. 1992. *English phonology: An introduction*. Cambridge: Cambridge University Press. https://doi.org/10.1017/CBO9781139166126.

Godfrey, John J. & Edward C. Holliman. 1993. *Switchboard-1 Release 2 LDC97S62*. Philadelphia: Linguistic Data Consortium. https://doi.org/10.35111/sw3h-rw02.

Godfrey, John J., Edward C. Holliman & Jane McDaniel. 1992. SWITCHBOARD: Telephone speech corpus for research and development. In *Proceedings of the International Conference on Acoustics, Speech, and Signal Processing (ICASSP-92)*, 517–20. San Francisco, CA. https://doi.org/10.1109/ICASSP.1992.225858.

Goldsmith, John A. 1976. *Autosegmental phonology*. Cambridge, Massachusetts: MIT Doctoral dissertation.

Hale, Kenneth. 1973. Deep-surface canonical disparities in relation to analysis and change: An Australian example. In Henry M. Hoenigswald (ed.), *Diachronic, areal, and typological Linguistics*, 401–458. Berlin, Boston: De Gruyter Mouton. https://doi.org/10.1515/9783111418797-018.

Hall, Nancy. 2006. Cross-linguistic patterns of vowel intrusion. *Phonology* 23. 387–429. https://doi.org/10.1017/S0952675706000996.

Hall, Nancy. 2011. Vowel epenthesis. In Marc van Oostendorp, Colin J. Ewen, Elizabeth Hume & Keren Rice (eds.), *The Blackwell companion to phonology*, vol. 3, 1576–1596. Malden, MA & Oxford: Wiley-Blackwell. https://doi.org/10.1002/9781444335262.wbctp0067.

Halle, Morris. 1992. Phonological features. In William Bright (ed.), *International encyclopedia of linguistics*, vol. 3, 207–212. Oxford: Oxford University Press.

Halle, Morris. 1995. Feature geometry and feature spreading. *Linguistic Inquiry* 26. 1–46. https://doi.org/10.1515/9783110871258.196.

Halle, Morris, Bert Vaux & Andrew Wolfe. 2000. On feature spreading and the representation of place of articulation. *Linguistic Inquiry* 31. 387–444.

Haspelmath, Martin & Andrea D. Sims. 2010. *Understanding Morphology*. 2nd edn. New York: Routledge.
Hayes, Bruce. 1986. Inalterability in CV phonology. *Language* 62(2). 321–351. https://doi.org/10.2307/414676.
Hayes, Bruce. 1989. Compensatory lengthening in moraic phonology. *Linguistic Inquiry* 20(2). 253–306.
Hayes, Bruce. 1995. *Metrical stress theory: Principles and case studies*. Chicago: University of Chicago Press.
Hayes, Bruce. 2009. *Introductory phonology*. Malden, MA: Wiley-Blackwell.
Heinrichs, Wolfhart. 1990. Introduction. In Wolfhart Heinrichs (ed.), *Studies in Neo-Aramaic*, ix–xvii. Atlanta, Georgia: Scholars Press. https://doi.org/10.1163/9789004369535_001.
Hellmuth, Sam. 2013. Phonology. In Jonathan Owens (ed.), *The Oxford handbook of Arabic linguistics*, 45–70. Oxford: Oxford University Press. https://doi.org/10.1093/oxfordhb/9780199764136.013.0003.
Itô, Junko. 1989. A prosodic theory of epenthesis. *Natural Language & Linguistic Theory* 7(2). 217–259. https://doi.org/10.1007/BF00138077.
Jastrow, Otto. 1993. *Laut- und Formenlehre des neuaramäischen Dialekts von Mīdin im Ṭūr ʿAbdīn*. 4th edn. Wiesbaden: Harrassowitz.
Kahn, Daniel. 1976. *Syllable-based generalizations in English phonology*. Cambridge, Massachusetts: MIT Doctoral dissertation.
Kaisse, Ellen M. & Patricia A. Shaw. 1985. On the theory of Lexical Phonology. *Phonology Yearbook* 2. 1–30. https://doi.org/10.1017/S0952675700000361.
Kalin, Laura. 2020. Morphology before phonology: A case study of Turoyo (Neo-Aramaic). *Morphology* 30. 135–184. https://doi.org/10.1007/s11525-020-09365-3.
Kalin, Laura. 2022. Infixes really are (underlyingly) prefixes/suffixes: Evidence from allomorphy on the fine timing of infixation. *Language* 98. 641–682. https://doi.org/10.1353/lan.2022.0017.
Khan, Geoffrey & Paul M. Noorlander (eds.). 2021. *Studies in the grammar and lexicon of Neo-Aramaic*. Cambridge: Open Book Publishers. https://doi.org/10.11647/OBP.0209.
Khattab, Ghada & Jalal Al-Tamimi. 2014. Geminate timing in Lebanese Arabic: The relationship between phonetic timing and phonological structure. *Laboratory Phonology* 5(2). 231–269. https://doi.org/10.1515/lp-2014-0009.
Kiparsky, Paul. 1982. Lexical morphology and phonology. In In-Seok Yang (ed.), *Linguistics in the morning calm*, 3–91. Seoul: Hanshin.
Kiparsky, Paul. 2003. Syllables and moras in Arabic. In Caroline Féry & Ruben van de Vijver (eds.), *The syllable in Optimality Theory*, 147–182. Cambridge: Cambridge University Press. https://doi.org/10.1017/CBO9780511497926.007.
Kisler, Thomas, Uwe D. Reichel & Florian Schiel. 2017. Multilingual processing of speech via web services. *Computer Speech & Language* 45. 326–347. https://doi.org/10.1016/j.csl.2017.01.005.
Ladefoged, Peter & Ian Maddieson. 1996. *The sounds of the world's languages*. Oxford: Blackwell.
Lahiri, Aditi & Jorge Hankamer. 1988. The timing of geminate consonants. *Journal of Phonetics* 16. 327–338. https://doi.org/10.1016/S0095-4470(19)30506-6.
Leben, William R. 1973. *Suprasegmental phonology*. Cambridge, Massachusetts: MIT Doctoral dissertation.
Lieber, Rochelle. 2009. *Introducing morphology*. Cambridge: Cambridge University Press.
Lindsay-Smith, Emily. 2021. *A phonological typology of modern Arabic varieties*. University of Oxford Doctoral dissertation.
Maddieson, Ian. 1985. Phonetic cues to syllabification. In Victoria A. Fromkin (ed.), *Phonetic linguistics: Essays in honor of Peter Ladefoged*, 203–221. New York: Academic Press.
McCarthy, John J. 1979. *Formal problems in Semitic phonology and morphology*. Cambridge, Massachusetts: MIT Doctoral dissertation.
McCarthy, John J. 1986. OCP effects: Gemination and antigemination. *Linguistic Inquiry* 17(2). 207–263.

McEnery, Tony, Richard Xiao & Yukio Tono. 2006. *Corpus-based language studies: An advanced resource book*. London: Routledge.
Moseley, Christopher (ed.). 2010. *Atlas of the World's Languages in Danger*. 3rd edn. Paris: UNESCO Publishing. https://unesdoc.unesco.org/ark:/48223/pf0000187026. (July 29, 2023).
Muller, Jennifer S. 2001. *The phonology and phonetics of word-initial geminates*. Ohio State University Doctoral dissertation. http://rave.ohiolink.edu/etdc/view?acc_num=osu1364226371.
Nespor, Marina & Irene Vogel. 2007. *Prosodic phonology*. Berlin, New York: Walter de Gruyter. https://doi.org/10.1515/9783110977790.
Paster, Mary. 2009. Explaining phonological conditions on affixation: Evidence from suppletive allomorphy and affix ordering. *Word Structure* 2. 18–47.
Payne, Elinor M. 2005. Phonetic variation in Italian consonant gemination. *Journal of the International Phonetic Association* 35(2). 153–181. https://doi.org/10.1017/S0025100305002240.
Pitt, Mark A., Laura Dilley, Keith Johnson, Scott Kiesling, William Raymond, Elizabeth Hume & Eric Fosler-Lussier. 2007. *Buckeye Corpus of Conversational Speech (2nd release)*. Columbus, OH: Department of Psychology, Ohio State University (Distributor). www.buckeyecorpus.osu.edu.
Plag, Ingo. 2018. *Word-formation in English*. 2nd edn. Cambridge: Cambridge University Press.
Pluymaekers, Mark, Mirjam Ernestus & R. Harald Baayen. 2005. Lexical frequency and acoustic reduction in spoken Dutch. *The Journal of the Acoustical Society of America* 118(4). 2561–2569. https://doi.org/10.1121/1.2011150.
R Core Team. 2021. R: A language and environment for statistical computing. R Foundation for Statistical Computing, Vienna, Austria. https://www.R-project.org/.
Reich, Sigismund. 1937. *Études sur les villages araméens de l'Anti-Liban* (Documents d'Études Orientales 7). Damascus: Institut Français de Damas.
Rihan, Emad. 2017. *Aramiyyat Maaloula al-muqaddasa: Al-aramiyya al-gharbiyya al-haditha [The holy Aramaic language of Maaloula: Western Neo-Aramaic]*. Vol. 1. Damascus: Muassasat Maaloula.
Rizkallah, George. 2010. *A grammar of the Syriac Aramaic language spoken in Maaloula*. (Translated by) Ghattas Eid. Damascus. (Original work published 2007).
Rizkallah, George & Bashir Saadi. 2016. Portrait of Jesus. The Aramaic Bible Translation Foundation. Text and audio available at https://www.rinyo.org/Bible. Metadata available at http://bethsaadi.com/bible/portraiteofjesus. (April 21, 2024).
Rosenthal, Franz. 1961. *A grammar of Biblical Aramaic*. Wiesbaden: Otto Harrassowitz.
Sagey, Elizabeth. 1986. *The representation of features and relations in non-linear phonology*. Cambridge, Massachusetts: MIT Doctoral dissertation.
Sarkar, Deepayan. 2008. *Lattice: Multivariate data visualization with R*. New York: Springer. http://lmdvr.r-forge.r-project.org.
Schiel, Florian. 1999. Automatic phonetic transcription of non-prompted speech. In *Proceedings of the 14th International Congress of Phonetic Sciences (ICPhS-14)*, 607–610. San Francisco. https://doi.org/10.5282/ubm/epub.13682.
Schiel, Florian. 2015. A statistical model for predicting pronunciation. In *Proceedings of the 18th International Congress of Phonetic Sciences (ICPhS-18)*. Glasgow.
Selkirk, Elisabeth. 1981. Epenthesis and degenerate syllables in Cairene Arabic. In Hagit Borer & Youssef Aoun (eds.), *Theoretical issues in the grammar of Semitic languages*, vol. 3. Cambridge, Massachusetts: MIT.
Spitaler, Anton. 1938. *Grammatik des neuaramäischen Dialekts von Maʿlūla (Antilibanon)*. Leipzig: F.A. Brockhaus. http://dx.doi.org/10.25673/36802.
Spitaler, Anton. 1957. Neue Materialien zum aramäischen Dialekt von Maʿlūla. *Zeitschrift der Deutschen Morgenländischen Gesellschaft* 107(2). 299–339. https://menadoc.bibliothek.uni-halle.de/dmg/periodical/titleinfo/93985. (April 21, 2024).

Uffmann, Christian. 2011. The organization of features. In Marc van Oostendorp, Colin J. Ewen, Elizabeth Hume & Keren Rice (eds.), *The Blackwell companion to phonology*, vol. 1, 643–668. Malden, MA & Oxford: Wiley-Blackwell. https://doi.org/10.1002/9781444335262.wbctp0027.

Watson, Janet C. E. 2002. *The phonology and morphology of Arabic*. Oxford: Oxford University Press.

Watson, Janet C. E. 2007. Syllabification patterns in Arabic dialects: Long segments and mora sharing. *Phonology* 24. 335–356. https://doi.org/10.1017/S0952675707001224.

Wiese, Richard. 1992. Was ist extrasilbisch im Deutschen und warum? In Karl-Heinz Ramers & Richard Wiese (eds.), *Prosodische Phonologie* (Zeitschrift Für Sprachwissenschaft 10), 112–133. Göttingen: Vandenhoeck und Ruprecht. https://doi.org/10.1515/zfsw.1991.10.1.112.

Wright, W. 1896. *A grammar of the Arabic language*. 3rd edn. Cambridge: Cambridge University Press. https://menadoc.bibliothek.uni-halle.de/publicdomain/content/titleinfo/293878. (April 21, 2024).

Zsiga, Elizabeth C. 2013. *The sounds of language: An introduction to phonetics and phonology*. Malden, MA & Oxford: Wiley-Blackwell. https://doi.org/10.1002/9781394260980.

Index

/ā/ rounding, 16–17, 59, 68–72, 102, 104, 105, 111, 118, **132–35**, 137, 150, 167, 180, 200, 206, 211, 219–37
/T/ palatalization, **93–95**, 105, 110, 180
/T/ spirantization, 72, **93–95**, 102, 105, 110, 111, 118, 165, 180, 200

affricates. *see* consonants
allomorphs, 10, 80, 93–96, 97, 102–5, 109–11, 140, 177, 235
analytical framework, **6–17**, 104
Arabic
– Cairene, 112, 126, 153, 154, 167–68, 172, 185, 187
– C-dialects, **154–55**, 168–69
– CV-dialects, **154–55**, 168–69
– Damascus, 126, 168, 172, 176, 178, 182
– Lebanese, 149, 195, 196
– Maltese, 126, 185, 187
– Moroccan, 154, 155, 172, 209
– San'ani, 112, 126, 199
– Standard, 126
– VC-dialects, **154–55**, 168–69
Aramaic varieties
– Biblical Aramaic, 66
– Turoyo, 37, 199, 208, 213
– Western Neo-Aramaic dialects of Jubbaadin and Bakhaa, 1–2
assimilation of consonants, 14, 48, 85, **106–29**, 143, 167, 186, 187, 192, 193, 212, 226
audio files. *see* the Maaloula Aramaic Speech Corpus (MASC)

Biblical Aramaic. *see* Aramaic varieties
bilabial stop devoicing. *see* devoicing of bilabial stops before a voiceless consonant
bilabial stop voicing. *see* voicing of bilabial stops in postvocalic position

Cairene Arabic. *see* Arabic
C-dialects. *see* Arabic
clitics, 15, 106, 107, 124, 125, 145, 181
consonants, **35–57**
– affricates, **44**
– coronals, 14, 36–39, 40–41, 45–50, 56, 93, 112, 113, 114, 123–28, 181
– dorsals, 37–40, 41, 45, 50, 56
– emphatics, 35–37, **37–38**, 40, 48, 54, 62
– fricatives, **44–52**
– glides, **54–55**
– glottals, 8, 16, 37–40, 42–43, 45, 51, 68, 69, 71, 77, 85, 144, 153–54, 166–67, 179, 199, 226, 228–29
– labials, 36–37, 40, 45, 64–79
– liquids, **53–54**
– nasals, **52–53**
– obstruents, 92, 93, 113, 149
– pharyngeals, 36–37, 45, 51, 56
– rhotics, 9, 35, 85, 91
– sonorants, 92, 149
– stops, **39–43**
coronal. *see* consonants
CV-dialects. *see* Arabic

Damascus Arabic. *see* Arabic
degemination
– phrase-final degemination, **208**, 213
– preconsonantal degemination, 8, 75, 84, 196, **199–201**
devoicing of bilabial stops before a voiceless consonant, **69–73**, 74, 75, 77, 79, 107–9
devoicing of geminate bilabial stops, **75–78**
diphthongs. *see* vowels
dorsal. *see* consonants

emphatic. *see* consonants
epenthesis
– glottal epenthesis, 8, 16, 43, 68, 69, 71, 77, 85, 144, **153–54**, **166–67**, 179, 199, 226, 228, 229
– vowel epenthesis, 4, 13–17, 33, 34, 62, 68–73, 107–9, 127, 128, 138, 144, **146–52**, **161–66**, **168–84**, 194, 199, 206, 208, 211, 229, 240

feature geometry, **36–38**, **55–57**, 63, 106–43

https://doi.org/10.1515/9783111447124-013

feminine marker, 4, 9, 13, 70, **80–95**, 95–99, 105, 109–11, 178
fricatives. *see* consonants

geminates, 75–78, **185–213**
- singleton-to-geminate duration ratio, 194–95, 201, 202, 212
- surface geminates, **192–93**
- underlying geminates, **188–92**
- word-final geminates, **203–8**
- word-initial geminates, **208–12**
- word-medial geminates, **199–203**

glides. *see* consonants
glottal consonants. *see* consonants
glottal epenthesis. *see* epenthesis

Iraqi Arabic. *see* Arabic

labial. *see* consonants
language consultant, **6–7**, 7–9, 21, 48, 49, 84, 98, 138, 139, 141, 149, 153, 156, 177, 189, 232, 234
language data, 3, **6–8**, 18, 83
Lebanese. *see* Arabic
lemmatized transcriptions. *see* the Maaloula Aramaic Speech Corpus (MASC)
lexical level, **15–16**, 68, 77, 79, 156, 159–66, 168, 173, 179
liquids. *see* consonants
loanwords, 22, 23, 59
long vowels. *see* vowels

Maaloula Aramaic Speech Corpus (MASC), 5, 6, 8, 9, **18–34**, 42–43, 49, 55, 59–63, 64, 66, 68, 71, 73–78, 80, 92, 98, 104, 112, 113, 118, 119, 122, 124, 126, 136, 139, 141, 143, 149, 159, 175, 177, 184, 215, 224–38, 239, 240
- corpus structure, 19–20, 24–26
- the (unannotated) transcriptions, 19–20, 20–22, 26–29
- the audio files, 19, 24, 31
- the lemmatized transcriptions, 22–23, 29–30
- the MASC dataframe, 9, **29**, 84, 98, 156
- the SQLite database, 32
- the time-aligned phonetic transcriptions, 24, 31, 33, 196, 211–12

Maltese. *see* Arabic
marginal phonemes. *see* phoneme inventory
MASC dataframe. *see* the Maaloula Aramaic Speech Corpus (MASC)
minimal pairs, **39–55**
moraic theory, 14, 56, 60, **156–57**, 160, 165, 184, 194, 199, 205, 209, 215–16, 235
Moroccan Arabic. *see* Arabic
morphology, 5, **10–13**, 16, 22, 70, 80, 83, 93, 97, 98, 103–5, 106, 150, 170, 176, 177, 183, 184, 187, **188–91**, 192, 212, 217, 238, 239, 240

nasals. *see* consonants
neutralization, 20, 66, 75, 76, 132, 133

obstruents. *see* consonants

pharyngeal. *see* consonants
phoneme inventory, **35–63**
- marginal phonemes, **42–43**

phonological processes. *see* phonological rules
phonological rules (summary), **238**
phonological word, **15**
phrase-final degemination. *see* degemination
plural marker, 4, 13, 80, 95–**105**, 240
postlexical level, **15–16**, 68, 73, 79, 108, 117, 120, 156, 161–81, 208
postvocalic voicing of bilabial stops. *see* voicing of bilabial stops in postvocalic position
preconsonantal degemination. *see* degemination
prefixes, 111–14
pretonic raising, 14, 97, 200, 214, **217–19**, 221–25, 229, 231, 235, 236
pretonic shortening, 16, 17, 68, 69, 97, 102, 134, 206, 214, **219–24**, 225, 226, 235
processes. *see* phonological rules
progressive umlaut. *see* umlaut

regressive umlaut. *see* umlaut
resyllabification, 14, 16, 156, **161–67**, 172, 173, 179–81, 203–13
rhotic. *see* consonants
rule ordering, 16, 17, 68–73, 108, 109, 128, 133–36, 166, 208, 221–23, 227–29, 235, 236, 238
rules. *see* phonological rules

San'ani. *see* Arabic
secondary articulation, 36, 37, 38, 40
segmental duration, 31, 185, **194–213**

short vowels. *see* vowels
singleton-to-geminate duration ratio. *see* geminates
sonorants. *see* consonants
speech corpus. *see* the Maaloula Aramaic Speech Corpus (MASC)
SQLite database. *see* the Maaloula Aramaic Speech Corpus (MASC)
Standard Arabic. *See* Arabic
stops. *see* consonants
stray consonants, 16, 17, **159–61**, 161–64, 168, 172, 179–81
stress algorithm, 148, 165, 204, **214–16**, 235
stress assignment, 16, 60, 68, 69, 156, 157, 164, 165, 180, 200, 206–8, 211, **214–16**, 219, 221–29
stress-dependent processes, **217–24**
suffixes, 12, 13, 81, 95, 114, 115, 116, 121–32, 135–41, 146, 151, 170, 176, 181, 234, 237
surface geminates. *see* geminates
syllabification, 13, 14, 16, 60, **144–45**, 146–49, 155, 156, **158**, 159, 160, 164–68, 172, 174, 179–84, 185, 199, 200, 206, 208, 211, 214–38
syllable structure, **144–45**, **154**, 161, 175, 179, 182, 199
syllable weight, 60, **156–57**, 185, 199, 205, 209

templatic patterns, **10–11**, 80–93, 104, 105, 215
time-aligned phonetic transcriptions. *see* the Maaloula Aramaic Speech Corpus (MASC)
transcription system, **7–8**, **35–36**, **55**, 153, 200
Turoyo. *see* Aramaic varieties

umlaut
- progressive umlaut, 129, **141–43**, 143, 234
- regressive umlaut, **129–41**, 143, 223, 224
underlying geminates. *see* geminates

VC-dialects. *see* Arabic
voicing of bilabial stops in postvocalic position, 16–17, **65–69**, 71–75, 77–79
vowel epenthesis. *see* epenthesis
vowels, **55–62**, 224–38, 236–37
- diphthongs, **59–61**
- epenthetic vowel. *see* epenthesis
- long vowels, **58–59**
- short vowels, **57–58**
- the distribution of vowels, **224–38**
- vowel allophones, **236–37**

Weight-by-Position, **156–57**
Western Neo-Aramaic dialects of Jubbaadin and Bakhaa. *see* Aramaic varieties
word-final /i/ deletion, **135–38**, 139, 140
word-final geminates. *see* geminates
word-initial geminates. *see* geminates
word-medial geminates. *see* geminates

zero-morph, **12**

www.ingramcontent.com/pod-product-compliance
Lightning Source LLC
Chambersburg PA
CBHW061710300426
44115CB00014B/2628
9783111447049